Ruth Knight
1355 Trappe Rd
Street MD 21154

P9-AZW-897

This
cherished volume
belongs to

_____

...a woman
who loves God.

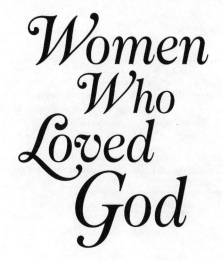

Women Who Loved God

Elizabeth George

HARVEST HOUSE PUBLISHERS
Eugene, Oregon 97402

Cover by Left Coast Design, Portland, Oregon

Elizabeth George and her husband, Jim, founded Christian Development Ministries, which reaches people internationally through Bible study materials, workshops, and tapes designed to nurture growth in the vital areas of Christian living. Through their extensive teaching ministry they have developed resources related to Bible study, leadership, discipleship, spiritual growth, marriage, and family.

If you would like more information about these study helps or you would like Elizabeth to speak to your group, or you want to share with Elizabeth how God has used *A Woman After God's Own Heart* in your life, write:

Christian Development Ministries
P.O. Box 33166
Granada Hills, CA 91394

Fax: (818) 831-0582
Toll Free 1-800-542-4611
www.elizabethgeorge.com

WOMEN WHO LOVED GOD
Copyright © 1999 by Elizabeth George
Published by Harvest House Publishers
Eugene, Oregon 97402

Library of Congress Cataloging-in-Publication Data

George, Elizabeth, 1944–
  Women who loved God / Elizabeth George
    p.   cm.
  Includes bibliographical references
  ISBN 1-56507-850-0
  1. Women—Prayer-books and devotions—English.   2. Women in the Bible—Meditations.   3. Devotional calendars.   I. Title.
  BV4844.G433   1999
  242'.643—DC21   98-5766
                                                                                    CIP

Printed in the United States of America.

99   00   01   02   03   04   /   DC   /   10   9   8   7   6   5   4   3   2   1

Come...
and Walk with God

Where does today find you? And what challenges does this day hold? How good it is to know that other women—the women of the Bible—have walked before us! And how wonderful to know that these women have left us sure guidelines, practical instructions, wise principles, and uplifting hope for managing life!

I invite you to journey along with these dear women today (and every day) through this unique daily devotional that follows the lives of the women of the Bible—the great women of faith who loved God, walked with God, and trusted God so long ago. And lest you think of these beloved saints as old-fashioned or out-of-date, remember God's Word to us: "All these things happened to them as examples, and they were written for our admonition" (1 Corinthians 10:11).

So come along—from Genesis to Revelation—and look to the Lord you love. Walk with Him and talk with Him along life's way. Grow in knowledge as you learn from these courageous women, from their lives, their trials, *and* their God, and grow in grace as you put their life lessons into practice yourself as a woman who loves God.

May we as women who love God continue to grow to love Him even more!

In His love,

Elizabeth George

God created man in His own image.
GENESIS 1:27

*D*o you know…that you are created in the image of God? When God created woman, He created her in His image. Let it sink into your heart and mind that you are creative, intelligent, and rational. In these ways you are created in God's image.

Do you know…that you are a reflection of God's glory? That's what being created in His image means. You reflect Him to other people. Every time you reach out in love, perform a deed of kindness, soften your heart in forgiveness, show a little extra patience, and follow through in faithfulness, other people experience the character of God through you!

Do you know…that you are created to have fellowship and communion with God? No other creature has been granted the privilege of communing with God except man—the creature made most like Him.

As a reflection of God's glory, why not:

Resolve never to worry about "self"-worth, but instead
Rejoice in your worth in God and your likeness to Him.

Resolve never to criticize or downgrade yourself, but instead
Rejoice that you are fearfully and wonderfully made (Psalm 139:14).

Resolve to seek a deeper relationship with God and to
Rejoice that He is near to all who call upon Him (Psalm 145:18).

Resolve to walk by faith paths you may not understand and to
Rejoice in the promise of His nearness as He directs the way.

Resolve to live your new year as a child of God through His Son,
  Jesus Christ, and to be a reflection of His glory, and
Rejoice that, as one of God's chosen, your name is written in heaven
  (Luke 10:20)!

Resolve to spend this year communing with God on a daily basis
  through prayer and the study of His Word, and
Rejoice in the strength He gives for each day and the hope He offers
  for all your tomorrows!

Resolve to reflect His glory and
Rejoice in His love!

Male and female He created them.
Genesis 1:27

*C*reation was complete. Well, almost! God had been busy for six days creating His beautiful new world. Now the stage was set. God's magnificent scenery stood finished and in place. His sun, moon, and stars lighted up His perfect planet. All creatures great and small enjoyed a perfect environment.

Yet all the universe stood at attention, awaiting God's final creations. At last God presented His masterpieces to the rest of nature. First the man Adam. Then—finally and dramatically—the woman Eve.

Devised by a perfect God, Eve reflected His divine perfection in her femaleness. Created for a position of honor, woman was born to life's loveliest, most lofty throne of glory: "the glory of man" (1 Corinthians 11:7). What can you do to join with Eve and revel in your lovely womanhood and femaleness?

1. *Accept your femininity.* There's no need to feel inferior, second-class, or second-rate. No, woman was God's last, best, most beautiful creation. You have manifold reasons for rejoicing. It was only after God presented woman that He proclaimed His creation was "very good." Adam and Eve were alike, yet they were different from one another. One was male and one female (Genesis 1:27), yet together as well as individually they reflected God's image and His glory.

2. *Embrace your womanhood.* Own your loveliness, your uniqueness, your beauty as a female. Delight yourself in God's handiwork—in being a woman.

3. *Cultivate your femininity.* This entire book is about the lovely, gracious, glorious, beautiful, prized-by-God women of the Bible. As you read each day this year, allow God's truths to permeate your understanding and transform your view of yourself as a woman until it matches the value God places on His women.

4. *Excel in your role as woman.* As God's woman, be the best of the best (Proverbs 31:29)! Delight in God's perfect design, in His good and acceptable and perfect will for your life (Romans 12:2). *He created you as a woman!* As such, you join Eve's exalted position of "fairest of creation."[1]

Eve…was the mother of all living.
GENESIS 3:20

"Guilty!" was the verdict God pronounced after Adam's wife listened to the tempter, ate of the forbidden tree, and involved her husband in rebellion. "Guilty!" was also the single word that reverberated in woman's own sad heart and mind. There was no doubt about her guilt. She would never argue that!

But just as darkness seemed to be settling in on her wonderful and perfect life, she heard Adam declare, "Your name shall be called 'Eve…the mother of all living.' " With those words, Eve glimpsed a fresh ray of light—and hope. Eve—the mother of all life!

Having been given a name filled with promise, Eve realized that she, the guilty sinner, could still serve her gracious and forgiving God. How? By bearing Adam's children and thereby becoming the mother of many generations (1 Corinthians 11:12). Her new name reflected the role she would have in spiritual history.

"Eve." From death sprang life; from darkness, light; from an end, a beginning; from the curse, a blessing; from her sentence to death, a hope for the future; from the stinging despair of defeat, the strength of a budding faith. Eve was the mother of all living!

Do you realize that your life, dear one, counts, too? And counts significantly? True, you share Eve's sentence of physical death (Romans 5:12), but whoever you are and whatever your circumstances, you have life to give to and pass on to other people. How?

- You give life through your physical efforts to care for others.

- You share spiritual life by telling others about Jesus.

- You are the life of your home, bringing the sparkle of laughter and joy to other people.

- You pass physical life on to your children.

- You can also pass eternal life on to your children by teaching them the gospel of Jesus Christ.

So this year choose to feed your spiritual life by sending your roots down deep into God's love. Eve's life came from the Lord, and so does yours. The Lord was the strength of her life, and He is your strength as well. All the energy of life, the purpose of life, all that you have of life to pass on finds its source in the Lord.

> *"I have acquired a man[-child] from the Lord."*
> Genesis 4:1

*I*t had never been done before. Never before had a woman given birth to a child. In fact, there had never before been a child—a baby! In fact, never before had the earth welcomed a baby.

But Eve wasn't worried. She knew she had all that she needed. She had the Lord.

Things had begun so well. How Eve cherished her memory of Adam's delighted face when God gave her to him (Genesis 2:21, 22). They had been so happy together in the beautiful perfection of the Garden of Eden. Yes, life had been wonderful until…

No, she wouldn't think about what she had done. About believing the serpent's lies. About causing her precious husband to join in her rebellious act of eating the fruit from the tree of knowledge (Genesis 3:5,6). She shuddered again, thinking of all the changes that had taken place…in her marriage…in her garden home…in her relationship with Elohim Himself… and in her heart.

Emotional pain had become a new part of Eve's daily life. And then there was the almost unbearable physical pain which accompanied childbirth. What could she do to ease the very real pain in both her mind and her body? Where could she turn for help?

She realized there was Someone she could turn to! And that Someone was the same God whom she had defied, yet who had come to her rescue.

"I have gotten a manchild with the help of the Lord" (NASB), Eve declared. "I've given birth to a baby—the first baby ever born—by the help of the Lord! He is all that I need!" How grateful she was—in her confusion, in her pain, in this new venture—to have the ever-present help of the Lord!

Fresh knowledge of God's love and trustworthiness soothed Eve's sore soul: She could lean on Him no matter what new challenges her life might bring. Eve was thankful.

And you can be thankful, too—

- Thankful that you can trust God in spite of how you have stumbled and fallen in the past.

- Thankful that you can trust God with any issue you are facing in the present.

- Thankful that you can trust God for whatever happens in the future.

Adam knew his wife...and she bore a son.
GENESIS 4:25

*L*oss tears at the heart, and Eve had suffered many losses! She had lost...

- Her perfect relationship with God (Genesis 3:8)
- The bliss of a sinless marriage (Genesis 3:12)
- Her ideal home in the Garden of Eden (Genesis 3:23)
- Her lack of acquaintance with evil (Genesis 3:22)
- Her son Abel, murdered by his brother
- Her son Cain, whom God sent away

She had little left to lose.

Eve had dipped into her barrel of hope more times than she could count. She seemed to have no hope left—another loss. It's been said that man can live 40 days without food, three days without water, eight minutes without air...but only one second without hope. And Eve's hope was gone.

But, oh, the goodness of the Lord (Psalm 31:19)! "Adam knew his wife again, and she bore a son and named him Seth, 'For God has appointed another seed for me.'" The gift of Seth, whose name means "appointed," refilled Eve's empty heart, and her equally empty barrel of hope. "Appointed" by God, Seth would be the one from whom God's Son would come, bringing bountiful and eternal hope to all mankind.

This Son brings hope to you, too—even in seemingly absolute hopelessness.

How do you handle your heartbreaking losses? Rather than plunge into depression or discouragement this year, place your faith and confidence in these hope-filled realities:

God's faithfulness—"'For I know the plans I have for you,' declares the LORD, 'plans to prosper you and not to harm you, plans to give you hope and a future'" (Jeremiah 29:11 NIV).

God's promises—Just one of the over 8000 promises in the Bible[2] assures that you can do all things through Christ who strengthens you (Philippians 4:13).

God's goodness—Your lack of hope can never negate God's goodness. Although weeping may endure for a night, because "the LORD is good; [and] His mercy is everlasting, and His truth endures to all generations" (Psalm 100:5), "joy comes in the morning" (Psalm 30:5).

"I will establish my covenant with you...and your wife."
Genesis 6:18 (NIV)

We don't know her name, so we'll call her "Mrs. Noah."

She spent her days loving her husband, Noah, raising their three sons, and caring for their home. Daily life was simple....

Until "the call" came from the Lord. Grieved in His heart over the wickedness of mankind, the Lord decided to destroy human beings, as well as the animals of the fields and the birds of the air. Noah, however, was a just man who walked with God, so God spared him and gave him a special twofold assignment: Make an ark and preach righteousness (2 Peter 2:5).

As Noah moved forward in obedience and full of faith, Mrs. Noah must have mused, "What can I do? How can I help him fulfill God's plan?"

Pray. She could pray—for mankind as God's judgment loomed; for her husband as he served the Lord; and for her family, that they would follow after God.

Choose. She could choose to enter into the righteousness of the Lord rather than go the way of the world.

Encourage. Every husband, including Noah, thrives on a wife's cheerful, steady, hope-filled words of support and affirmation. She could encourage Noah in his work.

Instruct. She could persist in sharing her faith with her sons and their wives. This was not the time to be silent and hope they learned from her example. She must speak up. Their lives as well as their souls were at stake!

Believe. She may have wondered about the "ark" and about the "flood of waters," but she chose to believe the prophecy.

Help. She could not help much with the building, but she could help gather the animals and the food they would need for their mysterious voyage of faith.

Follow. She could—by faith—follow her husband's leading day by day for 43,800 days...right into the ark of salvation that transported her family into an unknown future (1 Peter 3:20).

Prayer: Lord, is mine the kind of faith that prays persistently, chooses righteousness, encourages fellow believers, instructs others, believes always, helps Your kingdom come, and follows You faithfully? The kind of faith that willingly sails into the future? Help me find strength for today and hope for tomorrow by following in Mrs. Noah's footsteps of faith!

"Come into the ark."
GENESIS 7:1

*F*inally Noah had finished building the ark God had called him to prepare. And now the divine directive came from the Lord Himself: "Come
into the ark, you and all your household." Noah knew he would obey God,
and he thought he could count on his wife and three sons. But what about
his three daughters-in-law? How he must have prayed that their hearts
would respond to God's invitation and follow him into the ark, into salvation from the peril signaled by the gathering black clouds.

True obedience consists of three elements. And Noah's daughters-in-law
exhibited all three as they, too, acted in faith and entered the ark.

- *Element #1: Immediate obedience.* There appears to have been no
  delay or indecision. When it was time, these three women followed
  Noah and their husbands into the ark.

- *Element #2: Believing obedience.* Each daughter-in-law believed
  safety and salvation were to be found in the ark of God (1 Peter
  3:20).

- *Element #3: Personal obedience.* Not one of them was dragged,
  coerced, or carried into the ark. Each entered freely (Genesis 7:13).

God is issuing His divine invitation to you, too, dear one: "Come into
the ark of salvation." How are you responding to God's call of love and His
invitation to life—to eternal life?

- *With immediate obedience?* God is crying out to you now, "Behold,
  now is the accepted time; behold, *now* is the day of salvation" (2 Corinthians 6:2, emphasis added)!

- *With believing obedience?* Do you believe eternal safety and salvation are found in God through His Son, Jesus Christ (John 14:6)?

- *With personal obedience?* Salvation is "not of blood…nor of the will
  of man" (John 1:13). You are not born into salvation through your
  parents or the desires of others. You must personally respond to
  God's invitation. Have you walked into God's ark of salvation?

Just a note: Blessing always follows obedience. Noah's daughters-in-law
became the source of a new race. The numberless nations of the earth
sprang from these unnamed, but obedient women who loved God.

> *So Noah went out [of the ark]...and his wife.*
> GENESIS 8:18

At last Mrs. Noah's voyage was over! All 371 days of it! All 53 weeks of it! She shuddered, remembering the many years her faithful husband had preached and built, preached and built. Yes, those decades were difficult for her. Witnessing the rampant sin of mankind and the growing hostility toward her husband was almost unbearable. However, trusting in God, her husband—and his family with him—had followed His strange instructions to preach righteousness and build an ark.

To be sure, Noah's wife gladly followed her husband and three sons and their gallant wives into the finished ark. Relief surely flowed through her tense body and mind as she heard God shut the door behind them, sealing all eight members of her precious family and their animal cargo into the curious vessel Noah had built (Genesis 7:16).

But a part of her heart may have been sore. After all, she was leaving the only home she had ever known. Where was she going? What would her new home be like? And when would she see it?

Do her concerns sound familiar? Change brings lots of questions. How well do you handle change? Statistics place a household move near the top of the stress scale, yet no one else has ever experienced a household move that compares with Mrs. Noah's uprooting! No one! Yet she shows us how to manage any and all change. Learn her lessons well, for they are lessons for the changes of a lifetime.

By faith, choose to believe that...

- God is in control,
- God knows what He is doing,
- God has a plan and a purpose,
- God knows what is best,
- God will take care of everything...

Mrs. Noah stepped off the ark into the mud of her brave new world. As a special sign of encouragement, God hung a rainbow of promise in His heavens. That beautiful object shining through the clouds, a radiant expression of God's love, caused her own clouded heart to fill with fresh, warm hope!

But Sarai was barren; she had no child.
GENESIS 11:30

He maketh the barren woman…to be a joyful mother of children (Psalm 113:9 KJV).

Behold, children are a heritage from the LORD, the fruit of the womb is His reward (Psalm 127:3).

*B*ut Sarai was barren; she had no child." Eight words. A simple statement of a cold, hard fact. Sarai had no child.

Perhaps Sarai wondered, "What's gone wrong? What have I done? Why hasn't God blessed me with children?" On and on Sarai's questioning may have gone, and on and on went her pain. Nothing could relieve it, soothe it, take it away. Childlessness was a stigma that seared itself more deeply into Sarai's soul with each childless sunrise.

But Sarai, the wife and traveling companion of Abram and herself a follower of God, would—in the future—often remember a promise that would profoundly affecct her. God was about to promise to make Abram a great nation and to give the land to his offspring (Genesis 12:2,7).

Sarai would have to reach, reach back on many occasions the fingers of her faith to clutch God's promise. With aching heart and stinging tears, Sarai would trust God one more time, for one more day. She would have no other option. She must resist faithlessness, despite the great temptation to give up, succumb to bitterness, lash out at Abram, turn her back on God, or give in to the contentious spirit that hovered nearby as an easy option. Sarai would learn one thing, and that lesson was a beautiful flower that sprang forth from a pain-filled soil: Faith is the better way to face the distresses of life.

Speaking of facts, have you thought about the fact that, for 11 years, Sarai grabbed onto God's promise one more time, for one more day, until her son, Isaac, was born? Do you realize that those years add up to well over 4000 faith reaches? So Sarai blesses you with her example: Whatever impossible, unbearable, unusual, unchangeable test awaits you this day (or for 4000 days, or *forever!*), by faith, reach one more time for "the exceedingly great and precious promises" of God (2 Peter 1:4)! Yes, faith is the better way—indeed, the only way!—to face the distresses of life.

> *So Abram departed as the* LORD *had spoken to him.*
> GENESIS 12:4

*F*aith—what a price tag it has! The life of faith is not an easy one. And that's exactly what Sarai discovered. Life was going quite well for her in her hometown of Ur. True, she and Abram didn't have any children yet (Genesis 11:30), but that was more bearable as long as she was surrounded by friends, family, and the distractions of the sophisticated and prosperous city of Ur, located on the lush banks of the Euphrates River. How she loved home!

But then her world was turned upside down. Sarai was asked to leave behind all that was familiar and secure, to turn her back on all that she loved and knew, and go somewhere else. God had told her husband, Abram, to leave, to get out of Ur. And where were they to go? "To a land that I will show you," said the Lord. No preplanned itinerary offered here!

As it turned out, Abram—and Sarai with him—followed after God for the rest of his life, "not knowing where he was going," searching "for the city which has foundations, whose builder and maker is God," and "died in faith, not having received the promises" (Hebrews 11:8-13). His was a homeless family.

As it turned out, Sarai's minuscule seed of faith budded on that oh-so-difficult day when "they went out…from Ur of the Chaldeans" (Genesis 11:31). Possibly with pain in her heart and tears in her eyes, Sarai took an important step of faith, and that faith grew and ultimately earned her a place of honor in God's Hall of Faith (Hebrews 11).

Are you wondering, praying, "Dear God, how can I begin taking the heavenward steps Sarai took and develop even greater faith?" Try these important steps in faith today:

- *Trust the faith of those who lead you.* Whom is God using in your life to show you the path to greater faith?

- *Turn away from the pleasures of this world.* "Do not love the world or the things in the world" (1 John 2:15).

- *Turn toward the unknown, the unseen, the eternal, with a heart of faith.* "For we walk by faith, not by sight" (2 Corinthians 5:7).

Abram took Sarai his wife...to the land of Canaan.
Genesis 12:5

*O*h, the heartache! Will it ever go away?" Perhaps these words darkened Sarai's thoughts the day she followed her full-of-faith husband, Abram, out of Ur (Genesis 11:31). Ur was Sarai's home, her life, her joy, but God had told Abram to go to Canaan. Leaving Ur was bad enough, but going to the land of Canaan was worse!

What could have made it worse? First of all, Ur was beautifully situated along the rich and fertile Euphrates River. Canaan was so far away—600 miles!—from her beloved hometown. Abram may as well call it Nowhere Land!

Then, just when Sarai was getting used to Nowhere Land, a terrible famine struck, and it was time to move on again, this time to Egypt, another 300 miles away. Oh, if only she and Abram were still back in Ur! Then everything would be all right!

Maybe Sarai thought thoughts like these. We really don't know, but we do know that the backward gaze can be dangerous. It can impede and harm your progress in faith. So what can you do to continue...to look forward and faithfully follow God when the circumstances of your life seem to worsen?

> **F** *ace forward.* Real life happens in the present, and God's blessings happen there (and in the future), too.

> **A** *ccept your circumstances.* The circumstances of life are one primary way God works in you and works out His will for you. Therefore, "do all things without complaining and disputing" (Philippians 2:13,14).

> **I** *f your circumstances find you in God's will, you will find God in all your circumstances.*

> **T** *rust in the Lord.* God will keep you in perfect peace when your mind is stayed on Him in full trust (Isaiah 26:3).

> **H** *ope for the future.* Hope in God is the bright star that lights your path in the present darkness and into the unknown future.

Prayer: Dear God of Sarai, grant that such a one as I may see
the good in bad and the faith to be had...
following Thee!

"You are a woman of beautiful countenance."
Genesis 12:11

Every year women who desire greater beauty spend billions of dollars on makeup, hair treatment, dental work, cosmetic surgery, and physical conditioning. There seems to be no price too high for beauty. Do you yourself ever wish for greater beauty? Oddly, there were days when Sarai may have wished she were *less* beautiful!

God had blessed Sarai with great beauty. At her birth her proud parents had seen it and appropriately named her "princess." But beauty isn't everything! Sometimes Sarai's beauty was a blessing. Other times it was a curse.

Genesis 12 tells about one of those cursed times. As Sarai traveled with her husband, Abram, their caravan ran up against the powerful Egyptian Pharaoh. Although this impressive leader possessed massive military forces and great wealth, he wanted one more thing—the beautiful Sarai as an addition to his harem.

Amazingly, Sarai's husband had predicted this exact scene. (How had he known?) In fact, she and Abram had discussed such a possibility, and now it was reality.

Abram's solution? It went something like this: "Let's lie. We'll tell them you're my half-sister. Well it's not really a lie. After all, even though you are my wife, you're also my father's daughter. You know—a half-sister, a half-lie? At least *my* life will be spared!" Betrayal. Deception. And all because of beauty!

And yet the Bible says:

- Beauty is vain (Proverbs 31:30).

- Lust not after beauty (Proverbs 6:25).

- Inner beauty—not external beauty—is what God finds precious (1 Peter 3:4).

Why not pause right now and pray? Thank God that you are beautiful in His eyes—fearfully and wonderfully made exactly as you are (Psalm 139:14). Look long into the mirror of God's revealing Word (James 1:22-25). Decide to spend more time adorning your heart with the beauty of God's eternal jewel of a gentle and quiet spirit (1 Peter 3:4). In God's eyes that is the beauty beyond price!

The woman was taken to Pharaoh's house.
GENESIS 12:15

here is "a time to keep silence" (Ecclesiastes 3:7). Write this wise principle upon the tablet of your heart for life's seasons of testing. Sarai learned this costly principle on her journey toward greater faith.

Sarai's journey began in obedience. Faithfully following her husband, Abram, as he faithfully followed God, she had set out toward Canaan. Severe famine forced them south to the foreign land of Egypt. Fear for his life, mixed with fear of the famine, moved Abram, the great patriarch of Israel, to lie to the powerful Pharaoh about his exquisite wife: "She is my sister," Abram had said. So Sarai was taken to Pharaoh's house and into his harem.

Did fiery thoughts about Abram rage in Sarai's heart? Did she think him selfish to sacrifice her life to preserve his own? Did Sarai wonder with fear, "What will happen to me? Will Abram go on without me? Will I ever see him again? What will life be like as a member of a harem?" Scripture is silent. Don't you hope the silence indicated Sarai's faith as she sat in her harem prison and waited on the Lord?

Strength for today and hope for tomorrow are realized—by you as well as by Sarai—in the silent patience of faith.

- Wait on the LORD; be of good courage, and He shall strengthen your heart (Psalm 27:14).
- Rest in the LORD, and wait patiently for Him (Psalm 37:7).
- Truly my soul silently waits for God (Psalm 62:1).
- Those who wait on the LORD shall renew their strength (Isaiah 40:31).
- It is good that one should hope and wait quietly (Lamentations 3:26).
- Blessed is he who waits (Daniel 12:12).

Dear one, make it your practice to wait on the Lord, to trust in Him, to hope in Him...and to be blessed in your silence of faith.

> *But the LORD plagued Pharaoh.*
> GENESIS 12:17

*T*he cast is present:

- *Sarai*—the too-beautiful wife of Abram
- *Abram*—the waiting-to-be patriarch of the nation of Israel
- *Pharaoh*—the powerful heathen leader of Egypt
- *Pharaoh's household*—unsuspecting players

The stage is set:

- *Sarai*—shut up in the palace harem of Pharaoh
- *Abram*—free outside the palace walls
- *Pharaoh*—pleased with Sarai and busily lavishing gifts on Abram
- *Pharaoh's household*—innocently going about daily business

From all appearances, a sorrowful end is in sight for Abram and Sarai because of Abram's lie: "She is my sister." Following God hadn't quite gone the way Abram and Sarai had imagined. Famine in the Promised Land had led them to Egypt in search of food. And now it seems that Sarai will never share in the wonderful blessings God has promised.

But there is one more member of the cast! *The Ultimate One!* Yahweh, the God of Abram and Sarai, stands watching and waiting as the human drama unfolds. At the perfect moment, when things seem blackest, Yahweh makes His dramatic, miraculous appearance. Although He is never seen, His works are seen, heard, felt, and noted. It is God to the rescue! "But the LORD plagued Pharaoh and his house with great plagues because of Sarai, Abram's wife."

Do you realize that the God of Sarai is also your God? With God all things are possible (Matthew 19:26)—even deliverance from the impossible and the unbearable. Yahweh knows how to make a way of escape for His children (1 Corinthians 10:13). The Lord is able to deliver the godly out of trials (2 Peter 2:9). In His own time and in His own way, God rescues His people. So even when you feel awfully alone and your situation seems horribly hopeless, know that you are *never* alone and *never* without hope! "God is our refuge and strength, a very *present* help in trouble. Therefore we will not fear" (Psalm 46:1, 2, emphasis added).

The Angel of the Lord found her.
Genesis 16:7

*I*t wasn't *her* fault that she was carrying Abram's child! That had been Sarai's idea!

Hagar, the handmaiden of Sarai, was fleeing through the wilderness, her emotions reeling. Sarai had been so harsh! Hagar had tried to ignore her mistress's anger and mistreatment. But no more! She had decided to leave. After all, her name meant "flight," so she would live it out. She would run away—even if that meant running across a desert while she was pregnant.

But "the Angel of the Lord found her." God went looking for—and found—Hagar. Through His grace, God's "extended care" extended itself to Hagar, too. What did God do for this desperate woman?

- *God gave her instructions.* For her safety and well-being—and the baby's, too—God told Hagar to "return to your mistress." In Abram's tent she would have food and water, shelter and help during her pregnancy.

- *God gave her encouragement.* "You shall bear a son." All was not lost. However hopeless life looked, however hard life was right now, Hagar would one day have a son—a family.

- *God gave her a promise.* "I will multiply your descendants exceedingly, so that they shall not be counted for multitude." Yes, Hagar was a servant, but she would become the mother of many.

Could you use a little encouragement—a fresh, shining vision of hope for your tomorrows? Do you need instructions for a difficult situation—some clear, concrete guidance for a change in circumstances? Have you reminded yourself of God's promises lately? Instead of darting here and there, running to and fro…and away, spend time with your Bible and enjoy anew God's strength for this day and His hope for tomorrow. All Scripture—every word in the Bible—comes from God and is profitable for teaching you and instructing you, "for resetting the direction of [your] life,"[3] and for equipping you for every situation you encounter.

> *"The LORD has heard your affliction."*
> GENESIS 16:11

*A*lone. A fugitive. A *lonely* fugitive! Hagar, tired from running through the desert, rested beside a spring of water in the wilderness, her head filled with confused thoughts about her confused life.

Hagar was pregnant with Abram's child, as arranged by Sarai, her mistress and Abram's wife. The three-way arrangement—agreed on by all partners—had backfired. Hagar was prideful in her pregnancy; Sarai was jealous and angry; and Abram basically withdrew. Sarai dealt very harshly with Hagar, mistreating her so badly that she ran away.

"Now what?" Hagar cried out in bewilderment, helplessness...and hopelessness. But the Lord heard her affliction and inclined His ear to her. In fact, when her baby was born, Hagar called her little boy *Ishmael*, meaning "God hears"!

Throughout life's afflictions, you can pray many kinds of prayers, dear one, and God hears them all. Among the prayers you can rely on are...

- *Arrow prayers.* On the spot and at the very second Nehemiah needed God's help, he shot his arrow prayer upward to heaven, and God gave him the words he needed as he asked the king for permission to go to Jerusalem and rebuild the wall (Nehemiah 2:4).

- *Liquid prayers.* Psalm 56:8 reads, "Put my tears into Your bottle." Commenting on this verse, the early church father Augustine gave to our tears the lovely label "liquid prayers."

- *Wordless prayers.* You don't know what to pray? Is your affliction too heavy for words? Be encouraged: "For we do not know what we should pray for as we ought, but the Spirit Himself makes intercession for us with groanings which cannot be uttered" (Romans 8:26).

Prayer, dear woman of faith, is the answer to every problem there is because God always hears! Won't you learn to turn to Him? Indeed, His ears are open to your prayers (1 Peter 3:12). You can call upon "the God who hears" as long as you live (Psalm 116:2).

"I love the Lord, because He has *heard* my voice and my supplications" (Psalm 116:1, emphasis added).

"You-Are-the-God-Who-Sees…"
Genesis 16:13

A curse…or a blessing? Is the fact that God is omnipresent (He is everywhere) and omniscient (He knows everything) a curse or a blessing? Ask Hagar, one of the Lord's ladies who ran up against these two unfathomable attributes of God!

Hagar flew across wilderness territory to escape her difficult home life. When she was at the end of all human hope, "the Angel of the Lord found her."

There was no doubt in Hagar's mind what had occurred: She had seen none other than the preincarnate Lord Himself—a vision of strength and grace, of mercy and faithfulness, truly an angel of hope!

"Then she called the name of the Lord who spoke to her, You-Are-the-God-Who-Sees; for she said, 'Have I also here seen Him who sees me?' Therefore the well was called Beer Lahai Roi"—which translates, "the well of Him who lives and sees me."

Besides being omnipresent and omniscient, your God is immutable. That means He never changes. And that means the same God who ministered to Hagar ministers to you. Therefore…

- because God provides, you shall not want (Psalm 23:1).

- because God leads you, you are never alone (Psalm 23:3).

- because God is with you, you shall not fear (Psalm 23:4).

- because God comforts, you are always encouraged (Psalm 23:4).

Are you yet acknowledging that God's all-seeing, all-knowing eye is a blessing? When no other eye sees your struggles and difficulties and impossibilities, find hope and take comfort in the fact that your omniscient, omnipresent, immutable God is the God who sees. "The eyes of the Lord are on the righteous" (1 Peter 3:12). What a blessing that fact is!

Exactly what does God see? He sees:	*And how does God respond?*
• your affliction	• He is always at work.
• your struggles	• He is working out His purposes in your life.
• your mistreatment	• He provides for you.
• your faithfulness	• His help is on the way.
• your needs	• He is moved with compassion.

"You shall not call her name Sarai."
GENESIS 17:15

*P*romotions in the life of faith—like those in school—don't come easily. Required courses must be successfully completed before the diploma is beautifully scripted, signed, and sealed by the appropriate officials.

Genesis 17 offers God's snapshot of Sarai's promotion in the school of faith. On that day God said, "As for Sarai...you shall not call her name Sarai, but Sarah shall be her name."

Exactly what courses had Sarai completed that qualified her for this promotion? As you read along, grade yourself in the blanks provided. Then consider what you can do to grow in these areas and make plans for progress.

1. *Sarai had learned to follow her husband.* Sarai completed Faith 101 when she learned to trust and follow Abram as he followed after God (Genesis 12:1). True, her life had been one of radical moves and difficult change. But she had accepted her life-style as God's will and her husband as God's instrument in her life. _____

2. *Sarai had learned to trust the Lord.* Sarai almost failed that course, but by God's grace her faith held out up to the fingernail-scraping edge while she huddled alone with her fears—and faith—in Pharaoh's harem. Her own husband, Abram, had failed her. Would God fail her, too? She hoped...she prayed...she trusted He wouldn't (1 Peter 3:5,6). As she walked out of her hostage situation, amazed at God's miraculous solution (Genesis 12:15-20), Sarai's score on this exam of faith soared. _____

3. *Sarai had learned to wait on God.* Actually, she was still learning to wait. Already enrolled in Faith 102, Sarai was getting the instruction she needed to continue in her now 25-year wait on God's promise that Abram would have a son (Genesis 12:7). No, waiting was not—and never had been—easy for Sarai. _____

4. *Sarai had learned the importance of having a gentle and quiet spirit.* Yes, her name *Sarai* carried the connotation of "contention," as well as the meaning of "princess." And she had certainly been contentious with Hagar (Genesis 16:6). What a painful time of learning! How thankful she was to now be adorning herself regularly with the gentle and quiet spirit that pleases God (1 Peter 3:4,5). _____

Well, dear follower of God, how did you do on this quiz? Consider what you can do to grow in these areas and make plans for progress. After all, a lot more classes come after Faith 101 in this lifelong journey with the God you love.

"Sarah shall be her name."
GENESIS 17:15

*I*n God's eyes, Sarai's faith had grown and, as a sign that He was establishing a covenant with her and with her husband, Abraham, God changed her name: "Sarah shall be her name." Exactly what was the significance of Sarah's name change?

Her name was changed from	*Her name was changed to*
Sarai—meaning "my princess"	Sarah—meaning "princess"
Sarai—meaning "princely"	Sarah—meaning "chieftainness"
Sarai—meaning "contentious"	Sarah—a woman of godly faith

Did you know that God has also given you a new name that carries in it an expression of the character and plan He has for your life? If you are His child through Jesus Christ, the Bible says that you have:

- *New purpose.* Instead of being enslaved to sin, you are "His workmanship, created in Christ Jesus for good works" (Ephesians 2:10).

- *New direction.* Instead of wondering and worrying about your life, you are now to press heavenward, forgetting what lies behind and reaching forward to what lies before, following your upward call of God in Christ Jesus (Philippians 3:13,14).

- *New clothing.* Instead of the deeds of the flesh, you are to "put on the new man...according to the image of Him who created [you]" (Colossians 3:10).

- *New behavior.* As a "Christian" (Acts 11:26)—meaning "little Christ"— you are to be conformed to the image of Jesus (Romans 8:29).

- *New destiny.* Instead of possessing temporal life only, you have been given eternal life (1 John 5:11) and citizenship in heaven (Philippians 3:20).

- *New name.* Your new name is "written which no one knows except him who receives it" (Revelation 2:17). God's new name for you is an expression of Christ's love and guarantees your admission into eternal glory.

If you are a child of God, pause now and thank Him for your new name and its many blessings. If you're not yet His child, thank Him for sending His Son Jesus to die on the cross for your sin. Ask Jesus to become your Savior and Lord. With this prayer, you will receive a new name.

"I will bless her and...give you a son by her."
GENESIS 17:16

*H*ow many times had it already happened? Sarah could count at least five times when God had promised Abraham a son, a seed, offspring (Genesis 12–17)—and still no son! True, for a while they had thought Ishmael—Abraham's son born of their maidservant Hagar—was "the son of promise."

Yet now God was saying again to Abraham, "Sarah your wife shall bear you a son." She had heard the promise before, but this time there was a new twist: God spoke specifically of *her!* No wonder Abraham fell down and had a good laugh. After all, Sarah was 90 years old!

With her new name shining bright, Sarah undoubtedly wanted her deepening faith to shine equally as bright. Yet how, she may have wondered—just as you may—can one continue to believe God's promises when the situation seems impossible and the waiting endless? Note these answers, dear one:

By choice. The opposite of faith is disbelief—ugly, black doubt! When God presents you will one of His dazzling promises, He is offering you the choice of either accepting its brilliance and being led by its light or smothering it in the dark cloud of your doubt.

By faith. Strength for today and hope for tomorrow are realized only as you put your faith in His promises. Faith is "the evidence of things *not* seen" (Hebrews 11:1, emphasis added). We see God's answers and enjoy His strength and hope...only through the eyes of faith.

By exercise. Your faith is like a muscle: It grows with exercise and, over time, increases in strength and size. Every time you choose to exercise your faith, you gain further strength for each day and greater hope for each tomorrow.

Which area of your life, dear woman of faith, calls for you to choose to exercise your faith—by faith—today? Is it a physical problem like Sarah's was? A family problem? A personal struggle? A financial test? Does there seem to be no rhyme nor reason to the circumstances, no end to the waiting in sight, no solution to the predicament? Choose to wield your faith one more time! Stretch it! Strain it! Grow it! Trust in God because "there has not failed one word of all His good promise" (1 Kings 8:56).

> *"She shall be a mother of nations."*
> GENESIS 17:16

*B*ack in 1703 a godly woman named Esther Edwards gave birth to a son she named Jonathan. From this woman's son, who would become distinguished as a theologian and preacher, came an amazing line of offspring. More than 400 have been traced, and that number includes 14 college presidents and 100 professors. Another 100 were ministers of the gospel, missionaries, and theological teachers. Still another 100-plus were lawyers and judges, 60 were doctors, and as many more were authors and editors of high rank. What a tribute to this godly and prayerful mother!

Thousands of years before Mrs. Edwards, there was Sarah. God prophesied, "She shall be a mother of nations; kings of peoples shall be from her." In time, Sarah's ancestors became "as the stars of the heaven and as the sand which is on the seashore" (Genesis 22:17). The roll call of Sarah's descendants includes the patriarchs of the faith, kings of nations, and the Savior of the world, Jesus Christ—right on down to *you* if you've been born spiritually into the line of Abraham through Christ (Romans 4:16-25). The lowly Sarah, pilgrim from Ur and stranger in Canaan, became the progenitor of all the saints through all the ages!

Another woman can also become a mother of nations—and that woman is *you!* God's mandate to you is to faithfully teach your children the life-saving, life-giving truths of Scripture (Proverbs 1:8), which can bring your children into God's family. With Christ in *your* heart, you begin your own line of godly seed. As you pass on the gospel to your beloved children, they can, in turn, pass it on to the next generation. Your godly influence can continue through time and through generations as innumerable as the stars and the sand!

Are you thinking, "But I don't have children. This doesn't apply to me"? Oh, but it does! *You* can aid in the birth of spiritual children by sharing the truth about Jesus Christ. *You* can help bring many into the line of Christ. *You* can add fellow saints to God's great cloud of witnesses (Hebrews 12:1). And you can do so by speaking up at work, inviting your coworkers, neighbors, and family members to church, and sharing how Jesus has changed your life and given you His strength for today and His hope for tomorrow. You, too, can be a mother of nations!

"Is anything too hard for the LORD?"
GENESIS 18:14

*I*s anything too hard for the LORD?" How you answer this question indicates the level of your faith in God.

The angel of the Lord asked this question of Sarah, our great heroine of faith. Only she wasn't exhibiting much faith at the time. Here's what happened.

First, there had been the promise of a child, a seed, a son of Abraham to be born by Sarah. And Sarah had been hearing about that for 25 years! She had almost quit paying attention.

Then there were the facts. Sarah was 90 years old, well past the age of childbearing. Sarah was well aware that she had "grown old" (literally, worn out, withered, ready to fall apart like an old garment). At this point, having a baby would take a miracle!

Next, there was the laugh. "Sarah laughed within herself." As she thought about the absurdity, the impossibility of giving birth, her laugh of doubt rang forth.

Then came the question—the same question God asks of you and your faith: "Is anything too hard for the LORD?" Literally, "Is any word from God too wonderful, too impossible, for Jehovah?" With divine omnipotence a factor in the equation, the answer to that question resounds to the heavens and back: "NO!!!!!" Nothing promised by God is ever beyond His resources, His ability, His love!

So, with the flame of your faith, search your heart for any dark corner of doubt about God's ability to accomplish all things for you.

- Is this day of your life too hard for the Lord?
- Is the physical difficulty you are bearing too hard for the Lord?
- Is the heartache you suffer too hard for the Lord?
- Is the problem in your marriage or family too hard for the Lord?
- Is your financial condition too hard for the Lord?
- Is the path you're on too hard for the Lord?

No! Nothing you face is beyond the resources, the ability, or the love of your heavenly Father!

> *"At the appointed time...Sarah shall have a son."*
> Genesis 18:14

*T*here is no time lost in waiting...*if* you are waiting on the Lord!

Sarah, the one God had called "a mother of nations" (Genesis 17:16), waited on the Lord for 25 years! Clutching God's promise for a son, she had waited—right on past her childbearing years. The future looked hopeless, and although she had her moments of doubt, yet she hoped—hoped on the words the Lord Himself had spoken: "At the appointed time...Sarah shall have a son."

"At the appointed time." These words call us to the discipline of waiting on God's timing, of waiting until His "appointed time." These words call us to a deeper faith because, for everything, there is an "appointed time."

And nothing is harder than waiting. Yet all of us wait for something. And in God's School of Waiting, He teaches and transforms us as we wait. For what do you wait? Savor these special blessings while you wait on God's "appointed time":

Blessing #1: Increased value. Waiting increases the value and importance of the thing waited for. Whether you're waiting for deliverance from suffering, the discovery of God's purposes, direction for your confused life, a home at last, a wedding day, a family reunion, a prodigal's return, or a child's birth, waiting makes the desired object a greater treasure once it is received.

Blessing #2: Increased time. No one has enough time. But the one who waits is given the precious gift of time: time to embrace life's circumstances, time to press closer to God's loving and understanding heart, time to grow in the hard-won grace of patience, time to feel more deeply the pain of others who also wait with flickering faith.

Blessing #3: Increased faith. The writer of Hebrews defines faith as "the substance of things hoped for, the evidence of things not seen" (Hebrews 11:1). Please read the rest of Hebrews 11 and notice how the saints through the ages had their faith increased by waiting. Faith grows and is strengthened through time.

So while you wait, "be of good courage, and He shall strengthen your heart" (Psalm 27:14).

Abimelech king of Gerar sent and took Sarah.
Genesis 20:2

*A*s Sarah heard her husband, Abraham, say to Abimelech, king of Gerar, "She is my sister," her mind undoubtedly flashed back to a similar scene in Egypt 25 years earlier (Genesis 12). "Again, Lord?" she may have whispered.

Many lessons in faith require numerous review sessions! After all, trust in the Lord is like a multifaceted gem. A facet is cut, the gem turned, and another facet incised. So God once again turned Sarah's life in order to more clearly imprint the beauty of faith into her soul. The chisel of trial hurt, just as it had 25 years before when Abraham first put her life—and their future—in jeopardy. But God seemed to be asking Sarah to turn her face, her fears, and her faith once again toward Him and to, once again, trust Him.

After all, what had she learned those decades ago about trusting the Lord?

- *Lesson 1: Pray*—"The righteous cry and the Lord hears, and delivers them out of all their troubles" (Psalm 34:17).

- *Lesson 2: Trust*—"Trust in the Lord with all your heart, and lean not to your own understanding"—or anyone else's (Proverbs 3:5)!

- *Lesson 3: Believe*—"Faith is the substance of things hoped for, the evidence of things not seen" (Hebrews 11:1).

- *Lesson #4*: Wait—"I waited patiently for the Lord; and He inclined to me, and heard my cry" (Psalm 40:1).

As you enter into your new day, is something in your life a "repeat" problem? Are there daily difficulties you must constantly face? Are there people who regularly let you down or fail to follow through? Are there seemingly impossible hardships to be endured day after day?

Imagine the sheer beauty your faith will have as you allow God to, time after time and day after day, use life's difficulties and disappointments to lead you to deeper trust in Him. May these four lessons about living a life of faith—drawn from Sarah's journey in the presence of God—encourage you to once again lift your soul before the Author of your faith (Hebrews 12:2) and allow Him to add to the exquisite gem of your faith another sparkling facet.

And God said..."I did not let you touch her."
GENESIS 20:6

Sarah was alone again. Since their marriage in Ur, she and her husband, Abraham, had been almost inseparable, with him leading and her faithfully following. In those many years, Sarah had only been so alone once before. She cringed at the black memory of being separated from Abraham and taken into the harem of the mighty Pharaoh of Egypt (Genesis 12:15). And now it had happened again. Her husband had put their marriage—and the promise of their long-awaited son (Genesis 18:10)—at risk with four simple but half-true words: "She is my sister."

And so Sarah, earlier called the princess of a nation (Genesis 17:15), found herself alone again. The future looked hopeless. But Sarah was also the princess of faith (Hebrews 11:11). When God's promise seemed to be foiled and her future with Abraham finished, Sarah discovered afresh the one powerful truth she had experienced those decades ago in similar circumstances: She was alone...except for God—and what a great exception He is![4] She was alone, but—

- God protected Sarah, miraculously speaking to Abimelech in a dream by night.
- God preserved Sarah, threatening Abimelech's life because of her.
- God did not allow King Abimelech to touch Sarah.
- God miraculously intervened on Sarah's behalf and closed all the wombs in Abimelech's household because of her.
- God restored Sarah to Abraham.

And just like Sarah, you live your life in God's constant and powerful presence. No matter where you are, no matter what odds you encounter, no matter how alone you feel or appear to be, no matter who has let you down or forsaken you, you are never alone:

- Above you are God's overshadowing wings (Psalm 91:4).
- Beneath you are God's everlasting arms (Deuteronomy 33:27).
- All around you the angel of the Lord encamps to deliver you (Psalm 34:7).
- Inside, God's peace that passes all understanding guards your heart and mind (Philippians 4:7).

And the LORD did for Sarah as He had promised.
GENESIS 21:1 NASB

For Sarah and Abraham, the aged couple to whom God had for 25 years repeatedly promised a son, their time of waiting was finally over. In the quiet precision of His ordained, from-before-the-foundation-of the-world control, God did for Sarah exactly as He had promised. Divine grace and miraculous power were at work in Sarah's once-lifeless womb, and a baby son was on the way…exactly as God had promised!

What has God promised you, one of His precious women? The Bible contains as many as 8,000 promises. In difficulty and disaster, in trial, tragedy, trauma, and testing, in times of spiritual, emotional, and physical darkness, you can trust these promises. You can be assured that God will do for you, too, exactly as He has promised.

A young French woman once created a "promise box" to teach her children that the promises of God bring special comfort in times of need. The small box contained 200 handwritten promises copied out of the Bible onto small pieces of paper. Little did she know that her own trust in the Lord would be severely tested in war-time France!

With no food available for her family—her children emaciated and hungry, wearing rags and shoes without soles—she turned to her promise box. In desperation she prayed, "Lord, O Lord, I have such great need. Is there a promise here that is really for me? Show me, O Lord, what promise I can have in this time of famine, nakedness, peril, and sword." Blinded by tears, she reached for the box to pull out a promise and knocked it over. God's promises showered down all around her, on her lap, and on the floor! Not one was left in the box. What supreme joy in the Lord she found as she realized that *all* of the promises of God were hers—in the very hour of her greatest need![5]

He who has promised is faithful (Hebrews 10:23). God will fulfill His promises. Your responsibility is to believe His exceedingly great and precious promises and trust in the Promise Maker (2 Peter 1:4).

Sarah conceived and bore…a son.
GENESIS 21:2

*I*f there had been a newspaper in their day, the reporter assigned to the story of Abraham and Sarah's life would have received some amazing answers to his basic journalistic questions.

Who? Abraham, the 100-year-old-father, and Sarah, the 90-year-old mother, are proud parents of a baby boy (Genesis 17:17).

What? With God's blessing, Sarah conceived and bore a son.

When? At the appointed time, God fulfilled His promise to the elderly couple (Genesis 18:14).

Why? The miracle fulfilled what the "God, who cannot lie" had promised long ages before (Titus 1:2; Genesis 12:2).

How? "By faith Sarah…received strength to conceive seed, and she bore a child when she was past the age, because she judged Him faithful who had promised" (Hebrews 11:11).

This miraculous birth occurred because God fulfilled a promise made 25 years prior to His two believing saints, Sarah and Abraham. And it is no different for you, dear woman of faith. What has God promised to you, His believing saint? What do you, by faith, believe to be true of God?

- *Eternal life*—"I give them eternal life" (John 10:28).

- *Sufficient grace*—"My grace is sufficient" (2 Corinthians 12:9).

- *Strength for life*—"I can do all things through Christ who strengthens me" (Philippians 4:13).

- *His everlasting presence*—"The LORD your God is with you wherever you go" (Joshua 1:9).

Dearly beloved, these are but a few of the precious jewels of promise stored in God's Word. Open the Scriptures. Pour out its golden coins, stamped with the image of heaven's King. Let the treasure flow through your fingers. Count the diamonds of promise that flash like stars. Marvel over the royal rubies of guarantee. Imagine the worth of each single gem of promise. This treasure of promises is God's inheritance for you. By faith know and cherish what the Faithful One has promised!

Sarah…bore…a son.
GENESIS 21:2

Waiting. "To remain inactive in readiness or expectation." This is how the dictionary defines what Sarah had just spent 25 years doing: waiting. Oh, how difficult it must have been for Sarah to remain inactive in readiness and expectation of God's promised son (Genesis 12:2)! But the waiting meant precious treasure for Sarah. The riches at the end of her wait included:

- *The witnessing of miracles*—The 100-year-old Abraham fathered a child! The 90-year-old Sarah conceived and bore a son! And still another miracle followed as Sarah's worn-out body sustained the life of her little one as she nursed him.

- *The working of faith*—Sarah inherited the promise of a child by "faith and patience"; she exhibited the full assurance of hope until the end (Hebrews 6:11,12).

- *The fulfillment of God's promise*—Wrapped up in Sarah's little wrapped-up baby was God's fulfillment of His covenant with Abraham (Genesis 12:2), and the continuance of the family line which would give rise to God's own Son, Jesus Christ (Matthew 1:2,17).

- *A child to love*—God made the barren Sarah "a joyful mother of children" (Psalm 113:9).

For what are you waiting? For what are you remaining "inactive in readiness of expectation"? Are you waiting for a prodigal to return to his or her Father? Or are you waiting for release from some physical affliction? Perhaps you are waiting for a husband—or for your husband to return to the Lord, or to love the Lord more deeply, or to be the spiritual leader in your home. Could it be you are waiting, like sister Sarah, for a baby? Or are you waiting for vindication from some unfortunate misunderstanding, for God to come to your rescue and show forth His righteousness on your behalf (Psalm 37:6)? Are you eagerly waiting for heaven, for the groaning of your body to cease, for your ultimate victory, to go home to the heavenly abode for which you so long?

God bids you to wait—in readiness and expectation—on His riches, just as Sarah did, whose sister you are as you trust in God (1 Peter 3:5,6).

"God has made me laugh."
GENESIS 21:6

*T*he desert tent rang with sounds of joy! Sarah could not contain her gladness as she held her promised son. It was a season of joyous celebration. Sarah's shameful barrenness had ended (Genesis 11:29). Finally— *finally!*—after 25 years, after hearing the promise again and again, after a visit from God and two angels (Genesis 18:1, 2), little Isaac, pink and wrinkled, was born to the aged and wrinkled—but laughing—parents, Abraham and Sarah. And in their exultant joy, they named the babe *Isaac*, meaning "he laughs."

Once again Sarah was laughing. Oh, she had laughed before when the angels and the Lord had again promised the child. But then her laughter had been rooted in disbelief (Genesis 18:12). Now hers was the hearty laughter of joy upon joy! "Who would have dreamed?" Sarah marveled. Certainly not she! But God, who is always fully able, had accomplished the miracle. Others would no longer laugh at her—now they would laugh with her in joy.

This definitely was an occasion for joy. Isaac was the child of her own body, the child of her old age, the child of God's promise, the fruit of tested faith, the gift of God's grace, and the heaven-appointed heir. So Sarah sang a jubilant song of pure joy, the first-recorded cradle hymn of a mother's thankfulness and delight.

Dear woman of God, join with Sarah in this chorus of praise! Even if life is difficult *here,* you can know joy because of the hope you have in Christ. *Here* you have cause to sing even when you don't feel like singing, even when God's promises aren't yet fulfilled. At the appointed time—here or in heaven—God will give you reason to sing as He demonstrates His faithfulness to you. But sing now as you look forward to the fulfillment of all His promises to you and to your season of joy!

> Weeping may endure for a night,
>   But joy comes in the morning....
> You [God] have turned for me my mourning into dancing;
>   You have put off my sackcloth and clothed me with
>   gladness (Psalm 30:5,11).

God will "comfort all who mourn...give them beauty for ashes, the oil of joy for mourning, the garment of praise for the spirit of heaviness" (Isaiah 61:2,3)—and that "all" includes you! Rejoice!

The angel of God called to Hagar out of heaven.
Genesis 21:17

ecause you live your life in God's presence, you can never be anywhere that God isn't; He is always with you (Psalm 139:7-12). You can never be separated from the loving presence of the Lord (Romans 8:35-39). Wherever you are—dealing with whatever trial, facing whatever problem, enduring whatever difficulty—you can be assured that God knows, sees, hears, cares, and will provide for you. That's a reality Hagar, the handmaid to Sarah and the mother of Abraham's son Ishmael, experienced—twice (see January 16 and 17)! Here's how her second encounter with God went.

After Isaac, Abraham's God-appointed heir, was born, Abraham had sent Hagar and her son, Ishmael, away. With their water supply depleted, the two of them were dying in the desert as they lay atop the hot crust of the barren earth—cast out, crushed down, and beaten up by life. Their once-bright future now held only death—the brutal death that comes when water is not available to a parched body.

In despair, Hagar lifted up her voice and wept. Hers was a cry without hope, a wail of grief, a message of misery prompted by the deep anguish that was wringing her heart. And Ishmael cried out, too, his sounds of anguish joining with those of his mother.

Hagar had forgotten that the name of her handsome dying son meant "God hears." And indeed God does—and God did! "God *heard* the voice of the lad. Then the angel of God called to Hagar out of heaven…'God has *heard* the voice of the lad where he is'" (emphasis added).

Along with Hagar and Ishmael, delight yourself in the knowledge that God cares for His children and in the power of His attributes as set forth in Psalm 34:15-19. Your God is omnipresent, omnipotent, and omniscient:

> The eyes of the Lord are on the righteous,
>   And His ears are open to their cry….
>
> The righteous cry out, and the Lord hears,
>   And delivers them out of all their troubles.
>
> The Lord is near to those who have a broken heart,
>   And saves such as have a contrite spirit.
>
> Many are the afflictions of the righteous,
>   But the Lord delivers him out of them all.

"Fear not."
GENESIS 21:17

*W*hat are some of your favorite "fear nots" in the Bible? Perhaps your list includes these:

> "Fear not...I am thy shield" (Genesis 15:1 KJV).
>
> "Fear not...for I am with thee" (Genesis 26:24 KJV).
>
> "Fear ye not, stand still, and see the salvation of the LORD" (Exodus 14:13 KJV).
>
> "Fear not, little flock" (Luke 12:32 KJV).

You are wise to arm yourself with as many "fear nots" as you can find in God's powerful Word. They will help you stand strong through the years and fears of life. So why not add to your list the special "fear not" God gave to the suffering and destitute Hagar?

Hagar was afraid. Alone and homeless after being sent away from the shelter of Abraham's tent, Hagar and her son, Ishmael, were dying of thirst. The best Hagar could do was thrust her son under the scant shade of a desert scrub bush, distance herself from his pathetic sobs, and weep while she waited for death to come. And then, booming out of the heavens, the angel of God called out to Hagar, "Fear not!"

Any battle is won up front when you "fear not." So, as you enter the many battles of life, don the "fear nots" of the Bible as your armor. In days gone by, defensive armor was made of flexible fabric of interlinked metal rings. This chain mail was worn as a coat, forming a protective covering for those in battle. In fact, the metal mesh was perfected to the degree that it was scarcely possible to find a spot where the armor could be pierced.

Why not weave your own suit of armor against fear? Use the "fear nots" of the Bible as the links in your protective battle gear. Pull on God's perfect equipment—His "fear nots"—for fighting your own battle against fear. After all, "God has not given us a spirit of fear, but of power and of love and of a sound mind" (2 Timothy 1:7). Therefore, fear not!

"Arise, lift up the lad."
GENESIS 21:18

In the life story of Hagar, God gives you a powerful two-step plan for successfully enduring the distresses and overcoming the obstacles of life:

Step 1—A Negative: Fear not!

Step 2—A Positive: Do something!

In Hagar's case, her energy was spent—and so was her faith—when God Himself issued from heaven His orders for Step 1. Calling out to Hagar, now a single mother awaiting certain death in the desert with her son, the angel of the Lord commanded, "Fear not!"

Next, because faith must always be active, God spelled out Step 2: "Arise!" In other words, "Do something—do anything! Put feet on your faith!" God's message to the frail fugitive was, "Rise up! Don't give up—get up! Keep on keeping on! Go on! Muster your forces! Use any ounce of remaining strength! Proceed! Advance to the actions of faith!"

Why this call to action? Because action—continuing to try and doing what you can—conquers depression, staves off defeat, shakes off despair, and vanquishes discouragement.

What impossible challenge lies in your path today? What hopeless situation do you face? What insurmountable odds are before you? What disaster threatens your growth in faith? Tune your ear—and your heart and your strength—to God's voice of wisdom as He says, "Arise!" Move! Do something! Ask God for a plan of action and then plan your day. Make a to-do list. Get up off the ground or the couch, get out of the bed or the easy chair! Commit yourself to a day—and a life—of reaching forward to those things which are ahead and pressing toward the goal for the prize of the upward call of God in Christ Jesus (Philippians 3:13,14). Tap into the strength promised to you in Christ which enables you to do all things through Him (Philippians 4:13).

Assume a positive posture—one that moves you forward, up, and over your problem. Act! As a law of physics states, a body (human or otherwise) at rest tends to remain at rest, and a body in motion tends to remain in motion. Make sure yours is in motion!

"I will make him a great nation."
Genesis 21:18

As the utter darkness of Hagar's impending death immobilized her to a point of faithlessness, fear, and futility, God's sun of promise began its brilliant ascent. Truly, God's mercies and compassion fail not. They are new every morning (Lamentations 3:22, 23)—and so are His promises!

Picture the cast-out Hagar and her teenage son, Ishmael. In a stark, barren wilderness without water, these two pathetic people lay down to die. Casualties of cruel and unfair treatment, the two had been put out—defenseless—in the desert to make their way back to Egypt, Hagar's homeland. The end of life seemed near.

But Hagar's emergency became God's opportunity. Through the blindness of fear and the blur of hopelessness, Hagar found herself gazing at fresh, rising hope. It was a miracle! From the heavens, God's voice sounded forth His blessed assurance: "I will make him a great nation." Yes, there was hope for tomorrow! And, as God had promised, Hagar lived to see Ishmael grow up, marry, and become the ruler of a great nation (verses 20, 21; Genesis 25:12-18).

Are you enjoying the blazing glory of the many precious promises God gives you in Scripture, hope-filled promises for all your tomorrows? What wonderful promises from Him are you counting on? Thank God for this handful of glistening promises from His vast treasure house of hope:

- *His constant presence to cheer and to guide.* "I am with you always" (Matthew 28:20).

- *A new body.* He "will transform our lowly body that it may be conformed to His glorious body" (Philippians 3:21).

- *A life without sorrow or pain.* "God will wipe away every tear from their eyes; there shall be no more death, nor sorrow, nor crying. There shall be no more pain" (Revelation 21:4).

- *Eternal life in His gracious presence.* "I give them eternal life, and they shall never perish" (John 10:28).

- *Rest for your soul.* "Come to Me, all you who labor and are heavy laden, and I will give you rest" (Matthew 11:28).

And she saw a well of water.
GENESIS 21:19

*O*ne of God's many marvelous names is *Jehovah-jireh*, meaning "God provides." And Hagar came to appreciate that glorious truth when God graciously provided for her needs. Hagar was a needy woman who found herself on the receiving end of God's gracious provisions. As you consider what God supplied for Hagar, remember that He provides these very resources for you in your troubles.

- *Comfort*—Hagar and her son were alone and dying when God made His presence known. Taking the initiative, God rescued the forlorn and helpless pair. God saw the distressed mother and child, heard their cries of despair, and comforted them physically and emotionally.

When do you most need the comfort of God's presence and provision? Take heart! God sees your distresses, hears your cries, and comforts you in your troubles.

- *Encouragement*—Left alone to raise her son and care for him, Hagar was failing at the task. Their water was gone, and no one was around to help. But God called out encouragement to the exhausted Hagar. "Fear not!" He proclaimed, His words trumpeting hope from heaven.

Do you ever feel the despair of failure? Do you ever struggle with hopelessness? Fear not! The Lord knows your needs.

- *Instruction*—God's instruction accompanied His encouragement. God told Hagar: "Arise, lift up the lad and hold him with your hand." She was not to give up on life, on her son, or on God. Instead, Hagar was to get up, get the lad up, and go on!

Need guidance? God's Word is full of instruction and counsel. Jehovah-jireh ("God provides") gladly opens the windows of heaven to lavishly pour out His priceless wisdom to you in any situation. Just open your Bible.

God's love for you is unfathomable. These are but a few of the heavenly supplies He graces you with on your earthly journey. Pause, pray, and praise Him now for His comfort, encouragement, and instruction. And don't forget to read tomorrow to discover three more of the treasures God has for you!

And she saw a well of water.
GENESIS 21:19

*A*s we learned yesterday, our wonderful God is Jehovah-jireh, the God who provides, and one recipient of God's marvelous provision was Hagar. Life had not gone well for Hagar, who had been sent away into the parched, barren wilderness with her son, Ishmael. When their water supply was depleted and the pathetic twosome was near death, Jehovah-jireh heard their cries, noticed their dire condition, and met their many needs. Yesterday we noted the comfort, encouragement, and instruction God provided to Hagar. But His list of generous grace goes on:

- *Promise*—Indicating that all was not lost for her son, God promised Hagar, "I will make him a great nation." When no ray of hope was evident, God gave Hagar a promise to hold on to as she held on to her son's hand. Fueled by that promise, Hagar was energized to go on. Ishmael would live to rule a great nation.

Dear one, whatever your life situation, you have been promised "all things that pertain to life" (2 Peter 1:3). You, too, can go on through life, fueled by God's promise of great faithfulness.

- *Guidance*—Whether Hagar looked to God or not, God looked to her—and looked out for her. "God opened her eyes" and directed her to a nearby spring. God led Hagar, blinded by fear and exhaustion, safely to water.

God delights to lead you, too. He is constantly at work guiding you among the people and through the events and circumstances that make up your life. He is the Good Shepherd who leads His sheep (Psalm 23:2,3).

- *Provision*—When God opened Hagar's eyes, "she saw a well of water." In her frightening plight, God provided a spring, a fountain, life itself! At the point of Hagar's ultimate despair, Jehovah-jireh provided the abundance of a well—not just a cup—of water.

Your promise for today—and every day—as you walk in God's presence is His plentiful provision. You'll know as the psalmist did that: "The LORD is my shepherd; I shall not want" (Psalm 23:1)! And you can join in the chorus sung by generations of believers: "All I have needed Thy hand hath provided."

Sarah lived one hundred and twenty-seven years.
GENESIS 23:1

*D*id you know that Sarah is the only woman in the Bible whose actual age is given? God tells us, "Sarah lived one hundred and twenty-seven years; these were the years of the life of Sarah." Imagine what snapshots from the different seasons of Sarah's long life would reveal!

First, a season of leaving. How hard it must have been for the fair and educated Sarah to leave her beautiful, culturally advanced homeland in Ur (Genesis 12:1). Yet God, through her husband, Abraham, asked her to leave all that was splendid there along the lush Euphrates River valley and follow Abraham into the arid desert—and into the will of God.

Second, a season of learning. Sarah's lessons included learning to follow her husband as he followed God, "not knowing where he was going" (Hebrews 11:8). Her obedience meant she was a homeless nomad for 60 years.

Learning how to wait was also difficult for the impatient wife who had masterminded a plan for Abraham to have a baby with her handmaiden Hagar (Genesis 16:2).

Then there was the profound, often-repeated assignment of learning to trust in God's promise for a son. During those 25 years of waiting, Sarah's faith wavered and waned (Genesis 18:12).

Third, a season of leaning. Sarah is also the only woman in the Bible taken into the harem of a pagan ruler twice! First, Abraham told the Egyptian Pharaoh, "She is my sister" (Genesis 12:19). He then repeated his lie to King Abimelech (Genesis 20:5). Alone and cut off from her husband, Sarah learned to lean on God. She learned well that "God is our refuge and strength, *a very present help in trouble*" (Psalm 46:1, emphasis added)!

Finally, a season of loving. In His goodness and at the appointed time, God at long last miraculously gifted 90-year-old Sarah with Isaac, her own little baby boy (Genesis 21:7). How she must have cherished every second of the 37 years she was privileged to be a loving mother!

What season of life are you now experiencing? Learn well from these lessons of Sarah's life!

So Sarah died.
GENESIS 23:2

*A*s one wedding ceremony puts it, a marriage lasts "until death parts the partners." The day finally dawned when death did indeed part Abraham and his partner, Sarah. His faithful Sarah, his mate and friend for more than 60 years, slipped away. Death is certainly an end to temporal, earthly life, but for God's saints, death is the doorway to eternal life.

Have you thought about death? Does your perspective on death match what God says in His holy Word? Meditate on these truths about the death of a believer and embrace them for yourself.

Truth #1. How you die is as important as how you live. Paul writes, "For if we live, we live to the Lord; and if we die, we die to the Lord" (Romans 14:8). So how should you face death? Boldly and with unfailing courage so that "in nothing [you] shall be ashamed" (Philippians 1:20). Your goal is to glorify and exalt Christ by your life *and* in your death (Philippians 1:20).

Truth #2. How you view death is important. The world views death as the end, as the entrance into something unknown, something awful, something to be feared. But for God's saint, "to die is *gain*" (Philippians 1:21, emphasis added)! As someone has pointed out, in death "God strips me of everything to give me everything!"

Truth #3. How you define death is important. Death is simply a departure. In Philippians 1:23, Paul describes death as "depart[ing] and be[ing] with Christ." In the Greek, the imagery is one of loosening the ropes on a tent, pulling up the tent stakes, and moving on. Death is simply a moving on. Each day you live on earth is but another day's march nearer home until, in the end, camp in this world is forever struck and exchanged for permanent residence in a world of glory.

So the stakes on Sarah's tent were pulled up one final time, and Sarah went home to be with her heavenly Lord. "Precious in the sight of the LORD is the death of His saints" (Psalm 116:15)!

Milcah, the wife of Nahor...
GENESIS 24:15

*H*er name is listed in God's Word, but "nothing is recorded of the life and character of this daughter of Haran."[1] Yet what can we piece together about Milcah?

- Her name means *queen*.
- Her father was Haran, who was also the father of Abraham.
- Her brother was Abraham, the friend of God and the founder of the Jewish nation.
- Her sister-in-law was Sarah, the beautiful woman of faith.
- Her husband was Nahor, brother to Abraham.
- Her children included eight sons, the youngest one named Bethuel.
- Her lovely granddaughter was Rebekah, born to Bethuel and later married to Isaac.

Do you ever feel like a "nothing"? Like nobody special? Do you ever fear that nothing significant will be recorded of your life and character? Yet in your heart of hearts you know how much you love God, how you seek to obey Him and follow Him every step of the way. You also know the cost of such faithful following.

Perhaps Milcah was such a woman. Nothing about her life and character is recorded, but the missing details don't matter. Milcah stands as a quiet queen for you to emulate all the days of your life. How can you follow in her steps?

Be faithful to God. When Abraham needed a godly wife for his only son—the son from whom would arise the entire Jewish race—he knew exactly where to find her. She would be among the offspring of Milcah, his own brother's wife. Few believed in God, and Milcah apparently stood with those few.

Be faithful to your husband. Over the years, Milcah must have steadfastly loved and served her husband—through thick and thin, through better and worse, in sickness and health, until death claimed the first partner.

Be faithful to raise your children according to God's way. Eight sons are listed to Milcah's credit. One (Bethuel) bore Rebekah, who married the patriarch Isaac.

So when Abraham sought a wife to help build a people for God, the fruit of Milcah's life was harvested. This quiet queen had left a godly seed in a godless world.

"The daughter of Bethuel..."
GENESIS 24:24

$\mathcal{W}$e meet only a handful of single women in Scripture, but in Genesis 24 God presents Rebekah, a stunning woman of faith and service, who is single. Today, as you meet the lovely Rebekah, marvel at these qualities that make her one of God's special servants:

- *Rebekah's purity*—She was "a virgin; no man had known her."

- *Rebekah's busyness*—Rather than looking for a husband or languishing, moping, or mourning over the lack of one, Rebekah stayed busy serving her family and others.

- *Rebekah's hospitality*—Her home was open to those who needed care.

- *Rebekah's energy*—Abundant energy is a sign of happiness, and Rebekah's happiness empowered her with energy enough to serve other people far beyond the minimum. Rebekah ministered to the maximum!

Before journeying on with Rebekah, take a moment to note God's beautiful plan for His single women. God calls His special servants to a life of:

- *Purity*—A single Christian woman is to remain "holy both in body and in spirit" (1 Corinthians 7:34).

- *Ministry*—A single Christian woman is to live her life in a way that reflects her complete dedication to God. As one who is unmarried, she has the privilege of undistracted service to God and caring for "the things of the Lord" (1 Corinthians 7:34). Every day a woman is single is another glorious day to serve God wholeheartedly and without distraction. Her singleness is her "green light" from God to go all out in service to others.

Is singleness a reality for you today, dear woman of God? Although you may desire to be married, "let not [your] longing slay the appetite of [your] living....Accept and thank God for what is given, not allowing the *not-given* to spoil it."[2]

"…willing to follow me to this land."
GENESIS 24:5

*H*ow does a man find a wife? This was the predicament Abraham found himself in. But the wife he needed to find was not for himself. She was for his only son, 37-year-old Isaac. "Who?" and "How?" were the questions that plagued Abraham.

Realizing that the continuation of his family line and the fulfillment of God's promise to make his family a great nation (Genesis 12:2) were at stake, Abraham called in his oldest servant, the faithful Eliezer. After receiving a solemn oath from Eliezer, Abraham sent his 85-year-old servant on a 500-mile journey to find a wife for Isaac. This woman would have to be willing to follow Eliezer back across those 500 miles to an unknown future in order to serve God with a man she had yet to meet. What requirements did God and Abraham set down for such a woman?

- *She must not be a Canaanite.* Abraham carefully stipulated that his servant not "take a wife…from the daughters of the Canaanites." A wife from among these pagan, godless people would lead Isaac and his offspring away from the true God.

- *She must be from among Abraham's own family.* He instructed Eliezer, "You shall go to my country and to my family."

- *She must be willing to follow Eliezer* back to the land of Abraham and Isaac. A woman who would do this would be a woman willing to forsake all—in faith—for the glorious future God had ordained.

And now, dear friend, how would you describe your own devotion to God, your willingness to seek after and follow God's will for your life? Are you steadfastly renouncing the world and its influence, turning your back on its standards? Are you actively following the God of the Bible, the God you so love? As such a woman, you have a tremendous and godly influence on your husband, your children, and your world. And you have a glorious future in store!

"Let her be the one You have appointed."
GENESIS 24:14

Wanted: The Ideal Wife

Must be physically strong and healthy,
energetic and able to work hard.
must be friendly and industrious,
kind and compassionate,
generous and love to serve—
and devoted to God.

*A*braham's faithful servant Eliezer listed the qualities he was searching for in his quest for a wife for Isaac, his master's only son. Sent by Abraham on a 500-mile journey to find such a wife, Eliezer stopped to finalize his checklist. He was tired and thirsty after his extensive trip, and so were his ten camels. So Eliezer and his camel caravan stood at the well outside the city of Nahor.

At this point, Eliezer did one more thing with his "want" list: He lifted it up before his omniscient, omnipotent God in prayer. He knew that only God could lead him, a stranger in a strange land, to such a woman. So he asked God to "please give me success this day."

Considering the items on—and not on—Eliezer's list, how could God not answer his request!

- Eliezer did not mention outward appearance or material wealth.

- He asked only for godly character qualities.

- He asked for physical attributes that would enable a woman to endure an inevitably difficult life.

What does your "want" list look like? Who do you want to be? Single or married, are you focusing on godly character rather than on beauty or affluence? Would you rather be kind and loving (Galatians 5:22), or assertive and successful? Pray about your desires, and then adjust your standards to match the qualities God desires in His women.

Do not let your adornment be merely outward—arranging the hair, wearing gold, or putting on fine apparel—rather let it be the hidden person of the heart, with the incorruptible beauty of a gentle and quiet spirit, which is very precious in the sight of God (1 Peter 3:3,4).

Rebekah…came out with her pitcher…
Genesis 24:15

ightly or wrongly, we tend to evaluate a person's character based upon our first meeting with them. And that first impression can be very important.

It was no different when Abraham's servant first saw Rebekah. Tired from a long journey, on a mission to find a bride for Isaac, the only heir to Abraham's wealth and God's promise—Eliezer waited by the town well in Nahor for the young women to come draw water. Eliezer waited and prayed, asking God to bring a woman who would offer him a drink of water. And before he had finished speaking to the Lord, "Behold, Rebekah…came out with her pitcher on her shoulder."

What first impression of this young woman did Abraham's servant have? What does her initial appearance suggest about the lovely Rebekah?

Eliezer saw right away that Rebekah was a working woman. At the appointed time, probably twice a day, she took her heavy clay pitcher to the town's water source to draw some precious water and carry it back to her home within the walled city. Rebekah helped care for her family by regularly drawing the water they needed.

Dear one, take a long look at Rebekah. Gaze upon her beautiful qualities of diligence and faithfulness. Watch carefully her tireless industry and humble willingness to engage in menial work. Marvel at her fine ability to do very demanding work. Wonder at her servant heart that placed the needs of her family above any concern about what others would think of her.

Do you think hard work is degrading? Do you think hard work is to be done by other people, not you? Do you dread rolling up your sleeves and working hard on some necessary task? Here, in God's Word, God praises the enchanting Rebekah. So if you are ever tempted to disdain your work, allow God's thoughts about His beautiful woman of Proverbs 31 to correct your thinking: "She girds herself with strength, and strengthens her arms.… Strength and honor are her clothing" (Proverbs 31:17, 25). God values women who work hard to serve Him and the people He puts in their lives.

"I will draw water for your camels also."
GENESIS 24:19

esus told those listening to His Sermon on the Mount, "Whoever compels you to go one mile, go with him two. Give to him who asks you" (Matthew 5:41,42). Thousands of years before God's Son uttered these words, Rebekah was putting the principle into practice....

The scene opens with an old man and his ten thirsty camels lingering around a well in a city of Mesopotamia. The man had traveled 500 miles to the town of Abraham's family to find a wife for Abraham's only son. "O LORD God...please give me success this day," the tired servant had prayed. Before he affixed an "amen" to his request, the beautiful Rebekah came to the well with her empty water pitcher to draw water for her family.

A faithful servant, Eliezer hurried to meet her and said, "Please let me drink a little water from your pitcher." How did Rebekah respond? Ever gracious, helpful, and compassionate, she bade him, "Drink, my lord," and then she volunteered the second mile of service: "I will draw water for your camels also, until they have finished drinking."

How many draws of water from the well do you think Rebekah had to make to satisfy ten thirsty camels? A camel can drink as much as 25 gallons after a long journey. And yet the generous and energetic Rebekah "hastened" and "ran" back and forth from the well to the trough many times in order to satiate the weary animals. Rebekah went many "extra miles" on that extraordinary day!

No price can be put on the sterling qualities Rebekah exhibited in her attitudes and actions that day by the well. Her servant spirit shone like the sun, revealing her sincere and good heart. She was respectful, aware of those in need, willing to help, and generous. Giving drink to the tired old man only met a fraction of his needs. So Rebekah quickly acted to water his animals, too.

Just for today, won't you follow in beautiful Rebekah's footsteps and be on the lookout for some needy person...and then do more than is needed?

"We have...room to lodge."
GENESIS 24:25

*E*xactly how do you view your home? Do you see it as a gift from God to be used for the comfort and well-being of others? Such a perspective would please your God, who values the virtue of hospitality. Throughout the Bible, hospitality—or "stranger love"—is greatly valued because life in the desert depended on it.

Abraham's servant Eliezer had just traveled 500 miles in that desert. As he prayed beside the town well about his many needs, the lovely Rebekah appeared. After first drawing water from the cistern to satisfy his thirst, Rebekah offered him a place to rest and eat. In her welcoming way, Rebekah extended perfect stranger love, saying, "We have...room to lodge [you]." Inside Rebekah's family home, Eliezer would be the graced recipient of assistance, refreshment, shelter, and rest. His every need would be met.

A Christian home is earth's sweetest picture of heaven and a welcome relief in our stressed and weary society. Won't you open your arms, your heart, and your home to those in pain? Consider the teens you know who live where parents and siblings are seldom home, where few meals are served, and where it appears that no one cares. Think about the little ones next door who could heal for a moment in your warm kitchen, away from the endless, angry shouting under their own roof. Ponder the needs of a widow who has no one to talk to. Count the young singles you know who are away from their parents' home and hearth.

Why not serve a meal to a searching neighbor? Or sit over a cup of tea with a brokenhearted mother struggling over her child. Offer a listening ear, an encouraging word, and a heartfelt prayer to those in need. Hospitality is a matter of the heart—*your* heart! And your home can become a haven of rest for many wounded and needy souls. All who enter your door, cross your threshold, sit at your table, or rest in your bed offer you an opportunity to minister. Welcome them into your home sweet home—a home where Jesus lives in the heart of the hostess!

And she said, "I will go."
GENESIS 24:58

$\mathcal{T}$alk is one thing. Action is another—and action has always been a measure of true faith. Rebekah added her name to God's roll call of the truly faithful when she stepped out, trusting in Him.

The progression of events that culminated in that giant step of faith began with words spoken some 500 miles away by Abraham to his servant Eliezer: "Go...and take a wife for my son Isaac." When Eliezer reached his destination, the beautiful Rebekah, daughter of Abraham's distant relative Bethuel, invited him to stay in her family's home. While there, her father and brother agreed that Rebekah should marry Isaac.

However, when talk turned to a departure date for their cherished Rebekah, her mother and brother said, "Let the young woman stay with us a few days, at least ten; after that she may go." When Eliezer said that he needed to return now, they said, "We will call the young woman and ask her personally." When they asked Rebekah, "Will you go with this man?" the question really was, "Will you go now—or wait?"

Rebekah's faith evidenced itself as she said, "I will go." Her words revealed much about her faith. "I will go...with a stranger...to live in an unknown land...to be the wife of an unknown man. I will go...even though I will probably never see my family again...even though I have no time to prepare...even though the nomadic life of Abraham's family will be strenuous. I will go!"

Take a quick inventory of your own life of faith. Is there any act of faith you are postponing—even for "a few days"? Any decision you are putting off? Any step of faith you are delaying? Waiting may be easier, but the harder path of true faith is the path to greater blessing. Delayed obedience is in actuality disobedience, and delayed action delays God's blessing. Every step of faith is a giant step toward the center of God's will...and God's abundant blessings!

So they sent away Rebekah…and her nurse.
GENESIS 24:59

The Christian life is one of selfless service to others, and one picture in particular is worth a thousand words when it comes to understanding what selfless service looks like in God's great women through the ages. Deborah, Rebekah's lifelong maid, offers us a beautiful portrait of devoted service.

As a bond servant, Deborah was obligated to perform—without question or delay—her mistress's will. Whatever the order, Deborah was to respond quickly, quietly, without question.

That job description came to mean leaving the house of Bethuel, the only home she had ever known, to journey 500 miles with Rebekah to her new home—and doing so immediately! While Bethuel's family talked about this surprising turn of events, the devoted Deborah tried to get used to the idea that in the morning she was going to Canaan—forever!

But Deborah is a study in diligence as well as service. Her name, in fact, means "bee," suggesting industry and usefulness. We can imagine that she was constantly active, ever industrious and caring.

You, too, devoted follower of God, are called to serve many people in many places. How can you be industrious and willing like Deborah? Try these tactics as you tackle your work.

- *Tackle your work energetically.* Whatever chore you face, take on the challenge and "do it with [all] your might" (Ecclesiastes 9:10) and with "a mind to work" (Nehemiah 4:6). Remember to do your work "heartily" and "as to the Lord and not to men" (Colossians 3:23).

- *Tackle your work joyfully.* Choose to work with a joyful heart as well as a servant heart. You'll find great pleasure in your work when you approach it as a labor of love. Try to anticipate your work with joy instead of dread. See each task as an opportunity to serve, rather than as mere drudgery. Let the fact that you are ultimately serving God help you develop a positive attitude toward your work. Cultivate the habit of looking at each demanding task of life and deciding to do it, to do it well, to do it heartily, to do it as unto the Lord, and to enjoy doing it!

And they blessed Rebekah.
GENESIS 24:60

ℛebekah's beloved family stood on the road and called out their blessings for her life to come:

> Our sister, may you become
> The mother of thousands of ten thousands;
> And may your descendants possess
> The gates of those who hate them.

Twenty-four hours ago life had been so different for all of them. How
could Rebekah, her parents, or her brother have known that an ordinary
trip to the well would change the course of their history and, in fact, the
history of the world? Rebekah had simply gone—as she did every day of her
life—to draw water for the household. Yet, on that God-appointed day, a
stranger was waiting there. Sent by their kinsman Abraham to his family in
Nahor, the foreigner was to take back a bride for Abraham's son Isaac.

Dear, kind Rebekah gave the servant water and invited him to her family
home for the night. Over dinner her father and brother agreed that
Rebekah was the woman God had chosen to marry Abraham's heir.

As the sun rose the next morning, Rebekah mounted one of the
stranger's camels and left for the mysterious, faraway land of Canaan to be
married. Weeping and waving as the caravan carrying their precious
Rebekah filed out of sight, the family prayed and blessed the daughter and
sister they would probably never see again. Their prayers that Rebekah be
the mother of millions echoed God's promise that Abraham's many
descendants would be victors over all (Genesis 13:14,15; 15:5).

And now, dear one, if you are a mother, consider the potential impact of
that role. Your children are a blessing and a heritage from God (Psalm
127:3), a source of joy (Psalm 113:9), to be brought up in the training and
admonition of the Lord (Ephesians 6:4). After all, God can use a child of
yours to, through the ages, affect millions as he or she passes the baton of
faith to yet another generation.

And [Rebekah] followed the man.
GENESIS 24:61

*K*nowing God's will is our greatest treasure. As you pray, seek godly counsel, and live according to what is revealed in God's Word, you will discover His specific will for you in the everyday events of life. Learn more from the following simple ABCs, based on God's will for Rebekah and her marriage to Isaac:

Ask God. Through prayer and by reading God's Word, you can access the heart and mind of the Lord.

Ask God. Abraham's servant prayed fervently and specifically about finding the right wife for Isaac.

Be faithful. The need to make a decision is never a reason to neglect your duties. God leads His people as they remain obedient in the everyday events of life.

Be faithful. Rebekah was led to the next phase of God's will for her life while she was faithfully serving her family in the details of daily life.

Consult others. "Where there is no counsel, the people fall; but in the multitude of counselors there is safety" (Proverbs 11:14).

Consult others. Rebekah's father and brother were involved in counseling her and agreed to her marriage to Isaac.

Decide for yourself. You can be seeking, obedient, and asking, but ultimately you must decide whether or not you will heed God's will.

Decide for yourself. Family members agreed and the evidence of God's will lined up, yet Rebekah herself had to be willing to follow through in obedience.

Execute your decision. Once you know God's will, delayed obedience becomes disobedience. Take action immediately!

Execute your decision. Rather than lingering, Rebekah acted immediately and began her journey of faith…by faith!

She became his wife.
GENESIS 24:67

*W*hat a romantic and dramatic moment when Rebekah and Isaac are at last united!

After a bittersweet farewell to her family and a long journey through the desert, Rebekah caught the first glimpse of Isaac, her husband-to-be. He was in the fields that evening as her caravan moved oh-so-slowly toward the end of the grueling 500-mile trek from her home to his. Isaac, who was walking and meditating, praying and waiting, spotted the camels coming. "Could it be...?" he wondered. Was it possible the old servant had found a bride for him?

God be praised! The answer to both heart cries was "yes!" So Isaac "took Rebekah and she became his wife, and he loved her." One of God's great women of faith all those ages ago, Rebekah took the next step in God's divine design for her life. From that day forth, Rebekah would endeavor to be the kind of wife God wanted her to be. If you, too, are married, take to heart these guidelines from God:

- *Leave* your family and cleave to your husband. When you marry, you are freed forever from the authority of your parents to be joyfully bound to your husband. He—not your father or mother, brothers or sisters—is to be the most important person in your life (Genesis 2:24).

- *Help* your husband. God has ordained your role as one of helping, of using your energy to assist your husband with his responsibilities, his tasks, his goals (Genesis 2:18).

- *Submit* to your husband. Only one person at a time can successfully lead any organization or institution and, in your home, God has given that difficult role of leadership to your husband. Your role is to follow (Genesis 3:16; Ephesians 5:22).

- *Respect* your husband. How lovely it is to be in the presence of a wife who respects her husband! She shows her respect. She speaks it. She treats her husband as she would treat Christ Himself. This is God's lovely, high calling for you, too (Ephesians 5:33).

She was barren.
GENESIS 25:21

God's ways are not our ways (Isaiah 55:8,9), and God's timing is not always our timing (Ecclesiastes 3:1). Isaac's beautiful bride Rebekah had to learn these two lessons about God's plans.

The marriage of Isaac and Rebekah began in the right way: covered by prayer. It was truly a marriage made in heaven.

But there was one flaw. Twenty years passed and there was no baby. No baby to love. No baby to continue the family line. No baby to stand as a flesh-and-blood testimony of God's faithfulness to His promise (Genesis 12:2).

Consider how such heartache is often handled today. Doctors are consulted. Parents are informed. Best friends are updated daily. Husbands can become the target of much anger, blaming, belittling, and criticism. Emotions swing from shock to sorrow, from fear to panic. Arguments and complaints, mixed with tears of discouragement and depression, ring through homes where the happy blessing of children has been withheld.

What word of advice would God's couple, Rebekah and Isaac, have for us today when our dreams are thwarted?

In a word, *pray.* "Now Isaac pleaded with the LORD for his wife, because she was barren; and the LORD granted his plea, and Rebekah his wife conceived." Prayer was the means by which Rebekah entered into God's plan and His timing. Indeed, God's ways and His will come in His own perfect time.

> Like coral strands beneath the sea,
> So strongly built and chaste,
> The plans of God, unfolding, show
> No signs of human haste.[3]

For what are you waiting, dear one? Leave the desires of your heart with God through prayer and live each day in full contentment and confidence that your life—just as it is—is a part of God's perfect plan and His perfect timing. Enjoy God's peace that passes all understanding...for one more day.

She went to inquire of the Lord.
Genesis 25:22

*E*ach year of its life, a tree grows new wood. The new wood nourishes the very roots, fruit, and flowers, which are evidence that growth has occurred. Like a tree, Rebekah was also growing as she learned new lessons for life. One of those lessons was that prayer is the best way to handle the events and difficulties of life. The two major blessings in her life had indeed happened when people prayed:

- Blessing #1: Abraham's servant had prayed for a bride for Isaac—and God had led him to Rebekah (Genesis 24). Prayer was the key factor in Rebekah becoming Isaac's wife.

- Blessing #2: When Rebekah was still barren after 20 years of marriage, Isaac had prayed to God, and she had conceived. Prayer was the primary reason she was pregnant.

But now something was wrong. Rebekah was pregnant, but hers was a "problem pregnancy." Feeling an uneasy commotion in her body, she wondered, "If all is well, why am I like this?"

As the pregnancy and her worries continued, the blossoming fruit of spiritual growth burst forth: Rebekah "went to inquire of the Lord." Her understanding of God's power encouraged her to depend on Him more fully. And she was not disappointed. The Lord spoke to her.

You can be confident that God listens to your prayers when you call on Him (Psalm 4:3). Like Rebekah, you, too, can grow to depend more fully on God's power and His love by praying in your difficulties. Such asking in prayer helps you look at your problem in light of God's power, instead of looking at God in the shadow of your problems. Asking in prayer reaps other fruit, too:

- Prayer deepens your insight into what you really need.

- Prayer broadens your appreciation for God's answers.

- Prayer allows you to mature so you can use His gifts more wisely.[4]

Whatever your pain or problem, trial or temptation, suffering or sorrow, follow in Rebekah's footsteps of faith and inquire of the Lord. Ask in prayer. As the old hymn advises, "Take it to the Lord in prayer."

The Lord said to her...
GENESIS 25:23

*E*veryone struggles. We struggle in marriage, with finances, with health problems, with family members, in our career, in our job, with friends, and with temptation.

For the beautiful Rebekah, however, there was a literal and internal struggle. Finally pregnant after 20 years of marriage to Isaac, she knew something was not right in her pregnancy. An extraordinary physical commotion raged inside and made her uneasy.

How did Rebekah handle her anxiety? She went to the only Person who could help her: "She went to inquire of the LORD." The answer to her prayer—and the relief for her struggle—was in God's hands. No one else could help.

First, only God could know that Rebekah was carrying twins. God forms the inward parts of each child in the womb of its mother, and its frame is not hidden from Him. Rebekah's twins were the first recorded in Scripture, and only God could give her that information (see Psalm 139:13-16).

Second, only God could know the futures of her twin sons. God's answer to Rebekah's question, "Why am I like this?" contained a prophecy regarding her twins: "Two nations are in your womb, two peoples shall be separated from your body; one people shall be stronger than the other, and the older shall serve the younger." Her twins would reverse the traditional roles—the older would serve the younger—and the two would struggle as each became a great nation.

Rebekah exhibited her faith in God by praying to Him and inquiring of Him. When perplexed, disturbed, anxious, and distressed, she turned her anxiety into asking. Why not make it your practice to do the same—to turn your anxiety into asking? Why not take your struggles and routinely...

go into the sanctuary of God (Psalm 73:17),

spread out your case before the Lord (2 Kings 19:14), and

ask counsel at the Almighty's throne (Hebrews 4:16)?

"She is my sister."
GENESIS 26:7

$\mathcal{L}$ike any year of your life, each year of Rebekah's life brought many tests of her faith. So far, she had successfully weathered a series of significant faith tests.

- *Separation*—Rebekah had left family and homeland to marry the only son of Sarah and Abraham, the sole heir to God's promise to make Abraham's descendants into a great nation (Genesis 12:2).

- *Marriage*—In time, Rebekah had made the necessary adjustments to married life and to her marriage partner.

- *Childlessness*—Two decades passed as Rebekah waited for a child, waited for the promise, waited on God—and learned the lessons of faith that only waiting can teach (Genesis 25:21).

- *Motherhood*—Finally, not one, but two babies had been born! Being the mother of the world's first-recorded set of twins had stretched Rebekah's faith to greater lengths.

The only thing about Rebekah that wasn't weathering with time was her exquisite appearance. But her enduring beauty presented yet another test of faith for Rebekah.

The setting for the test was a famine in the land. God specifically instructed Rebekah's husband to stay where he was during the famine. So Isaac—by faith—had stayed, but—in fear—he had lied about Rebekah. He said to the king of the Philistines, "'She is my sister'; for he was afraid to say, 'She is my wife,' because he thought, 'lest the men of the place kill me for Rebekah, because she is beautiful to behold.'"

What would you have done? How do you normally face fear? Do you panic? Flee? Crumble? Through the ages, God's women have chosen to trust God. The next time you are frozen with fear, fight it with God's formula for your faith:

Trust in God—not your husband (1 Peter 3:1, 2).

Refuse to succumb to fear (1 Peter 3:6).

Understand that God always protect you (Psalm 23:4).

Strengthen your spirit with God's promises (2 Peter 1:4).

Thank God for His promised protection (Isaiah 41:10).

"Rachel is coming."
GENESIS 29:6

*I*n Washington, D.C., the Smithsonian Institute houses the portraits of our country's first ladies. The wife of every president is shown wearing her inaugural ball gown. Gazing into the faces of the women who stood behind our leaders is a moving experience.

God, too, has His own portraits of great women. They are housed in the Word of God, and you are invited to look long at His women of faith through the ages and learn much from them—today and throughout your life—as you stroll through the pages of the Holy Scriptures. So far in this devotional, you have admired the portraits of many of God's beautiful women, most recently, Sarah and Rebekah. Soon we'll see God add Rachel to His museum masterpieces.

How does a woman gain a place in God's great hall of faith? More importantly, how can your portrait find a position alongside God's faithful women through the ages? John 1:12 tells you how: "But as many as *received* Him, to them He gave the right to become children of God, to those who *believe* in His name" (emphasis added).

> *Receive*—To become a child of God, you must receive Jesus Christ as your personal Savior and acknowledge His death on your behalf for your sins.

> *Believe*—Jesus Christ is the living Word of God, and God calls you to acknowledge His claim to be God-in-flesh and place your faith in Him as Savior and Lord.

Are you a child of God? Have you yielded your life to Jesus Christ? Have you received God's grace gift of salvation and eternal life through Jesus? When you believe in Jesus as God-in-flesh and receive Him into your heart and life by faith, you can claim the exalted title of "God's child." Only the precious status of "God's child" qualifies you for a place in the portrait halls of heaven.

Rachel came with her father's sheep.
GENESIS 29:9

*E*xperts on proper etiquette tell us to include some kind of personal information when we introduce ourselves. At this point in our journey through the Bible, God introduces us to another of His wonderful single women, Rachel, and He tells us some personal information about her:

- *Her family*—Rachel was the daughter of Laban, Rebekah's brother, and therefore in the line of Abraham.

- *Her occupation*—Rachel was a shepherdess. In fact, the name *Rachel* means "ewe."

- *Her appearance*—"Rachel was beautiful of form and appearance." Like her Aunt Rebekah, she was lovely to look at.

God also introduces us to Jacob, another person who is important to Him and who will soon be important to Rachel, too.

- *His family*—Jacob and his twin brother, Esau, were the sons of Isaac, grandsons of Abraham. His beautiful mother, Rebekah, had come from Rachel's homeland.

- *His predicament*—Favoritism, jealousy, and deceit had led Jacob to flee to Rachel's homeland to escape being murdered by Esau. Furthermore, Isaac had advised Jacob to find a wife from among his own people (Genesis 28:2).

Through God's sovereign providence, these two singles are introduced to each other. How did He bring Rachel and Jacob together? 1) God used *people.* Rachel and Jacob's family ties qualified them to marry one another. 2) God used *events.* During the routine events of daily life, Rachel came to the place where Jacob stood. 3) God used *circumstances.* Forced to leave his home, Jacob met Rachel in her homeland.

Take inventory of the *people, events,* and *circumstances* unique to your life. Even if these elements are not ideal, you can thank God that He has promised to work "all things"—including the problem people, traumatic events, and difficult circumstances of your life—together for your good (Romans 8:28). God is always at work—sometimes in the open, sometimes in the shadows.

Rachel came with her father's sheep.
GENESIS 29:9

The day began like every other day of her life. As Rachel mentally ran through her list of chores, she saw no hint that today her life would be dramatically transformed. Yet something happened that day which changed everything—forever.

At the top of Rachel's to-do list was one very necessary responsibility: "Water father's sheep." As she approached the well that afternoon, Rachel noticed a stranger. He stood with other shepherds, waiting until the large stone across the well's mouth would be removed so the sheep could drink. Rachel was surprised when the handsome stranger ran to the well, lifted off the rock, and began watering her sheep. Then he kissed her, wept, and explained that they were relatives.

That scene was the beginning of the courtship of Rachel and Jacob. Rachel's ordinary day had become extraordinary, marking the start of a changed life. The stranger would become her husband.

How does a single woman meet the man of her dreams? Learn from Rachel's experience.

Rachel was busy. She was where she was supposed to be (at the town well), doing what she was supposed to be doing (watering her father's sheep), when Jacob arrived.

Rachel was faithful. "God has no higher ground for those who are unfaithful where they are," observes an unknown sage. Tending and watering her father's sheep were Rachel's responsibilities. As she faithfully discharged her duty, God led her to another level of responsibility—that of wife and mother.

If you are single and looking for a marriage partner, don't look for miracles. Don't look for the extraordinary. Look to the most seemingly ordinary incidents in life. God usually reveals His divine plans in the small, ordinary events of life. He orders your steps when you stay busy and remain faithful to your present duties. So be concerned with Him—pleasing the God of the universe—instead of being concerned with "him"—finding a husband.

Leah's eyes were delicate.
GENESIS 29:17

Do not let your adornment be merely outward—arranging the hair, wearing gold, or putting on fine apparel—rather let it be the hidden person of the heart, with the incorruptible beauty of a gentle and quiet spirit, which is very precious in the sight of God (1 Peter 3:3,4).

These few verses from God's Word give God's women through the ages His personal standards for the kind of beauty He values. Take to heart His beauty tips:

Nurture the beauty of your heart. God values truly godly character, which always shines forth in outward conduct. So concern yourself with fashioning your heart after the likeness of Jesus.

Cultivate the beauty of a gentle and quiet spirit. It is your most prized ornament. God treasures the soft graces of a calm, quiet spirit—not costly clothes and jewels.

Concern yourself with inner beauty, which is precious in the sight of God. God is the One you must seek to honor. Your supreme goal in life is to be pleasing in *His* sight.

One of the Lord's ladies, Leah was destined to live her life in the shadow of her sister Rachel's exquisite beauty. Not only was Leah—whose name means "wearied" or "faint from sickness"—less than beautiful, but she had a physical defect. The Bible tells us her eyes were delicate, weak, pale, and dull. And eyes like that were considered a serious blemish.

Aren't you glad for Leah—and for yourself—that our God is more concerned about inner beauty? Aren't you glad that "the LORD does not see as man sees; for man looks at the outward appearance, but the LORD looks at the heart" (1 Samuel 16:7)?

Resolve to nurture your inner beauty, which is precious in the sight of God, by spending time each day in the presence of the Lord, beholding His beauty (Psalm 27:4). Then, as you behold the glory of the Lord, you will be transformed into His image by the Spirit of the Lord (2 Corinthians 3:18). Then you will be truly beautiful…in God's eyes!

He took Leah…and brought her to Jacob.
Genesis 29:33

$\mathcal{L}$eah's father, Laban, was a master of deception, and unfortunately, he used Leah as a pawn in one of his most cunning schemes. Thanks to her own father, Leah was used, mistreated, and rejected. Note these details:

- Jacob, a distant cousin to Leah and Rachel, had come to their home in Padan Aram to seek a bride (Genesis 28:2).

- Rachel, Leah's beautiful sister, met Jacob at the city well, and the two instantly loved one another.

- Laban, Rachel's father, contracted Jacob for seven years of indentured service in exchange for Rachel's hand in marriage. On Jacob's wedding night, Laban secretly substituted Leah, who had a physical defect, for Rachel.

- The result? Leah was used by her father, unloved by her husband, and envied by her sister (Genesis 30:1).

Disappointment is a fact of life, yet with God you can triumph in spite of it. How has your life gone? What disappointments have you encountered? Have you ever been unfairly used by someone? Deceived by a friend or family member? Rejected by someone you trusted and loved?

Be comforted by the fact that God turns the ashes of your life into beauty (Isaiah 61:3). Leah wasn't beautiful—and neither were her life circumstances—but God gave her beauty in exchange for those ashes. Look ahead to the end of Leah's life and see the beauty that emerged from the ashes of her disappointment:

- She had a husband. With her imperfect eyes, she might not have ever married.

- She had children. She might never have had children.

- She was the mother of six of the dozen men who led the 12 tribes of Israel (Genesis 35:23).

- She was the mother of Judah, through whom the Savior, Jesus Christ, would come (Revelation 5:5).

- She—not Rachel—was the recognized wife of Jacob (Genesis 49:31).

So gather up the ashes of your life. Offer them to God. Allow Him to transform them into something beautiful…in His time.

The LORD saw that Leah was unloved.
GENESIS 29:31

*T*he lowly. The downtrodden. The suffering. People who know affliction also know the protection of God's promises. Indeed, we are assured that "the LORD is near to those who have a broken heart, and saves such as have a contrite spirit. Many are the afflictions of the righteous, but the LORD delivers him out of them all" (Psalm 34:18,19)!

Leah knew affliction. She was deceived, used, and rejected; her heart was broken and crushed. As the less-than-beautiful sister of the stunning Rachel and the daughter of the deceptive Laban, Leah ended up in a loveless marriage. To make matters worse, her husband, Jacob, later married her sister, Rachel—"and [Jacob] loved Rachel more than Leah."

But God, in His omniscience, knows all there is to know about His beloved children and sees all that touches their lives, all that harms or hurts them, all that causes them pain. God took note of the lowly condition of Leah: "The LORD saw that Leah was unloved." And God did something about her condition: "He opened her womb" and allowed Rachel to remain barren.

As you suffer, remember the eyes of the Lord. Nothing that happens to you goes unnoticed by God. He sees all that goes on in your life.

> For the eyes of the LORD run to and fro throughout the whole earth, to show Himself strong on behalf of those whose heart is loyal to Him (2 Chronicles 16:9).

> Behold, the eye of the LORD is on those who fear Him, on those who hope in His mercy (Psalm 33:18).

As you suffer, remember that, in His time, God acts on your behalf: "He shall bring forth your righteousness as the light, and your justice as the noonday" (Psalm 37:6).

As you suffer, remember to look to the Lord. Pray these heartfelt words of another saint who looked to the Lord: "[We] do [not] know what to do, but our eyes are upon You" (2 Chronicles 20:12).

> *"The LORD has surely looked on my affliction."*
> GENESIS 29:32

*W*hat's in a name? Plenty! In Bible times, the names given to new-borns were very significant. A name expressed the parents' feelings and many times alluded to actual circumstances in the family's history. Often the relationship the parents enjoyed with God was evident in their baby's name. Through the name they bestowed, mothers and fathers would pass on to their child their expectations, their faith, or a bit of their hard-earned wisdom. Such is the case of Leah, one of God's special women through the ages. As you follow Leah on her journey to spiritual maturity, you'll see that just as the rings in the trunk of a tree mark its growth, so the names of Leah's children mark her own spiritual growth in the Lord.

Now Leah had the misfortune of sharing her husband, Jacob, with her sister, Rachel. The Bible tells us that Jacob "loved Rachel more than Leah" and that "Leah was unloved." Both Leah and Rachel were barren, but the Lord opened Leah's womb, and she conceived and bore a son.

When she held her new little baby, Leah christened him *Reuben*. His name meant, "See, a son!" or "Behold a son!" Leah said, "The LORD has surely looked on my affliction. Now therefore, my husband will love me."

So what's in a name? In the name *Reuben* we see Leah's desires and long-ings for her marriage. She hoped that the near 90-year-old Jacob would turn his heart toward her as he held his firstborn child, a son! That was her human hope.

But buried deeper in the naming of her tiny boy was her joyful surprise at God's compassion for her. God had taken pity on her. "Behold a son!" In the name *Reuben*, Leah thankfully acknowledged God's kindness and His providence. He had noticed her trouble, and He had looked favorably upon her. Leah treasured that thought so deeply that she passed it on to her son. To Leah, unloved by her husband, Reuben would always be personal proof of God's loving care.

Prayer: Thank You, Lord, that the absence of earthly blessings reveals the presence of Your eternal love.

"The Lord has heard that I am unloved."
Genesis 29:33

*T*hen she conceived again and bore a son." So the story of Leah, the unloved wife, continues.

Sharing her husband with her sister, Rachel, was becoming increasingly difficult for Leah. Neither Leah nor Rachel had been able to have children…until the Lord opened Leah's womb. How she had hoped her firstborn son would help her win her husband's love! But nothing had changed.

Perhaps, Leah wondered as she realized she was pregnant again, a second child—a second son—would make a difference. Just maybe Jacob would begin to care. But still nothing changed. In fact, things were worse. The message was clear: Jacob did not love Leah. In fact, sometimes she felt he hated her (kjv).

But, swaddling her second infant son, Leah called him *Simeon*, meaning "hearing." She said, "Because the Lord has heard that I am unloved, He has therefore given me this son also."

Is there any difficulty, any trial, any lack in your life? Are there sorrows you must bear from sunup to sundown each and every day? Are there any unbearable burdens weighing down your body and soul? Allow Leah to show you a path through your pain.

Hidden in the name that Leah selected for her new baby is evidence of her budding prayer life. With her first child, she hoped to gain her husband's love. When those hopes died, Leah turned to prayer. Evidently, Leah had been troubled by her husband's rejection and had prayed about it. A second baby had come because God heard Leah's prayer. For Leah—and for you—the name *Simeon* stood as a lasting monument to answered prayer.

Are you praying, precious friend? Pour out the contents of your troubled heart. Water the soil at the foot of the cross with your tears. Lift the details of your difficulties up to God's throne. Call upon the Lord—and behold His great and mighty answers. Cast your burden on the Lord…knowing He cares for you and hears your prayers.

As one who has gone before you shares, "Trouble and perplexity drive me to prayer and prayer drives away perplexity and trouble."[1] Oh, dear lover of the Lord, look to Him now!

"I have borne him three sons."
Genesis 29:34

*Y*ear by year Leah's problem intensified. Her husband Jacob seemed to love her less and her sister Rachel more.

But year by year Leah's family grew. First Reuben was born, then Simeon, and now she held yet another newborn in her arms.

And year by year Leah's faith grew. While waiting for her first two children, she had come to know God better and trust Him more. He had removed her barrenness and opened her womb for Baby #1, and her choice of the name *Reuben* reflected her deep gratitude to God. The name sounds like "the Lord has surely looked on my affliction" and means "Behold a son." She knew that Reuben was a gift from God. Then Baby #2 arrived, God's answer to her prayers, and with his name—*Simeon*—Leah again gave credit to God: "The Lord has heard that I am unloved."

But with her third baby, Leah seemed to forget about God, and hope instead in human accomplishment. Perhaps she thought, "Surely now that I've given Jacob three sons he will love me! I know he's thrilled with the children. Maybe now I'll win favor in his eyes and heart."

Brimming with hope and confident in her physical ability to bear children, Leah looked at her new little one and named him *Levi*, meaning "joined, attached." "Now this time my husband will become attached to me, because I have borne him three sons." Surely with Levi's birth, she thought and hoped, she would be more closely united to her husband.

After taking two steps forward in her growing faith, Leah now seems to take one step back. Let's focus on her two giant steps forward, though, and draw out two principles that will help us base our hopes and focus our faith on God rather than on ourselves and our human efforts.

Step 1: Always acknowledge God in each event of life.

Step 2: Always ask God for direction and wisdom about each event of life.

Making these two steps a part of your approach to life will help you center your heart and mind on God.

"Now I will praise the Lord."
Genesis 29:35

There can be no rainbow without clouds and storms. And Leah, one of God's cherished women, lived a life filled with clouds and storms. Maybe you can relate.

If you were to describe your life, the account would certainly include some clouds. Everyone experiences disappointment and lack, loss and sorrow. Everyone has thwarted dreams and hopes that are dashed. Everyone has storms to contend with—problems and conflicts with a spouse or child, with in-laws or a neighbor, with a boss or coworkers. Whatever clouds and storms you have encountered, your victory over them stands as a brilliant rainbow of God's grace. When God makes something lovely out of a life filled with disadvantages, it becomes a tribute to His goodness.

Aren't you glad that Leah finally enjoyed such a brilliant victory in her problem-filled life? Locked into a loveless marriage, Leah was forced to share her husband, Jacob, with her younger sister. Yet, as determined by God, Leah was the wife who bore Jacob child after child.

> Child #1 was named *Reuben.*
>
> Child #2 was christened *Simeon.*
>
> Child #3 was called *Levi.*
>
> Child #4 was named *Judah,* meaning "praise." Finally the arch of the rainbow was clear and complete as pure praise rang through Leah's tent: "Now I will praise the Lord!"

Yes, praise—prophetic praise—leapt from Leah's lips. Truly this fourth son would be great, for, through Judah, the Messiah would come. Every generation would praise the name of Judah!

What made the rainbow's arch complete at this point was Leah's apparent submission to the Lord and, with that, victory over her circumstances. Leah finally ceased fretting over the absence of Jacob's love for her and rested instead in the Lord's love. She no longer needed people to make her happy. She found in God a source of joy and reason to praise. The rainbow was complete!

Will you follow Leah's path to victory, dear one? Will you praise your all-wise, ever-loving, forever-faithful Father…even through tears and in dark times? Will you choose to rest in God's love and offer to Him the praise that fills out the vivid, joyful colors of the rich rainbow of His grace to you? Pause now for a moment…pray for a bit…and praise Him always!

"Now I will praise the LORD."
GENESIS 29:35

 hat does it take to become strong in the Lord? Why not glean answers from the following insights?

> The support of a healthy root system is vital for standing strong in the Lord. In bygone days there was a process used for growing the trees that became the main masts for military and merchant ships. The great shipbuilders first selected a tree located on the top of a high hill as a potential mast. Then they cut away all of the surrounding trees that would shield the chosen one from the force of the wind. As the years went by and the winds blew fiercely against the tree, the tree only grew stronger until finally it was strong enough to be the fore-mast of a ship. When you have a solid root system, you, too, can gain the strength needed for standing firm in spite of the pressures of life.[2]

For Leah, as the years increased so did the fierce winds that blew in her life. Her father's mistreatment, her husband's hatred, and her sister's envy (Genesis 30:1) hurled against her. As God cut away every thing and every person that might shield her from the full force of adversity, Leah found strength as she deepened her roots in God and received from Him the nourishment and sustenance she needed. Standing firm in her newfound strength in the Lord, she shouted, "Now I will praise the LORD!"

> Stand up in the place where the dear Lord has put you, and there do your best. God gives us trial tests....Out of the buffeting of a serious conflict we are expected to grow strong. The tree that grows where tempests toss its boughs and bend its trunk often almost to breaking, is often more firmly rooted than the tree which grows in the sequestered valley where no storm ever brings stress or strain. The same is true of life. The grandest character is grown in hardship.[3]

Dear one, welcome the buffeting, the conflict, the tempest, the storm, the stress, and the strain. See these hardships as God's prods to greater faith, making you strong in the Lord.

And [Rachel] gave him Bilhah her maid.
GENESIS 30:4

Jesus cried out, "Blessed are the meek, for they shall inherit the earth" (Matthew 5:5). Paul wrote, "When I am weak, then I am strong" (2 Corinthians 12:10). Hannah prayed, "The LORD...brings low and lifts up" (1 Samuel 2:7). Mary praised, "[The Lord] has...exalted the lowly" (Luke 1:52). David explained, "God...puts down one, and exalts another" (Psalm 75:7).

Do you see the common theme in these thought-provoking statements? They tell us that, in God's economy, might comes from meekness. If you find yourself in a lowly position, or if you are struggling under some kind of oppression, or if you are living in a God-ordained season in the shade, take heart and "humble your[self] under the mighty hand of God, that He may exalt you in due time" (1 Peter 5:6).

Sentenced to a life of slavery, Bilhah had nothing to look forward to. Her life simply was not her own. In fact, she was passed from person to person, given to Rachel by her master when Rachel married Jacob (Genesis 29:29). Yet Bilhah discovered God's blessings in the midst of her lowly existence.

Bilhah could not help but notice the domestic tensions in her new home. Jacob married Rachel, but he also married Rachel's sister, Leah. And as Leah gave birth to son after son, the barren Rachel burned with envy. Finally, during a heated argument between Jacob and Rachel, she announced, "Here is my maid Bilhah; go in to her, and she will bear a child on my knees, that I also may have children by her." Bilhah had just been passed on again. But from meekness arises might.

> Dan was Bilhah's firstborn by Jacob. From Dan sprang the mighty Samson, the renowned judge and deliverer of Israel, whose exceptional physical strength was greatly used by God (Judges 13–16). Naphtali was Bilhah's second son by Jacob. He, too, grew to might as the founder of a very large tribe of people.

The lowly maid Bilhah was blessed with two sons who legally inherited a portion of Jacob's vast wealth and became the powerful leaders of two of the 12 tribes of Israel. From meekness came might.

[Leah] took Zilpah her maid and gave her to Jacob.
GENESIS 30:9

*I*n Proverbs 31:25, wise King Solomon describes the ideal clothing for women throughout the ages: "Strength and dignity are her clothing, and she smiles at the future" (NASB).

Now meet a woman most *un*likely to be clothed with such splendor: Zilpah, whose Arabic name does in fact mean "dignity." Nothing in Zilpah's life, however, hinted that she would ever be important. She was a slave, owned by Leah's father, Laban, and given to Leah when she married Jacob (Genesis 29:24).

Little did Zilpah know that being Leah's servant would require her to bear children by Leah's husband. But "when Leah saw that she had stopped bearing, she took Zilpah her maid and gave her to Jacob as wife." And God blessed her, an insignificant servant, with two sons who became great men of strength and the fathers of two tribes of Israel. Each definitely contributed to the development of Israel as a nation.

Gad, meaning "fortune," was the forefather of a strong, warlike race which bravely defended their country and aided their brethren in the conquest of Canaan (Joshua 4 and 22). *Asher*, meaning "happiness," caused Zilpah to smile with happiness. That smile extended throughout history as his line brought forth Anna, another woman of strength and dignity. Anna was a godly woman who devoted her life to prayer—a prophetess who recognized that the infant Jesus was the Messiah (Luke 2:36-38).

Regardless of your situation, as God's child you may clothe and carry yourself with the strength and dignity that is available to you by God's great grace. As you devote yourself to developing the character and the conduct that is pleasing in God's sight (1 Peter 3:4) and pour your life into your family and church family, you contribute mightily to God's plan in ways that only He knows and only time will reveal. Like Leah, you can pass on your faith to your children. Like Gad, you can aid and assist your brothers and sisters in Christ in their tasks for the Lord. Like Asher, you can bring happiness and encouragement with sweet words of comfort and cheer to those who are cast down. And, like Anna, you can apply yourself to prayer…for others and for God's church.

God listened to Leah, and she conceived.
GENESIS 30:17

$\mathcal{L}$ eah's name may have meant "faint" and her eyes may have been dull (Genesis 29:17), but centuries later Leah's life still shines like a brilliant star that left its sparkling trail across the span of God's velvet sky—a sky sparkling alongside His people throughout the ages. Here we take our last close look at Leah's radiant star. She wasn't beautiful, she wasn't loved, and she wasn't wanted (Genesis 29:31), but her star nevertheless shines in the pages of Scripture. And left behind in her luminous train of light were six more stars in their own right: her six sons.

The background against which Leah's star shines was indeed black. On the night of her sister Rachel's marriage to Jacob, Leah's scheming father had replaced the beautiful Rachel with his less-than-lovely daughter, Leah (Genesis 29:17, 23). Trickery, lies, scheming, and deception were the starting point of her loveless marriage to Jacob.

But out of her dark and difficult circumstances, Leah began to shine as—through prayer—she pressed herself closer to the awesome, dazzling glory of God (Genesis 29:33). Four sons—Reuben, Simeon, Levi, and Judah—followed as she looked to God for His understanding, His mercy, and His help.

Leah's season of luster slowed as "she stopped bearing" children (Genesis 29:35). Once again with no friend but God, Leah applied the most important lesson she had learned about handling all the heartaches of her life: Pray!

So Leah prayed. She prayed passionately for the blessing she most desired: to be a part of God's promise to Abraham and now to Jacob (Genesis 28:13,14). She prayed that Jacob's seed would be as the stars of heaven (Genesis 22:17), and perhaps even that one of them would be the Messiah.

"And God listened to Leah, and she conceived and bore Jacob a fifth son...Issachar...[and] a sixth son...Zebulun."

Is your life blazing a trail of faith across a dark sky, dear one who loves God? Is your faith something for others to marvel at, to wonder at? Something that reflects God's radiant glory and the luster of His brilliant presence in your life? Pray to shine...for Him.

> *God remembered Rachel, and God listened to her.*
> GENESIS 30:22

$\mathcal{S}$econd only to suffering, waiting may be the greatest teacher and trainer in godliness, maturity, and genuine spirituality most of us ever encounter."[4]

Rachel was one of God's women through the ages who definitely put in her time waiting. She learned much in its classroom as she waited a long time for a child of her own. Rachel's expectation that she would one day be a mother grew out of God's promise to Abraham that his seed would become a great nation equaling in number the stars in God's sky and the grains of sand on God's seashores (Genesis 12:2,3; 22:17). Yet Rachel, the wife of Abraham's grandson, waited…and waited…and waited for a son that didn't come.

How long did Rachel wait? For her, the wait probably seemed to last forever. First she waited seven years before marrying Jacob (Genesis 29:18). Then she waited while ten other children were born to Jacob by her sister, Leah, and two servant girls. It's possible that a quarter of a century passed while Rachel waited…and waited…and waited.

What lessons in godliness, maturity, and spirituality did she learn while she waited? And how can they help you in your own journey of faith?

- *The lesson of prayer*—Evidently, Rachel discovered the beauty of prayer in the waiting process because the Scripture says, "Then God listened to her and opened her womb." Prayer stills your fretting heart before the Lord as you look to God for what is lacking in your life, and prayer sculpts your heart into the beautiful bowed posture of humility.

- *The lesson of faith*—In naming her long-desired son, Rachel exhibits extraordinary faith: "She called his name Joseph [meaning "God will add"], and said, 'The LORD shall add to me another son.'" Rachel's faith—enshrined in the name of her son—is a faith that reaches out and presses on for more than God has yet given. "Faith is the substance of things hoped for, the evidence of things not seen" (Hebrews 11:1). What unseen future blessings are you reaching for by faith?

> *"Whatever God has said to you, do it."*
> GENESIS 31:16

*F*rom the very beginning of time—and marriage—God has given us His divine principle of "leaving and cleaving" as a guideline for that unique relationship of husband and wife: "Therefore a man shall leave his father and mother and be joined to his wife, and they shall become one flesh" (Genesis 2:24).

The time came when Rachel and Leah had to decide whether to leave and cleave to their husband, Jacob, or remain in their homeland. God had promised to make Jacob into a great nation, but first Jacob must leave his father-in-law's home and return to the land of his grandfather Abraham— the land of God's promise.

But Jacob wanted to take a willing family with him on his pilgrimage into God's will—a family filled with faith. Detailing God's leading and pointing to God's hand of blessing, Jacob called upon Rachel and Leah to join him in following after God.

The two women had to choose: Would they leave their father's house and their familiar home and, with their husband, follow after God?

Leaving and cleaving is always a test of faith.

- It tests our obedience to God's Word and His way.

- It tests our faith in God's leading through our husbands.

- It tests our trust in our husbands' wisdom.

- It tests our commitment to our husbands.

Rachel and Leah's answer—"Whatever God has said to you, do it"—was evidence of their faith in God. They joined with other women of faith through the ages as they left the familiar, stepped out into the unknown, and followed after God.

Are you a wife? Have you determined in your heart that your husband (not your parents) is number one in your life? Consider signing an agreement which spells out the status between you and your parents. The wording might go something like this: "I am no longer accountable to obey my parents. I am freed from that authority to be bound, joyfully and securely, to my mate."[5]

Are you a mother? If so, consider signing such a statement, releasing your married children to follow after God with their mates.

Deborah, Rebekah's nurse, died.
GENESIS 35:8

$\mathcal{L}$ ife is a journey, and Deborah found her life's journey to be made up of many actual journeys.

As Rebekah's faithful nursemaid (Genesis 24:59), Deborah first traveled the 500-mile trip from Haran to Hebron as Rebekah went to marry Abraham's son Isaac. Deborah weathered not only the arduous trip, but also the 20 years of waiting for her beloved Rebekah to have a child Deborah could nurse and serve. When Rebekah's twin boys arrived, Deborah lovingly and tenderly cared for Jacob and Esau, who eventually grew up and left home to start their own families. Jacob married in Haran, and his family quickly grew into a large one. It's probable that Isaac and Rebekah gave Deborah to him to help nurse along a third generation—a duty that required a tedious trek back to Haran. She had cared for Rebekah, Rebekah's children, and now Rebekah's grandchildren. Truly, Deborah is a portrait of true devotion.

Age, however, brought an end to Deborah's active role of care-giver, but then Jacob's family cared for her. She had loved them, and they had loved her—and continued to do so until she died on yet another journey back from Haran to Hebron. After 100 years of life, Deborah was buried under "the oak of weeping" and was lamented with the kind of sadness and tears reserved for family members.

Deborah—the woman who spent her entire life as a nursemaid—offers us a portrait of true devotion. Her noble life is a call to you to live a life of love—of selfless love. Are you following in her steps? Oh, the situations and the people will change, but as a representative of God's great, selfless love— the love that gave His only begotten Son for you—you are called upon to love long and hard, to love any and all, to give God's kind of to-the-end love. Love means service, which is the ultimate expression of your love. Learn these lessons of love from the Bible:

> Love bears all things,
> Love believes all things,
> Love hopes all things,
> Love endures all things,
> Love never fails (from 1 Corinthians 13:7,8).

"You will have this son also."
GENESIS 35:17

Died: Rachel, wife of Jacob, while giving birth to her second son, Benjamin. Buried near Bethlehem. Her grave is marked by a pillar raised in her memory by her devoted husband, Jacob. She is survived by her husband, Jacob, her sister, Leah, her firstborn son, Joseph, and her new baby, Benjamin.

Rachel's hypothetical obituary offers us two fascinating firsts.

One point of interest is that Rachel's death is the first instance of death during childbirth recorded in the Bible. Journeying from Bethel to Ephrath, Rachel's labor began, and "Rachel [travailed] in childbirth, and she had hard labor." In an effort to encourage and comfort the distraught Rachel, her midwife said, "Do not fear; you will have this son also." Her words were true, but the beginning of Rachel's second son's life marked the end of her own. As the little son was being born and Rachel's "soul was departing (for she died)," Rachel cried out instructions to name her infant *Ben-Oni*, meaning "son of my sorrows." But the baby's father, Jacob, called him *Benjamin* instead, meaning "son of the right hand."

Second, the pillar which the grieving Jacob set up on Rachel's grave is the first on record in the Bible. It's true that the life of Rachel was sad, marred by many struggles and growing pains, but in the end, we can remember her for two phrases that could well have been engraved on that pillar. Rachel was:

- *A loved wife:* Rachel was Jacob's true love for as long as they were married and she was alive.

- *A loving mother:* At one time Rachel had demanded that her husband, Jacob, "give me children, or else I die" (Genesis 30:1). Eventually God gave Rachel the opportunity to pour her love into her older son, Joseph, who grew to become the godliest and greatest of the 12 sons of Jacob.

We see, in the end, that Rachel's chief contribution to God's kingdom happened in her home and in the hearts of those nearest and dearest to her: her family. Could these truths be written and remembered of you?

"She was a loved wife and a loving mother."

"There I buried Leah."
Genesis 49:31

Sometimes a life ends in great drama, but Leah's life ended quietly, like a slow-burning wick that simply stops burning. No sputter. No flicker. Only the quiet of death. The only mention of her death is found in the words her husband, Jacob, spoke as he lay dying: "I buried Leah."

What a sad life Leah had lived! Although married to the patriarch Jacob, Leah never enjoyed his love. Hers was a life filled with pain and sorrow, discouragement and disappointment, setbacks and letdowns. Yet, as Leah gallantly lived her life in the shadow of Jacob and Rachel's bright love, she did enjoy three unspeakable blessings:

- Leah was blessed by God with six sons to love. One of those sons was Judah, through whose line the Savior Jesus Christ came.

- Leah was buried with her husband. It was not Rachel, but Leah, who lay next to Jacob in the family tomb.

- Leah was listed in God's *Who's Who*. The name *Leah*, meaning "weak" and "faint," stands next to those of the powerful giants of the faith—Abraham, Isaac, and Jacob—and their honored wives, Sarah and Rebekah.

Every life—including yours—has its darkness, its valleys, its shadowlands. How can you forge ahead through heartache and heartbreak? Learn from Leah the following lessons which she learned from God in the shadowlands of life.

Lesson #1: Take a long-range view of life. God's grand purposes are achieved through the whole of your life, not in the fragments of a moment, a day, a year, even a decade. What counts most is the sum total of your contributions, not the deficits along the way. Being a devoted wife, a loving mother, and a benefit to those around you are contributions to His kingdom that can never be fully measured.

Lesson #2: Give your love along the way. Give it generously, liberally, lavishly, bountifully, as much as you can to as many as you can. It's not what you get, but what you give that is God's true measure of a life.

"There I buried Leah."
GENESIS 49:31

*F*ar better than reading a volume of *Who's Who in Church History* is reading the *Who's Who* lists of men and women who shaped the nation of Israel. One such list appears in today's reading from the end of Genesis. And please note that the name of lowly Leah is included in this roll call of very important people, which shows us something very important about who matters in the kingdom of God!

As Jacob, the son of Isaac and grandson of Abraham, lay dying in Egypt, he first blessed his 12 sons. Then, having pronounced his blessing, Jacob charged his sons to bury him in the field of Machpelah in the land of Canaan and explained why:

> There they buried Abraham and Sarah his wife,
> There they buried Isaac and Rebekah his wife,
> And there I buried Leah.

At long last Leah is honored by her husband! In life, Jacob had never pretended to love Leah, and he had never hidden his deep love for her sister, Rachel (Genesis 29:18). But in the end, he requested that he be buried alongside Leah. In the end, Leah—not Rachel—was buried next to her husband at the family burial grounds. In the end, Leah—not Rachel—is listed in the *Who's Who* of patriarchal couples through whom God extended the promise of a Savior. Leah is mentioned right beside Abraham, Isaac, and Jacob, right next to Sarah and Rebekah. In the end, the faithful Leah received honor she never knew during her days on this earth.

Your calling—like Leah's—is to remain faithful…to the end. Honor is not always bestowed along life's way. Flowers may be thrown across your path, but the winner's wreath is not awarded until the end of the contest. Regardless of seeming barriers or obstacles en route to glory, regardless of sorrow or mistreatment on your journey to paradise, you are to look only to the Lord. He is standing…at the end, to receive you…at the end, and to reward you…at the end. Wait, dear one. Wait for God's "well done." It will come, but not until…the end.

Israel took his journey with all that he had.
GENESIS 46:1

*I*n a country ruled by a king or queen, a royal crown is usually passed down from monarch to monarch. The crown—often magnificent, ornate, and bejeweled—serves as an emblem of the ruler's exalted position and title. But no position or title is more exalted or prestigious than "woman of faith," and through the ages many women who loved God have worn that crown—a crown of eternal righteousness.

Before you leave Genesis, look back at some of the many women who loved God and walked with Him—women who were honored to wear God's glorious crown of faith and grace. Gaze again at these women and their journey with God as recorded in God's book of beginnings:

- Eve fell in sin but went on to walk with God.
- Noah's wife accepted God's invitation to salvation.
- Sarah followed where God led her husband.
- Hagar cried out to God twice and He preserved her.
- Rebekah prayed to God for a child.
- Bilhah and Zilpah entered into God's blessings despite the fact that they were servants.
- Rachel died giving Israel a godly leader.
- Leah shone brilliantly in the shadows of suffering.

The Lord blessed each of these women and made her beautiful. These beloved women endured times of hardship, adversity, deprivation, shame, and failure. All were called upon by God to make choices—hard choices, seemingly unbearable choices, but choices by which they demonstrated their faith. Many showed their faith in God by a forward gaze, by a decision to not look backward at loss, at things forsaken, at failure, at mistreatment. Most chose to greet every sunrise with fresh hope rather than to stare backward at their sunsets of defeat and be immobilized. All in all, each endured, pressing on and drawing great strength from the Lord as she donned His crown of grace.

Is your name among God's great women of faith through the ages? And are you actively looking to the Lord for His help, His wisdom, His enabling, and His grace? As one writer has remarked, "Our part is to trust Him fully, to obey Him implicitly, and to follow His instructions faithfully."[6] In doing so, you live life in a way that points to the crowning, majestic beauty of faith and grace.

"You shall kill him."
EXODUS 1:16

*E*very problem requires a solution, and the Pharaoh of Egypt had a rapidly growing problem. As the Book of Genesis closed, Joseph, the son of Rachel and Jacob, was a powerful leader in Egypt. During a devastating famine, the only food available was in Egypt. Therefore, Jacob and his other 11 sons moved to Egypt where his family was reunited with Joseph, enjoyed many wonderful years together, and grew greatly in number.

"Now there arose a new king over Egypt, who did not know Joseph. And he said to his people, 'Look, the people of the children of Israel are more and mightier than we.'"

- *The problem:* The rapid increase in the number of Israelites.
- *The solution:* Murder every male baby as he is born.
- *The means:* The Hebrew midwives, Shiphrah and Puah.

These two Hebrew women were professionals who assisted women with childbirth and the initial care of their newborns. Such a command to kill the very babies they were helping to bring into the world presented them with a problem of their own.

- *The problem:* Ordered to kill every male baby born to the Hebrews.
- *The solution:* "The midwives feared God, and did not do as the king of Egypt commanded them, but saved the male children alive."

Every problem in life tests the mettle of your allegiance to God. Every problem asks the question, "Whom will you obey?" Take courage from those who have gone before you and made the choice to obey God rather than man. Take courage from the apostles who were ordered not to preach the gospel of Jesus Christ but answered, "Whether it is right in the sight of God to listen to you more than to God, you judge....We [will] obey God rather than men" (Acts 4:19; 5:29). Take courage from Shiphrah and Puah (two women who feared and revered the Lord as you do), who risked their lives by disregarding Pharaoh's command to kill children because they feared God. Take courage every time you must answer the question, "Whom will I obey?"

The midwives feared God.
Exodus 1:17

$\mathcal{W}$hat does it mean to "fear" God? Two Hebrew words help us understand: One points us to reverence, and the other to terror. As a woman of God—a woman who fears the Lord—your life should be characterized by the kind of evidence listed below. Notice how both reverence and terror are reflected in these qualities that (hopefully) describe you and your attitude toward God. The woman who fears the Lord...

• Dreads God's displeasure

• Desires His favor

• Reveres His holiness

• Submits cheerfully to His will

• Is grateful for His benefits

• Sincerely worships Him

• Conscientiously obeys His commandments[7]

As a woman who fears the Lord, your reverence for God should spring from your love for Him and should prompt you to take care not to offend Him and to endeavor to please Him in all things.

Shiphrah and Puah show us something of what it means to fear God. Hebrew midwives by profession, they were assigned by the Pharaoh of Egypt the task of killing every male child born to any Hebrew woman. What would you do in such a situation?

Scripture tells us that Shiphrah and Puah "feared God, and did not do as the king of Egypt commanded them, but saved the male children alive." Their choice to disobey Pharaoh's command revealed their great courage and their tremendous love for God. They counted the cost (and the cost was their lives!), but because they feared the Lord, they obeyed God rather than man. They lived out their "fear of the Lord" in practical piety and developed admirable virtues of godly character.

Are you a woman who fears the Lord? Is your love for God obvious in the practical details of your daily life? Spend some time in sincere prayer now and commit yourself to the Lord—to more fervently revere His holiness, submit to His will, and obey His Word. And pour out your gratitude for His many blessings. O worship Him now! For "the mercy of the Lord is from everlasting to everlasting *on those who fear Him*" (Psalm 103:17, emphasis added)!

[God] provided households for them.
EXODUS 1:21

$\mathcal{D}$ark days had fallen on God's people....

The number of Israelites in Egypt was greatly increasing, so the Pharaoh of Egypt ordered the Egyptian midwives who assisted the Hebrew women in childbirth to kill every male baby as he was born. But Shiphrah and Puah, the two women who may have been in charge of the other midwives, refused to murder the newborn babies. Shiphrah and Puah "feared God," so they risked their own lives in order to save many Jewish infants.

The kindness these two midwives showed to God's people did not go unnoticed by the Lord. God saw their tenderness toward His chosen race and blessed them for obeying His ways. He opened the windows of heaven to reward the two women who refused to harm His children. With what did God honor and bless Shiphrah and Puah?

Blessing #1: God protected them against Pharaoh. Because they chose to disobey Pharaoh's edict, "God dealt well with the midwives." He preserved their lives. Those who fear the Lord receive His protection: "The angel of the LORD encamps all around those who fear Him, and delivers them" (Psalm 34:7). Indeed, those who fear the Lord "abide under the shadow of the Almighty" (Psalm 91:1).

Blessing #2: God provided them with families. "Because the midwives feared God...He provided households for them." Shiphrah and Puah were probably older, unmarried women, so in return for their goodness, God blessed them with what they most wanted: families of their own. He gave them husbands, built them up into families, blessed their children, and prospered them in all they did. *Shiphrah* means "prolific" and *Puah* means "childbearing," and, in the end, God blessed each according to her name.

What does God require of you so that He may abundantly bless you, His child? In a word, obedience. Shiphrah and Puah feared the Lord and obeyed Him. What will you do to cultivate such a life of obedience? Ask and answer the following questions—and then obey!

- What does God command in His Word?
- What is the right thing to do (James 4:17)?
- What would Jesus do?

She hid [her baby] three months.
EXODUS 2:2

*M*any wonder what true faith looks like in real, everyday life. As you meet Jochebed, God's next noble woman in the Bible, you find a picture of faith in action. Note a few key facts about this great woman of faith.

Her heritage: A daughter of Levi, Jochebed married Amram, a man of the house of Levi (Exodus 2:1; 6:20). Through Levi, Jochebed and Amram inherited the faith of Abraham, Isaac, and Jacob.

Her situation: As the mother of a newborn boy, Jochebed was faced with a frightening dilemma. She knew that the Pharaoh had ordered that every son born of the Jews should be cast into the Nile River (Exodus 1:22), but could she let her son die?

Her faith: Motivated by her trust in God and her love for her child, Jochebed took a step of faith and hid her little Moses instead of murdering him. This singular act of faith qualified her as one in the great cloud of witnesses whose lives testify of faith in God. Only three women—Sarah, Rahab, and Jochebed—are noted among God's heroes of faith. Of Jochebed it is eternally written, "By faith Moses, when he was born, was hidden three months by his parents, because…they were not afraid of the king's command" (Hebrews 11:23).

Her decision: Jochebed's faith fueled her courage. Deciding to neither obey the Pharaoh's command nor fear him or any consequences, Jochebed trusted in God and hid her baby.

Your faith: What would people point to in your life as evidence of your faith? What acts or choices of faith (James 2:22) might they have noticed?

Dear one, look to your *heritage:* You are a child of God! Hold up your frightening, seemingly impossible *situations* to your Father in heaven. Realize that worry ends when *faith* begins…and that *faith* ends when worry begins. Make a *decision* to face your trials with courage fueled by faith. Make a *decision* to refuse to fear and to instead place your trust in God. Declare with David, "Whenever I am afraid, I will trust in You" (Psalm 56:3). Join with Jochebed in a life of real, everyday faith.

She took an ark...and laid it...by the river's bank.
Exodus 2:3

$\mathscr{T}$he wise writer of Ecclesiastes calls us as women who love God to "cast your bread upon the waters, for you will find it after many days" (11:1). This principle for living a life of faith alludes to the agricultural practice of throwing seed upon water or soggy ground and then waiting for it to produce a harvest. Like that farmer, at times you must take a faith-risk in order to enjoy the rewards of your faith. At times you must step out in faith before you can receive God's blessing.

Like a farmer, Jochebed was forced to take a chance with her seed, but her "seed" was her tiny baby, Moses. The Pharaoh of Egypt had ordered every male baby born to the Jews to be drowned in the Nile River (Exodus 1:22). Jochebed, however, put her faith to work at once and hid her dear little one for three months.

Then she had to take another risk of faith. Realizing she could no longer hide a vigorous infant, and trusting God, Jochebed "took an ark of bulrushes...put the child in it, and laid it in the reeds by the river's bank." She was casting her bread—her beloved son—upon the waters.

In His great providence, God brought Pharaoh's own daughter to the riverbank. She found the ark and had compassion for the infant inside. Needing a nursemaid for the baby, the princess found Jochebed—further evidence of God's providence. Jochebed was allowed to keep and nurse the precious babe she had placed into the hands of God when she had placed him in the river. Truly—and literally—Jochebed had cast her seed upon the waters...and it came back to her!

What challenge in your life requires a risk of faith from you? Are you sending your own child off to school or college, off to a new married life, off to a job in another city or state, off to serve God on the mission field? Do you feel like you are losing him or her? Have the faith of Jochebed—the faith that casts your bread upon the water. Trust God that you will eventually reap benefits and blessings because of your risk of faith.

The daughter of Pharaoh…had compassion on him.
EXODUS 2:5,6

*T*oday's meditation offers one more stunning instance of God's providential use of people, events, and circumstances in the lives of His children. The times were dark—deathly dark!—as the wicked Pharaoh of Egypt sentenced every Jewish baby boy to death by drowning in the Nile River (Exodus 1:22). One of God's women of faith, however, defied Pharaoh's order: Jochebed hid her baby boy for three months and then hid him in a handmade basket on the river's edge.

By God's sovereign providence, into this grim scene waded the Pharaoh's very own daughter. Walking along the riverbank, she spotted the basket and fetched it out of the water. She knew of her father's detestable edict, but his evil could not harden her tender and noble heart—a heart of compassion that prompted her to respond to the baby's cries and later to adopt the crying baby as her own. Imagine, the daughter of the Pharaoh saving the life of a baby her father had ordered killed! Only God could design such an amazing rescue.

As God's child, you are the apple of His eye (Deuteronomy 32:10). As such, you are guarded, protected, and kept by God just as Jochebed and her baby were. Despite the appalling edict of one person (the Pharaoh), God used another person (ironically, the Pharaoh's daughter) to honor Jochebed's faith and save her baby. In the midst of Israel's difficult circumstances, God was at work preparing for their future deliverance under the leadership of that little three-month-old baby found by a princess in the bulrushes.

And now for you, precious friend! What's going on in your life today? Are you facing unfair treatment from someone, perhaps someone cruel and evil? Are you oppressed? Do you face harsh daily trials? Cling in faith to God's gracious providence and overruling power. Trust that He is going before you, as He went before Moses and Jochebed, to use all people, each event, and every circumstance to deliver you, the apple of His eye! With His great power, God will keep you, care for you, guard you, and guide you…and afterward receive you to glory (Psalm 73:24).

The daughter of Pharaoh…had compassion on him.
Exodus 2:5,6

Two things stand like stone:
Kindness in another's troubles;
Courage in one's own.[8]

$\mathcal{L}$ittle is known about the mysterious daughter of Pharaoh, but her kindness and courage stand like stone through the ages.…

The Scriptures tell of that sunny day when this nameless princess approached the Nile River for her bath. While wading along the river's edge, she caught sight of a floating basket which she discovered held a small baby boy. God tells us that "she had compassion on him." Pharaoh's daughter knew that the baby was "one of the Hebrews' children." She was also well aware that her own father, the powerful Egyptian Pharaoh, had ordered all male babies born of the Hebrews to be thrown into the river to die.

Although we know little about the Pharaoh's daughter, we see much about her heart:

- *Pharaoh's daughter was compassionate.* Compassion is a response of sorrow or pity on those in distress or misfortune. Hearing the baby's cries, the daughter of the powerful Pharaoh had compassion on the helpless infant, drew him out of the water, and named him Moses (meaning "drawn out") "because I drew him out of the water."

- *Pharaoh's daughter was kind.* Kindness is a tender concern for the welfare of another. And even at the risk of jeopardizing her relationship with her father, Pharaoh's daughter thought it too cruel to murder the little infant she held. She offered kindness to someone in trouble.

- *Pharaoh's daughter was courageous.* Courage is a quality of mind and spirit that enables one to meet danger and difficulty with valor. Compassion and kindness kindled courage in the princess and overshadowed any fear she had of disobeying her father.

Although Pharaoh's daughter was a pagan idolater, God used this great woman's kindness and courage to benefit His people. This tender woman of the past—whose name we don't even know—challenges God's women today. Won't you pray to be, as she was, more kind to others in their distress? And won't you ask God to give you greater courage to act in kindness?

His sister stood afar off.
EXODUS 2:4

*H*ow can you nurture family values in your home? How can you pro-mote concern for one another among your children? How can you raise your children to love each other? Before we look at some of God's answers to these vital questions, note how one devoted sister models family values for us.

Miriam was a 12-year-old girl who undoubtedly adored her new baby brother. For three months Miriam had helped her mother, Jochebed, hide little Moses and care for him as their family defied the Pharaoh's edict to kill every newborn Hebrew boy (Exodus 1:22). Then her mother had placed the infant into a floating basket which she set among the reeds of the Nile River. Miriam "stood afar off, to know what would be done to him." When the opportunity arose—when the Pharaoh's daughter discovered the baby—Miriam offered to find a nurse for the infant, thereby arranging for her baby brother to be cared for at home again.

Where do you think young Miriam developed such family loyalty? Prob-ably from her wonderful mother. As the mother in your home—or as a devoted grandmother or aunt—you, too, can help instill such values in your family. Daily efforts to do the following will help:

- Teach siblings to love one another (John 15:12,17). Encourage brothers and sisters to pray for one another and to do secret acts of kindness for one another.

- Openly express kindness and concern for others (Proverbs 12:25). Children repeat what they hear and mimic what they see. So be a living model of Jesus Christ, acting with His kindness and compas-sion.

- Express love openly. Be affectionate and verbal. Say "I love you" every time you say good-bye or talk on the phone to your children.

- Cultivate strong family ties. Develop a "three musketeers mentality" of "one for all and all for one." See that each family member sup-ports and encourages the others.

- Pray for God's love to be made manifest by your children (Galatians 5:22).

And remember, too, that the effective, fervent prayer of a righteous mother avails much (James 5:16)!

So [Miriam] went and called the child's mother.
Exodus 2:8

Traditionally, Jewish girls remained under the care and guidance of their mothers until marriage. So for a dozen years already, Jochebed had taught and trained her daughter, Miriam, in the valuable qualities of diligence, faithfulness, responsibility, and wisdom—and young Miriam clearly exhibited each of these virtues. She became a mirror of her mother's marvelous merits. Here's how her opportunity to shine unfolded.

Pharaoh had commanded that every boy born to the Hebrews be drowned in the Nile River (Exodus 1:22), and Moses' parents had defied that edict. Instead, they had hidden Moses until he could no longer be kept secret. Then came the sad day when they placed Moses in a basket on the river—and into the hands of God.

Perhaps Moses' mother couldn't bear to watch what might happen to her dear baby. Or perhaps her presence at the riverbank would be too obvious. Or perhaps Jochebed asked her daughter, Miriam, to stand nearby and watch over the basket. Or perhaps the spunky and devoted sister felt compelled to stay and look out for her baby brother. However it happened, the young girl "stood afar off, to know what would be done to him."

As Miriam peered through the reeds, the daughter of Pharaoh came to bathe. Curious about the floating basket, the princess opened it up, and Moses began to cry. The baby needed milk.

At that moment Miriam stepped forward and cleverly asked, "Shall I go and call a nurse for you from the Hebrew women, that she may nurse the child for you?" Given permission by the princess, Miriam brought Jochebed—her mother and Moses' mother—to feed him. Because of Miriam's quick thinking, a triple blessing was reaped by her family:

- Moses' life was saved.

- Jochebed received her baby back.

- Jochebed received wages from Pharaoh's daughter for nursing Moses.

Teaching your children love, mercy, caring, and compassion along with diligence, faithfulness, responsibility, and wisdom—the kinds of traits we see in Miriam—begins with you, dear mom. Your children will mirror your merits. What are they seeing in you and learning from your actions? Whatever you sow, that shall you also reap (Galatians 6:7)!

> *"Take this child away and nurse him for me."*
> EXODUS 2:9

*D*o you have any little ones in your life? If you are a mother, grandmother, or aunt, God's high calling for you is to devote yourself to those children during the first few years of their lives. God has given you the important role of teaching His little ones about Him, of nurturing them up for Him, of giving Him a godly man or woman to use for His great purposes.

Today's look at the life of Jochebed focuses on such faithful mothering.

Her name: Jochebed is the first person in Scripture to have a name compounded with *Jah,* or *Jehovah.* *Jochebed* means "glory of Jehovah," "Jehovah is her glory," or "Jehovah is our glory." It was to such a woman of God—a woman whose glory is Jehovah—that the pagan daughter of Pharaoh said, "Take this child away and nurse him for me."

Her son: Little did Pharaoh's daughter know that the three-month-old infant she had just taken out of the basket she had found floating in the Nile River was Jochebed's own baby. To save her child from a death decree, Jochebed had placed him into that homemade basket and, by faith, positioned the ark and its precious cargo in the water at the river's edge.

Her assignment: The opportunity to nurse little Moses gave Jochebed approximately two and a half years to teach her son the great truths about Jehovah, "her glory." Jochebed had just these few years to give God a man who would lead His people. Then she would have to deliver him to Pharaoh's daughter to be raised in a godless home.

Just a few years. Do you know that 50 percent of a child's character and personality development takes place by age three and 75 percent by age five? The first years of a child's life are critical years for input and training. Jochebed was one of God's faithful mothers who used those first critical years to train her son in the ways of the Lord. Indeed, the only time that she had with her little boy was those few years. Won't you take seriously your calling as a mother? Just a few years devoted to God's little ones make a world of difference!

> *[Jochebed] took the child and nursed him.*
> Exodus 2:9

*G*od has given Christian mothers the sacred assignment of training up their children for Him. Proverbs 22:6 spells it out this way: "Train up a child in the way he should go."

One godly mother, Jochebed, trained up her little Moses for his first three years, and we can be sure her heart was heavy the day she gave him over to Pharaoh's daughter for the rest of his life. But we clearly see that Jochebed's faithful training lasted because, later, Moses' life exemplified the second half of Proverbs 22:6—"When he is old he will not depart from it." At 40 years of age, Moses chose to identify with God's people rather than remain in Pharaoh's palace (Hebrews 11:24-26), and that was the first step toward the important role God had for him.

Deuteronomy 6:5-7 gives mothers like Jochebed two basic guidelines for training up children:

> *Love God:* "You shall love the Lord your God with all your heart, with all your soul, and with all your strength." Devote yourself to your heavenly Father; love Him more than anyone or anything else.

> *Teach God's Word:* "You shall teach [My words] diligently to your children and shall talk of them when you sit in your house, when you walk by the way, when you lie down, and when you rise up." Faithfully communicate the truths of Scripture to your children.

An axiom of teaching warns, "You cannot impart what you do not possess." To impart the great truths about God to your children and to train them up in the way they should go requires that God be the focus of *your* life! Is pleasing your heavenly Father the overarching concern of your life? With a deep love for God as the foundation of your life and His Word hidden in your heart, you definitely have something to impart to your children.

So in the day-in, day-out routines of home life are you consciously—and constantly—talking to your children about God? By doing so, you train a child for God.

Every single day counts in training up a child for God. Jochebed had only about 1000 days with her little Moses. How many do you have left? Are you making each one of them count?

She brought [Moses] to Pharaoh's daughter.
Exodus 2:10

*T*urn on the news. Read any newspaper. Evil is a fact of life in this fallen world. But *you* can make a difference. Learn how from Jochebed, a godly mother from ages ago.

Jochebed lived in an evil world that was growing darker every day. When her third baby was born, the Pharaoh in Egypt put forth his evil hand of oppression to harm God's people (Exodus 1:11). He ordered that every boy born to the Jews be murdered (Exodus 1:16, 22). What could Jochebed—a godly woman and devoted mother—do against such evil? Her solution was to put to work all that God had worked in her:

- *Courage*—Jochebed decided to keep her baby rather than kill him, thereby preserving him to bless the world.

- *Creativity*—Jochebed made a basket from bulrushes, covered it with tar and mud, and then put her baby in it to keep him alive as he floated upon the Nile River.

- *Care*—During the brief time she had him, Jochebed lovingly nursed and diligently trained her little son in the ways of the Lord.

- *Confidence*—Having acted with courage and creativity and having offered the loving care of a godly mother, Jochebed then placed her son in Pharaoh's household and placed her confidence in God, trusting that He would care for her boy.

In the end, God used Jochebed's courage, creativity, care, and confidence to position her son Moses inside the house of Pharaoh. God would use Moses to fight against evil and save His people from Egyptian oppression.

Moses' mother, Jochebed, therefore belongs to a sorority of mothers who first trained and then gave their sons to God to use in the fight against evil. Hannah contributed her little Samuel (1 Samuel 2:28), Daniel's mother gave him up (Daniel 1:6), and Mary offered her son Jesus to die on the cross.

If you are a mother, "do not fret because of evildoers" (Psalm 37:1). Instead, devote yourself to raising godly children. The prince of darkness is helpless against the power of the truth you plant in your child's heart and mind. Be courageous, be creative, care for your children, and place your complete confidence in God.

> *She brought [Moses] to Pharaoh's daughter.*
> EXODUS 2:10

The famous woman described in Proverbs 31 excelled in her God-given role of mother, so it is no wonder that "her children rise up and call her blessed" (verse 28). What this expression means is that her grown children lived in a way that brought honor, blessing, and credit to their mother—and these words could be said of Jochebed. The Bible doesn't say much about this godly mother, but the lives of her three children speak volumes about her. Exactly who were her celebrated children?

- Aaron, her firstborn, became Israel's first high priest, marking the beginning of the Aaronic priesthood (Exodus 30:30).

- Her daughter, Miriam, was a gifted poetess and musician who led the Israelite women in a victory song after God delivered them from Pharaoh's army (Exodus 15:20) and who, with her brothers, was intimately involved in God's deliverance of Israel from Egyptian oppression. (You'll get to know her better starting on April 2.)

- Moses, the small baby that Jochebed gave to Pharaoh's daughter in order to save his life, was used by God to lead His people out of the land of Egypt and to communicate to them His fundamental commands for life (Exodus 4:11,12; 24:3).

From whom did these three inherit their flame of faith? From their mother, Jochebed. She had taken seriously her relationship with God and her calling as a mother. She had lived her life as unto the Lord, and her sons and daughter lighted their torches of faith at her flame.

You and I are called to light the fires of faith in our homes. To do so, we ourselves must burn energetically with a hot love for the Lord, with the bright joy of our salvation, with a shining commitment to our family. Being such a fire of faith is costly; light comes at the cost of that which produces it. But as we give our lives to fuel the flame of faith in those we love most, as we burn brilliantly and intensely, our children will have the opportunity to inherit the flame of our love for God and our faith in Him.

She brought [Moses] to Pharaoh's daughter.
EXODUS 2:10

Take a moment to look into the heart of Jochebed, one of the great and godly mothers found in the Bible. Her vocation and passion can be summarized in a single word: *Mother.* And Jochebed was a *fierce* mother!

Now consider these modern-day "commandments" for mothers as you think of Jochebed's fierce, godly mother-heart and as you nurture your own:

Commandment #1: Begin early. "Let every Christian parent understand when the child is three years old that they have done more than half they ever will for his character."[9]

Commandment #2: Embrace motherhood as an occupation. "The most important occupation on the earth for a woman is to be a real mother to her children. It does not have much glory in it; there is a lot of grit and grime. But there is no greater place of ministry, position, or power than that of a mother."[10]

Commandment #3: Live a life of integrity. "Only as genuine Christian holiness and Christlike love are expressed in the life of a parent, can the child have the opportunity to inherit the flame and not the ashes."[11]

Commandment #4: Partner with God. "Parenthood is a partnership with God. You are not molding iron nor chiseling marble; you are working with the Creator of the universe in shaping human character and determining destiny."[12]

God's calling to teach and train those little ones He gives to us is truly a high and noble calling. And because we cannot impart what we do not possess, it is vital that we nurture in our heart a fierce passion for God's Word and His wisdom!

Therefore, consider these checkpoints: Do you treasure God's truth, laying it up in your own heart (Psalm 119:11)? Do you spend time each day feasting on His Word and sharing that life-giving truth with your children? Are you giving God's Word a reigning position in your home and family life? What steps are you taking, dear mother, to ensure a regular time for teaching, reading, studying, discussing, memorizing, and even reciting passages from the Bible? Your time in God's Word is time He can use to give you the heart of a mother, and therefore is time well invested for your children.

[Moses] became [Pharaoh's daughter's] son.
Exodus 2:10

everal days ago we considered a few of the beautiful character qualities of Pharaoh's daughter. We saw that this nameless daughter of the cruel Egyptian ruler was compassionate, kind, and courageous as she defied her father's death sentence for every Jewish baby boy and drew Moses out of the water. To this kind and fearless daughter's credit, we now add yet another virtue: *Pharaoh's daughter was generous.* Not only did she save Moses' life, but she took him into Pharaoh's own palace as her son and raised him as royalty.

Count the blessings and benefits that Moses enjoyed as the adopted son of Pharaoh's daughter:

1. Her care helped to provide Moses with a solid foundation for his effective leadership of God's people. Being raised in the Pharaoh's home, he saw government up close.

2. Her kind act was God's means of delivering the child who would one day lead His people out of Egypt.

3. Her adoption of Moses afforded him all the privileges of a royal son.

4. Her parentage meant an education and knowledge of the Egyptian language for the man who would one day negotiate with the Pharaoh, lead Israel out of Egypt, and write the first five books of the Bible.

Through the actions of one noble woman, God moved His servant Moses from the reeds along the Nile River into the royal household of Pharaoh; from the simple home of persecuted Israelite parents to the luxurious palace of the Egyptian ruler; from a future of shepherding and brick-making to his role as leader of the Hebrew nation.

Have you thought about the many advantages and blessings you have received at the hands of others? Have you expressed gratitude to your parents or foster parents; to any special teachers, benefactors, or mentors? Pause now, thank God for His gifts to you in these people, and then take time to express your sincere appreciation to the people God has used to make you into the woman of God that you are.

He gave Zipporah his daughter to Moses.
EXODUS 2:21

*M*eet Zipporah, the woman married to Moses, the friend of God. God does not tell us much about Zipporah's life, but we can glean some things from a few facts.

Facts about Moses: Moses was taken into the palace to be raised and educated, but his special status there deteriorated the day he murdered an Egyptian who was beating a Hebrew man. When Pharaoh sought to kill Moses, he fled to the land of Midian.

Facts about Reuel's daughters: Moses' first encounter with his distant relatives in Midian was at a well where the daughters of Reuel, the priest of Midian, came to water their father's flock. After Moses helped these seven women with their task, they invited him to their home.

Facts about Zipporah: Piecing together the facts about Zipporah (whose name means "little bird") reveals that she was:

- A distant relative to Moses—Kin to Moses through Abraham, Zipporah was the daughter of a priest who was probably a God-fearing man (Exodus 18:12,13).

- A faithful worker—When we first see Zipporah, she is at work. In her day, men tended to the camels and women to the flocks. So Zipporah had come to the well to draw water for her father's flock.

- An obedient daughter—Not only did Zipporah serve her father in her daily duties, but she was content to marry Moses, the man to whom her father gave her.

- A hospitable woman—After Moses helped Zipporah and her sisters with their watering chore, they called him to come to their father's house for food and shelter.

Are you single? Are you wondering how…when…if…you will ever meet the man of your dreams? Cultivate for yourself the admirable character qualities exhibited in Zipporah's life. Nurture your relationship with God, become more faithful in your responsibilities, be obedient to your parents, and develop a spirit of generous, thoughtful hospitality.

"Let…every [woman] ask [silver and gold] from her neighbor."
EXODUS 11:2

udson Taylor, the founder of China Inland Mission, once boldly and rightly declared, "God's work done in God's way will never lack God's supplies." Again and again in the case of the Israelites, God indeed provided for His work and His people. In one instance He did so by instructing the Jewish women to ask the people of the land for provision.

Moses had been leading God's people. At this point, he and the Jews had made nine unsuccessful attempts to escape their bondage in Egypt. Then, with His decisive final stroke against the Egyptians remaining, God told Moses, "I will bring one more plague on Pharaoh and on Egypt. Afterward he will let you go from here." That last plague was death—death to the first-born man and beast in every Egyptian household.

Before the death plague occurred, God instructed Moses, "You shall not go empty-handed. But every woman shall ask of her neighbor…articles of silver, articles of gold, and clothing" (Exodus 3:21, 22). The women were to ask openly and intentionally, not deceitfully, for the Egyptians' gold and silver jewelry, drinking vessels, and clothing. What was the outcome of the women's obedience? The Egyptian people showered them with gifts galore!

Whatever God requires of you, He will see that you are suitably equipped for the task and that your needs are, by His providence, abundantly supplied. Trust that you, God's child, will never lack the supplies you need to do His work. Indeed, God your heavenly Father has promised to "supply all your need according to His riches in glory by Christ Jesus" (Philippians 4:19).

Are you remembering to ask God for His supply—and are you asking faithfully?

Perhaps "you do not have because you do not ask" (James 4:2).

Are your motives pure? Are you most concerned about God's purposes and His glory?

See that you do not "ask amiss, that you may spend it on your pleasures" (James 4:3).

> *Miriam...the sister of [Moses and] Aaron...*
> EXODUS 15:20

*M*iriam, what advice do you have for a single woman?"

Imagine an interviewer today asking this question of Miriam, one of God's supersingles of yesterday. What wisdom do you think Miriam would offer after her 90-plus years of singleness?

Perhaps Miriam would say simply, "Devote yourself to ministry." The Bible provides no evidence that Miriam ever married. In all of Scripture, no husband or children are mentioned. But apparently, rather than pining away or giving in to feelings of inferiority, hopelessness, or loneliness, Miriam viewed her singleness as an opportunity to give herself fully to ministry. As a result, she blossomed into one of the Bible's strongest female leaders (Micah 6:4). Throughout the deliverance of God's people from Egyptian bondage and their journey into the Promised Land, Miriam accompanied and assisted her brothers, Aaron and Moses, in their leadership of the Israelites.

If you are unmarried as you read these words today, may you, dear lover of God, join the ranks of Miriam. Oh, you may have your job, your career (which, remember, is also an important opportunity for ministry), but the rest of your time is labeled by time-management experts as *discretionary time*. And you are in complete control of how you use your discretionary time—that time which is yours to manage at will because it is *your* time.

So, single or married, take some time to pray about these questions:

• How effectively am I using my "free" time—my evenings, my weekends, my children's naptime—for God's kingdom?

• What doors of ministry are open to me now?

Just think of the myriad ministries you could have during your free time! You could disciple or mentor another woman in the faith. You could write or e-mail a lonely missionary. You could take a meal to a cancer patient. You could visit a shut-in. You could help your church prepare for Sunday morning worship services. Add your own ideas to this list of suggestions and then take a bold step...right into the realm of selfless ministry and devote yourself to helping others!

Miriam…the sister of [Moses and] Aaron…
EXODUS 15:20

*W*e saw the delightful, quick-thinking Miriam hide among the reeds along Egypt's Nile River. Holding her breath, she quietly watched the tiny floating basket that held her baby brother, Moses, and waited to see what would happen to him (Exodus 2:4).

But Miriam's devotion to her brother Moses didn't end there on the riverbank. In response to God's call to live her life as a single woman, Miriam chose to devote herself to serving her two brothers, Aaron and Moses, as they served God and His people (Micah 6:4).

Yesterday we began a fictitious interview with Miriam, one of God's supersingles, by asking the question, "What advice do you have for a single woman?" Based on how Miriam lived her life, we imagined that her first piece of advice would be, "Devote yourself to ministry." Today we add her second pearl of wisdom: "Devote yourself to family."

Miriam, a woman who had no husband or children, devoted her heart, her love, her energy, and her wit to helping her brothers in the massive undertaking of leading the Jewish nation—over two million people!—out from under the oppression of Pharaoh and into the freedom of the Lord. Apparently, as Aaron and Moses led the entire company, Miriam was looked upon—and acted as—the premier leader of the women.

So now to you, dear one. Are you single? If so, in what creative ways can you serve and support your own family members in their various endeavors, especially those laboring for God's kingdom? No one more than family deserves your loyalty and understanding!

Or are you a mother? If so, are you nurturing family unity among your children? Try to engage your family in joint service to God. Your family could, for instance, adopt a missionary family, serve a meal at a local soup kitchen, labor shoulder to shoulder during a church workday, attend a family camp, teach Sunday school, and fill a new backpack with school supplies for a child who wouldn't have one otherwise. As you encourage mutual service to God and mutual ministry to one another in your family, your children will be well on their way to joining together in service to God, just as Moses, Aaron, and Miriam did.

Miriam, the prophetess...
EXODUS 15:20

A prophetess is a woman who acts as a mouthpiece for God, receiving a message from Him and proclaiming it in accordance with His commands.[1] Only a handful of women in Scripture have received that honored role and title. They include Miriam, Deborah (Judges 4:4), Huldah (2 Kings 22:14), Anna (Luke 2:36), and Philip's four daughters (Acts 21:9). Miriam, the sister of Aaron and Moses, was the first woman to be given this rare honor as the Lord spoke through her to His people (Numbers 12:2). One of those occasions was a great day in the history of the Jewish people.

Times were tense. The years before Miriam's prophesying included her people's bondage under the oppressive hand of the Egyptians (Exodus 1:11-14). When the sons of Israel cried out to God for help, God sent Moses and Aaron, Miriam's brothers, to lead His people to freedom (4:27-31). After ten encounters with Moses and numerous plagues choreographed by God Himself, Pharaoh finally allowed the Israelites to leave Egypt.

Yes, times were tense when Pharaoh increased the Jews' workload, withheld the supplies they needed, repeatedly changed his mind about their release, and finally, after the death of every firstborn Egyptian male, consented to their departure. But even then Pharaoh was so angry that he sent an army of warriors in pursuit of the Jews (Exodus 14:7).

This dramatic situation was the backdrop for one more mighty and supernatural act. As soon as all of the Jewish people walked through the miraculously parted Red Sea waters, God just as miraculously closed the waters over the entire Egyptian army (Exodus 14:28).

What wonder! What relief! What deliverance! Moses erupted into a song of sheer praise. Miriam offered her own God-inspired song, too. Hear the joyous words of Miriam the prophetess as she, with tambourine in hand and followed by all the women who were dancing and playing their own tambourines, exulted: "Sing to the LORD, for He has triumphed gloriously! The horse and its rider He has thrown into the sea!" Amen!

All the women went out after [Miriam]....
EXODUS 15:20

*D*o you have aspirations for leadership? If leading other women is one of the desires of your heart, or if leadership is something you wish to pray about, consider a few principles of spiritual leadership and ask God to help grow them in your life.

- *A leader is a follower.* The adage is true that to be a leader you must first be a follower. Leadership is a discipline, and it is in the process of being a faithful follower that you gain the discipline necessary for effective leadership.

- *A leader is a pray-er.* Prayer brings to leadership the power and energy of the Holy Spirit. Missionary and leader Hudson Taylor was convinced that "it is possible to move [others], through God, by prayer alone."

- *A leader is an initiator.* It is only the authentic leader who is willing to take risks and move out courageously as venturesomeness is applied to vision.[2]

If you are looking for a model of a leader of women, God shows you in Miriam one of His very special women of faith who lived out these principles of leadership.

- *Miriam was a follower.* She faithfully followed and assisted her two brothers, Aaron and Moses, as they led God's people to freedom (Micah 6:4).

- *Miriam was a pray-er.* As a prophetess and a pray-er, Miriam was filled with the Holy Spirit, who inspired her words.

- *Miriam was an initiator.* Moved by God's miraculous defeat of the Egyptian army in the midst of the Red Sea, Miriam "took the timbrel in her hand; and all the women went out after her with timbrels and with dances."

May God's Spirit at work in your life and the example of Miriam inspire you to serve as a leader for His kingdom.

All the women went out...with timbrels and with dances.
EXODUS 15:20

*H*ave you ever felt like a rubber band: stretched...and stretched... and stretched some more...until the only step remaining is to snap? Well, that's exactly the kind of tension that had been building among the Israelites. For over 350 years God's people had suffered oppression and persecution in the land of Egypt (Exodus 1). Even when God sent Moses to deliver His people, the tension increased as the Pharaoh of Egypt refused again and again to let God's people go (Exodus 10:27).

The Jews had worked hard. They had waited long. They had worried about much. They had wondered about Moses' leadership and God's faithfulness. They had witnessed many of God's powerful miracles. They had at last won their freedom by yet another of God's miracles.

Now and at long last, on the other side of the Red Sea, they worshiped! Their release from bondage, and the long-awaited relief from tension, created an occasion for celebration! In a spontaneous outburst of praise, Moses and the people of Israel sang to the Lord, and all the women went out after Miriam playing their timbrels and dancing.

God tells us in Ecclesiastes 3:4,7:

There is a "time to weep, and a time to laugh;"
There is a "time to mourn, and a time to dance...."
There is a "time to keep silence, and a time to speak."

Well, it was time for the Israelite men and women to laugh, dance, speak, sing, shout, and celebrate! So, with their lips, they exalted Jehovah, spoke of His wonders, and sang His praises.

Can you add your voice of celebration to the Israelites' mighty chorus of praise to God? Can you celebrate...

- your release from certain trials?
- your deliverance from bondage?
- your escape from eternal darkness?

The Bible urges you to magnify the Lord and exalt His name (Psalm 34:3). Give thanks to the Lord, and let the redeemed of the Lord sing His praises (Psalm 107:1, 2).

Let's celebrate the goodness of the Lord!

Miriam…answered [the men's song].
EXODUS 15:21

*C*onsider this thought-provoking idea: "Music is God's gift to man. It is the only art of heaven given to earth, and the only art of earth we take to heaven."[3]

Throughout time God's people have expressed their praise and worship and joy to God through music and song. In fact, the Bible charges everything that has breath (and that includes you!) to "Praise the Lord!"—and to do so not only with your voice but also with the trumpet, lute, and harp, with the timbrel, stringed instruments, flutes, and cymbals (Psalm 150:1-6). It's natural to want to sing and shout whenever you experience an unspeakable blessing, and music allows you to express the purest praise to God and to participate in an activity of heaven.

Miriam, the sister of Moses and Aaron, brought a little bit of heaven down to earth through music oh-so-many thousands of years ago. Miriam was the leader of the women in that two-million-plus assembly of God's people who escaped from bondage to the powerful Pharaoh of Egypt. After they fled through the miraculously dry floor of the Red Sea—which just as miraculously closed in, on, and over Pharaoh's pursuant army (Exodus 12–14)—Miriam sang! Inspired by God, she sang and praised His power and faithfulness: "Sing to the LORD, for He has triumphed gloriously! The horse and its rider He has thrown into the sea!"

What was at the heart of Miriam's song? And how can you follow her joyous example of praising God in unashamed exaltation?

- *Praise God spontaneously.* Miriam grabbed a tambourine and spontaneously answered the male singers with a chorus of joyful praise.

- *Praise God for who He is.* Miriam celebrated God's power and His unchallenged supremacy, justice, truth, and mercy.

- *Praise God heartily.* Miriam and the Israelite women sang and danced as they praised the Lord. We New Testament believers are told, "Whatever you do, do it heartily, as to the Lord" (Colossians 3:23). Miriam is an Old Testament example of what doing something heartily as unto the Lord can look like.

So follow in her footsteps and praise the Lord! Let all that is within *you* bless His holy name!

Miriam…answered [the men's song].
EXODUS 15:21

$\mathcal{Y}$esterday we reveled in the joyous, grateful heart of Miriam as she expressed her appreciation to God in exultant song. But the Scriptures tell us of another kind of singing. Both the psalmist and Job, two men who knew dark times of suffering and distress, speak of "songs in the night" (Psalm 77:6; Job 35:10). Just as music is a wonderful avenue for sharing joy, it is a blessed avenue for expressing pain.

Two modern-day women have found that singing songs in the dark nights of their trials has helped them in their sorrow. Let me introduce you today to Elisabeth Elliot.

In 1956 Elisabeth's husband, Jim, was martyred by savage Auca Indians in Ecuador. Later, when an interviewer asked this woman why hymns are an important part of her life, Elisabeth Elliot responded:

> I came from a home where we not only read the Bible every day, but we sang a hymn every day. I have learned as a result of that [practice]…hundreds of hymns. They are as much a part of my life as the Scriptures, and they have been a tremendous blessing to me in times of distress.

Elisabeth Elliot went on to say that, upon hearing that her husband might be dead, a verse of Scripture and the words of a hymn came to mind and ministered to her soul. Mrs. Elliot shares,

> Isaiah 43 says, "When thou passest through the waters, I will be with thee; and through the rivers, they shall not overflow thee." That idea is also taken up in the great hymn "How Firm a Foundation." As the stanza says, "When thro' the deep waters I cause thee to go, / The rivers of sorrow shall not overflow. / For I will be with thee, thy troubles to bless, / And sanctify to thee thy deepest distress."[4]

Consider how biblical truth and how expressing that truth in "psalms and hymns and spiritual songs" (Ephesians 5:19) can undergird you, too, during your dark nights. In times of distress and discouragement, of heartache and heartbreak, in pain and in sorrow, remembering to sing songs in the night will bring comfort and hope.

Miriam…answered [the men's song].
EXODUS 15:21

*H*ave you noticed that women who love God tend to sing? Miriam sang when God gloriously delivered His people. Yesterday we noted the "songs in the night" which Elisabeth Elliot sang after her husband was martyred for Christ. And today we meet yet another woman who loved God and sang His praises—in the darkness.

Fanny Crosby was an American hymn writer who lived from 1820 until 1915. That's 95 years—and Fanny Crosby spent all but six weeks of those 95 years in complete blindness. When she was six weeks old, a doctor unwittingly caused Fanny's blindness, yet Fanny, through the eyes of her Christian faith, saw that doctor's apparent mistake as "no mistake of God's." She wrote, "I verily believe it was [God's] intention that I should live my days in physical darkness, so as to be better prepared to sing His praises and incite others to do so."[5] Note the path Fanny Crosby's life of singing in the darkness took:

- At age eight, Fanny Crosby began writing poetry.
- When she was 11, one of her poems was published.
- When Fanny was 24, she published her first book of poems.
- Throughout her life, Fanny wrote a large number of religious poems, a few cantatas, and many songs.
- At the time of her death, the total number of her hymns and poems of praise to her God exceeded 8000!

Truly, Fanny Crosby was a woman who loved God and trusted in His wisdom and His ways (Romans 11:33). Rather than succumb to bitterness or resentment, self-pity or regret, Fanny sang. She became God's songbird. Like the nightingale, she sang in the darkness…for 95 years.

Today, if you are facing what seems to be a tragedy, then lift a song of praise to God in that darkness, worship Him while wandering in fogs of uncertainty, and bless God despite the blindness of your incomprehension. Your song of faith gives clear tribute to the goodness and greatness of God.

"Sing to the Lord."
EXODUS 15:21

One of the most encouraging characteristics of the women in the Bible who loved God is that they loved Him and served His people until they died. Dear Sarah loved and served God and her family to the age of 127 (Genesis 23:1), and Rachel's devoted nurse, Deborah, lived and loved her charges for a century.

Today we say farewell to yet another one of God's terrific senior saints, Miriam. In your last look at this woman who loved God so fervently, please notice the many wonderful ways the 92-year-old-plus Miriam gave of her energies until the end of her life. Be sure to make her pattern for senior sainthood a personal lifetime goal.

- *Miriam was still in love with the Lord.* As the Israelites emerged from the parted waters of the Red Sea and witnessed God's destruction of their enemies, Miriam's heart burst into praise and song as she worshiped the Lord.

- *Miriam was still leading the women.* Ever the leader, when Miriam's hands reached for a timbrel and her soul sang in tribute to God, the other women joined her.

- *Miriam was still serving with her brothers.* In her later years she assisted both Moses and Aaron as these three siblings led God's two million people out of Egypt and through the desert. Not only did the young Miriam care about her baby brother, Moses, as his little basket floated along the Nile River (Exodus 2:4), but the spunky, energetic Miriam continued to help Moses and Aaron by attending to the needs of the women as the Israelites moved through the wilderness.

- *Miriam was still praising God.* She was never too old or too tired to praise Jehovah for His goodness and for His wonderful works to the children of men.

- *Miriam was still singing praises to God.* Her worship was public, expressive, exuberant, and heartfelt as she came before His presence with song.

Whatever your age, dear sister, continue to the end to be a woman who loves God and serves His people!

"Honor your...mother."
EXODUS 20:12

*J*ust hear "Mother's Day" mentioned, and you immediately think of bouquets, balloons, and bonbons. Add to that the traditional phone call, and you've just celebrated Mother's Day one more time. But why is it that we tend to applaud our mothers only one day of the year when they are as worthy of our appreciation the 364 other days as well?

God, who created the family as His instrument for stability in society and for raising children in the knowledge of the Lord, is very concerned about how you treat your mother. In the Book of Exodus, God gives His people—then and now—the Ten Commandments He desires us to follow. Number five is "Honor your father and your mother, that your days may be long upon the land which the LORD your God is giving you."

Because God commands you to honor your mother, why not set out to honor her today and each day for the rest of this year—and then each day for the rest of your life? Here are some practical, loving ways you can honor your Mom:

1. *Pray for your mother.* It's a fact: You cannot neglect, much less hate, a person you are praying for!

2. *Speak well of your mother.* A part of honoring your mom includes speaking well of her to others (Titus 3:2).

3. *Speak politely to your mother.* Good manners are always a sign of respect, and love "does not behave rudely" (1 Corinthians 13:5). In other words, love has good manners!

4. *Treat your mother with courtesy and respect.* Rush to help. Open her door. Stop, look, and listen when she speaks.

5. *Exhibit open affection to your mother.* A hug, a pat, a squeeze of the hand, an arm around the shoulder, or a sweet kiss speaks volumes!

Take these five suggestions to heart and to prayer. Commit now to honoring your mother, and then meet here again tomorrow for five more suggestions!

Prayer: May our thoughts honor every remembrance of ***Mother.***

> *"Honor your...mother."*
> EXODUS 20:12

*D*o you want a life that is blessed by God? Well, God promises it to you—and He does so in a most unusual way.

When God delivered His law to His people through Moses, one of His Ten Commandments carried with it a promise: "Honor your father and your mother, that your days may be long." Parents have a special place in God's eyes, and He will bless with a life of peace those offspring who honor their parents. When you honor your *parents*, God blesses *you* (Ephesians 6:1-3)!

Yesterday we considered the first of half of our ten suggestions for honoring your precious, God-given mother. Today please enjoy the remaining five. As you pay tribute to your mother, may your life be filled with God's richest blessings and may your days be long!

6. *Shower your mother with thoughtfulness.* How much does a stamp cost? How many minutes does it take to write a few sentences on a postcard? If the hours are right (and the rates, too), how can the joy of a quick phone call cost too much?

7. *Master the art of giving "little" gifts to your mother.* Do you know her hobbies? Would she enjoy that little bookmark? Was there a cartoon in the paper today that would give her a chuckle? Can you loan her one of your favorite books? Drop off a few homemade cookies? Share your latest favorite recipe? Mail her an extra photograph?

8. *Seek to be a giver to your mother, rather than a taker.* Call her when you don't want or need anything. Let her know you just wanted to say, "Hello!" and hear her voice. Also be careful about filling up her "free" time with "free" baby-sitting for your children.

9. *Consider this proverb a word to the wise:* "A foolish man despises his mother" (Proverbs 15:20).

10. *Honor your mother now!* As a few lines of poetry remind us:

> If you have a smile for Mother, give it now.
> If you have a kindly word, speak it now.
> If you have a flower for Mother, pluck it now.
> Give [your honor] while she is living,
> If you wait 'twill be too late.[6]

[Women] came...as many as had a willing heart.
Exodus 35:22

The Dead Sea is a vast body of water located in the desert land of Israel. Forty-nine miles long, 10 miles wide, and 1300 feet deep, the Dead Sea is fed by the Jordan River at the rate of six million gallons of fresh water a day. Despite that influx of clean water, the Dead Sea is—dead! Even with its abundant supply of fresh water, the Dead Sea is useless and lifeless because its water has no outlet.

Today we meet a splendid group of women who made sure there was an outlet for their resources. They are a lovely sorority of women referred to by many as "the willing-hearted women." Note the setting for their generous giving: Before the Israelites left Egypt, the women had asked for— and received—gifts of gold and silver jewelry from the Egyptians (Exodus 11:2). Now Moses issued a call from God for an offering to finance and furnish a place of worship for the Hebrew nation (Exodus 25:8).

How did these willing-hearted Israelite women who loved God respond to Moses' call to give? They contributed freely to the work of God. Those with willing hearts responded, bringing earrings, nose rings, rings, necklaces, and other gold jewelry as an offering to the Lord.

How lovely to have a generous heart! You see, like flowing water, money and possessions are less useful when they become stagnant, when they are no longer moving. You don't want to be like the Dead Sea—useless and dead—because your assets have no outlet! Prayerfully consider these questions:

- What is my attitude toward my belongings (Matthew 10:8)?
- Do I have a plan for regular giving (1 Corinthians 16:2)?
- What can I contribute to the Lord's work today?

Oh, yes—don't fail to note the way this story ends! The Bible reports that the people gave much more than what the Lord had commanded. So Moses had to tell the people to stop giving. They had all the material they needed for the work to be done. In fact, they had too much!

[Women] came…as many as had a willing heart.
Exodus 35:22

ow does a woman who loves God thank Him for His faithfulness and love? More than 3000 years ago, a group of grateful Jewish women modeled one way to express heartfelt appreciation to God. God had miraculously spared their firstborn children (Exodus 12:27) and orchestrated the deliverance of the Jews after long years of anguish in the land of Egypt. Now Moses, their leader, was calling out, "Whoever is of a willing heart, let him bring…an offering to the LORD" (Exodus 35:5).

These women who loved God so deeply responded very generously! Their striking example offers us several precepts for giving to God from our heart. Note the first precept today, and then meet here again for the next few days to find out more about heartfelt giving.

Precept #1: Give your treasure. When the call came for an offering, the Israelite women brought treasures of earrings and nose rings, rings and necklaces, jewelry of gold and silver and bronze, fine linen of blue and purple and scarlet, goats' hair, badger skins, the red skins of rams, and acacia wood. God's women brought out any and all of the treasures they possessed and willingly gave them for the Lord's work. Remember that they had spent 400 years as slaves who had nothing. Now that they had treasures, they chose to give rather than keep!

Dear one, consider your own treasures and remember where they come from. The Bible speaks to this issue:

- "And what do you have that you did not receive?" (1 Corinthians 4:7). The answer to this question is a loud and clear, "Absolutely nothing!" After all, "It is [the Lord your God] who gives you power to get wealth" (Deuteronomy 8:18).

- In the New Testament, the apostle James prompts us to remember that "every good gift and every perfect gift is from above, and comes down from the Father of lights" (James 1:17).

- The apostle Paul reminds us that "we brought nothing into this world, and it is certain we can carry nothing out" (1 Timothy 6:7).

Now make these words of Jesus the prayer and the attitude of your heart: "Freely you have received, freely give" (Matthew 10:8). Amen!

All the women who were gifted artisans spun...with their hands.
EXODUS 35:25

⟨esus speaks this truth about possessions: "Where your treasure is, there your heart will be also" (Matthew 6:21).

In this scene from Exodus, the women of Israel were given an opportunity to evaluate exactly where their hearts were. As one saint of old muses, they were forced to choose God or gold[7] when Moses called for a freewill offering to support the building of a tabernacle for worshiping God. Many of the willing-hearted women practiced Precept #1 of giving: *Give your treasure.* Their generous hearts overflowing with gratitude to God, they gave liberally of their possessions. Others among them followed yet another precept for giving to God:

Precept #2: Give your talent. Supplied with raw materials by those women who gave of their treasure, others gave their special God-given talents. Those women who could spin and weave put their hands to work and brought forth fine linens and spun fabrics as an offering to God.

How do you, dear woman, view your God-given talents? Do you realize that talent, too, is treasure you can use to bring glory to God? Imagine the beauty these Israelite women contributed to the house of the Lord. They worked the hair of goats and the skins of rams and badgers into gorgeous hangings to adorn their place of worship! They dedicated their talents and abilities to God. Putting their hands to work, they revealed the generosity of their hearts...beautifully!

Evaluate your own aptitudes, skills, abilities, and expertise. Do you regularly acknowledge that your giftedness comes from God? Do you regularly pray about how to use your abilities for His purposes? And do you regularly share your talents to benefit people and perhaps even to enhance the worship of God?

Consider some examples. If you have a flair for arranging flowers, why not volunteer to supply pulpit flowers each week? If you know how to clean, consider tidying up the ladies' room between services. If you're an artist, could you embellish the church bulletin? If you crochet, why not drop off an afghan made with love to one of your church's shut-ins? Determine to give back to God the talents He has given you!

> *All the women whose hearts stirred*
> *with wisdom spun yarn of goats' hair.*
> EXODUS 35:26

*N*ineteenth-century essayist and poet Ralph Waldo Emerson likened the minutes of our life to uncut diamonds. Just as uncut diamonds gain value by being cut and used in jewelry-making, our minutes are indeed a raw commodity that increases in value as they are shaped and used for the Lord.

Imagine how brilliantly the diamond-like minutes—and hours—that the Israelite women gave to God preparing for His tabernacle shine in heaven! When God told their leader Moses to involve the people in outfitting a place for worship, God's faithful women answered His call. In so doing, they present us as women who love God with yet another precept for our own giving.

Precept #3: Give your time. The women of Israel generously donated their time as they diligently worked to furnish the tabernacle. With grateful hearts and busy hands, they set about to work and weave raw materials into masterpieces of beauty fit for God! It's hard to conceive of the time these women spent weaving 10 curtains of fine twined linen (highlighted with blue, purple, and scarlet yarn and decorated with cherubim) and making the 11 curtains of goats' hair, goats' skins, and rams' skins needed for a top covering. Each curtain measured 42 feet long and 6 feet wide—large enough to cover the 30-foot-high, 75-foot-wide wooden framework of the tabernacle![8]

Yes, time is a precious gift from God that you can graciously and joyfully give back to Him. Consider the gifts of time that you can give from the hourglass of your life: time at a church workday to make your place of worship a little more beautiful; time at a prayer meeting to make the lives of those you pray for more beautiful; and time in God's Word (perhaps a time-tithe of your waking hours) to make your soul even more beautiful in God's eyes.

Resolve to watch your minutes. Ensure that you spend them wisely. As a little poem declares, "Just a tiny little minute, but eternity is in it!" Seek to use your time for timeless endeavors.

All the...women whose hearts were willing...
Exodus 35:29

ifteen hundred years after the wonderful events of Exodus 35, another woman who loved God—Mary, the mother of Jesus—would utter an inspired line of prayer and praise that surely expressed what was on the hearts of the Israelite women: "He who is mighty has done great things for me" (Luke 1:49).

Before we count the blessings the dear women of Israel enjoyed from the hand and heart of God—the very blessings that moved them to offer up to God the sacrifices of treasure, talent, and time—please pause right now, bow your head before Him "who is mighty," and note a number of the "great things" He has done for you. Don't hesitate to take a full five minutes (or more!) in praise, worship, and thanksgiving to your awesome God....

Now, after your time of personal reflection, you may be able to more fully appreciate and identify with the hearts of God's women in Genesis 35. Note a few of God's rich and miraculous blessings in their lives:

- *Safety:* God protected the Israelites through the ten plagues He sent to the land of Egypt (Exodus 7–12).

- *Family:* God spared the Hebrews' firstborn sons during the final plague, the death plague (Exodus 11–12).

- *Life:* God saved His people's lives by allowing them to cross the Red Sea on dry land (Exodus 14).

- *Deliverance:* In these miraculous ways, God put an end to the bondage and affliction His people had long experienced at the hands of the Egyptians (Exodus 14:30,31).

The Almighty has done wonders for you, too, dear friend. Why not echo the response of the Israelite women to God's overwhelming blessings? Give unto the Lord...

> *Volume*—they gave generously,
>
> *Value*—they gave their best,
>
> *Variety*—they gave treasure, talent, and time, and
>
> *Vigorously*—they gave enthusiastically.

The bronze mirrors of the serving women...
Exodus 38:8

When God speaks, His people need to make sure that they listen—and obey! In the days of the patriarch Moses, God spoke to him about using the gifts of the people to build a tabernacle for worship (Exodus 35:5). The hearts of the Israelites were so moved that they brought more than enough and had to be instructed to stop their giving (Exodus 36:6,7). Once the materials were gathered, the preparations began.

First, the coverings and structure were assembled. Next, the inner and outer veils were made (Exodus 36). Then, oh so carefully, the articles for the Holy Place—the ark of the covenant, the mercy seat, the table of showbread, and the golden lampstand—were fashioned (Exodus 37). Finally, the altar of incense and the altar of burnt offering were crafted from acacia wood (Exodus 37–38).

One last utensil remained to be created, and that was the laver where the priests could wash their blood-stained hands and soiled feet after offering the required animal sacrifices and before going into the Holy Place to worship and serve the Lord. For this most important basin, Moses "made the laver of bronze and its base of bronze, from the bronze mirrors of the serving women."

God records forever in His Word this selfless act of the Israelite women who gave up their highly prized possessions for the priests' washbasin. They freely surrendered their beautiful brass mirrors—undoubtedly fine examples of Egyptian handiwork. From these melted-down objects of personal vanity, Moses formed an item that provided for the priests' purity and holiness before God. The women who loved God more than their possessions—and more than their outward beauty!—demonstrated their devotion to Him and to His causes by seeking the higher beauties of holiness.[9]

Have you dedicated to God all that you own? Would you gladly give up and over to Him any asset or belonging for His use and purposes? Is all that you are and have His? If this is the attitude of your heart, then you, precious sister, possess the highest beauty of all: the beauty of devotion and dedication to God.

...a woman...take[s] the vow of a Nazirite...
NUMBERS 6:2

*A*s a believer in Jesus Christ, you are a woman set apart unto God. You have been delivered from the power of darkness and translated into the kingdom of God's Son (Colossians 1:13). Jesus has accomplished these wonders for you! Oh, praise Him now!

In the time of Moses, a group of women chose to be set apart unto God. God provided for ritual sacrifices to atone for their sin, but He also allowed for a special heart offering—a vow—for those laypeople who wished to consecrate themselves to God and His service for a specific period of time. The law stated, "When either a man or woman consecrates an offering to take the vow of a Nazirite, to separate himself to the Lord, he shall separate himself from [certain items and practices]." Indeed, the word *Nazirite* itself means "one separated" and signifies dedication by separation.

What were some of the particulars a woman who took a voluntary Nazirite vow was to avoid? God's unusual list included wine, grape products, haircuts, and the touching of dead bodies. By electing to submit to these restrictions in their daily life, the women (and men) who took a Nazirite vow evidenced visibly and publicly their separation from the world and their dedication to God. They became something of a "wonder" (the meaning of the word *vow*), something out of the ordinary.

And now, dear woman who loves God, as one already set apart unto the Lord, consider these questions:

- Are you set apart to God in your heart and in your practices?

- Can others tell by your behavior, words, and attitudes that you are set apart from the world?

- Do people sense an otherworldliness about you, an aura of holiness?

- Have you set your affections on things above, not on things of the earth? Is your heart seeking those things which are above where Christ is seated at the right hand of God (Colossians 3:1, 2)?

- What will you do today to dedicate yourself afresh to God?

Miriam died there and was buried there.
Numbers 20:1

*W*hy is it so easy for us to let the memory of one negative action in a person's entire lifetime overshadow all of the good accomplished in that life? Consider the case of Miriam.

We've noted along the way Miriam's life of service to God. Four books of the Bible—Exodus, Leviticus, Numbers, and Micah—tell us something about Miriam, an amazing woman who dearly loved God. Just look at her list of outstanding accomplishments for God:

- Miriam cared for her baby brother, Moses (Exodus 2:4).

- Miriam served God shoulder to shoulder with her two VIP brothers, Moses and Aaron, as they led God's people to freedom (Micah 6:4).

- Miriam prophesied for God, speaking and acting under His inspiration (Exodus 15:20).

- Miriam led the Israelite women in joyous worship after their deliverance from the Egyptian army (Exodus 15:20, 21).

- Miriam served God into her nineties, earning for herself the tribute of "senior saint."

Yet there was that one terrible incident when, in her jealousy, Miriam attacked Moses and was severely punished by God (Numbers 12). As a further result of her action, Miriam did not enter the Promised Land with God's people. But neither did her two famous brothers, Moses and Aaron, because each of them had also participated in one unforgettable sin when they failed to honor the Lord in front of the Israelites. Yet we don't remember either Moses or Aaron in a bad light, and we shouldn't remember dear Miriam in a bad light, either.

Don't you think words like these should have been engraved on Miriam's gravestone?

Here lies a woman who loved God
with all her heart, soul, mind, and strength.

Beginning today, make an effort to graciously note and remember all that is good in other people, rather than focusing on one unfortunate misstep or significant sin. As the Bible reminds us, "Whatever things are...noble...lovely...of good report...[and] praiseworthy—meditate on *these* things" (Philippians 4:8, emphasis added)!

Then came the daughters of Zelophehad.
Numbers 27:1-11

Question: What happens to a man's property when he dies without sons?

The five daughters of Zelophehad found themselves asking this very question. Their father died before the Israelites took possession of the Promised Land, and now these young women—who had no father, no brothers, and no husbands—wondered about their inheritance. Going to Moses, they asked their godly leader to issue a ruling on the matter.

Answer: In response to their predicament, Moses consulted the Lord, and God gave Moses a new statute: The daughters of Zelophehad should receive their father's inheritance. This decision by the Lord—that a daughter could inherit her father's wealth—became the legal basis of a perpetual statute in Israel governing inheritances.

The record of their request stands forever in praise of these women who loved God. Mark well their positive qualities. They knew why, when, and how to ask. The daughters of Zelophehad were:

Bold—They asked boldly and courageously. As women without any relative to protect them, they took their case directly to Moses and so before God. With boldness they made their request known to God (Hebrews 4:16), who values each of His children and considers each one's cause worthy of attention.

Balanced—To the credit of these daughters, their request was not a matter of greed. They did not ask for their father's possessions. They asked instead for their father's property—the land that would have been assigned to him when Canaan was settled. They wanted their father's name attached to that land, which would not only provide for them but also be handed down from generation to generation.

Believing—These brave and wise and believing daughters of Zelophehad never doubted that every man among the Lord's people would receive his portion in the land of promise (Joshua 21:43). By faith they looked to God to fulfill His promises.

Blessed—This group of sisters received the reward of faith: They received the inheritance of their father!

What can you, dear daughter of the King, learn from these godly women about approaching your heavenly Father? Follow their example and go *boldly* before God, *believe* He will answer prayer, and receive the *blessings* that come with depending on Him.

> *If a woman makes a vow to the Lord...*
> NUMBERS 30:3-16

A few days ago our hearts were stirred when we saw the devotion of the Israelite women who expressed their love for God by voluntarily taking a Nazirite vow.

Today we learn more about the vows we women make—and want to make—to God. Be sure to read for yourself Numbers 30 (it's an exciting, thought-provoking chapter) and then consider the nature of our vows to God.

- *The definition of a vow*—The Hebrew word for *vow* means "a bond" or "a binding obligation." In the Greek language, *vow* means "a prayer to God."

- *The significance of a vow*—A vow is a pledge or oath religious in nature. It is a transaction between man and God in which man dedicates himself, his service, or something valuable to God.

- *The kinds of vows*—Besides being promises made to God, vows can also be voluntarily imposed self-discipline for building character and reaching certain goals.[10]

At the core of a heart that desires to make a vow to God is a tremendous dedication to Him and a longing to be more faithful and to grow in holiness. Before you consider making a vow, please take these two guidelines to heart:

- *Guideline #1: Keep your word.* In the New Testament, Jesus continually emphasized the importance of keeping your word. Whether vows, oaths, or promises, Jesus charges, "Let your 'Yes' be 'Yes,' and your 'No,' 'No' " (Matthew 5:37).

- *Guideline #2: Take your vows seriously.* God does! Before you make a vow, weigh the consequences of breaking or failing to fulfill it. The Bible says, "It is a snare for a man...to reconsider his vows" (Proverbs 20:25). In today's language, this proverb would mean, "It is better not to make a vow or a promise than to make one and then break it."

In light of these two guidelines, is there a promise you've made or an area of self-discipline you're struggling with that you need to commit to God today? Do so now and ask Him to give you the grace to follow through.

They…came to the house of a harlot named Rahab.
JOSHUA 2:1

ahab-the-harlot." Throughout the Bible, these three words have been used as one to refer to a remarkable woman who loved God. The very fact that Rahab-the-harlot appears in faith's Hall of Fame (Hebrews 11:31) signifies to us that she has a before-and-after story to tell. Consider the Bible's account of her life.

Before—Before Rahab became a believer in the one true God, she was an idolatrous Amorite. *Ra* was the name of an Egyptian god, and Rahab's full name meant "insolent and fierce." Besides her less-than-positive name, the Bible reports that Rahab was a harlot.

But God—who, according to the pleasure of His good will, chooses His children before the foundation of the world, that they should be holy and without blame before Him (Ephesians 1:4-8)—touched Rahab's heart and transformed her into a new creature (2 Corinthians 5:17). For Rahab, old things passed away, and behold, all things became new!

After—After God's grace touched and cleansed the soul of Rahab-the-harlot and after her many heroic acts of faith, God opened the windows of heaven and poured out His rich, abundant blessings upon her life. What were some of the tangible blessings Rahab received as a child of God?

- Rahab married Salmon, a prince in the house of Judah.
- Rahab bore Salmon a son named Boaz…whose son was Obed… whose son was Jesse…whose son was David (Ruth 4:20-22)… through whose line Jesus was born (Matthew 1:1,5).

Pause now and thank God for your personal before-and-after story. The little epistle of Ephesians reminds us that in times past (before), we all walked in disobedience according to the course of this world (Ephesians 2:2). But to the praise of the glory of His grace, God (after) has made us accepted in the Beloved, accepted in His Son Jesus Christ, in whom we have redemption through His blood, the forgiveness of sins (Ephesians 1:6,7)! Selah! Think on this!

The woman took the two men and hid them.
Joshua 2:4

*E*very woman admires a delicate and carefully crafted cameo, but few of us are aware of how that piece of jewelry comes to be so unique and beautiful.

The process begins with a multilayered stone or shell. An engraver first etches a design (usually the profile of a woman) on the piece and then sets about carving a relief in the top layer. Lower layers serve as the background for the portrait. Cutting through the tiers of colors in the stone or shell can create a striking effect, and cameos are the most breathtaking when a light color is set against a dark background.

The life of Rahab offers us one of the Bible's most dramatic cameos of courage, and what is true of a cameo was true of Rahab: Her beauty is brilliant because of the dark background against which it shines. Consider her situation.

The future was dark for Rahab and her hometown of Jericho as Joshua sent his warrior spies into the Promised Land. The Israelite army was planning to cross the Jordan River and take possession of their new kingdom, beginning with the godless city of Jericho.

But God, the Master Artist and Engraver, shows us in the harlot Rahab a stunning relief against the grim backdrop of godlessness, war, and impending death. We are astonished at the layer upon layer—and act upon act—of faith displayed by this unlikely woman who truly feared God.

How was Rahab's faith evidenced? What were the lovely layers of her precious faith? When Joshua's spies entered Jericho, Rahab revealed her faith in God by hiding the two spies, helping them escape, and eliciting from them a promise of future protection. Within the rough stone walls of a dark and godless city, the faith of one woman—a moral leper in her day—creates an elegant cameo of courage for us to admire.

Dear one, where do you live? What dark events, circumstances, and trials serve as the backdrop for your daily life? How will your own precious faith shine against such layers of darkness to create an exquisite cameo of courage?

> *"...for the LORD your God, He is God...."*
> JOSHUA 2:11

*I*n its own statement of faith, almost every church and Christian organization officially declares what it believes about God, His Son, and its role in the world.

Every woman who loves God should also have a statement of faith. She should know and be able to clearly state exactly what she believes. Rahab was able to say what she believed, and one day her statement of faith saved her life. Here's how it happened.

The time had come for God's people to enter the land God had promised them. Joshua, God's appointed leader, sent two of his warriors to survey the walled city of Jericho. While these spies were staying at Rahab's house, the king of Jericho sent a message to Rahab, commanding her to hand over the men thought to be at her house. Rather than turn in the spies, though, Rahab hid them.

Why did this harlot and resident of a godless town take such a risk? Hear Rahab's words to the godly spies...and her heart of faith:

- I know that the Lord has given you the land.

- I have heard how the Lord dried up the water of the Red Sea for you when you came out of Egypt.

- The Lord your God, He is God in heaven above and on earth beneath.

Rahab's statement of faith clearly reveals her knowledge of God. She obviously knew who God is and what He had done for His people. She knew of His plan to give the land to His chosen race, and she knew that God was the God of all heaven and earth. Rahab definitely had her facts about God straight!

And now for you, dear woman of faith. How would your own statement of faith read? How much do you know about God and His dealings with His people? How many of His attributes are you familiar with? How thoroughly can you spell out your knowledge of God? Take time to think...and pray...and articulate your beliefs. Search the Scriptures, too. Make it your goal to know what you believe...and then, as Rahab did, declare your faith to others!

She let them down by a rope.
JOSHUA 2:15

*D*id you know that only three women are included in God's honor roll of Old Testament saints found in Hebrews 11? Standing tall in this lineup—with Sarah, the mother of faith (verse 11), and Jochebed, Moses' faithful mother (verse 23)—is Rahab (verse 31). But there is one glaring, and even shocking, difference between Sarah and Jochebed...and Rahab.

—Sarah was married to Abraham, the friend of God (James 2:23).

—Jochebed was married to Amram, of the house of Levi, in the line of Abraham, Isaac, and Jacob (Exodus 2:1).

—Rahab wasn't married at all, but was a harlot, a pagan prostitute.

Rahab had no religious background, no godly heritage, no devout husband, and no pious parents. But Rahab's *choices* qualified her to join the ranks of Sarah and Jochebed.

It's been said that choices, not chance, determine human destiny. We could add that, to some extent, our choices also determine our eternal destiny. Ponder the truth of these lines of poetry:

> To every man there openeth a way
> And the high soul climbs the high way
> And the low soul climbs the low...
> To every man there openeth
> A high way and a low;
> And every man decideth
> Which way his soul shall go.[11]

Rahab exhibited her faith by her choices, and those choices affected her human—and her eternal—destiny. On that notable day in Jericho, when God sent His agents to Rahab's house, two ways opened up to her. The choice was hers: Would she choose the way of faith—the high way? Or would she continue on the way of the world—the low path? Note over these next few days a handful of Rahab's brave choices—choices that revealed her remarkable faith and reaped for her a fulfilling future and eternal life.

But now consider what choices *you* are making that will affect *your* destiny. How high are your sights—and your faith—set? Are you choosing the high way?

She let them down by a rope.
JOSHUA 2:15

$\mathcal{M}$ost of the days of our lives move along in a predictable rhythm. We get up at a predicted time. We work our way through the day doing predictable tasks. We go to bed, finishing yet another predictable day filled with familiar people, familiar situations, and familiar activities.

Rahab's life followed its own predictable paths until one dramatic day when she was suddenly confronted by new faces, new circumstances, and a new choice. She had heard about God and the wondrous miracles He had performed for His people, about the parting of the Red Sea, and about the destruction of two Amorite kings. But then, on one ordinary day, Rahab came face-to-face with two Israelite men…and with a serious decision to make: Would she choose to turn the two spies over to the king's men, or would she choose to help them?

Choice #1—Rahab helped the spies. Such courage and such faith! Rahab risked her own life to protect her nation's enemies—the spies Joshua had sent in preparation for battle. Hers was an act of treason, punishable by death, yet Rahab feared God more than she feared man, and so her choice revealed these fine qualities:

- *Kindness*—The two spies were in need. Rahab's king had found out about their presence. But when he asked her to deliver the men over to him, Rahab could not sacrifice their lives. Instead, she was willing to sacrifice her own.

- *Courage*—To stand up against her king and to betray her own city unto death and destruction took courage. Yet she acted boldly, choosing to save the two men who represented God's people.

- *Faith*—Rahab believed. She believed that her country was destined for destruction and that God and His people would prevail.

- *Creativity*—Thinking quickly, Rahab hid Joshua's spies, sent their pursuers in another direction, and then secretly let the spies out of the city.

The New Testament exhorts us to "do good to all, especially to those who are of the household of faith" (Galatians 6:10). Is yours a heart that chooses to act toward God's people with kindness, courage, faith, and creativity?

"According to your words, so be it."
Joshua 2:21

$\mathcal{T}$he tiny book of James explains to us that "faith by itself, if it does not have works, is dead" (James 2:17) and that "by works faith [is] made perfect" (verse 22). And our works are guided by our choices.

Have you ever thought about faith being like a chain—a series of choices linked together? Rahab, who loved God, continued to make choices that evidenced her love and her faith. We saw the first faith-link in her chain of choices yesterday: Rahab chose to help the spies who entered Jericho, rather than turn them over to the king. Then Rahab made another faith choice.

Choice #2—Rahab believed the spies. When Joshua's scouts said the Israelites would cross the Jordan River and take the land, Rahab believed them. By faith, she said, "I know that the Lord has given you the land." Rahab had heard of God's miraculous care for His people, was convinced of the supremacy of Jehovah, and so believed, fastening another faith link onto her growing chain of faith.

How long—and how strong—is your chain of faith? Are you an ever-growing woman of faith? And is that fact evident in the faith choices you make?

For starters, do you believe God's Word? It's important that you do because what you believe will determine how you behave, how you work out your faith. These two men of faith serve as good examples:

- Abraham, the father of our faith, believed God when He promised, "I will make you a great nation" (Genesis 12:2; 15:6).

- The apostle Paul exhibited this same faith during a storm he encountered as he sailed to Rome. He declared, "I believe God that it will be just as it was told me" (Acts 27:25).

Won't you follow in Rahab's and Abraham's and Paul's footsteps of faith and believe God's Word? The next time you have the choice of faith or doubt, choose to believe...and fasten one more faith-link onto your increasing chain of faith.

> *Doubt* sees the obstacles. *Faith* sees the way.
> *Doubt* sees the darkest night. *Faith* sees the day.
> *Doubt* dreads to take a step. *Faith* soars on high.
> *Doubt* questions, "Who believes?" *Faith* answers, "I."

> *"According to your words, so be it."*
> JOSHUA 2:21

*P*lease sit back a moment and admire Rahab's amazing faith! Everything about her situation seemed to work against Rahab ever becoming a woman who loved God and trusted in Him. She was a pagan, and she was a prostitute. And yet, in Hebrews 11, the chapter of the Bible considered "God's roll call of faith," dear Rahab appears among the great men of faith, alongside only two other women: Sarah and Moses' mother.

She earned that place because of her choices. Today we look at brave, believing Rahab-the-harlot confirm her faith by yet another choice:

Choice #3—Rahab secured a promise. Believing in the ultimate triumph of Jehovah, Rahab asked for and received a promise from the spies that they would save her life and all her family members when they returned to annihilate the city.

A promise is defined as "the declaration of some benefit to be conferred."[12] Well, dear one, many of the thousands of promises in the Bible apply to you! What a blessing and a joy to partake of the many promises—those declarations of benefits to be conferred (on you!) that are based on the very nature and character of God! So make it your choice to believe these few promises:

- Jesus promised, "I will never leave you nor forsake you" (Hebrews 13:5).

- Paul promised, "My God shall supply all your need according to His riches in glory by Christ Jesus" (Philippians 4:19).

- Jesus promised, "My grace is sufficient for you" (2 Corinthians 12:9).

- Paul promised, "If you confess with your mouth the Lord Jesus and believe in your heart that God has raised Him from the dead, you will be saved" (Romans 10:9).

Let us again follow in the footsteps of God's beautiful woman of faith, Rahab. Let us secure and appropriate God's promises for ourselves. What is God promising you today? Why not spend some time reading His Word... and look for one of His precious promises? Then, in faith, make the choice to trust.

> *Joshua spared Rahab...and all that she had.*
> JOSHUA 6:25

*A*s we leave the month of April, we also leave Rahab's heroic life, but first notice how God worked in her heart.

Rahab's life before faith

- Place of residence: Jericho
- Occupation: Prostitute

Rahab's acts of faith

- She helped the spies. Rather than turn Joshua's spies over to the king of Jericho, Rahab hid them, diverted the king's soldiers, and helped Joshua's men escape out of the city (Joshua 2:4).

- She believed that the spies were God's people and that they would surely possess and destroy her city of Jericho (Joshua 2:9).

- She secured the promise that, because of her kindness to the spies, she and her family would be spared when the soldiers returned to take the city (Joshua 2:12-14).

- She acted on the promise. Immediately after the spies departed, Rahab followed their instructions and tied scarlet cord in the window of her house—a signal that they were to save everyone in that house before destroying the city (Joshua 2:21).

Rahab's blessings for faith

Rahab's remarkable story of transformation doesn't end here. Oh no! As a woman of faith (Hebrews 11:31), Rahab was greatly blessed. She and her family were spared during Jericho's destruction, she lived in Israel the rest of her days, she married Salmon (Matthew 1:5), and she was the mother of Boaz...who married Ruth...who bore Obed...whose son was Jesse, the father of David...through whose line came Jesus, the Messiah and Savior of the world (Matthew 1:5,6)! Thus, by God's rich grace, Rahab's life changed.

Rahab's life of faith

- Place of residence: Israel
- Occupation: Wife and mother

Of course, your life of faith and your list of blessings will differ from Rahab's, but you are indeed a recipient of "every spiritual blessing in the heavenly places in Christ" (Ephesians 1:3)! Rejoice!

> *Joshua read...before all the assembly of Israel*
> *...with the women...among them.*
> Joshua 8:35

*A*t last! God's people had crossed the Jordan River, the final obstacle between them and the Promised Land. This red-letter day, however, had been slow in arriving. At times the waiting had seemed unbearable. Consider...

- The hundreds of years of bondage in Egypt (Exodus 12:41),
- The ten plagues God sent against the Egyptians (Exodus 7–12),
- The pursuit of Pharaoh's forces as Israel fled (Exodus 14:9),
- The miraculous crossing of the Red Sea (Exodus 14:22),
- The total destruction of Pharaoh's army (Exodus 14:27), and
- The 40 years of wilderness wanderings (Deuteronomy 1:3).

Even when the Jewish people finally entered Canaan, they faced battles and wars, death and destruction as they fought opposing forces first at Jericho (Joshua 6) and then at Ai.

And then Joshua stopped. He built an altar, and the people worshiped the Lord God of Israel. Then Joshua read—so that the entire congregation of Israel, including all the women and children, could hear him—every word of God's law. The Word of the Lord offered guidance to the Israelites as they began life in the new land. Exactly what kind of guidance did it provide the women specifically?

Guidance for family—Every mother needs help when it comes to raising her children. God's Word includes specifics for training children in the way of the Lord (Deuteronomy 6:6,7).

Guidance for one's heart—Inside the heart of every woman who loves God is a desire to please Him. The Bible contains instructions for nurturing a heart that is pleasing in His sight (Psalm 139:23, 24).

Guidance for eternal life—There is only one way to heaven, and that is by faith in God. Every page of the Scriptures points to the reality of God and builds our faith in Him (Hebrews 11).

Guidance for life on earth—Job mourned, "Man is born to trouble" (Job 5:7). Trouble is a fact of life, but God's Word contains direction, hope, and comfort for us.

Today, before you go into battle, stop, worship, read God's Word for guidance, and then proceed in the strength and power of God's Spirit.

"Give me also springs of water."
JOSHUA 15:19

$\mathcal{P}$roverbs 31 paints a portrait of God's ideal woman—a woman of virtue and wisdom who, among other admirable traits, works diligently to improve her property (verse 16). Achsah was such a woman.

The daughter of Caleb, Achsah had learned from him to ask for what she wanted. Caleb had served faithfully under Moses (Joshua 14:7), and, as a reward for his allegiance, Moses had assured Caleb of a specific piece of land. Finally, when the Promised Land was divided, Caleb reminded Joshua, "Give me this mountain" (verse 12).

When Achsah married, the dowry that Caleb gave the groom included a portion of his land in the south. Because water was of utmost importance in that hot and arid climate, Achsah boldly said to her father, "Give me also springs of water." Like father, like daughter!

Although Achsah is easily overlooked in the Bible, her life offers important messages for our lives.

Message #1: Watch. In describing God's ideal woman, the wise writer of Proverbs 31 points out, "She watches over the ways of her household" (verse 27). Responsible for taking care of her household and home, Achsah realized that water on her property would improve the welfare of her family.

Checkup: Are you watching over your home? Are you aware of any necessary home improvements that would enhance the welfare of your precious family?

Message #2: Improve. As we noted above, the Proverbs 31 woman enhances her property. In her case, "she plants a vineyard" (verse 16). Achsah noticed what her property needed and desired to make it better.

Checkup: Are you in the process of improving your place of residence (your house, room, or dorm room)? Do you have a plan of action (even for a good cleaning), and are you taking action?

Message #3: Ask. Achsah knew what she wanted and what she needed to make her home improvements happen, and she knew whom to ask to make it happen. In her case it was her father, Caleb, who owned the upper springs!

Checkup: Are you asking God for wisdom, direction, and provision? …Your husband for his input and support?…Any others who might help you better your situation?

Deborah, a prophetess…was judging Israel.
JUDGES 4:4

$\mathcal{R}$emarkable! There is no other word to describe the life and ministry of Deborah. Hers was truly an uncommon and extraordinary existence. For the next few days we will be stringing together the many lovely pearls that comprised the remarkable beauty of Deborah, a woman who loved God. Several things make her stand out so dramatically:

1. *A remarkable woman*—The Book of Judges introduces Deborah as a prophetess, a wife, and a judge. We also learn that Deborah went out to war with the Israelite army, sang her own song to the Lord (5:1), and was called "a mother in Israel" (5:7). No other woman in the Bible is described by such titles.

2. *A remarkable calling*—Deborah is referred to as "a prophetess." Only a handful of women in the Bible have been called to this lofty position.

3. *A remarkable wife*—Despite the unique roles God called Deborah to fulfill for His people, she is also described as "the wife of Lapidoth." Deborah's training ground for remarkable leadership had been at the hearth where she served as a wife.

4. *A remarkable leader*—Deborah served not only in her home, but also as one of God's judges over His people. Her leadership extended beyond her place of judgment—"the palm tree of Deborah"—to the plain of the battlefield where she was shoulder to shoulder with Barak, the commander of the army.

5. *A remarkable faith*—Although others wavered—including the warrior Barak—Deborah's faith in God's sure victory over His enemies did not falter, even when the odds were greatly against Israel.

6. *A remarkable poet*—Inspired by God and speaking from a heart of gratitude, Deborah sang! She lifted her spirit and her stanzas to the heavenly gates as she offered her musical tribute to God for His great victory (Judges 5).

Remarkable! Do you, too, want this rich word to describe your life? While the specifics will differ, your commitment to God and your heart attitude can match Deborah's. How? Be diligent. Be devoted. Be dedicated. Be available. Be prepared. The rest is up to God!

Deborah…the wife of Lapidoth…
JUDGES 4:4

*H*ave you ever noticed what people say when they introduce you to someone? What, for instance, do they say about your achievements? If you are married, consider yourself successful if you are introduced as the wife of your husband! Those words of tribute may mean that you have become known as a faithful, dedicated, and supportive wife, and such a wife is more valuable than rubies (Proverbs 31:10).

When God introduces us to Deborah, He introduces her as "the wife of Lapidoth." Oh, Deborah was a prophetess and a judge, but she was also a wife. While nothing is known about Deborah's husband, we can safely assume that the godly Deborah extended every form of respect and honor that was due to Lapidoth as her husband. After all, she was known as his wife.

God used Deborah so mightily on behalf of His people because she was a woman who loved God. As such, we can be sure that she obeyed God's Word and followed His guidelines for her as a wife. Note this quick overview from both the Old and the New Testaments of our God-ordained role as wives:

A wife is to help her husband. "And the LORD God said, 'It is not good that man should be alone; I will make him a helper comparable to him'" (Genesis 2:18).

A wife is to submit to her husband. "Wives, submit [subordinate yourselves, learn to adapt yourselves] to your own husbands, as to the Lord" (Ephesians 5:22).

A wife is to respect her husband. "Let the wife see that she respects [praises and honors] her husband" (Ephesians 5:33).

A wife is to love her husband. "Admonish the young women to love [to be affectionate to] their husbands" (Titus 2:4).

As some wise person reminds us, "God has no greater ground for those who are unfaithful where they are." To become like Deborah—a woman used powerfully by God, a woman entrusted with leadership responsibility, a woman given a great ground for service to the kingdom—you must first be faithful as a wife. After all, God is honored when you help, submit to, respect, and love your husband (Titus 2:5)!

The children of Israel came up to [Deborah] for judgment.
JUDGES 4:5

Visit any art museum, look at any painting there, and you will see that the background sets off the subject and gives the painting its impact. As we look at Deborah, today's outstanding subject and a woman who loved God, we can't help but notice the background against which her dazzling life is lived out:

- *The period*—"In those days there was no king in Israel; everyone did what was right in his own eyes" (Judges 21:25). These words paint the background of the Book of Judges. Clearly, it was a bleak time for Israel, a time characterized by disobedience, idolatry, and defeat. Israel had entered the Promised Land, but because of the many pagan strongholds that remained, the Israelites suffered spiritual decline and the ever-present threat of battle.

- *The problem*—During these turbulent times, God let the children of Israel fall into the hands of Jabin, the king of Canaan, who harshly oppressed the Israelites for 20 years.

- *The prophetess*—God's solution to Israel's problem was Deborah. She became His witness, His prophetess. As such, Deborah discerned and declared the mind of God. She ministered as a mediator between God and His people. Inspired by God to speak for Him, she poured out His wisdom, knowledge, and instruction when the people came to her for help.

- *The purpose*—God's purpose in using Deborah as a judge was to lead His people into successful battle against the Canaanites and ignite spiritual revival in their hearts. Hearing God's Word awakened God's people to their sagging spiritual condition and stirred up their hearts. As God's witness, Deborah was used by the Lord to bring the Israelites back to Him.

How clear and useful is your witness for God? You, too, live in spiritually dark times. Throughout the world, people need God. In your church, Christians need encouragement and believers need exhortation. God's Word and wisdom need to be proclaimed, and you can share the Word of the Lord with needy people each time you speak and share truth from Scripture. Make it your aim to follow in the footsteps of godly Deborah. First open God's Word so that your own heart is encouraged. Then turn around and spur on another's faith.

She said, "I will surely go with you."
JUDGES 4:9

"$\mathcal{W}$isdom is oftentimes nearer when we stoop than when we soar." These words of English poet William Wordsworth perfectly describe a key to the fame and success of Deborah, the only female judge of Israel. Exactly how did Deborah's remarkable wisdom exhibit itself? In a word, through her *humility.* Take these characteristics of her life:

1. *Deborah did not seek to be a judge.* The judges of God's people—including Deborah—were "raised up" by God Himself (Judges 2:16) to administer the laws of the Lord and help deliver His people from their enemies.

2. *Deborah called upon Barak to lead the people.* When times were tough and Israel suffered at the hands of the king of Canaan, Deborah sent for Barak, told him to deploy troops, and shared with him God's promise: "I will deliver him into your hand."

3. *Deborah warned Barak about the consequences* of her going into war with him. Despite God's promise of sure victory, Barak refused to go to battle without Deborah. Reluctant to do so, Deborah explained that if she were present, "there will be no glory for you...for the LORD will sell Sisera into the hand of a woman."

4. *Deborah went up with Barak to support him and God's people.* Ever the patriot, Deborah declared, "I will surely go with you." Only after calling upon a male leader and then advising him of the consequences of her presence on the battlefield did Deborah go to the front lines.

Dear lover of God, Deborah shows us the way of wisdom. She truly lived out the adage that the way up is down. The way to greatness in God's kingdom is the way of humble service. Never seeking, never aggressive, never too assertive, Deborah waited on God, encouraged others to take the lead, and assisted only when needed. What would God's advice be to you?

- Be submissive to one another, and be clothed with humility, for "God resists the proud, but gives grace to the humble" (1 Peter 5:5).

- Humble yourself under the mighty hand of God, that He may exalt you in due time (1 Peter 5:6).

Then Deborah arose and went with Barak [to war].
JUDGES 4:9

*G*od asks the question, "Who can find a virtuous woman?" (Proverbs 31:10 KJV). Well, in Deborah He has found one! A virtuous woman is a woman who possesses power of mind (moral principles and attitudes) and power of body (ability and effectiveness).

Deborah, a judge in Israel, had both. Strong in mind and morals, Deborah administered God's law and managed and counseled His people; strong in body, she accompanied Barak into war. While the mental image of a woman with a sword in her hand may not sound too appealing or admirable, God has nothing but praise for this remarkable woman and warrior (Judges 4–5).

The Hebrew word for *virtuous* is used more than 200 times in the Bible to describe an army, and, as you'll agree, it aptly describes Deborah. This Old Testament term refers to "a force" and means "able, capable, mighty, strong, valiant, powerful, efficient, wealthy, and worthy." The word is also used in reference to a man or men of war and men prepared for war. Simply change the masculine to the feminine, and you begin to understand the power at the core of a virtuous woman,[1] the power at the core of Deborah! To lead God's people into battle against their oppressors, Deborah called upon her complete store of mental toughness and physical energy. Such toughness and energy are the primary traits of a successful army, and they also characterize Deborah, God's prophetess.

And now for you, dear woman of God. Don't you, too, desire to be identified by God (and others) as a virtuous woman? The day-in, day-out duties you encounter call for you to possess a significant store of power of mind and body. Mental toughness and physical energy will keep you from giving up, giving in, dropping out, or quitting short of God's goal for you as you, like Deborah, serve as His remarkable warrior even on the homefront!

Right now take a moment to whisper a plea to God for strength—for *His* strength. Declare to Him your desire to become a woman who, like a warrior, moves through the challenges and duties of life with valor, courage, bravery, stamina, endurance, and power—*His* power.

Then Deborah...sang.
Judges 5:1

ow does one chronicle important events in a day and age when the instruments and media for writing are cumbersome and crude? This was the predicament Deborah, the prophetess and judge over God's people, found herself in. The important event was God's victory over Israel's enemies (Judges 4:23). The day and age was a time when the law of Moses was still being written on stones (Joshua 8:32). Yet, when God "fought from the heavens [and] the stars from their courses fought against" Israel's adversaries (5:20), Deborah's full heart yearned to keep the memory alive forever. So how did she do that?

Deborah sang. Deborah not only had a sword in her hand, but she also had a song in her heart. Just as Moses and Miriam (Exodus 15) and David (2 Samuel 22) sang after God's mighty conquests, Deborah sang, too. She sang a song detailing God's triumph over His foes. Judges 5 contains Deborah's poem of praise—the words of a joyful heart overflowing with gratitude and worship. Deborah, the writer, gave testimony to God and praised Him in song for

- marching against the opposing armies,
- His righteous acts, and
- acting on Deborah's behalf.

Jesus tells us that "out of the abundance of the heart [the] mouth speaks" and "a good man out of the good treasure of his heart brings forth good" (Luke 6:45). Clearly, Deborah's song spilled forth from a heart filled with "good treasure." Her song reveals all that was in her heart: the worship and reverence, the honor and love, the joy and exultation, the praise and adoration. Deborah was a woman after God's own heart. Hers was a heart "fixed" on God (Psalm 112:7).

Thought: What is in your heart, dear one? What words would you put to the song of your heart?

Consider these "writing guidelines" from Scripture:

Let the words of my mouth and the meditation of my heart be acceptable in Your sight (Psalm 19:14).

With...psalms and hymns and spiritual songs, be singing and making melody in your heart to the Lord (Ephesians 5:19).

Deborah arose...a mother in Israel.
JUDGES 5:7

$\mathcal{D}$o you think Golda Meir, former prime minister of Israel, knew about Deborah, the female judge and leader of Israel (Judges 4–5)? It's possible. Golda Meir once said, "I have no ambition to be somebody," and yet Mrs. Meir became great in her own lifetime as she dreamed of a Jewish state and then witnessed its birth![2] In her own day, Prime Minister Golda Meir was something of a mother to Israel.

The title "a mother in Israel" was originally attributed to the prophetess Deborah by God Himself. Because of her role among God's people as a leader, judge, warrior, motivator, deliverer, and protector, Deborah became like a mother—a spiritual mother—to all in Israel. Her remarkable faith gave strength and courage to all Israel. Her remarkable dedication to God and His purposes enabled her to arouse the Israelites from their spiritual lethargy and despair. Her wholehearted commitment to God energized her to serve Him, His people, and His purposes for a long time. Under Deborah's reign as judge, Israel enjoyed 40 years of rest.

All women who love God desire, deep in their souls, to possess and display the same remarkable, wholehearted devotion to God that Deborah had. Do you desire this? Pause now and give thought to a few of the factors that contribute to a fervent and unqualified commitment to God, that foster a life of great faith, deep commitment, and abundant spiritual energy:

- *A life spent in God's Word*—All Scripture is profitable for instruction in righteousness, and God's Word thoroughly—*thoroughly!*—equips you for a lifetime of good works (2 Timothy 3:16,17).

- *A life spent in prayer*—Do you want to do great things for God? Then ask great things *of* God. Scripture says, "You do not have because you do not ask" (James 4:2). So ask...for greater strength and perseverance, greater faith and devotion.

- *A life spent in obedience*—As you dedicate your life to being "a doer of the word," God promises that you will be blessed in all you do (James 1:22, 25).

"Most blessed among women is Jael."
JUDGES 5:24

*T*oday we meet a woman whose story can, at first glance, cause confusion. The woman's name is Jael, and Scripture sings her praise for the act of assassination. Let's unravel a few facts about Jael before we consider God's description of this woman who loved Him and showed that love in a most unusual way:

- Israel was at war against the king of Canaan (Judges 4:10).
- Jael and her husband, Heber the Kenite, were dwelling in a tent about 15 miles from the battle site (verse 11).
- As Israel routed the Canaanite army, God's people pursued Sisera, the captain of the enemy forces (verse 16).
- A tired and famished Sisera arrived at Jael's tent (verse 19).
- While Sisera slept, Jael took a tent peg and drove it into his temple with a hammer (verse 21).

Although Jael's actions are startling and anything but lovely, God has nothing negative to say about her! Indeed, we see through the words of praise which Deborah and Barak sang that God considered Jael to be a heroine, a woman who loved Him, a woman who was "the friend of Israel." In their God-inspired song of tribute, Deborah, the reigning judge of Israel, and Barak, the captain of Israel's army, offer up praise for Jael, the woman who was God's instrument in His victory over His enemies. They praise the faith of Jael, a foreigner who acted out that faith in her family's tent, by herself, in the only way that she, a Bedouin tent-woman, knew. Using the tools and skills of her daily life, Jael did battle for God in a time of war.

Through the voices of Deborah and Barak, God gave praise where praise was due. Perhaps to truly understand Jael's act, you had to be there! But file this "friend of Israel" away in your heart and pray for opportunities where you yourself can be a "friend of Israel" and be used to help God's people and purposes.

His daughter [came] out to meet him.
Judges 11:34

$\mathcal{W}$hat does every parent who loves God dream for their children? The desire that their children will come to love God with all their heart, soul, and might is at the top of every godly parent's prayer list! If you have children and if you long to raise them to love God, be diligent to:

- Live a life that reveals your love for God (Proverbs 23:26).

- Nurture them in the training and admonition of the Lord (Ephesians 6:4).

- Speak continuously of the Lord. Talk about Him when you're at home and in the car, before you go to sleep and right when you wake up (Deuteronomy 6:6,7).

Jephthah, the ninth judge of Israel, proved to be a godly father. Called upon to lead God's people into battle, Jephthah exhibited a heart of faith (Hebrews 11:32), "spoke all his words before the Lord," was visited by "the Spirit of the Lord," and "made a vow to the Lord": If God would give him victory in battle, he said, then "whatever comes out of the doors of my house to meet me…shall surely be the Lord's, and I will offer it up as a burnt offering." Unfortunately, when victorious Jephthah returned home, his daughter—his only child—was the first to come out of his house to meet him!

How did this godly father and daughter react? Jephthah tore his clothes and explained, "I have given my word to the Lord, and I cannot go back on it." Jephthah's daughter affirmed his vow: "If you have given your word to the Lord, do to me according to what has gone out of your mouth."

Jephthah had successfully trained his daughter to love God, and such training cost him dearly as the two honored God by honoring the vow he had taken. Jephthah's daughter lived out every parent's desire to have children who love God—regardless of the price tag. Her devotion to God was a devotion that cost.

Sometimes when our children live for God, it costs them, too. Nevertheless, pray that your children's devotion to God will be ever increasing—regardless of the price tag.

"Do to me according to what has gone out of your mouth."
JUDGES 11:36

It was a time of rampant sin, defilement, confusion, anarchy—and painful judgment from God as "everyone did what was right in his own eyes" (Judges 21:25). Yet Jephthah and his daughter proved to be a vein of gold, shining bright for God amidst the dirt and darkness of the era of the judges.

The black background against which they shone was God's punishment of His people's sin and rebellion. A part of God's retribution was war with their surrounding heathen neighbors. At just such a time, Jephthah was summoned to lead the Israelites into battle against their persecutors. It was then that Jephthah and his daughter's golden vein of faith suddenly emerged as a dazzling light in Israel, glistening brilliantly against the age's dark faithlessness. What was it about their confidence in God that sparkled so splendidly?

- Jephthah invoked God as a witness to his agreement to serve his country as judge and warrior.

- Jephthah was graciously empowered by the Spirit of the Lord to benefit His people.

- Jephthah vowed to God to sacrifice whatever came out of the doors of his house if he experienced victory in battle.

- Jephthah's daughter—his only child—was the first creature to exit the doors of Jephthah's home, yet she nobly accepted her role as a sacrifice and encouraged her father to follow through on his vow. This woman of golden character viewed her destiny as a worthwhile price to pay for God's victory over Israel's enemies.

You, dear one, are also called to be a shining vein of gold. That's what a woman who loves God is—a light in darkness, a witness of the Light, a city set on a hill, the light of the world. Therefore, "let your light so shine before men, that they may see your good works and glorify your Father in heaven" (Matthew 5:16)!

His wife was barren and had no children.
JUDGES 13:2

 o you love flowers? Can the sight of a beautifully arranged floral bouquet take your breath away and stir your soul? As we spend the next few days strolling through the life of another woman who deeply loved God, we'll be noticing a few of the flowers which God, the Master Gardener, selected to make her life a lovely tribute to Himself.

How fitting that the first flower picked for this lovely woman's bouquet is the most fragrant: the flower of humility. Just as the fragrance for perfumes comes from crushed flowers, so the beauty and godliness of the wife of Manoah came from her humbling life circumstances.

She had no child. God's details about the life of Manoah's wife are sad words: "Now there was a certain man...whose name was Manoah; and his wife was barren and had no children." These words are brands that burn and sear their way into a woman's heart, causing her head to hang and her soul to sigh. You see, in the day of Manoah's wife, many people looked with reproach at those without children. Others thought childlessness a form of punishment from God.

So what does a woman without children do? Manoah's wife probably spent time praying. We know that her husband prayed—and his prayers that the angel who had appeared to his wife would reappear were answered. Like other childless women of the Bible (Sarah, Rebekah, Hannah, and Elizabeth), this woman's inner pain presumably pressed her more closely to the heart of God.

What is your life situation? Is there something you deeply desire that has so far been denied? Is there something you yearn for? Seek to imitate this precious woman who loved God. A life of faithful prayer has the lovely fragrance that comes only from godly humility and kneeling before the Almighty God. So bow your head, submit your soul, and allow God to begin His exquisite arrangement of the bouquet of your life with the unequaled beauty of His flower of humility.

And the Angel of the LORD appeared to the woman.
JUDGES 13:3

The vase is large. The container God has selected for the flowers with which He will grace the life of Manoah's wife is fit for an abundant bouquet. Yet right now, it contains only a single stem, a bending-but-fragrant flower, the flower of humility which we admired yesterday.

But the Master has not finished arranging the lovely existence of Manoah's wife. A second rare blossom is now added: the flower of faith. Note its beauty:

- "The Angel of the LORD appeared to the woman." Whenever "the Angel of the LORD" appeared to anyone in the Bible, the occasion was significant—and Manoah's wife paid attention!

- The angel of the Lord announced, "You shall conceive and bear a son." Certainly this barren woman's heart leaped!

- Next the angel of the Lord gave Manoah's wife some specific personal instructions: "Please be careful not to drink wine or similar drink, and not to eat anything unclean." These restrictions made up a Nazirite vow and set a person apart for God's purposes.

- The angel of the Lord offered further instructions regarding the baby-to-be: "No razor shall come upon [your son's] head, for the child shall be a Nazirite to God from the womb."

Such an overwhelming moment! How did our dear friend cope with it all? Simply put, she handled it by faith. She asked no questions, requested no signs, and showed no hint of doubt. She responded with the rare and precious silence of belief, and one more gracious flower was added to the vase of her life.

Don't you yearn for the gracious presence of the flower of faith in your life and character? Pray about your answers to these questions: Do you love God and obey His Word? Do you trust in the promises of the Bible? Is your faith marked by a quiet silence (no questions asked), a gentle spirit (no details needed), and a sweet submissiveness (no struggling against the unknowns)? If so, rest assured that God has slipped the flower of faith into your personal bouquet of beauty.

"[He] shall be a Nazirite to God."
JUDGES 13:5

*D*o you have a vision for your children and grandchildren? Do you pray that they will be useful to God and His people? Do you dream of an extraordinary existence for your beloved offspring? Do you faithfully encourage godly character and virtuous deeds in their lives? *Someone* in their lives must have a vision that looks beyond any obvious boundaries and magnifies the possibilities. May that *someone* be you!

In the most striking of floral designs, several stalks of flowers shoot out far beyond the others. These big, bold flowers contribute height and interest to the arrangement, magnifying the bouquet's impact. For the wife of Manoah, one far-reaching, radiant blossom was God's flower of vision for her son.

As we've noted these past few days, God has been busy transforming Mrs. Manoah's life into the kind of beautiful masterpiece that can come only from His holy hand. Into the empty life of oppression (the Lord had delivered the Israelites into the hands of the Philistines for 40 years) and sadness (this woman had no children), God has already positioned two glorious blossoms of His grace. God's fragrant flower of humility and His precious blossom of faith stand in place, arranged and waiting on His wise selection of still more beauty.

Today we see God add the dramatic flower of vision to the life of Manoah's wife. When the angel of the Lord appeared to this childless woman who loved God, he announced that she would bear a son and that he would be "a Nazirite to God from the womb; and he shall begin to deliver Israel out of the hand of the Philistines." What a wonderful blessing to the long-aching heart of this mother-to-be!

- *Blessing #1: Her son had a special calling.* He would be a Nazirite from the womb to the day of his death.

- *Blessing #2: Her son had a special career.* He would deliver God's people from the reign of the Philistines.

God's vision for her son gave Manoah's wife immense hope for the future. Pray now and every day for such a God-given vision for your offspring!

"[He] shall be a Nazirite to God."
JUDGES 13:5

$\mathcal{W}$hat kind of flower do you imagine when you think of obedience? How about a blossom that is sturdy and solid, hardy and long-lasting? After all, obedience is evidenced by a strong will and a commitment to the long haul.

The obedient spirit of Manoah's wife, the soon-to-be mother of Samson, was yet another flower in her bouquet of godly traits. Exactly what did God ask of Manoah's wife?

1. *To follow the law of the Nazirite.* She was to "be careful not to drink wine and not to eat anything unclean. Compliance to these commands placed this nameless wife and mother alongside Hannah (1 Samuel 1:11) and Elizabeth (Luke 1:15) in terms of their calling.

2. *To be sure that her son followed the law of the Nazirite.* "No razor shall come upon his head, for the child shall be a Nazirite to God from the womb." This godly mother's obedience ensured her son Samson partnership in the purposes of God along with fellow Nazirites Samuel (1 Samuel 1:11) and John the Baptist (Luke 1:15).

Consider where Mrs. Manoah's obedience led. What was in the heart of God was passed on to the mother. What was in the heart of the mother was passed on to the child. What was in the heart of the child was passed on to God's people.

Dear one, how does your heart check out? Are you a passionate listener to the heart of God and a committed doer of His Word (James 1:22)?

Do you faithfully pass on what is in your heart to the child of your heart? One mark of an obedient mother is the constant, steadfast training of her children in the things of the Lord (Ephesians 6:4; 1 Timothy 2:15).

Do you pray faithfully for your child to pass on to other people what is in his or her heart from the Lord? The mother of the famous evangelist Billy Graham set aside time every day to pray that what Billy preached would meet with God's approval.[3]

Pray to gather God's flower of obedience so that what is dear to the heart of God is passed on to your children from your full, rich, obedient heart!

So Manoah…offered [an offering] to the LORD.
JUDGES 13:19

O, let us worship the Lord and bow down (Psalm 95:6)! Let us worship the Lord in the beauty of holiness (Psalm 96:9)! Let us worship at His footstool (Psalm 99:5)!

Worshiping the Lord in response to these charges reveals a true heart of worship: bowing down before God, falling down in homage, rendering honor to Him, the Almighty. As Manoah and his wife offered up to God their heartfelt worship, God added the final radiant flower to the glorious spray representing the life of this unnamed woman. As she bows in worship, God completes Mrs. Manoah's bouquet.

A quick review leads us to join Manoah and his lovely wife in worshiping God:

- The couple was childless.

- The angel of the Lord appeared to Manoah's wife.

- They were promised a son who would serve God.

- The angel next appeared to Manoah *and* his wife.

- The promise for a son was repeated.

- The angel was "wonderful" and did "wondrously" (KJV).

When Manoah and his wife saw the wondrous act of the angel of the Lord, they fell facedown on the ground and worshiped! They worshiped God for who He is: the Giver of blessings, the Answerer of prayers, the Protector and Deliverer of His people, the Sovereign Ruler of all time, the Keeper of promises, and the transcendently wonderful God of the universe.

Why not add your own thoughts and praise to this list of God's great attributes and glorious character? Why not fall on your face in honor of the Almighty God? Take to heart this definition of worship and make it your goal to spend time in earnest worship:

Worship is an inward reverence, a bowing down of the soul in the presence of God, an awesome dependence on Him…a solemn consciousness of the Divine, a secret communion with the unseen.[4]

So the woman bore a son.
JUDGES 13:24

*I*n America we often honor our mothers with a single rose on Mother's Day. Today we want to honor Manoah's wife with a single beautiful stem: the flower of motherhood. This blossom has been long in coming, and we rejoice as we see God present it to her!

Known throughout reference books only as "Manoah's wife," at last another phrase can be used to describe this lovely lady: Now she is known as "Samson's mother." This gentle woman, who lived out her life in the shadow of two men—her husband, Manoah, and her famous son, Samson, the judge of God's people and the strongest man who ever lived—was apparently content and fulfilled without personal fame. The wife of Manoah was a mother, and that seemed to be enough for her happiness and fulfillment.

Aren't you glad the Bible offers such a positive picture of parenthood? From the Holy Scriptures we learn these divine truths about motherhood:

- Behold, children are a heritage from the LORD (Psalm 127:3).

- The fruit of the womb is [His] reward (Psalm 127:3).

- He maketh the barren woman…to be a joyful mother of children (Psalm 113:9 KJV).

And aren't you glad the Bible gives God's precious mothers sound advice for child-raising? Here are a few bits of wisdom:

- Train up a child in the way he should go (Proverbs 22:6).

- Bring your children up in the training and admonition of the Lord (Ephesians 6:4).

- Love your children (Titus 2:4).

If you have children, know that your calling of motherhood is a high and noble one, a sacred stewardship as God entrusts your precious children—His special creations—to you. Therefore, pray daily for your children. Teach God's Word diligently. Model Christlikeness. Worship together regularly.

[He and his wife]…went to dwell in…Moab.
RUTH 1:1

 he famous opening words of Charles Dickens' *A Tale of Two Cities* declare, "It was the best of times, it was the worst of times."[5] These words also aptly describe ten years of the life of a woman named Naomi.

The best of times. Naomi and her family—her husband, Elimelech, and their two sons, Mahlon and Chilion—left their hometown of Bethlehem and were strangers in the land of Moab. Because of famine in Judah, the family settled in Moab where there was food. Yes, times there were good. They feasted while others endured famine. And, oh, how Naomi must have rejoiced when her two sons were married! Each had met his mate in Moab. Those days had truly been sweet!

The worst of times. But soon the death knell sounded. First, Naomi's beloved husband died, and then she lost her two precious sons. It was a triple blow to the heart and the life of this wife and mother. How could something that had been so good turn so sour? Naomi seemed alone in the world except for her sons' wives.

Dear one, have you ever felt like Naomi must have felt? Have you ever moved into what was supposed to be an ideal future, experienced temporary bliss and blessing, and then faced great loss and pain? Please take these two strong promises of the Lord into your tender heart:

> "For I know the thoughts that I think toward you," says the LORD, "thoughts of peace and not of evil, to give you a future and a hope" (Jeremiah 29:11).

> And we know that all things work together for good to those who love God, to those who are the called according to His purpose (Romans 8:28).

Now, clinging to the One who made those promises, won't you walk the path of "a future and a hope" with Naomi? Won't you, for the next few days, follow Naomi's trail of tears that led her straight into the discovery of the good, acceptable, and perfect will of God (Romans 12:2)?

She went out from the place where she was.
RUTH 1:7

$\mathcal{W}$hen you are in a hard place in life, it is not the time to collapse, to cave in, to fall apart, or to break down. It is time to trust God.

When her life caved in, Naomi, a woman who loved God, began learning how to trust God more. During her decade in the foreign land of Moab, Naomi lost her husband and her two sons. Earlier when famine struck, the family had left their home in Bethlehem for the land of Moab, where there was food. The day she had left her hometown to go to the new land, Naomi "went out full." But in Moab things had changed dramatically!

Then Naomi heard the news. The Lord had once again given bread to His people in Bethlehem, so she left Moab to return to the land of Judah. But it was a long road home, and much happened between Point A (Moab) and Point B (Bethlehem)! Note these stops—and changes—along the way:

- Naomi's two daughters-in-law started out with her.
- Naomi urged these two young widows to return each to their mother's house.
- Naomi kissed the two women good-bye.
- Naomi's daughter-in-law Orpah returned to her home.
- Naomi's daughter-in-law Ruth stayed with Naomi.

Certainly this was not how Naomi had expected her life to unfold, but she was (as we noted earlier) learning to trust God more, to trust Him to work in her life through unexpected people, events, and circumstances.

- *The people?* Where once Naomi had depended upon her husband and sons, now she was to depend upon one lone, young, and widowed daughter-in-law.
- *The events?* Certainly Naomi would have chosen to have God work through the lives of her menfolk, but she was now trusting Him to work through their deaths.
- *The circumstances?* Never had Naomi imagined that she would be going back to Bethlehem without her husband or sons, but she was headed in that direction. It was a long road home. She would have to trust God.

The two of them went until they came to Bethlehem.
RUTH 1:19

*A*ll the world loves a reunion! Relatives from far away regularly gather for family reunions. Best friends rendezvous to catch up on each other's lives. Military squadrons meet and renew their war-time friendships. High schools and colleges host get-togethers and homecoming events so graduates can stay in touch.

A different kind of reunion, however, took place thousands of years ago. It was not by choice. It was not for pleasure. And it was not with joyful anticipation. Instead, it was by necessity. You see, Naomi, formerly of Bethlehem, had left that town with her husband and children, but dreams had turned to disaster. Naomi's husband and both her children had died. So Naomi was returning to Bethlehem as a widow with Ruth, a daughter-in-law from a foreign land. Naomi was "empty."

Naomi, whose name means "pleasant," walked 70 dusty miles home to the town of Bethlehem. As her former friends greeted her with, "Is this Naomi?" she could only reply, "Do not call me Naomi; call me Mara [Mara means "bitter"]....I went out full, and the LORD has brought me home again empty."

God works in our lives through people, events, and circumstances, but never to make us bitter—only to make us better! Remember these two promises: God's thoughts toward us are "thoughts of peace and not of evil, to give [us] a future and a hope" (Jeremiah 29:11), and "we [can] know that all things work together for [our] good" (Romans 8:28).

Other than remembering such promises from God, what can you do to "be fruitful in the land of [your] affliction" (Genesis 41:52)?

Give thanks always—It is impossible to be bitter and thankful at the same time (Ephesians 5:20).

Pray without ceasing—Even through tears, prayer is the heart's song to God (1 Thessalonians 5:17).

Reach out to others—Comfort others with the comfort God has given you (2 Corinthians 1:4).

She happened to come to...the field belonging to Boaz.
RUTH 2:3

 ethlehem was the place.
Food was the pressing need.
A field of grain was the setting.

Ruth was the woman, and she "happened to come to the part of the field belonging to Boaz, who was of the family of Elimelech."

There is no such thing in the life of God's children as happenstance or coincidence. There is only the great sovereignty of God Almighty, who watches over His children and guides their steps, sometimes quite obviously and other times not. God's sovereignty was at work in Ruth's life on that particular day when she ventured out in search of food and later discovered that the field belonged to Boaz, and that the man Boaz was related to her by marriage.

Ruth went out to glean in her new homeland. She went without a guide, without a companion, alone—except for God, who directed her steps to one particular field, owned by one particular relative, who later became her husband (Ruth 4:13). As you consider these happenstances in Ruth's life, ponder these words by seventeenth-century writer and minister Matthew Henry:

> God wisely orders small events; and those that seem altogether...
> [conditional] serve his own glory and the good of his people. Many a
> great affair is brought about by a little turn, which seemed...[lucky or
> accidental] to us, but was directed by Providence with design.[6]

As a woman who loves God, why not seek to see the hand of God in all of the events, the coincidences, the chance happenings, the luck and flukes of life? If you believe in a sovereign God, if you believe in His loving providence, choose to consider all that touches your life as Him at work once again. Learn to:

- *Look* for the hand of God.

- *Believe* that God works in your life, in all that you encounter and all that you experience.

- *Trust* that God works *all things* together for your ultimate good (Romans 8:28).

> *"...under whose wings you have come for refuge."*
> RUTH 2:12

*T*he tiny book of Ruth includes a pair of heartfelt hymns beautifully sung by two people who took refuge under the wings of God.

Ruth's hymn—A woman who loved God, Ruth had only recently placed her trust in the Lord of Israel. Although raised in the pagan nation of Moab, Ruth gave her heart and allegiance to the God of Israel, the one true God. In her faith-filled declaration to Naomi, her bereaved mother-in-law, Ruth uttered words of devotion that read like a hymn:

> Wherever you go, I will go;
> And wherever you lodge, I will lodge;
> Your people shall be my people,
> And your God, my God.
> Where you die, I will die,
> And there will I be buried (Ruth 1:16,17).

Boaz's hymn—Boaz was a man who loved God. He was also a landowner and a distant relative of Ruth through her dead husband's father. Upon meeting Ruth, he blessed and encouraged her in her newfound faith in God with words that also sound like a hymn:

> The Lord repay your work,
> and a full reward be given you
> by the LORD God of Israel,
> under whose wings you have come for refuge.

What beautiful words! Perhaps Boaz saw the struggling Ruth—a woman who had wandered into his field and labored so diligently in the hot barley fields to gather one more day's worth of food for herself and her widowed mother-in-law—as a fragile baby chick. His song pictures this woman who loved God finding refuge under His wings—His wings of protection and safety, wings of care, strength, and warmth. In the Holy Scriptures, God is indeed portrayed as a mother bird who shelters her young chicks with her wings (Psalm 36:7), and Boaz uses this metaphor to bless one who has placed remarkable trust in God and found refuge there.

Do you trust in God and God alone? Do you depend totally on the One who protects and provides for His own? And are you resting under His wings of love? God, your heavenly Father, is responsible for protecting you. Your responsibility is to trust in Him and to rest under the shadow of His wings.

"...under whose wings you have come for refuge."
Ruth 2:12

$\mathcal{W}$hat a blessing it was yesterday to read the outpourings of two hearts so full of love for God—the hearts of Ruth and Boaz. Their words were so heavenly that it seemed Ruth and Boaz were speaking forth songs and hymns (Ephesians 5:19). And couched in the words of Boaz was the comforting thought of finding refuge under the wings of God.

We simply cannot leave this rich image of resting under the shadow of God's wings (Psalm 17:8) without appreciating a hymn written by William O. Cushing in 1896. Enjoy Mr. Cushing's personal expression of trust. And remember, please, that these words were wrung from a heart that knew pain and sorrow. Doctors had told this gentleman, a preacher of the gospel, that his voice was gone. After crying out the words to Psalm 17:8 in prayer ("Hide me under the shadow of Your wings"), this saint wrote more than 300 gospel hymns.[7] Whatever difficulties and pain you face, may you, too, find your refuge "under His wings."

Under His Wings

Under His wings I am safely abiding,
Tho the night deepens and tempests are wild;
Still I can trust Him—I know He will keep me,
He has redeemed me and I am His child.

Under His wings, what a refuge in sorrow!
How the heart yearningly turns to His rest!
Often when earth has no balm for my healing,
There I find comfort and there I am blest.

Under His wings, O what precious enjoyment!
There will I hide till life's trials are o'er;
Sheltered, protected, no evil can harm me,
Resting in Jesus I'm safe evermore.

Refrain: Under His wings, under His wings,
Who from His love can sever?
Under His wings my soul shall abide,
Safely abide forever.

"The LORD…has not forsaken His kindness."
RUTH 2:20

*W*hat would you do if…

- You were a widow,

- Your sons had died,

- Your daughter-in-law was your only companion, and

- You needed food?

This was exactly the predicament Naomi found herself in after all the menfolk in her family died (Ruth 1:3-5), and she returned to Bethlehem with Ruth, her daughter-in-law (Ruth 1:22). Too old to labor herself, Naomi had to depend solely on Ruth for the basics of life. Times were hard when Ruth gleaned barley from the harvested fields. The law of Moses stipulated that any grain dropped by the reapers as they brought in their crops could be gleaned by the poor (Leviticus 23:22). This law was tailor-made for those like Naomi and Ruth.

But beyond this law, the kindness of the Lord was at work. Unknowingly, Ruth "happened"—by God's sovereign design—into the field of a relative named Boaz. As Boaz blessed Ruth for finding refuge under the wings of the Lord, he then took both Ruth and Naomi under his own wings and gave Ruth extended privileges in the reaping of his fields. Boaz also extended his hand to the two destitute women in the form of extra food, extra grain, and protection.

When Ruth reported to Naomi the goodness of Boaz on their behalf, Naomi's heart warmed for the first time in many months. Hope and joy began to push their way up through the bitter, hard crust that encased Naomi's once-happy heart (Ruth 1:20). Her mouth opened to offer the praise, "Blessed be he of the LORD, who has not forsaken His kindness to the living and the dead!" In Naomi's cold heart there appeared a glimmer of understanding of God's sovereign working in her life, of His steadfast lovingkindness, and of His mercy being showered on them through Boaz.

God's gracious dealings with these two needy widows who loved and trusted Him offers you at least two messages:

- *Message 1:* Look for the kindness of the Lord extended to you through the good deeds of others.

- *Message 2:* Extend the kindness of the Lord to others through your own good deeds.

"All that you say to me I will do."
RUTH 3:5

*W*e have very little knowledge of the customs in the small town in Israel where Ruth and Naomi lived, but Ruth 3 gives us some interesting clues.

As you remember, Naomi was Ruth's mother-in-law, and both women had lost their husbands. Returning to Bethlehem, Naomi and Ruth found themselves looking straight into the face of a dim future...until Boaz came on the scene. This long-lost relative generously graced the lives of these two women with food from his fields.

Now consider the actions of these two women who loved one another. Each looked out for the cause of the other (Philippians 2:4), and each sought the best for the other ("Love...does not seek its own"—1 Corinthians 13:4,5).

Naomi wanted the best for Ruth—Naomi noticed the budding respect Ruth and Boaz had for each other. Perhaps rather than resisting the thought of someone else taking her dead son's place as husband to Ruth, Naomi saw a hopeful future for Ruth as a married woman. Therefore, this older, wiser woman coached the younger in the customs of her land—customs for securing a marriage partner. Naomi told Ruth:

- Exactly how to look ("wash yourself and anoint yourself, put on your best garment") and

- Exactly how to act ("when he lies down...uncover his feet...and he will tell you what you should do").

Ruth wanted the best for Naomi—By now Ruth knew that Boaz could—and wanted to—provide for the aged and needy Naomi (Ruth 2:16). Ruth, too, wanted that security for Naomi. Therefore the younger woman obediently followed through on Naomi's instructions to propose marriage to Boaz.

Naomi and Ruth offer us two beautiful portraits of selflessness. Each clearly wanted what was best for the other. What sort of picture are you painting with your life? Are you truly loving other people? Do you consistently desire what is best for others? Pray today for a more generous, a more selfless attitude toward others.

"You are a virtuous woman."
RUTH 3:11

*W*hat joy I find in Dr. John MacArthur's words about Ruth, one of the women in the Bible who loved God!

Ruth was not from Israel; she was a Moabite. Ruth was not Jewish; she was a pagan. Ruth had no husband; she was a widow. Yet Ruth left her homeland, her family, and her religion to follow Naomi back to Bethlehem. Everyone there saw in Ruth's hard work her concern for her widowed mother-in-law (Ruth 2:11). As the landowner Boaz declared to Ruth, "All the people of my town know that you are a virtuous woman."

Precious sister, take a moment to open your Bible and read Proverbs 31:10-31, God's portrait of a godly woman, "a virtuous woman," and then read below Dr. John MacArthur on "Ruth: The Proverbs 31 Wife."[8]

> The "virtuous" wife of Proverbs 31:10 is personified by "virtuous" Ruth of whom the same Hebrew word is used (3:11). With amazing parallel, they share at least eight character traits....Each woman was:
>
> 1. Devoted to her family
>   (Ruth 1:15-18//Proverbs 31:10-12, 23)
>
> 2. Delighting in her work
>   (Ruth 2:2//Proverbs 31:13)
>
> 3. Diligent in her labor
>   (Ruth 2:7,17, 23//Proverbs 31:14-18,19-21, 24, 27)
>
> 4. Dedicated to godly speech
>   (Ruth 2:10,13//Proverbs 31:26)
>
> 5. Dependent on God
>   (Ruth 2:12//Proverbs 31:25b,30)
>
> 6. Dressed with care
>   (Ruth 3:3//Proverbs 31:22, 25a)
>
> 7. Discreet with men
>   (Ruth 3:6-13//Proverbs 31:11,12, 23)
>
> 8. Delivering blessings
>   (Ruth 4:14,15//Proverbs 31:28, 29,31)

Pray now and ask God to work each of these eight godly virtues into your heart and life, that all the people of your town would see that you, too, are a virtuous woman!

Boaz went up to the gate.
RUTH 4:1

*I*n both Ruth 3 and Proverbs 31 we meet "a virtuous woman," but did you know that Ruth 4 details for us the qualities of a virtuous man? The man was Boaz, a hardworking landowner who became Ruth's husband. Note well God's list of the virtues exhibited by Boaz's sterling life. He was:

- *Diligent*—Boaz is described as "a man of great wealth" (Ruth 2:1), and we see him carefully and thoughtfully overseeing his property.

- *Friendly*—Boaz greeted his workers with warmth, and even welcomed the stranger named Ruth (2:4,8).

- *Merciful*—Noticing Ruth at work, Boaz asked about her situation and acted on her behalf (2:7).

- *Godly*—Boaz asked Jehovah to bless Ruth in return for her care for Naomi (2:12).

- *Encouraging*—Boaz pointed out Ruth's strong qualities and spoke of them to cheer her on (2:12; 3:11).

- *Generous*—Although Ruth needed food and was willing to work for it, Boaz gave her extra (2:15).

- *Kind*—When Ruth reported the considerate ways of Boaz, Naomi thanked God for His kindness shown to both of them through Boaz (2:20).

- *Discreet*—Boaz exhibited wise discretion by sending Ruth home before daylight (3:14).

- *Faithful*—Following through on his promise to Ruth, Boaz "went to court" to clear the way to marry her.

Are you single? If so, look for these qualities in the man you may seek to marry. Don't settle for less than the best—a virtuous man who is godly, diligent, faithful. You know the list!

Are you married? Remember to prize, praise, and pray for these qualities in your beloved husband.

Are you a mother? Be sure to instill these qualities in the hearts and minds of your daughters (your young Ruths) and your sons (your young Boazes). Point your children to God's high standards and teach them to embrace His ways as their own. Train each son to be a virtuous man and each daughter to appreciate men who possess godly virtues.

Ruth...became his wife; and...bore a son.
RUTH 4:13

*H*ere's a thought to tape over the kitchen sink, stick on the refrigerator door, attach to your computer, and affix to your bathroom mirror:

True service is love in working clothes.

Ruth, the precious woman we've been getting to know these past few days, is certainly a woman of many virtues. But perhaps Ruth's most outstanding distinction is her servant heart. We've seen her consistent ministry to her widowed mother-in-law, Naomi. For weeks Ruth rose before dawn, put on the work clothes of love, gleaned in the barley fields during the daytime heat, and returned home late at night carrying food and grain so Naomi and she could eat (Ruth 2:17,18). When God gifted Ruth with a wonderful husband and a precious baby, Ruth's joy was full and complete! She had a family to love and serve!

Yes, Ruth possessed the heart of a servant. Like her, you, too, can put on the work clothes of love and engage in:

Service to others—Nurturing a servant's heart begins with the decision to serve others—anyone and everyone. Jesus Himself models this heart attitude for us, for He "did not come to be served, but to serve" (Matthew 20:28).

Service to your husband—God's Word is clear: "Whatever you do [including serving your husband], do it heartily, as to the Lord and not to men" (Colossians 3:23).

Service to your children—As a familiar kitchen plaque reads, "Divine services rendered here three times a day!" It's true that not only every meal prepared, but also every piece of clothing washed, every room tidied, every floor swept, every ride given is love in action.

Service to your church—Married or single, you can exercise your servant heart at your church. There are always meals to take to those in need, pew racks to stock, chairs to set up, and Sunday school classes to teach.

The New Testament points out the beautiful service rendered by the godly women who gave strangers a place to stay, washed the saints' feet, relieved the afflicted, and diligently performed good works (1 Timothy 5:10). May you join their inspiring ranks!

Naomi took the child and...became a nurse to him.
RUTH 4:16

During her life, Naomi traveled from a mountaintop existence of bliss into a deep and dark valley of sorrow. Those many years ago when Naomi had left Bethlehem she "went out full"; but when she returned, she came "home again empty" (Ruth 1:21). In Moab her family of four had grown to include two daughters-in-law, but death had made a triple appearance and claimed Naomi's cherished husband and two beloved sons. It was a bitter, empty day when the bitter, empty Naomi walked the road into Bethlehem with only one daughter-in-law, Ruth, and announced, "Call me Mara," meaning "bitter" (1:20).

But blessed be the Lord! He did not leave Naomi in her valley of despair, hopelessness, and emptiness. God blessed Naomi with a grandchild, a grandson, and she knew happiness again. How she must have welcomed the warmth of fresh-flowing love and life as God began to grow in her the heart of a grandmother.

Tiny Obed was Naomi's first grandchild. Decades had passed since she had held a little one in her arms. What did this signify to her?

- A continuation of the heritage of her dead husband (4:17).
- A person to love since losing her own two sons (verse 15).
- A child to care for and serve as a nursemaid.
- An offspring who would help care for Naomi in her old age.
- A "restorer of life" and a hope for the future!

The role of grandmother is a great privilege God grants women. When you talk to any grandmother, you better be prepared for many glowing tales and a plethora of cherished photographs! But being a grandmother also gives a woman who loves God new opportunities, challenges, and responsibilities. The heart of a godly grandmother is dedicated to the practices listed below—and many more! If you're a grandmother, are you living out the "grand"? If you're not a grandmother, pray for your own dear grandmother.

Give a godly example.

Remember important occasions.

Always love your grandchildren's parents—no matter what!

Never show favoritism.

Develop a personal relationship with each grandchild.

Now this is the genealogy of...Boaz.
RUTH 4:18,21

*P*roverbs 12:4 proclaims, "A virtuous woman is a crown to her husband" (KJV). And Ruth was such a woman of virtuous character. She married a man named Boaz, a man of virtuous character (see May 28). It was a grand day when these two who loved God married one another!

The union of this noble man and woman continued the line of descendants who also loved God. Through their marriage a wonderful, godly lineage extended through time and for eternity, and each offspring became another star in Ruth's crown of virtue. Take a moment to admire these gems in Ruth and Boaz's genealogy:

> *"Boaz begot Obed"*—As one Bible scholar has noted, "Through the birth of Obed, God wove the thread of Ruth's life most intricately into the web of the history of His people. She became the chosen line through which later the Savior of the world appeared."[9]

> *"Obed begot Jesse"*—Just as Isaiah had prophesied, "There shall come forth a Rod from the stem of Jesse, and a Branch shall grow out of his roots" (11:1). That Rod and that Branch was the Lord Jesus Christ.

> *"Jesse begot David"*—The hope of a messianic king and kingdom was fulfilled in the Lord Jesus Christ through the lineage of David, his father Jesse, and his grandfather Obed, who was born to Boaz and Ruth.

> *Jesus Christ*—The family tree or "the book of the genealogy of Jesus Christ, the Son of David" includes these noble names: Boaz, Obed, Jesse, and David (Matthew 1:1,5,6).

Do you have children or grandchildren? Blessed be the Lord if you do! They are precious treasure, stars in your crown. Pray for them—fervently! Encourage them in the Lord—mightily! Ensure that they know about Jesus—abundantly! Support their spiritual growth—heartily!

> *[Her] name…was Hannah.*
> 1 SAMUEL 1:2

$\mathcal{G}$et ready to meet one of the most gracious women in the Bible. Her name is Hannah, and her very name means "gracious, graciousness, grace, and favor." Hannah is one of the few women in the sacred Scriptures about whom nothing negative is reported.

How did Hannah become such a testimony to God's great grace? Short, simple answers to that question include a series of bitter words—words like *difficulty, pain, suffering, sacrifice.* For Hannah—and for all women who love God (including you, dear one)—God used some dark threads when He wove the rich tapestry of her life.

Before we look closely at the various threads running through Hannah's life, take to heart the poignant words of this bit of poetry written by an unknown lover of God and aptly entitled "The Divine Weaver":

> My life is but a weaving
> Between my Lord and me;
> I cannot choose the colors
> He worketh steadily.
>
> Ofttimes He weaveth sorrow
> And I, in foolish pride,
> Forget that He seeth the upper,
> And I the under side.
>
> Not till the loom is silent
> And the shuttles cease to fly,
> Shall God unroll the canvas
> And explain the reason why.
>
> The dark threads are as needful
> In the Weaver's skillful hand,
> As the threads of gold and silver
> In the pattern He has planned.

Rest assured that the Master Weaver is weaving the threads of your life, too, one event at a time, one moment at a time. He alone knows the pattern. Won't you trust Him as He graciously makes an exquisite work of your life?

He had two wives: the name of one was Hannah.
1 SAMUEL 1:2

*Y*oung girls often dream of someday getting married. They may even spend years imagining and planning the perfect wedding day, honeymoon, and life. In fact, most bridal magazines and books are purchased by young women who don't even have a prospect for marriage! They are simply fantasizing about their future.

If, as a young girl, Hannah had dreamed of the perfect marriage, her dreams were eventually met by a rather harsh reality. Hannah did marry, and her husband's name was Elkanah, a Levite from one of the most honorable families of priests. Hannah's husband may have been a wonderful man, yet there were some not-so-wonderful facts about Hannah's marriage to Elkanah. Those became the dark threads of pain woven throughout Hannah's life.

- *Hannah shared her husband with another woman.* Hannah's husband had two wives. Hannah's name is listed first, indicating that she was probably Elkanah's first wife and that later a second wife was added to the family.

- *Hannah had no children.* Hannah did not receive the blessing of a happy marriage and a happy family which she had hoped for. Instead of ringing with the laughter and noise of active children, Hannah's house may have echoed with muffled sobs and tears. The Bible simply states, "The LORD had closed her womb."

- *Hannah was harassed by her husband's other wife.* Insult was added to injury for the lovely Hannah. Peninnah, Elkanah's second wife and Hannah's "rival…provoked her severely, to make her miserable."

Dark Threads the Weaver Needs[1] is the title of an insightful book about suffering, and a title that speaks to precious Hannah's life. Can you gather together the dark threads of pain in your life and then lay them oh so carefully into the wise and wonderful hand of God? He will use those dark threads to make your life a beautiful masterpiece and testimony to His glory!

She went up to the house of the LORD.
1 SAMUEL 1:7

*W*oven into the texture of Hannah's soul alongside the dark thread of pain was the glorious gold thread of reverence for God. Hannah's life was filled with problems, but it was also filled with fervent worship. At the appointed time each year, Hannah journeyed with her husband to the house of the Lord to worship and make sacrifices to Him.

Such devotion to worship is clear evidence of a woman's love for the Lord. Regularly, sincerely, and reverently, women who love God offer to Him their reverent worship. Consider what worship is and some of its benefits:

1. *Worship is fellowship with God.* We don't know whether Hannah talked to her husband about the relentless aggravation she suffered from his other wife. But we do see that Hannah worshiped God and fellowshipped with Him. Jehovah was definitely One she could tell her troubles to.

2. *Worship is the first step toward wisdom.* How do you handle a hard situation? Hannah went to God for wisdom about how to deal with the daily difficulties of her life. As she worshiped, God led her in the path of wisdom—*His* wisdom.

3. *Worship is inward reverence.* It's relatively easy to do things for God— to give money, to serve in church, to regularly attend events. But true worship is personal, a matter of the heart rather than external activity.

4. "*Worship quickens the conscience* by the holiness of God, feeds the mind with the beauty of God, opens the heart to the love of God, and devotes the will to the purpose of God."[2] Can any other activity be more important?

Dear one, when you suffer, worship! When you are confused, worship! When you are lonely, worship! When you are anxious, worship! When you are criticized, worship! Make it your daily habit to liberally fill God's hand with the golden threads of your reverential worship. Allow Him to weave an abundance of gold among the darker threads of the tapestry He's making of your life.

She...prayed to the Lord.
1 Samuel 1:10

*W*hen a tapestry is complete, the weaver hangs it by a cord strong enough to support its weight. For the splendid weaving of Hannah's life, that cord was the rope of prayer, and here's how it came to be.

Hannah's afflictions were heavy: She shared her husband with his second wife; she had no children; and she was relentlessly provoked by that other wife. Tears had become her diet: She wept and would not eat. Bitterness of soul and anguish of heart clouded her spirit. Many people in her place would have given up...or blown up! But Hannah prayed. Her soul may have been dark, but her faith was radiant as she knelt down and poured out her distress and disappointment to God in prayer.

The Hebrew language has many words for the act of prayer, but the specific Hebrew term used to describe Hannah's heartfelt prayer in the house of the Lord is *palal*, meaning "to entreat, to make supplication."[3] You see, Hannah pleaded with the Lord in her trouble. She petitioned the Almighty. She made her request known unto God.

Beloved woman of God, take inventory of your life. Hannah had marital problems. Do you? She was denied motherhood—something she sorely desired. What do you long for but have not been given? Provocation, cruelty, and ridicule were part of Hannah's everyday life. Do you regularly suffer any kind of mistreatment?

Suffering from what she did not have, precious Hannah grabbed onto what she did have—the rope of prayer—and drew herself and her situation up to God's heavenly throne. Though weak from sadness and weeping, Hannah found her fingers of faith strong enough to seize her one link to God, and she pulled the rope of prayer.

You can, too, and when you do, you can enjoy the benefits of doing so:

- Holding onto the rope of prayer helps bring you into the will of God.

- Handling the rope of prayer develops strong spiritual muscles.

- Hanging onto the rope of prayer in turbulent times gives you an anchor, however rough or long-lasting the storm.

- Hitching yourself to God by the rope of prayer moves you along His path for your life.

She made a vow.
1 SAMUEL 1:11

The threads have been gathered, and the shuttle is flying. God is at work weaving His divine design for Hannah's life. He has included dark threads—the black and charcoal-gray hues of trial—as well as the glittering golden threads of Hannah's worship. We've also noted that the sturdy, powerful rope of prayer securely attaches Hannah to her God. Now, as we hear her speak to God, sterling silver makes its appearance as Hannah utters a vow to her Lord.

Terrible tension had been mounting in her home. Hannah's marriage hadn't gone the way she had hoped. Her family life hadn't either: She had borne no children. And her relationship with her husband's other wife was unbearable.

Hannah's situation seemed hopeless, as did the situation of her people, the nation of Israel: "There was no king in Israel; everyone did what was right in his own eyes" (Judges 21:25), and "the word of the LORD was rare" (1 Samuel 3:1). What had happened to God's plan for His chosen people? What about all He had promised them? Where were the leaders He had said He would provide? God was silent, and His people were lost.

True, Hannah's longing for a baby was a very personal desire. A baby would bring joy to her heart, brighten her life, and silence her critics. But as time—the preordained and perfect timing of God's plan—went on, Hannah's desires slowly grew beyond her personal yearnings and focused instead on God. The time Hannah spent wanting and waiting gave Him time to work in her a desire for something more worthy than a child merely for herself. She came to desire a man for God.

So Hannah vowed: "O LORD of hosts, if You will…give Your maidservant a male child, then I will give him to the LORD all the days of his life." If God would give her a son, she would give that son back to God.

Do you as a woman of faith want what you want for selfish purposes, to "spend it on your pleasures" (James 4:3), or do your desires focus on God and His ultimate purposes? Take time today to evaluate…and adjust…your desires and the motives behind your prayers.

"I am a woman of sorrowful spirit."
1 Samuel 1:15

*B*ut you don't understand!" "Wait a minute! That's not what happened!" "Let me tell you *my* side of the story!" Note the exclamation points. Words like these are usually spoken with a raised voice by someone who has been misunderstood or falsely accused.

Hannah, a woman who loved God and was so completely devoted to Him, was both misunderstood *and* falsely accused. Yet we see in her response how the softer hues of the virtues of grace and graciousness are woven into the tapestry of her life, despite her difficult circumstances.

In her pain—the pain of childlessness and the pain that comes from the cruel, relentless goading of another woman—Hannah turned to God for refuge. Weeping in anguish and bitterness of soul, Hannah prayed to the Lord, crying out in her heart rather than lashing out with her mouth. Never had Hannah felt such agony, and never had she prayed so passionately. Never had she made such a serious vow to God as she made that day.

Yet even as Hannah poured out these most fervent prayers in sincere worship of her Lord, she was totally misunderstood! Eli the priest, who sat nearby and saw Hannah silently mouthing her cries to God, concluded that she was drunk. "How long will you be drunk? Put your wine away from you!" he accused.

Learn a lesson or two from Hannah about those soft-hued threads of grace and graciousness. She didn't argue or get defensive; she softly explained her situation: "I am a woman of sorrowful spirit." She knew and lived the truth of Proverbs 31:26: "She opens her mouth with wisdom, and on her tongue is the law of kindness." Hear God's rules for virtuous speech:

1. Speak with wisdom and kindness (Proverbs 31:26).

2. Think before you speak (Proverbs 15:28).

3. Learn to speak softly (Proverbs 15:1).

4. Add sweetness to your speech (Proverbs 16:21).

5. Be instructive when you speak (Proverbs 16:23).

6. Err on the side of less (Proverbs 10:19).

Do you want to know how Eli responded to Hannah's gracious speech? He gave her his priestly blessing!

Her face was no longer sad.
1 SAMUEL 1:18

*A*t long last Hannah's ordeal was over! After the trials of sharing a husband with another wife, dealing with the heartbreaking inability to have children, being incessantly harassed by the other wife, and finding herself misunderstood by the temple priest, Hannah suddenly found her misery pushed aside by joy.

What prompted this radical change of emotions? The Scripture tells us that Eli gave Hannah this priestly blessing: "Go in peace, and the God of Israel grant your petition which you have asked of Him."

And what was Hannah's petition? Dear Hannah had long wanted and long prayed for a child. She had even vowed to God that if He gave her a son, she would give that son back to God "all the days of his life."

At this point in the weaving of Hannah's life story, the color blue appears in the tapestry, denoting her confident faith in the Lord—a faith that spanned the blue skies and connected her to her heavenly Father. But note this stunning fact about the moment marking the end of Hannah's sadness and the beginning of the joy, which was evidence of her great faith:

Nothing had changed!

Nothing in her life had changed, but Hannah believed, and so found joy in the promise. What great faith, indeed! After Eli had pronounced his blessing, this woman who had fasted, wept, and prayed in anguish and bitterness of soul "went her way and ate, and her face was no longer sad." She didn't have a baby—she wasn't even pregnant yet!—but she believed in faith that one day she would have a son.

Beloved woman of God, are heavenly blue threads of faith woven throughout the warp and woof of your existence? Does your faith, revealed in the everyday events of life, evidence a trust in God that shoots to the heavens? When God speaks to you through His Word, do you believe Him? Do you hold on to the "exceedingly great and precious promises" of God (2 Peter 1:4)? Do you trust what God says, even when nothing about your situation seems to be changing for the better? As a children's song reminds us, "Faith is just believing what God says He will do."

Hannah conceived and bore a son.
1 SAMUEL 1:20

*J*oy is brightest in the person whose life has been darkest. And what dark, sad colors appear in the life tapestry of Hannah, one who loved God so!

But then we are surprised by a sizable splash of brilliance! At the edge of the blackest black, a new color—the riotous threads of joy—appears. And quite a sizable patch it is!

As you know, despite her deep love for God, Hannah had known dark times. She had problems at home where her husband, Elkanah, divided his love between her and another wife. She had personal problems as, year after year, she bore no children to love. She had people problems as the other wife—who had given Elkanah several sons and daughters—relentlessly mocked and reviled her. And she had problems in public when the temple priest scolded her after she prayed.

Joy, however, burst on the scene when Hannah received the priest's blessing and later conceived a child and gave birth to a baby boy. Never, never, never would Hannah forget who had given her this precious baby. She had prayed, and God, the Creator of life, had heard her prayers and answered with the gift of her son. So Hannah named him *Samuel*, meaning "name of God" and "asked of God," saying, "Because I have asked for him from the LORD." Samuel would continually remind his devoted and prayerful mother of God's mercy toward those who call upon His name.

Do you share Hannah's joy? Even if the weaving of your life contains many dark threads, can others see the brilliance of joy? Can you thank the Lord for His goodness and mercy? The psalmist calls himself and you and me to "bless the LORD, O my soul, and forget not all His benefits" (Psalm 103:2).

Even if your life is dark right now, consider the charge that Paul gives us believers on this side of the cross. We are to rejoice in the Lord always (Philippians 4:4)—to rejoice in the forgiveness, redemption, and relationship with God that Christ made possible on the cross through His death for you and me. May the brilliant threads of that joy brighten whatever darkness you now know!

The woman…nursed her son until she had weaned him.
1 Samuel 1:23

*R*ich and warm are the red tones, the violets, and the roses in God's spectrum of colors. And those are the perfect tints for the threads of love woven into the spectacular masterpiece of Hannah's humble life.

A baby was born! And this was no ordinary miracle of birth. A baby was born to the long-barren Hannah—and she had work to do, and do quickly!

You see, Hannah only had a few brief years to train her son for God. After all, her Samuel had not only been "asked of God" (the meaning of his name) and given *by* God, but he had also been vowed to God and so must be given *to* God. Exactly how long did Hannah have to pour her love and God's truth into little Samuel? An oh-so-brief two or three years, only until he was weaned.

> *Question:* How does a mother—in Hannah's time or ours—train a child for God?
>
> *Answer:* By following God's guidelines for child-raising.

1. *Love the Lord with all your heart* (Deuteronomy 6:5). Training a child for God requires that you, dear mother (or grandmother!), love God supremely. You can only give away what you yourself have.

2. *Teach your child God's Word* (Deuteronomy 6:7). God's Word will teach, convict, guide, and train your young one as he or she grows (2 Timothy 3:16).

3. *Teach your child God's ways.* Proverbs 22:6 advises, "Train up a child in the way he should go." A mother is to "educate a child according to his life requirements" and "give instruction to a youth about his way."[4] God's way *is* "the way he should go"!

4. *Remember the Lord at all times* (Deuteronomy 6:7). Your own devotion to God and His Son points your child to eternal life. So, in the moment-by-moment unfolding of everyday life, acknowledge God's lordship and power, His sovereignty and love, His protection and provision. Your children will take note!

5. *Worship the Lord* (Deuteronomy 6:13). Your devotion to God, and to Jesus also, points your child to eternal life.

Dear loving mother or grandmother, let not another minute slip by! Set about *now*—do whatever you can *now*—to train each child your life touches for the God you love.

> *"I…have lent him to the LORD."*
> 1 SAMUEL 1:28

*H*annah's love flowed warm and full. How she cherished her little boy, never forgetting for a day that Samuel had been asked of God and given to her by Him!

Hannah also never forgot that Samuel must be handed over to God's high priest to serve the Lord every day of his life. You see, when the child-less, heartbroken Hannah had petitioned God for a son, she had also promised to give him back to God for a lifetime of service. At last that day arrived.

As she and her husband approached the house of the Lord with their son and the sacrifice required for the fulfillment of her vow, Hannah knew that today she would give God the most personal sacrifice of all, the source of her greatest joy. She was giving God her best, most costly gift: her only child, her son, Samuel.

As you picture this little family walking toward Shiloh, imagine the rich red yarns added into the tapestry of Hannah's noble life to mark her costly offering. Red seems the most suitable color for sacrifice—the deep, costly, rare red of genuine sacrifice.

What can you give to God that costs? Will it be your…

- *Children?* God gave His only Son (John 3:16), and Hannah gave hers. Have you given your children to God for Him to use in any way and in any place for His service and His purposes?

- *Obedience?* It was Samuel himself who later said, "Has the LORD as great delight in burnt offerings and sacrifices, as in obeying the voice of the LORD? Behold, to obey is better than sacrifice" (1 Samuel 15:22). To what obedience is God calling you?

- *Time?* Time wasted is a theft from God.[5] As every thread is valuable, so is every moment of time.[6]

- *Money?* As he placed his silver on an altar to the Lord, King David revealed his heart for God: "I…[will not] offer…to the LORD my God…that which costs me nothing" (2 Samuel 24:24). Gifts of love cost.

Hold all things lightly and nothing tightly when it comes to God, and that "all" includes your best, most costly treasures!

And Hannah prayed.
1 SAMUEL 2:1

*W*hat really counts in the Christian life? Hannah is a woman who knew the answer to this question. She shines forth from the pages of Scripture as a woman who knew pain and problems (barrenness, persecution, misunderstanding, loss), yet gave glory to God when she spoke. As our brave Hannah entered her hardest hour—the hour appointed for her to leave her long-awaited and much-prayed-for son at the house of the Lord to be raised by another—we see that her focus was not on herself, not on her problems, and not on her sacrifice, but instead on her great God. Expressions of exultation and glory tumbled out of Hannah's thankful heart as she heralded: "My heart rejoices in the LORD.... I rejoice in Your salvation" (1 Samuel 2:1).

Clearly, Hannah's heart was riveted on God, so we shouldn't be surprised by her worship and praise even at this difficult moment. Her lips revealed her heart, and her words are recorded in the pages of God's Holy Scriptures for women through the ages—women just like you—to read, to enjoy, to learn from, and to imitate. Note the content of Hannah's impassioned prayer:

- *God's salvation*—"I rejoice in Your salvation" (verse 1).
- *God's holiness*—"No one is holy like the LORD" (verse 2).
- *God's strength*—"There [is no] rock like our God" (verse 2).
- *God's knowledge*—"The LORD is the God of knowledge" (verse 3).
- *God's power*—Only God has the power to make the mighty weak, the full hungry, the barren fertile, the dead alive, the sick well, the poor rich, and the humble exalted (verses 4-8).
- *God's judgment*—"The adversaries of the LORD shall be broken in pieces" (verses 9,10).

What blazing glory you, too, bring to God as you, who love and serve Him, pray and praise as Hannah did! So why not memorize parts of Hannah's psalm of praise and make it your own? Meditate on the attributes and actions of God she mentions there. And make sure that in every event or difficulty you focus on the Person and power of God, not on your circumstances. Be confident of God's sovereign and loving control over the events of your life.

His mother used to make him a little robe.
1 SAMUEL 2:19

*H*ow does a woman who loves God and her family fill her days when her nest is empty? That's the next challenge Hannah faced. After her many years of suffering, grief, and prayer (1 Samuel 1 tells the whole story), God at last graced Hannah with a son. As she loved and trained Samuel, her days were happy, full, and rich. But Hannah had wanted Samuel so badly that she had vowed to "give him to the LORD all the days of his life" (1 Samuel 1:11). Because her love for God was genuine, Hannah kept that promise and took her young son to the house of the Lord 16 miles away.

Again, how does a woman who loves God and her family fill her days when her nest is empty? Note Hannah's example. Rather than give in to sadness, Hannah worked on long-distance love. Each year she made him a little robe and took it to him.

Hannah, whose life was such an exquisite weaving, became a weaver herself—weaving for the next generation. Imagine the rich variety of colors Hannah carefully selected for Samuel's warm and beautiful coats. And imagine the lifetime memories evoked by the necessary darks, the splashes of blue, the sparkling silver and gold, the brilliant yellows, and the crimson reds—memories of the lessons she had learned from the Lord throughout the years. And don't you think Hannah, who prayed so fervently for a son, prayed for him still as she wove his robes? There's no more secure investment in the next generation than your prayers for your children!

Now consider how you can follow Hannah's example. What can *you* do today to love your children and grandchildren across the miles? The mother of writer Elisabeth Elliot prayed and she wrote letters. For more than 45 years, she wrote to each of her six children twice a week (that's 12 letters a week—before computers!).[7]

As a loving, praying mother, reach out to your children today—and every day!—with your prayers and your love. Your faithful efforts are indeed a secure and vital investment in the next generation.

Hannah...bore three sons and two daughters.
1 SAMUEL 2:21

*J*esus said, "Unless a grain of wheat falls into the ground and dies, it remains alone; but if it dies, it produces much grain" (John 12:24). In Hannah's situation, the "grain of wheat" that fell into the ground and died was her young son, whom she left with the priest at Shiloh (1 Samuel 1:28). Oh, Samuel didn't die in the literal sense, but Hannah, who was childless for so long, had prayed fervently to God for a son, vowing in the midst of her impassioned prayers to give her baby back to God all the days of his life. Faithful to her word, Hannah did experience, in a sense, the death of her son.

Yet *after* Hannah acted on her vow, *after* she gave her little boy to God, *after* she had apparently lost her only child, "the LORD visited Hannah, so that she conceived and bore three sons and two daughters." Five more children filled Hannah's empty home after Samuel left. The grain of Hannah's sacrifice sprouted and bore fruit—much fruit! Hannah's faith grew, her family grew, her love grew, her joy grew, and her influence grew as she had the opportunity to raise five additional children.

Hannah learned many lessons that are represented by the vibrant green threads of growth running throughout the weaving of her life. In this final look at the tapestry of Hannah's life, allow her to pass on to you several of her lessons in growth for your own tapestry.

1. Hannah learned firsthand the heartache that accompanies barrenness. Are you sympathetic and sensitive to those around you who have no children?

2. Hannah learned to take her problems to God. Do you tell God your problems, or only your friends?

3. Hannah learned about petitioning the Lord. Have you learned the value of earnest prayer and petition (James 5:16)?

4. Hannah learned that children are gifts from the Lord. How does the fact that your children are gifts to you from God impact your parenting (Psalm 127:3)?

5. Hannah learned the importance of training up a child for God. Are you diligently training your children—on loan to you from God—for service in His kingdom?

Michal let David down through a window.
1 SAMUEL 19:12

*M*eet Michal, the younger daughter of Israel's first king, Saul, and the first wife of David, the Old Testament hero, warrior, and king. And see how rough life was for Michal and David:

- *David was to marry Merab*, Saul's first daughter. But instead, Saul gave Merab to another man (1 Samuel 18:19).

- *David was to die.* Saul required a premarital test for David: He was to kill 100 Philistines, and David was sure to die in the process. But instead, David slew 200 Philistines and lived (18:20-27)!

- *David was targeted for murder* by his bride's father. Saul sent messengers to David's house "to watch him and to kill him." But Michal acted quickly to help her husband escape.

Although Michal was hardly an ideal match for David, she most certainly contributed to God's purposes by following one of the Lord's principles for marriage: A bride is to leave her father and mother and cleave to her husband (Genesis 2:24). Because Michal helped her husband escape her father's men, the righteous David was spared. Far from being a "snare" to David, as her father had hoped (1 Samuel 18:21), Michal was instrumental in saving his life. At this point in her relationship with David, Michal displayed a covenantal love and faithfulness to her husband.[8]

Consider your loyalty to your husband. Do you support him in his role as leader and provider? Do you refrain from criticizing him in front of your parents and others? Do you stand with him, presenting a solid front to your parents and his? Do you follow your husband as he leads your family in the direction of his choice?

You can nurture a more solid union with your precious husband when you:

1. *Speak well of your husband.* The Bible says to speak evil of no one (Titus 3:2), and that includes your husband!

2. *Look for positive qualities in your husband,* and don't forget to praise him for them!

3. *Pray for your husband.* Prayer changes both husband *and* wife!

> *"Let my...mother come here with you."*
> 1 SAMUEL 22:3

*I*magine having a son who was a man after God's own heart—in the making! David was such a boy, and his mother must have been a mother after God's own heart who contributed greatly to her son's heart. Note these facts and fine features about her son David from 1 Samuel:

- David was one of the eight sons of Jesse (16:10,11).
- David was a responsible shepherd (16:11).
- David was a singer (16:18).
- David faithfully delivered food to his brothers (17:17).
- David obeyed his father (17:20).
- David trusted God as he stood against the giant Goliath (17:40,41).
- David was a blameless fugitive (19:12).
- David sent for and protected his mother, father, and brothers (22:1-3).
- David was "a man after [God's] own heart" (13:14; Acts 13:22).

Consider for a moment other mothers of great men. Mrs. Graham described herself as "a simple dairy farmer's wife" but gave to the world evangelist Billy Graham. Mrs. Briscoe never taught a Bible lesson, never led a women's meeting, and never served at the local mission, but gave the world Stuart Briscoe, a pastor, Bible teacher, evangelist, and Christian leader. And Mrs. Bright, who is described as "an ordinary woman," gave the world Bill Bright, founder of Campus Crusade for Christ International.

How does a mother like you become a mother of a man or a woman who wholeheartedly loves God, a man or woman who does great things for the kingdom? You partner with God to give the world a godly child when you:

- *Pursue* God with your whole heart (Luke 10:27).
- *Plant* the seed of faith in your child's heart (1 Corinthians 3:8).
- *Pray* for your child (Proverbs 31:2).
- *Prepare* your child for greatness in God's service by training him or her in God's ways (Proverbs 22:6).

Abigail…was a woman of good understanding.
1 SAMUEL 25:3

*A*bigail. Mark this woman's name well. Over the next few days, you'll be delighted to learn from this gallant woman who loved God. Abigail, whose name means "cause of joy," will bring great joy to your heart as you discover diamonds in the dust—jewels of godly virtue mined out of the adversity that filled Abigail's daily existence.

As we consider Abigail's plight, we find little cause for joy in her life. Several difficult, joyless facts made up the soil—the dust—of dear Abigail's life. Her marriage appears to have been loveless and childless, and her husband, Nabal (whose name literally means "foolish"), was indeed a fool, "harsh and evil in his doings," "a scoundrel," and a drunk.

Yet the first dazzling, diamond-like quality we gather from the dust and dirt of Abigail's life is faithfulness. We see it in her loyalty, trustworthiness, steadfastness, and reliability; in her faithfulness to God's Word and to the people in her life. The Scriptures, for instance, instruct God's women to build their homes (Proverbs 14:1) and to watch over their households (Proverbs 31:27). And dear Abigail faithfully did both. When her husband foolishly endangered the lives of everyone in her household by refusing to be kind to the powerful David, Abigail acted quickly to appease the angry David and to save the lives of her husband, her servants, and herself. The flashing diamond of Abigail's faithfulness glistens through the dust of her difficulties. Even in her problem-ridden situation, Abigail was faithful to her husband, to her household, to her work in the home, and to the God she loved.

And now for you, dear woman of God. Your life, too, may sometimes seem buried beneath generous layers of dust and dirt, yet your own faithfulness to God—whatever your circumstances—will shine brightly as you remain "faithful in all things" (1 Timothy 3:11). May you never underestimate the brilliance and beauty of faithfulness in the eyes of God. After all, God is more concerned about us being faithful to His standards than He is about us being successful in the eyes of the world!

Then Abigail made haste.
1 SAMUEL 25:18

*H*ow could he do it! How could my husband say *no* to David?"

Perhaps faithful Abigail had thoughts like these. She learned from her loyal servants—who also couldn't believe what Abigail's husband, Nabal, had done—that her household was at risk. David's band of men needed something to eat. His messengers had come in peace, treating her servants with respect as they asked for food. Rather than turning David away, Nabal should have helped him, for everyone knew that the mighty warrior David could annihilate any and all in his path! After all, he had slain tens of thousands of people (1 Samuel 21:11)!

"What do I do, Lord?" dear Abigail may have prayed. God granted her wisdom, benefiting all her household, including the arrogant Nabal. "Abigail made haste." With the help of her servants, she quickly sent to David the food he had requested: bread, wine, meat, grain, fruit, and cakes, as much as he and his men needed.

And Abigail went beyond providing food for the angry David. She also humbly laid herself before David, falling on her face and bowing down to the ground. One more thing Abigail laid before this powerful man was the request that he spare her husband and his household with him.

When crises arise, we must act as Abigail did: We must act as women of wisdom. Praise God that He has given us all that we need to live our lives as Christians, and that "all" includes wisdom! What sources of wisdom are available to you, precious imitator of Abigail?

1. *Knowing the Lord:* "The knowledge of the Holy One is understanding" (Proverbs 9:10).

2. *Fearing the Lord:* "The fear of the LORD is the beginning of wisdom" (Proverbs 9:10).

3. *Acknowledging the Lord:* "In all your ways acknowledge Him, and He shall direct your paths" (Proverbs 3:6).

4. *Asking the Lord:* "If any of you lacks wisdom, let him ask of God...and it will be given to him" (James 1:5).

Make it your habit to ask God to guide...before you act!

So she fell at his feet and said...
1 SAMUEL 25:24

*C*onsider first the paradoxical principle for our speech found in Proverbs 25:15—"A gentle tongue breaks a bone"—and then, in light of that thought, Abigail's situation....

A woman with beauty and brains, Abigail found herself caught in the face-off of two powerful men. One of those men was her husband (who had acted foolishly), and the other was the famed warrior David (who was about to act foolishly). What had happened? When David had needed food for his band of men, Nabal refused to provide it, so David was determined to slay Nabal and destroy all that was his.

If ever there were a time to speak soft words that could break strong bones (and strong wills), it was now! Yet another bit of biblical wisdom reminds us that there is "a time to keep silence, and a time to speak" (Ecclesiastes 3:7).

With David—Abigail opened her mouth with God-given wisdom and the utmost respect. She spoke intelligently, appealing to his future kingship, which was a purpose much higher than getting into a physical skirmish with her husband as revenge for his foolishness.

With Nabal—Abigail wisely waited to open her mouth because Nabal was "very drunk" and wouldn't be able to understand his narrow escape from death at the hands of David.

Today God shows us the discretion that is among the diamond-like qualities in precious Abigail. The situation was critical. Abigail was about to lose everything—including the lives of her innocent servants—and she acted discreetly. She exhibited good judgment in her timing (*when* she spoke), her choice of words (*what* she spoke), and her manner (*how* she spoke). Her gracious speech was effective against two men stubbornly opposed to one another. Their granitelike wills were broken by a gentle tongue!

Discretion is hard-won, but you, beloved of God, can become more discreet and enjoy its benefits. How?

- *Value discretion*—Understand its importance in human relations.

- *Desire discretion*—A mark of the wise is the desire for godly traits.

- *Learn discretion*—Study wise Abigail's discretion.

- *Use discretion*—Call on the Holy Spirit to help you exercise restraint, calm your emotions, and enable you to act with discretion.

- *Pray for discretion*—Ask God to give you this diamond-like quality.

So Abigail…became his wife.
1 SAMUEL 25:42

*T*ake a moment to consider our Lord's majesty and magnificence! As a popular chorus celebrates, "Our God is an awesome God!" As the Omniscient One (the One who knows all there is to know), our God knows every detail about our personal situation. He knows why it exists and how He will use it to accomplish His work in our lives. So pause now and ponder that fact about our God…and then consider how He worked in Abigail's life.

An End. Gentle Abigail's husband was a vile, unreasonable, and disrespectful fool who endangered those in his care by offending the powerful David. Quick thinking, fast action, and wise words from Abigail, however, saved the day for all, including David. In the end, neither Abigail nor David—nor anyone else!—had to do anything about Nabal the fool. The Bible simply reports, "The LORD struck Nabal, and he died." *God* came to Abigail's rescue. In her case, *God* acted in judgment and ended her difficult situation.

A Beginning. With the end of Nabal's life came Abigail's marriage to David and a welcomed new beginning: "Abigail…became his wife." In God's plan—and in His time—Abigail went from marriage to a beast to marriage to God's best. David, a man after God's own heart (Acts 13:22), took care of Abigail for the rest of her days.

A Blessing. Apparently, Abigail and Nabal had no children together, but God blessed her marriage to David with a beautiful son named Chileab, meaning "God is my Judge" (2 Samuel 3:3). Surely Abigail knew the truth of this name well!

God carefully crafted the details of Abigail's life, and you can be sure that He is busy doing so in yours as well. Take comfort. As God commands, "Be still, and know that I am God" (Psalm 46:10). There is a time to act, but there is also a time to trust, to be still and know that in His time and in His way God makes all things beautiful. Be still as you wait to behold the hand of the Lord at work in your life!

So Abigail...became his wife.
1 SAMUEL 25:42

*I*t's hard to say farewell to Abigail! Her life has been a model of true feminine grace, as her mosaic of character reveals. Whenever Abigail is spoken of—whether in Bible commentaries, reference books, or Bible notes; in sermons or Sunday school lessons; in Jewish circles or Christian ones—the words are always glowing. Abigail is described as intelligent and beautiful, warm and winsome, a prudent manager, and the beautiful voice of reason and of faith that God would provide wisdom and protection. And Abigail earned these accolades as she walked the tightrope challenges involved in managing the household of a foolish, alcoholic husband.

Before we move on to a host of other women who loved God, take one final gaze at the lovely mosaic of Abigail's character. As you may know, a mosaic is a surface decoration made by laying small pieces of colored glass or stone in patterns to make up a picture or design. In Abigail's life, beauty arose from the arrangement of the following character traits:

- *Wisdom*—Not only did Abigail act wisely, but she spoke wisely, approaching the job of peacemaking according to God's ways.

- *Discretion*—Rising above the din of David's haste, strong emotion, recklessness, and rage, Abigail's sweet and clear voice of reason calmed all. Ever so carefully and humbly, Abigail reminded David of God's sure justice, His ability to act on David's behalf, and His great future for David. Her sweet speech tamed a lion. In fact, it actually tamed two lions: the angry David *and* the foolish Nabal! God also gave Abigail the right words and a sense of the appropriate timing when she dealt with her contemptible husband.

- *Faithfulness*—In all things, Abigail was faithful—as a wife to Nabal, as a mistress to her servants, as a messenger to David, later as his wife, and as a woman who loved God.

When others look at the qualities that make up the mosaic of your character, what do they notice? Hopefully, as we see in Abigail, they see in you the qualities of gracious humility, wisdom, discretion, faithfulness, and godliness—and find their beauty breathtaking!

His nurse took him up and fled.
2 SAMUEL 4:4

Confusion and fear reigned in Israel. The Philistines were on the move! King Saul was dead on the battlefield. So were his sons, including fair Jonathan (1 Samuel 31). When word of their deaths reached the ears of a certain woman, she had a critical decision to make. We don't know her name, but we do know that she held the important position of nurse to Mephibosheth, the five-year-old son of Jonathan and grandson of Saul.

Acting quickly to save the young boy's life, this loyal and brave servant snatched up the young boy and fled for safety. In their haste, however, the young prince fell and became lame for life.

How did this courageous woman handle such a disastrous consequence? We don't know for sure, but we can imagine that she may have blamed herself and carried the guilt all her days. Yet she had tried to do what was right, and she had acted with a pure heart of love and devotion.

Has any act of your own devotion ever failed, backfired, or turned out in a negative way? Have you ever been forced to live with the consequences of a good intention that went bad? Then take heart! Just look at the actual outcome of this dear nurse's heroic deed, according to God's balance sheet:

NEGATIVES	POSITIVES
• Mephibosheth was permanently maimed.	• Mephibosheth's life was saved.
	• The line of Saul and Jonathan continued.
	• Mephibosheth enjoyed the favor of David's care for life (2 Samuel 9).
	• David was blessed to be able to fulfill a vow he had made to his friend Jonathan, the father of Mephibosheth (1 Samuel 20:15).

Consider now the balance sheet of your life and what God is doing despite, or even with, the negatives you may list. Also ask yourself whether you might be allowing one negative in your life to blind you to the many positive and redemptive blessings that come from His hand. As the comforting truth about God's power assures us, He uses all things—including the negatives in our lives—for our good, for His supreme purpose of making us more like Christ (Romans 8:28, 29).

So she bore a son....
2 SAMUEL 12:24

*F*orgiveness! The mere sound of this precious word brings joy to the heart of each and every repentant sinner. How we rejoice to know that our gracious and merciful God has declared, "I will forgive their iniquity, and their sin I will remember no more" (Jeremiah 31:34)! Praise Him!

Let's take a moment today to consider Bathsheba. The initial facts we learn about her life hardly glow with godliness! In fact, Bathsheba is best known for being an adulteress, the woman involved in infidelity with King David. This sin resulted in her pregnancy, her husband's murder, and her newborn baby's death. These are indeed dark, ugly details!

Yet, like the sun after the rain, God's cleansing forgiveness shone brilliantly and warmly once Bathsheba's new husband acknowledged their sin. Hear her husband's words, flowing from a penitent heart:

> I acknowledge my transgressions....
> Create in me a clean heart, O God....
> Restore to me the joy of Your salvation (Psalm 51:3,10,12).

After David's restoration to a right relationship with God, Bathsheba seems to have received that same divine forgiveness and lived to enjoy the goodness of the Lord. Soon He blessed her with another baby, whom she named *Solomon*, meaning "beloved of the Lord." God chose Solomon to be king of Israel, and he is numbered among the ancestors of Jesus Christ (Matthew 1).

Beloved of the Lord, everyone's life is spotted and stained with sin. Yet we women who love God and are loved by Him can enjoy the promise and reality of His forgiveness. As one commentator has written about forgiveness, "When we brood over sins God has said He will remember no more against us, we actually doubt His mercy and rob ourselves of spiritual power and progress."[9] No single sin, however dark, should ruin an entire life. Instead, acknowledge your transgressions before God, receive His cleansing and forgiveness, and, with renewed joy over the salvation you have through Jesus Christ, enter a bright future.

So Bathsheba went into the chamber to the king....
1 KINGS 1:15

A lovely line of Scripture prompts us women who love God to adorn our hearts with "the incorruptible ornament of a gentle and quiet spirit" (1 Peter 3:4). This is a beautiful concept, but many women (and perhaps you're one of them!) wonder, "Does this mean I can never speak up?" In Bathsheba we see once again that there is "a time to keep silence, and a time to speak" (Ecclesiastes 3:7). Dear Bathsheba acts with discernment according to five principles that signal a time for speaking up:

- *First, find the right time.* David had promised Bathsheba that their son Solomon would reign as king after him. Yet David lay dying without having named Solomon as his successor and unaware that a political uprising was in progress. It seemed to be the right time to speak up.

- *Second, choose the right issue.* If David's kingly line were to continue through Solomon, he must act. The successor to the throne seemed to be the right issue to speak up about.

- *Third, act out of the right motive.* God Himself had designated Solomon as the man to build the house of the Lord instead of David (1 Chronicles 22:9,10). How could this happen if Solomon weren't on the throne? This grand issue seemed to qualify as a right motive for speaking up.

- *Fourth, be sensitive to the right prompting.* As Proverbs 20:18 tells us, "By wise counsel wage war." Nathan the prophet had approached Bathsheba, advised her to speak up, and even told her what to say. The counsel of this godly man seemed to be the right prompting.

- *Fifth, speak in the right manner. How* we say what we say is usually more important than *what* we say! And how did Bathsheba say what she had to say? She first bowed respectfully, paying homage to her husband with her face on the ground, and then waited until he asked her to state her business.

These principles are good for us to follow, too. Wait for the right time. Discern the right issues. Pray for the right motives. Act in response to the right advice. Ask in the right manner. Try this approach the next time you must take care of business!

The queen of Sheba...came to test [Solomon]...
1 KINGS 10:1

*I*n the sixth century B.C. there was no network news coverage of Israel's King Solomon. Instead news traveled slowly, ever so slowly—as slowly as people walk, camels amble, and donkeys shuffle. Slowly, word of this wise king who served a powerful God made its way to Sheba, some 1200 miles south of Jerusalem. Sitting in her palace, the queen of Sheba must have mulled over the various reports. Surely no person could be so wise and no god so remarkable! And yet...what if? The reports just might be true! She must see for herself.

The trip to Jerusalem was long and expensive. Scholars estimate the progress of soldiers, gifts, animals, supplies, and attendants at 20 miles a day for 75 days. But no matter! No effort is too great and no price too high in the quest for true wisdom! And so, perhaps with some curiosity about Solomon and definitely with a deep hunger for wisdom (Matthew 12:42), this queen set out for Israel.

The greater the effort, the sweeter the prize. And the greater the cost, the more valuable the treasure. So it is with wisdom—as you, dear seeker of wisdom, may discover for yourself.

Consider the effort you are willing to make to gain wisdom. Do you spend five minutes a day reading a chapter of Proverbs, the Bible's book of wisdom? Do you make the effort to attend a class, lecture, or seminar taught by a wise and godly person? Do you reserve time in your schedule to seek counsel or mentoring from someone you know to be wise? Do you gladly spend a weekend at a conference that can help make you wise in God's ways?

We live in a drive-through, instant-gratification society. We want all things without effort—and we want them *now!* Yet, in the example of this famous queen, we see a willingness to seek and sacrifice, to give whatever it takes to find answers to life's questions. Just for today, follow her example. Try to obtain one precious pearl of wisdom...and then add another to your priceless strand tomorrow...and then another the next day. Wisdom is truly an ornament of grace to the soul!

She came to test [Solomon] with hard questions.
1 KINGS 10:1

*Y*ou may know the scene well. You're planning a vacation. The calendar is in front of you. You've contacted the travel agent. You've gathered brochures, maps, and guidebooks. And (hopefully) you've saved the money. You need a break!

Exactly why do we take vacations? Top on most people's list is R&R—a little rest and relaxation. But we may also go for the adventure of sight-seeing, a dip into history, or a photographic safari.

The queen of Sheba, however, offers the noblest of all purposes for taking a trip. You see, she was a true seeker of wisdom. Jesus reports that this "queen of the South...came from the ends of the earth to hear the wisdom of Solomon" (Matthew 12:42). Her journey from southern Arabia to Jerusalem by camel caravan across some 1200-plus miles of desert serves as a model for all of us. Why? Because she journeyed to see and hear the wisdom of King Solomon—the wisdom of the Lord—and to learn more about this God he relied on.

Known for her legendary beauty, wealth, and magnificence, the queen of Sheba appeared to have everything. But her greatest asset was a heart that desired wisdom. She gladly spent what she had to obtain the invaluable wealth of wisdom. This queen went on a quest not for transitory pleasure; her quest had a purpose. She did what all of us who love God need to do: She sought wisdom.

Proverbs 16:16 says, "How much better to get wisdom than gold!" So why not plan your own quest? First review the checklist below for resources that will help you nurture a heart of wisdom, and then add your own ideas.

✓ Books to read

✓ Bible studies to complete

✓ Seminars or conferences to attend

✓ People to meet with and learn from

✓ Classes to take at a Christian college

Truly, "he [or she] who gets wisdom loves his own soul" (Proverbs 19:8).

Then she gave the king...talents of gold.
1 KINGS 10:10

*I*t's hard to imagine the fortune belonging to the queen of Sheba. This remarkable woman gave Israel's King Solomon the equivalent of 3.5 million dollars in gold and an unheard-of abundance of spices and jewels. Why? Because this rich sovereign from southern Arabia had lacked one thing: true knowledge of God and the wisdom it brings. No price tag can be put on the knowledge of the holy, for "the fear of the LORD is the beginning of wisdom, and the knowledge of the Holy One is understanding" (Proverbs 9:10). The material abundance this wise queen presented to Solomon was nothing compared to her newly found wisdom and understanding of God!

We've already noted some details of the trip this queen-full-of-questions took in order to talk to King Solomon about life and the Lord. And this sovereign from Sheba was well rewarded for her costly efforts. Hearing Solomon's answers to her hard questions, watching him worship, and seeing the order of his home and government gave her the wisdom she sought. Afterward, when the queen's caravan trekked back to Sheba across the same 1200 miles of sand, this queen carried with her the most priceless treasure of all: a heart of wisdom.

Acquiring wisdom doesn't always require much money. A seeking heart and an eternal perspective on what matters are the basic requirements. But consider these daily dollar costs:

- One drive-through trip for fast food: about 10 dollars for two people

- One bottle of makeup: about 10 dollars

- One new videotape: about 20 dollars

- One month of cable TV reception: about 30 dollars

We often think very little about spending our money for everyday items like these—items that have no significance in eternity. Why not, then, gladly put such amounts of money to work obtaining God's matchless wisdom? Why not spend the same 10 dollars on a good book, the 20 dollars on a study Bible, and the 30 dollars on a Bible course? As Jesus pointed out, "Where your treasure is, there your heart will be also" (Matthew 6:21). Make sure yours is a heart that seeks wisdom!

*King Solomon gave the queen of Sheba
all she desired, whatever she asked.*

1 KINGS 10:13

*W*hat a joy it's been to journey alongside the great queen of Sheba on her pathway to wisdom. How we praise her and thank God for her! She is truly worthy of admiration. Jesus Himself praised this exceptional "queen of the south." Why? Because when she learned of the wisdom of Solomon and the fame of his God, the queen of Sheba was determined to find out for herself and "came from the ends of the earth to hear the wisdom of Solomon" (Matthew 12:42).

As one scholar has noted, the queen of Sheba walked the pathway to wisdom by taking these seven steps:[10]

Step #1 She heard—her ears were open (Proverbs 20:12).
Step #2 She came with no regard for effort or expense.
Step #3 She communed with the wisest man of her day.
Step #4 She saw—her eyes were open (Proverbs 20:12).
Step #5 She said, "Blessed be the Lord your God!"
Step #6 She gave in gratitude for priceless wisdom.
Step #7 She returned home, filled with the knowledge of God.

Since you, like the queen of Sheba, desire a heart of wisdom, take a moment now and thank God that His wisdom is available to you, too. Then follow these steps from the Bible and continue on your pathway to wisdom today…and for the rest of your life. If you do, you will not only be a woman who loves God, but also one who possesses the true riches of wisdom and knowledge.

- *Ask*—"If any of you lacks wisdom, let him ask of God…and it will be given to him" (James 1:5).
- *Grow*—"…in the grace and knowledge of our Lord and Savior Jesus Christ" (2 Peter 3:18).
- *Desire*—"…the pure milk of the word, that you may grow thereby" (1 Peter 2:2).
- *Seek*—"…those things which are above, where Christ is" (Colossians 3:1).
- *Set*—"…your mind on things above, not on things on the earth" (Colossians 3:2).

Walk this path, dear friend, knowing that God will honor your efforts and bless you with His wisdom.

"I have commanded a widow there to provide for you."
1 KINGS 17:9

*T*errible, foreboding words—words like *drought, poverty, leanness, famine, death,* and *despair*—describe the backdrop against which the next woman who loved God eked out a dreary life. The setting of this dear widow's tale was the parched land of Zarephath. The drought God's prophet Elijah had prayed for (James 5:17) had worked its way up the coast of Israel to the Gentile Baal-worshiping town of Zarephath.

This woman's almost-depleted food supply meant that she and her young son would not live to see another sunrise. But as she gathered one last bundle of sticks for one last fire to bake one last bread cake from her last handful of flour and last dollop of oil, Elijah arrived. Could he really be asking her for a piece of bread to eat? Ha!

But the coming of Elijah was actually the coming of light into darkness for this poor, fatherless family. God had sent Elijah, whose name means "the Lord is God," to enjoy the widow of Zarephath's provision. Yet, in order to provide for Elijah, she had to trust Elijah's God and pour out—in faith—her final handful of earthly goods.

And you? What are your circumstances and needs today? Are you suffering leanness of soul? The leanness of physical nourishment like this widow in Zarephath? Or the bitter taste of despair? The Bible tells us to "be strong and of good courage; be not afraid, neither be thou dismayed: for the LORD thy God is with thee" (Joshua 1:9 KJV). In light of that truth, you can choose to...

Stop! Stop fretting and start putting your faith to work! Be anxious for nothing and instead let your requests be made known to God. Then you will experience the peace of God (Philippians 4:6,7).

Look! Look to the Lord in faith. Call upon the Lord, and He will answer you and show you great and mighty things which you do not know (Jeremiah 33:3).

Listen! Listen to the promises of the Lord. He promises to supply all your needs according to His riches in glory by Christ Jesus (Philippians 4:19).

Go! Go on being a generous, giving woman of faith. Give...and it shall be given unto you (Luke 6:38).

So she…did according to the word of Elijah.
1 Kings 17:15

"Where our bread is concerned, it is a material matter. Where our neighbor's bread is concerned, it is a spiritual matter."[11]

What started as a material matter for the widow of Zarephath quickly became a spiritual matter as God's servant Elijah strode toward her and boldly asked for food. Did he know that she was gathering sticks for a fire to make the last meal for herself and her little boy before they died of starvation? All this poor woman had was a handful of flour and a little oil—just enough for one final meal for the two of them.

Yet, in faith, choosing to trust the God this man followed, this brave woman decided to share her depleted supplies with Elijah. She opened her hand and her heart to him.

Others who, like the widow of Zarephath, have known hard times have also chosen to trust God and love people by opening up their hands and hearts to share:

- *The widows in the early church* offered the ministry of hospitality. Just as the widow of Zarephath did for Elijah, they fed and lodged those in need (1 Timothy 5:10).

- *Corrie ten Boom* risked her life to hide and feed Jews in World War II Europe—a "spiritual matter" that led to her interment in a German concentration camp.

- *George Muller* faithfully called upon God's sharing hand to provide daily bread for 2000 orphans—and he did so for 20 years!

Precious sister, through the example of such men and women of faith and generosity, God is calling you to a life of spiritual giving, of sharing what you have. Start by looking around at the needs of others. Then…

- Begin at home by faithfully providing meals for your family.

- Expand this spiritual ministry at home into a ministry of hospitality (meaning "stranger love"), and open your door to others.

- Help stock your church's food closet for those in need.

- Take a turn at your city's downtown mission project.

- Pray for God to give you a vision for how you can be involved in feeding the hungry of the world.

> *So she...did according to the word of Elijah.*
> 1 Kings 17:15

ood and faith. We don't normally think of these two words together. Yet, in the actions of the widow of Zarephath, faith is at the core of a food issue. Living in a time of severe drought and famine, everyone in the land was scraping to survive—including this widow and her young son. Yet God brought together His prophet Elijah and this widow, for the good of them both.

To live, this woman must simply give her last handful of meal to God's messenger. But this small act would require great faith! The Bible defines faith as "the substance of things hoped for, the evidence of things not seen" (Hebrews 11:1), and this dear woman hoped and acted in faith by...

- *Believing* Elijah's words: "Do not fear...for thus says the Lord God of Israel: 'The bin of flour shall not be used up...until the day the Lord sends rain on the earth' ";

- *Opening* her hand; and

- *Giving* all she had left to the man of God.

What resulted from such faith? This widow *and* her son *and* Elijah were blessed by God. For more than 1000 days, He miraculously supplied food for the three of them. She discovered firsthand that God's people walk by faith, not by sight (2 Corinthians 5:7).

By sight...	*But by faith she trusted and...*
There was no more food.	God provided daily bread.
Supplies were limited to one handful of meal.	God supplied for three years of meals.
Everyone was perishing.	God sustained these three faithful people.
Death was certain.	God preserved life.

Are you walking by faith? Is there any step you need to take, trusting God for the results? Is there something you need to release your hold on and let God handle? Do you possess even a tiny handful of faith? Fear not, precious friend. You can be rich in faith even when you have nothing, for it is through faith that we inherit the promises. So right now pray, "Lord, I believe; help my unbelief" (Mark 9:24) as you pour your little handful of faith into His almighty hands for His use and your blessing.

"Now…I know that…the word of the LORD…is the truth."
1 KINGS 17:24

*H*ave you ever sat on the seashore and enjoyed the rhythm of the waves as they roll up onto the beach and kiss your feet? The ocean's waves break regularly and unceasingly. As one breaker swells and curls over, the next whitecap is forming on its heels, sometimes with little pause in between.

Keep this image in mind as you remember the poor widow of Zarephath, and as you consider your own life. You see, our lives have a rhythm, too—the rhythm of trouble and trust. As the trials of life roll in, regularly and unceasingly, we have the opportunity to trust the Lord afresh for each new situation.

The widow of Zarephath trusted God for a trial that threatened her very life. When she had only enough flour for one last meal before she and her young son would die due to lack of food and an inability to get more, this dear woman used that tiny bit of flour—and her tiny bit of faith—to first make a bread-cake for God's prophet Elijah. Only then did she make one for herself and her son. In honor of her faith, God opened the windows of heaven and fed her, her son, and Elijah…for three years!

But then a new trial struck this widow and single mother. Her little boy, her only child, died. As this wave of trouble washed over her fragile life, this desperate widow was called upon to pour out another measure of faith and trust anew that God would help her again. After Elijah raised the child from the dead, her heart full of faith declared, "Now I know that…the word of the LORD in your mouth is the truth" (1 Kings 17:24).

Our troubles are never over, dear one. Our trials never cease. They roll in as surely as the surf brings new waves, regularly and unceasingly, day in and day out. What new or different trial or struggle are you facing today that you can commit to Him now? As you face new troubles and trials, remember that God's mercy and compassion are new every morning. He is there for you—to provide new showers of His grace for each new problem (Lamentations 3:22, 23).

"Now…I know that…the word of the LORD…is the truth."
1 KINGS 17:24

*G*ive, and it will be given to you: good measure, pressed down, shaken together, and running over" (Luke 6:38). Although these words were spoken by Jesus, the widow of Zarephath experienced the truth of their promise more than 800 years before they were uttered. Her test of faith came when the prophet Elijah asked her for the final little bread-cake she was preparing for her child and herself before they lay down to die of starvation. Would she give the food to Elijah, or feed her son and herself?

Giving her food to Elijah was the beginning of God's great giving to this trusting woman. Note some of the blessings He bestowed:

1. *The blessing of feeding Elijah.* God used this poor widow to provide for His servant Elijah as she gave him bread made from her final handful of meal. How wonderful to be used for God's kingdom purposes!

2. *The blessing of life.* After the widow of Zarephath shared with Elijah the last flour she had—an act of faith in God—He miraculously provided for her. That minuscule portion of meal was given back to her and her young son in good measure, pressed down, shaken together, and running over for three years as God fed her, her son, and Elijah!

3. *The blessing of a resurrected son.* When tragedy struck and her little son died, Elijah called upon God, and the boy was miraculously revived.

4. *The blessing of the wonderful knowledge of God.* The physical provision of food became the avenue by which the woman received the spiritual provision of a clear knowledge of God and a firm faith that His word is truth.

5. *The blessing of Jesus' praise.* To this woman who loved God, Jesus bestowed His "Well done!" with these words: "Many widows were in Israel in the days of Elijah…but to none of them was Elijah sent except to Zarephath…to a woman who was a widow" (Luke 4:25, 26).

To quote a few lines of poetry, "Give to the Lord the best that you have, and the best will come back to you."[1] What will you, as a woman who loves God, give Him? Give it now, and begin to reap a heap of blessings!

> *"Now…I know that…the word of the Lord…is the truth."*
> 1 Kings 17:24

*G*od's tale of two women recorded in 1 Kings 17–19 opens with the spotlight on Elijah. This faithful prophet encounters two women who were radical opposites in heart and in deed: a humble widow in Zarephath, and Queen Jezebel, the wife of wicked King Ahab. Note the three phases of Elijah's experience:

- *Phase 1—Prophecy.* Told by God to condemn the evil deeds of Ahab and Jezebel, Elijah delivered the message: There would be no rain for three and a half years (1 Kings 17:1).

- *Phase 2—Poverty.* Soon the fulfillment of God's message affected God's messenger, and Elijah, too, knew life-threatening hunger and thirst.

- *Phase 3—Provision.* As Elijah struggled to survive the drought and famine, God guided him to the home of a poor, starving widow in Zarephath. Not only did she open the door of her home to Elijah, but this widow first opened her hand, feeding him with her last bit of food. She ultimately opened her heart to embrace Elijah's God.

The Bible tells us that "the eyes of the Lord are in every place, keeping watch on the evil and the good" (Proverbs 15:3). We see both evil and good in the tale of these two women:

The Widow of Zarephath	Jezebel
Was poor, but kind	Was wealthy and evil
Cared for Elijah	Vowed to kill Elijah
Believed in God Almighty	Believed in Baal
Had nothing, yet had everything	Had everything, yet had nothing
Lives on in God's Word	Died a brutal death

Before we leave the wonderful widow of Zarephath, consider her splendid example for us. Whom can you help today? How can you serve the people of God? What can you do to extend kindness to someone in need? Remember that the "little that a righteous man has is better than the riches of many wicked" (Psalm 37:16). So open your heart…and your hand…and your home. Dedicate yourself to relieving the afflicted and giving to the needy, no matter how little you have. Discover both the joy of giving and the blessing of God as you serve Him in this way!

A certain woman…cried out to Elisha.
2 KINGS 4:1

𝒯he Bible reveals a God who cares about the everyday needs of His children. In the touching miracle of mercy recorded in 2 Kings 4, we see an example of God's tender care for His own as He provides for a prophet's widow and her fatherless family. Here's what happened.

This woman approached God's prophet Elisha with her plea: "The creditor is coming to take my two sons to be his slaves" (2 Kings 4:1). This widow who loved God had a twofold problem: She owed a debt she could not pay, and she had a family she could not feed. With an outstanding bill and no husband, the servitude of her sons seemed inevitable. But Elisha had instructions for her: "Borrow vessels from all your neighbors, go into your house, shut the door, and pour out your last tiny amount of oil."

Filled with hope and acting in faith, the widow went to work. With her neighbors' pots surrounding her, she began to pour…and pour…and pour! Her meager amount of oil filled every container she had gathered as God miraculously made little into much, supplying enough oil for the widow to pay her debts *and* care for her sons until they were old enough to work. How she and her desperate family must have praised God as, behind closed doors, He grandly revealed to them His power, His love, and His provision!

God extends His love for you, too, dear friend. Think about how God touches your life with His mercy. Does He provide your daily bread? When have you tasted His comfort in your sorrows? At what moments have you recognized His presence in your times of trouble? How has His grace proved to be sufficient…enough…all you need in all your trials? In what ways have you noticed that His mercies are new every morning? As a woman who loves God, you are indeed privileged to enjoy God's provision for your every need and His solution for your every problem. As the psalmist declares, "The LORD is my shepherd; I shall not want" (Psalm 23:1). Or, as another has rendered these words: Because "the Lord shepherds me, I shall never be in need."[2]

She constrained [Elisha] to eat some food.
2 KINGS 4:8

*Y*esterday we watched God provide food for a woman in need as she followed the instructions of the prophet Elisha. Today, the gracious provision is reversed as this woman who loved God, but whose name we never learn, provided food for Elisha.

This generous woman is described in various translations of the Bible as a "notable," "prominent," and "great" woman from Shunem. She had a home, and she used it for the Lord, opening its doors as well as her heart to Elisha. When she noticed that the prophet regularly passed through her town, she persuaded him to stop in and share a meal—anytime! This Shunammite woman excelled in the fine art of biblical hospitality—the practice of "stranger love," the custom of entertaining strangers and showing them kindness. And she did it "without grumbling" (1 Peter 4:9)!

We are struck by this woman's kindness (she noticed that Elisha had no place to eat) and her goodness (she acted on what she had noticed and swung wide the doors of her heart to welcome this stranger to her hearth and home). How lovingly hospitable she was as she provided the best she could for Elisha!

Do you want to add your name to the roll call of God's hospitable women like the Shunammite woman…Mary and Martha who opened their hearts and home to Jesus (Luke 10:38)…and those women we read about in 1 Timothy 5:10 who lodged strangers, washed the saints' feet, and relieved the afflicted? As the New Testament exhorts, "Do not forget to entertain strangers" (Hebrews 13:2).

Hear the wisdom of early church father Augustine: "Love has hands to help others. It has feet to hasten to the poor and needy. It has eyes to see misery and want. It has ears to hear the sighs and sorrow of men." Ask God to work in you and open your heart to those in need and fill it with "stranger love." Pray for…

> ❦ A heart that cares,
>
> ❦ Eyes that see,
>
> ❦ A soul that is compassionate,
>
> ❦ Funds to provide,
>
> ❦ Resources to share,
>
> ❦ Hands that open, and
>
> ❦ Energy to serve.

She constrained [Elisha] to eat some food.
2 KINGS 4:8

If you've ever wondered what kindness and compassion look like, the Shunammite woman is one of God's answers to your question. In her we find a truly grand woman of noble character and great kindness. Ever observant, her heart was fine-tuned to the needs of others, and God's prophet Elisha was one blessed by this great lady's kindheartedness. Since his journeys regularly took him through the Shunammite's town and past her home, she realized that he probably had nowhere to eat. Moved with compassion, she insisted that he take all his meals at her table.

Dear woman, also of noble character, our love for God and His love for people is lived out as we love others and are kind to them. In fact, expressing God's lovingkindness is a calling of every believer:

- "Put on a heart of...kindness" (Colossians 3:12 NASB).
- "Walk in the Spirit...[and] the fruit of the Spirit is...kindness" (Galatians 5:16, 22).
- "Be kind to one another" (Ephesians 4:32).
- "Be kind to all" (2 Timothy 2:24 NASB).
- "Encourage the young women...to be...kind" (Titus 2:4,5 NASB).

In the Shunammite woman we see that...

Kindness notices. Her habit was to watch and listen to those around her, to pay attention and be on the lookout for people's needs.

Kindness cares. This woman genuinely cared about Elisha's welfare and the fact that he had no place to eat or sleep.

Kindness takes action. She noticed Elisha's situation, wondering, "How can I make his life easier? How can I lift his burden?"—and then invited him to dine with her family whenever he passed through their town.

A kind heart is a garden that cultivates the roots of kind thoughts, the flowers of kind words, and the fruits of kind deeds. Why not put the following time-honored practices to work and cultivate your own heart of kindness?

- Pray for others.
- Confess any ill will toward anyone.
- Ask God to fill your heart with His lovingkindness.
- Look at the life of Jesus, God's kindness in human flesh.
- Practice kindness at home.

> *"Let us make a small upper room...so*
> *...he can turn in there."*
> 2 Kings 4:10

A popular praise chorus declares the biblical truth, "They will know we are Christians by our love."[3] If your heart is filled with the goodness of the Lord, you can be sure that the people around you will know of your love for God and His place in your heart. Everyone around you will notice and be blessed by the very real presence of His love in you.

The presence of God's love was certainly apparent in the Shunammite woman as she cared for the Lord's beloved prophet Elisha. Noticing his need for nourishment and rest, this godly woman went into action because, you see, goodness of heart naturally leads to goodness in deeds. First, she insisted that he allow her to provide his meals. Then she asked her husband if they could make a little room where this man of God could sleep, study, and pray. When the chamber was finished, Elisha had a home away from home. How he must have looked forward to stopping in Shunem on his exhausting trips!

Look closely at the Shunammite woman and notice the godliness of her actions:

- She took the initiative in order to meet specific needs.
- She set aside her own comfort and willingly worked to provide for the needs of another.
- She advanced the well-being of another person.
- She gave every good thing she could think of to help Elisha.

Do you want to know what God is like? Then look to His goodness, which is considered to be the sum of all God's attributes, expressing the supreme benevolence, holiness, and excellence of the divine character.[4] Bask in the presence of this character so that the light of His goodness may transform you.

You can reflect in your own life what you see as you look at God's goodness, helping others see for themselves its breathtaking beauty. Simply show by your own good acts what God is like and that you know Him personally. As the apostle Paul prompts, "Let us do good to all" (Galatians 6:10). Whom will you help today?

And the woman…bore a son.
2 KINGS 4:17

*N*ever did the Shunammite woman slip a bill under Elisha's door during his stays at her family's home. She had no reason to because the account never changed:

Room	$ 0.00
Board	$ 0.00
Balance Due	$ 0.00

Deeply touched by this godly woman's hospitality, Elisha wondered aloud to his servant, "What can be done for her?" Perhaps Elisha's servant had been pondering the same question since he, too, had been blessed by her graciousness. He said: "She has no son, and her husband is old."

"That's it! A son for her to love, who will care for her in the future! Call her in now!" Elisha exclaimed. Then he announced to this generous but childless woman, "About this time next year you shall embrace a son" (verse 16). And it happened just as Elisha said: She conceived and bore a son. In the words of the psalmist, "He maketh the barren woman…to be a joyful mother of children. Praise ye the LORD!" (Psalm 113:9 KJV).

The story of the Shunammite woman has a happy ending, but please don't miss its remarkable message: Apparently this precious sister was content even before she had children. She seems content to dwell with her own people, content to live her days without children, content to lavish her love upon her husband, content to extend her welcoming care to the likes of Elisha and his servant. In this godly woman we sense no bitterness or regret about how her life is going. She had apparently "learned" to be content.

Nevertheless, she undoubtedly knew ecstatic joy at the birth of her infant son! But she had learned greater lessons in the days and the decades preceding that wondrous event. Surely this woman had learned that…

> …contentment is understanding that if I am not satisfied with what I have, I will never be satisfied with what I want.

> …contentment is realizing that God has already given me everything I need for my present happiness.[5]

Learn the lessons this woman learned and know a heart of peace and contentment. Then, right where you are, praise the Lord whatever your circumstances!

[Her son] sat on her knees till noon, and then died.
2 KINGS 4:20

*G*one was her joy, and her soul began to mourn. Gone was the sound of laughter, and she began to weep. The Shunammite woman's little son was dead.

After years of her childless marriage, Elisha had prophesied to this godly and hospitable woman that a baby would grace her home. How the halls of her home must have rung with joy as she and her husband praised God for this great gift! But now sorrowful sounds filled the corridors instead.

The day had been hot as her little boy helped his father reap the harvest of the fields, and soon he was screaming, "My head, my head!" After being carried to his mother, the lad sat on her knees until he died. The reaper whose name is death had unexpectedly visited the happy home in Shunem.

Exactly what does one do with a heart filled with sorrow and a soul in deep distress? There are certainly no easy answers, but we can trust that God will provide for us in those times.

The provision of God's grace—Whatever your day—or your life—holds, God promises you that His grace is sufficient for you (2 Corinthians 12:9,10). Do you suffer from…

- Infirmities, weaknesses? God's grace is sufficient for you.
- Reproaches, insults? God's grace is sufficient for you.
- Needs, hardships? God's grace is sufficient for you.
- Persecutions, oppression? God's grace is sufficient for you.
- Distresses, difficulties? God's grace is sufficient for you.

The provision of God's compassion—What a blessing to know that, whatever we face in life, we have Jesus as our great High Priest. He, who Himself has walked this earth and been tempted as we are, can sympathize with us in our weaknesses (Hebrews 4:15).

The provision of God's comfort—Be not dismayed, dear suffering one. For the "God of all comfort…comforts us in all our tribulation" (2 Corinthians 1:3,4)—*all* our tribulation!

The provision of God's promises—When there is nothing else to stand on, stand on the promises of God. They cannot fail. As one hymnwriter put it, "Tho' the howling storms of doubt and fear assail, / By the living Word of God, you shall prevail, / When standing on the promises of God!"[6]

So she...went to the man of God...
2 KINGS 4:25

*T*he expectation of good." That's how *hope* is defined for us believers.[7] And *hope* is the next golden and godly quality revealed in the life of the noble woman of Shunem. But the road to hope is often the path of sorrow and adversity.

Tragedy struck the happy heart and home of the Shunammite woman when her only child—a little boy who undoubtedly brought unspeakable joy to her childless home, who would carry on her elderly husband's name, and who would care for her in the years to come—suddenly died as she held him in her arms.

"The expectation of good." Energized by hope, the Shunammite decided to go to God's prophet and see if Elisha could do something about the tragedy that had darkened her happy life. She hoped—and she acted! As she hoped, she acted on that hope in faith.

- Faith laid her limp, dead son on the prophet Elisha's bed...and hoped.

- Faith answered her husband's inquiry with an "It is well"...and hoped.

- Faith saddled a donkey and traveled the 30 miles to Mount Carmel to Elisha, the man of God...and hoped.

- Faith answered Elisha's servant's inquiry with an "It is well"...and hoped.

- Faith fell on the ground and grasped Elisha's feet...and hoped.

- Faith refused to follow the prophet's servant and instead waited on the prophet...and hoped.

- Faith waited outside the bedroom door as Elisha prayed to God seven times...and hoped.

- Faith *and* hope were rewarded as the Shunammite woman took up her son—alive!

"The expectation of good." The Bible tells us that "he who comes to God must believe that He is, and that He is a rewarder of those who diligently seek Him" (Hebrews 11:6). God's role is to reward faith in Him. Your role is to act in faith and to bring all your hopes, all your expectations of good, to the "God of hope" (Romans 15:13), the Rewarder of a believer's expectations of good.

She waited on Naaman's wife.
2 KINGS 5:2

I tell you, half my work is taking away—rather than putting on—the paint!" So says award-winning *Reader's Digest* cover artist Nita Engle,[8] stating in her own words a basic principle of art: *Less is more.*

Today we pause to appreciate another in the portrait gallery of women who loved God. First, note that the Lord uses only 20 words to describe her (be sure and read them!), but these few precise strokes are all we need to "get the picture." Second, consider that this woman who lives on in eternity is an unnamed masterpiece.

Now notice how much we glean from little as we study the canvas of this young servant girl's life:

Her Circumstances—Taken with the spoils of war as a slave for Naaman, the conquering Syrian general, this maidservant had lost all that she had: her freedom, her land, her people, her family, her place of worship, the people of God. She had lost all but her faith. Yet please notice the absence of malice toward her leprous master. Instead, like a caged songbird, this young woman sang the song of the Lord in a strange land, telling Naaman's wife about the power of the God of Israel to heal her suffering husband.

Her Heart—Although just a girl, her heart was full of love for God, loyalty to Him, and faith in Him. Therefore, when she spoke, people listened!

Her Influence—True, the Master Artist has not included much detail in this unnamed masterpiece, yet this young girl's faith influenced people in her day and inspires us today. Because this woman who loved God spoke of the prophet Elisha's healing powers to her mistress (who spoke to her leprous husband, who spoke to the king of Syria, who wrote to the king of Israel, who spoke with Elisha, who gave Naaman instructions for healing), Naaman was healed and all of Syria witnessed God's power.

Like this unnamed masterpiece, how can your heart of faith and your influence for the Lord affect the people around you? Ask God to take away any ill will rooted in losses you've experienced and to make you a striking masterpiece, a source of relief and blessing to others—even to those who have caused you pain.

The woman…did according to the saying of the man of God.
2 KINGS 8:2

$\mathcal{T}$he generous Shunammite woman we met several days ago knew blessings from the Lord: She had a husband to love, a home to enjoy, a friendship with God's prophet Elisha, and a son after years of barrenness.

But a heart of faith is grown in the dark, and there were dark times aplenty for this godly woman! Childlessness was a humbling experience, and the death of her only child a dismal ordeal. (Thank God that Elisha had miraculously raised him from the dead!) But then death visited her happy home again, and she slipped into the shadows of widowhood. And Elisha was predicting dark skies once again: A seven-year famine was approaching, and the widow must move out of Israel in order to survive.

The Bible teaches that "he [or she] who heeds counsel is wise" (Proverbs 12:15). Well, dear sister, the Shunammite woman displayed her wisdom and her faith by acting on Elisha's counsel. With a heart of faith, she believed Elisha's words and acted. With a heart of faith, she disregarded all personal cost and inconvenience, packed up house and home, and did what Elisha advised. With a heart of faith, she stepped out of her comfort zone, out of the land she loved and had been so content to dwell in (2 Kings 4:13), out of her home, away from her property, her inheritance, her security…and into the unknown will of God.

But that's not the end of her story! Rewards aplenty accompanied her faith. After surviving the famine, this courageous widow returned to Israel, petitioned the king of Israel for her property, and received everything she owned *plus* what the land had earned during her absence. With a heart of faith, this noble woman first believed the Word of God for what she could not see and later was rewarded by seeing what she had trusted Him for.

Dear follower of God, behold the beauty and the strength of a heart of faith! Oh, that it were ours! Is there any dark difficulty in your life today? Then nurture your own heart of faith by choosing to believe God's Word, trust in Him, and follow His instructions—and then enjoy faith's many rewards.

But Jehosheba...stole him away.
2 KINGS 11:2

$\mathcal{H}$ow did it happen? How did the house of David, the tribe of Judah, the lineage of the awaited Messiah come to stand on the brink of extinction?

This huge question points to a solitary woman: the evil Athaliah. Hoping to fulfill her dream of ruling Israel, she murdered all her grandchildren who were in line for the crown. Imagine killing your grandchildren! The heirs to the throne were gone—all except one.

The quick-thinking Jehosheba had preserved one last heir. The wife of God's high priest, Jehosheba snatched up her infant nephew Joash, rescued him from Athaliah's massacre of the royal seed, and hid him in the house of the Lord for six years until he could safely be crowned king. Today we can thank God for this daring woman and her valor because the Messiah, our Lord, came through the line of Judah, the family line that Jehosheba saved.

Athaliah and Jehosheba offer a stark contrast between good and evil:

Jehosheba	*Athaliah*
—Name means "Jehovah, her oath"	—Name means "afflicted by God"
—A worshiper of Jehovah	—A worshiper of Baal
—Devoted to the things of God	—Dedicated to establishing Baal worship in Judah
—Married to a godly high priest	—Daughter of the wicked Ahab and Jezebel
—Acted to save life	—Sought to destroy life
—Used by the Lord to save the line of Judah	—Attempted to extinguish the the line of Judah

Now take a peek into the future and see what little Joash went on to accomplish for God. Joash became king of Judah and reigned 40 years in Jerusalem. He was one of the kings who "did what was right in the sight of the Lord," and he commanded and oversaw the repair of the neglected house of God (2 Kings 12:1-16).

If you've ever desired to do great things for God, simply focus on doing what is good! Because of one woman who worshiped God and acted out of her love for God and her devotion to His purposes, good triumphed over evil. As eighteenth-century British philosopher Edmund Burke observed, "All that is necessary for the triumph of evil is that good men do nothing."

So [they] went to Huldah the prophetess…and…spoke with her.
2 Kings 22:14

*I*f you ever visit the Holy Land, be sure to spend time in the Old City of Jerusalem. A highlight there for all who love God is the Temple Mount, the site of the temple first built by King Solomon in 950 B.C. As you walk around the perimeter of this awesome area, you will see a beautiful double-gated entrance on the south side of the city walls called "Huldah's Gate."

Who was Huldah? Referred to as the wife of Shallum, the keeper of the royal wardrobe, Huldah belonged to a small group of women given the rank of "prophetess." Seldom did God speak to His people through a woman, but when, during King Josiah's campaign to clean up and repair the house of the Lord, workers unearthed "the book of the law," the king sent immediately for Huldah. Three traits made her—and make you—useful to God's people:

A—Available. Sitting in the central part of the city, Huldah was ready to counsel any and all who wished to inquire of Jehovah.

Are you available? Can others get to you? Do you return your phone calls and answer your mail? Do you walk where other women walk? Are you available to be used by the Lord?

B—A Believer. Huldah held fast to God's truth. What God's Word said, she believed—and spoke! Graced by God, Huldah prophesied the doom of the kingdom of Judah that would come because people disobeyed God's commands. Because she genuinely believed and boldly spoke the truth, the people responded, and the kingdom experienced revival, reform, and renewed spiritual life.

Are you an ardent believer in God's Holy Scripture—every single word of it? Do you passionately believe it, love it, live by it, and share it?

C—A Counselor. Everyone accepted Huldah's words as received from the Lord. She spoke God's truth—His wisdom, the precepts of His Word—and called for obedience.

And you, precious sister? When others share a problem, do you call upon God for His grace and then speak forth the wisdom of God rather than the wisdom of men?

Make these ABCs of ministry your guide to greater usefulness in God's kingdom!

God gave Heman…three daughters…
for the music in the house of the Lord.
1 Chronicles 25:5,6

What would our worship be like without music? As an anonymous observer has noted, "Hymns breathe the praise of the saints!"

Mentioned in only a few verses of Scripture is a trio of women who loved God, and each one was a musician. Their father, Heman, was the musician assigned by King David to lead the temple music, and this father had his 14 sons and three daughters sing the songs of the Lord and play instruments during worship. Theirs was the honored ministry of assisting in the praise of the sanctuary, of participating in the service of song in the Lord's house.

Through the ages, women who loved God—women like Heman's daughters—have participated in formal worship. When describing worship in his day, for instance, David reported, "The singers went before, the players on instruments followed after; among them were the maidens playing timbrels" (Psalm 68:25). When reporting on the first captives to return to Jerusalem, Nehemiah wrote of the presence of 245 men and women singers (Nehemiah 7:67).

Consider this an open invitation to you, faithful follower, to join the ministry of Heman's daughters in worshiping the King of kings with psalms and hymns and spiritual songs and singing (Colossians 3:16). How?

Participate—Do you have a talent? Can you play an instrument, carry a tune, sing a solo? Offer your gift to the Lord and to His people.

Cooperate—Some might call this "audience participation," but when your congregation sings, cooperate by singing wholeheartedly, by making "a joyful noise" unto the Lord (Psalm 66:1)!

Appreciate—Learn more about the music of worship through the centuries. Every hymn has a story, was written for a purpose, and sprang from the creator's personal relationship and life experiences with his or her Creator.[9]

Incorporate—Make hymns of praise and worship a part of your daily life.

- Study them to be pure in heart;
- Sing them to be joyful in spirit;
- Store them in the mind to possess a treasury of worship.[10]

He and his daughters made repairs.
Nehemiah 3:12

"Who can find a virtuous woman," a woman who is strong in mind, character, and body? So asks Proverbs 31:10 (KJV). Well, rejoice, dear one! Hang out a banner that declares, *"Found: Virtuous Women!"* Shout it out for all to hear!

And where were these women found? Standing by a broken-down wall in ancient Jerusalem. And what were they doing? Working. Repairing. Serving under the leadership of Nehemiah. Helping the men of Israel rebuild the wall around Jerusalem.

Seventy years after that beautiful city was destroyed and God's people were carried away captive to Babylon, the Jews returned to their homeland and rebuilt the temple in Jerusalem. Later, Nehemiah organized the reconstruction of the protective walls around the city of God…and these women helped.

These wonderful women—all daughters of Shallum, these women who loved God—teach us much today:

1. *These daughters of the wall set an example*—Ever zealous for the things of God, these women voluntarily worked for the glory of God. Oh, as God's women we take care of house and home, mate and offspring, but we must also care about the larger issues of our faith and the bigger picture of what God is about. Are you concerned about the things of the Lord—concerned enough to work vigorously for His purposes, for His truth, His values, His reign here on earth?

2. *These women who loved God serve as a reminder*—God notices our good works, and here in Nehemiah 3, the names, details (including gender), and accomplishments of individuals are recorded for all eternity. This roll call implicitly asks, "Are you doing your part, doing it well, and doing it heartily for God's kingdom?"

3. *These daughters of Shallum issue a challenge*—In the face of opposition and ridicule, threats and discouragement, they looked to the Lord and drew upon the force of their moral virtues, powerful character, and physical strength. Are you a persevering woman, looking in faith to the Lord for His grace, determining to press on, and moving forward in your work for Him?

Prayer: Lord, may my heart be devoted to You and Your causes. May no task for Your kingdom be too great and no effort too small.

"Give [Vashti's] royal position to another who is better."
ESTHER 1:19

*O*nce upon a time there was a queen named Esther. She was the most beautiful woman in the vast Persian empire of King Ahasuerus."

This may sound like a fairy-tale opening, but the story of Esther—which comes right out of the Bible—begins with similar words, "Now it came to pass in the days of Ahasuerus…"

But wait! Before we launch into Esther's story, we must consider the history leading up to the scenes we'll look at. The drama actually begins with another woman, another queen, whose name is Vashti. Briefly stated, Vashti, queen to King Ahasuerus, refused a command from her husband, the king, and was removed from her position as queen, so that "another who is better" could be found.

We're not told all the details of Vashti's dismissal, but we do know that behind the details (in anyone's life!) God reigns with absolute sovereignty and is at work in the lives of His people. The first step in His perfect plan was the removal of the existing queen to make way for Esther. Vashti's banishment created a vacancy on the throne and opened the doors of the palace to Esther, a lowly Jewess, an outsider, a commoner.

Consider for a moment the people, events, and circumstances of your own life, and then acknowledge that God is at work through these daily particulars. As a woman who loves God, is yours a faith that believes God is working out His purposes in and through the people, events, and circumstances that He allows to touch your life? Although the details may not be clear now, you can be confident that God reigns in absolute sovereignty and is bringing about His perfect plan in His perfect time and perfect way. Such confidence is the beauty of faith.

Why not make the sentiment of an unknown saint the beautiful prayer of your own heart and life?

> I love to think that God appoints
> My portion day by day;
> Events of life are in His hand,
> And I would only say,
> "Appoint them in Thine own good time
> And in Thine own good way."

So [the king] made her queen.
Esther 2:17

*W*hat does it take to acquire the beauty of being useful to God? We get an idea from the life of Esther, the Old Testament heroine whose name means "a star," the woman God used so dramatically to save the Jews. Your usefulness to God springs from the same foundation as Esther's:

Heritage—Esther, a Jew from the tribe of Benjamin, was taken to Babylon when her people were led away captive around 600 B.C.

> *Consider your own heritage.* What life lessons have you learned from what your ancestors stood for, fought for, believed in, and endured?

Parentage—Both of Esther's parents died while she was young, but a faithful and loving uncle took her in and brought her up as his daughter.

> *Consider your own parentage.* And if you, too, have "missing" parents, gratefully acknowledge those whom God has provided in their place to shape your life.

Tutelage—All of us have been taught by many teachers, and Esther is no exception. She learned not only from her Uncle Mordecai, but also from Hegai, a heathen eunuch in King Ahasuerus's palace who taught her the ins and outs of pleasing the king.

> *Consider your own tutelage.* Give thanks for the variety of teachers God has sent your way to instruct you and guide you to the present point of being useful to Him.

Advantage—Esther was gifted with physical beauty, Mordecai's wisdom, and Hegai's preferential treatment.

> *Consider your personal advantages.* Identify those conditions, circumstances, and opportunities God sovereignly arranged to make you useful in His kingdom.

Homage—All said and done, Esther's heritage, parentage, tutelage, and advantage added up to homage when she was presented as King Ahasuerus's queen.

> *Consider the homage you will one day enjoy* because you are a member of a royal priesthood (1 Peter 2:9 KJV), a daughter of the King of the universe!

Dear one, Esther's God is your God, too. As the Omnipotent One, He is always at work in every detail of your precious life. Thank Him now for His active, transforming, loving presence in your life.

"If I perish, I perish!"
ESTHER 4:16

oday let's gaze upon the beauty of two women whose courage reflects their mature faith in the Lord.

The first woman is Queen Esther. This beautiful Jewess who loved God was married to a temperamental pagan king. When she learned of a plot to kill all Jews, she knew she must go—unsummoned—before her husband and plead for their lives. Her plan put her in danger because no one (not even a wife) went before the king uninvited without risking death. Yet her courage, rooted in her faith in God, empowered Esther to boldly say, "If I perish, I perish!" Both the urgent need to act on behalf of God's people and her fearless faith in the God she loved inspired Esther's heroism. The result? Esther's life was spared—and so were God's people.

The second woman is Betty Scott Stam. Betty Stam lived only a few brief decades because, in 1931, her courage and fearless faith led her to serve in China as a missionary. Caught in a Communist uprising, this woman—whose life verse was "To me, to live is Christ, and to die is gain" (Philippians 1:21)—knelt beside her husband, bowed her head, and was decapitated. Later, 700 students at Moody Bible Institute stood at Betty Stam's memorial service and consecrated their lives to missionary work whenever and wherever God might call them.[11] As the gifted English preacher C. H. Spurgeon noted, "Suffering saints are living seed."

Can you put your name alongside this remarkable pair of women who loved God and brilliantly displayed the beauty of courage rooted in that love and in their faith in Him? Do you value the things of God more than the things of this world? Do you embrace the stance of faith that "for me, to live is Christ, and to die is gain"? Could you cry out in the face of death, "If I perish, I perish!"? Allow the following words, cherished by Betty Stam, to urge you to a life of greater courage:

> Afraid? Of what?
> To feel the spirit's glad release?
> To pass from pain to perfect peace,
> The strife and strain of life to cease?
> Afraid—of that?[12]

"What is your petition, Queen Esther? It shall be granted you."
ESTHER 7:2

𝒜 bit of biblical wisdom states, "By long forbearance a ruler is persuaded" (Proverbs 25:15), and God's beautiful Queen Esther offers us an
example of this powerful precept put into practice.

Esther was a Jew who learned that Haman, the right-hand man to her
husband, King Ahasuerus, had received permission "to destroy, to kill, and
to annihilate all the Jews" (Esther 3:13). Esther also knew that only her husband, the ruler, could intervene to save her life and the lives of her people—
and that she must persuade him to do so!

What a beautiful picture of grace, wisdom, and patience God paints in
Esther's life as she shows us how to effectively persuade other people by following some practical steps of wisdom.

> *Step 1: Stop*—Before trying to rightly handle a wrong situation,
> Esther paused. She didn't rush headlong into just any course
> of action.

> *Step 2: Wait*—Time is a precious asset which cannot be bought later.
> Waiting gave Esther time to gather the facts (Esther 4:5).

> *Step 3: Consult*—Waiting also meant important time for Esther to
> seek counsel from her wise Uncle Mordecai (Esther 4:12-14).

> *Step 4: Pray*—Waiting gave Esther time to fast and pray about her
> task and how she would approach the king (Esther 4:16).

> *Step 5: Decide*—Time, counsel, and prayer moved Esther to choose a
> plan of action and move forward with the triumphant atti-
> tude of "If I perish, I perish!" (Esther 4:16).

> *Step 6: Act*—Before she asked for what she wanted, Esther prepared
> a special dinner for King Ahasuerus and Haman to test the
> waters and assess the king's frame of mind (Esther 5:5).

> *Step 7: Adjust*—Discerning and sensitive to the situation, Esther
> wisely waited and prepared yet another dinner before asking
> her husband to save her people (Esther 5:8). During this
> second banquet Esther made her request, and the king acted
> to protect the Jews!

Esther's path of wisdom can be yours, too. Why not follow that path
when you next face a challenge? Relying on God's wisdom enables you and
Him together to accomplish His will in His way.

"What is your petition, Queen Esther? It shall be granted you."
ESTHER 7:2

$\mathcal{T}$he Proverbs teach, "By long forbearance a ruler is persuaded, and a gentle tongue breaks a bone" (25:15). As you will discover today, when we act with wisdom and patience, softness can indeed accomplish hard things.

Yesterday we admired the wisdom of God's Queen Esther as she figured out how to persuade her powerful husband, King Ahasuerus, to overrule a death edict against her people, the Jews. Today we will come to appreciate her use of sweet speech—"a gentle tongue"—to turn the heart of her husband *against* Haman, his second-in-command and the instigator of the evil plan to annihilate the Jews, and *toward* the Hebrew people.

But it's important to notice first what Esther did *not* do when she learned of her people's plight. Nowhere in the ten chapters of Esther's story will you find anger or agitation, violence or panic, rashness or reaction. Esther knew that out-of-control emotions would not help her avert disaster. So she chose as her weapon gentle, persistent, persuasive, and sweet speech.

What were some of Esther's "sweet-speech patterns"? And, more importantly, what are your speech patterns like?

- *Words of respect*—When Esther addressed her husband, she said things like, "If it pleases the king..." "If I have found favor in [your] sight..." and "I will do as the king has said" (5:4,8).

- *Words of welcome*—The gracious Esther sweetly invited, "Let the king...come today to the banquet that I have prepared for him" (5:4).

- *Words of caution*—Sensing that the timing for her request was not right, Esther wisely requested that the king "come to the banquet which I will prepare...tomorrow" (5:8).

- *Words that were direct*—When the time was right, Esther boldly asked: "Let my life be given me at my petition, and my people at my request" (7:3).

- *Words few in number*—Esther uttered words that were respectful, welcoming, cautious, and direct—words that were carefully chosen and precise. She spoke only what was necessary—and, of course, she did so graciously.

May God grant us the beauty of sweet speech!

So Esther arose and stood before the king.
Esther 8:4

Where has God planted you? What might your fresh new day hold? You may not be waking up to ideal circumstances, and you may not be in a place you would have chosen for yourself. But wherever you are today, whoever fills your life today, and whatever happens to you today, remember that it is God's plan for you in His larger picture and bigger purposes. Esther learned about the beauty of God's plan as her usefulness to Him and His people grew from seeds sown in the soil of sorrow and pain. Just look at the liabilities in this quick biographical sketch of Esther's life:

> *Born:* A stranger in a strange land, born of captives
> *Parents:* Both her mother and father had died
> *Address:* The king's harem; taken there against her will
> *Position:* Queen to an alcoholic and impulsive pagan king

Although these details suggest that she is an unlikely candidate, God used Esther mightily in His plan. In a time of crisis when the Israelite nation was threatened with extermination, Esther realized that she was the only direct link between the king and her people, the Jews. As queen, Esther occupied an important place at court, so she was exactly the person God could use as an instrument for delivering His people. She had truly "come to the kingdom for such a time as this" (4:14).

You, too, can be used by the Lord today by simply being faithful to Him wherever you are *today*, to the people in your path *today*, in your circumstances *today*. Take the hope of these words to heart *today*. Discover the beauty of being part of God's plan by doing the heroic, as defined below:

The Hero

The hero does not set out to be one. She is probably more surprised than others by such recognition. She was there when the crisis occurred...and she responded as she always had in any situation. She was simply doing what had to be done! Faithful where she was in her duty there...she was ready when the crisis arose. Being where she was supposed to be...doing what she was supposed to do...responding as was her custom...to circumstances as they developed...devoted to duty—she did the heroic![13]

The Jews established…that these days should be remembered.
ESTHER 9:27,28

A good time-management principle advises us to write all special events on a 12-month calendar at the beginning of each new year. This practice ensures that we remember important occasions with each passing year.

More than 2400 years ago, Queen Esther and her Uncle Mordecai did something similar when they established a way of remembering how God had once again delivered the Jews from peril. It had been a dark time for God's people. King Ahasuerus had issued an edict giving his subjects permission "to destroy, to kill, and to annihilate all the Jews, both young and old, little children and women…and to plunder their possessions" (Esther 3:13).

Imagine the heartache! The fear! The mourning! The dread! Life was over for God's people! They could do nothing to save themselves. But, trusting in the Lord, Esther found the courage to ask her husband, King Ahasuerus, to give her people two days to defend themselves against the onslaught. He granted her wish, and the Jews overpowered their enemies.

Now imagine the joy! The jubilation! The sweet taste of victory! The relief! Life was *not* over for the Jews! And to celebrate, the Israelites made the day following their triumph a holiday, a day of feasting and gladness, a day of gift-giving.

To make sure the Jews now and in generations to come would never, *never* forget how God had turned their sorrow to joy and their mourning to a holiday, Esther and Mordecai instituted the annual observance of the Feast of Purim. To this day, 2400 years later, Purim is still celebrated by Jews around the world. Every year the faithful Jews remember God's merciful act of salvation.

And you? Do you make every effort to remember the goodness of the Lord to you and to celebrate His work in your life? Remembering Christmas (God's coming in flesh) and Easter (God's atoning work for your sin) is worthy of your efforts and inconveniences. Spiritual birthdays and baptism dates are other opportunities to commemorate God's involvement in your life. As the psalmist reminds us, "Bless the LORD, O my soul, and *forget not all His benefits*…who redeems your life from destruction" (Psalm 103:2,4, emphasis added). May we indeed remember His great goodness and love!

Esther the queen…wrote with all authority.
ESTHER 9:29 (KJV)

*H*asn't it been lovely to get to know Queen Esther? The Bible tells us about her exquisite physical beauty—that she "was lovely and beautiful," one of the "beautiful young virgins…sought for the king" (Esther 2:7,2). But the primary focus of the Bible's account of Esther's rise to fame and God's use of her to save His people—and the lesson from her life that we women who love God want to take with us—is that only the Lord can create the true beauty that comes from within the heart of a woman like Esther.

Before we end our look at Esther's story, consider again her timeless beauty:

- *The beauty of acceptance*—Although Esther's parents had died, we see in her no hint of bitterness or resentment to spoil her beauty. She accepts her circumstances with grace.

- *The beauty of character*—Scholars describe Esther with words like *faithful, courageous, pious, wise,* and *resolute*—each a reference to inner character.

- *The beauty of spirit*—Clearly Esther possessed the beauty of a gentle and quiet spirit, which we know is very precious in the sight of God (1 Peter 3:4). Esther exhibited a gracious, cautious, patient, and discreet spirit.

Where does such beauty come from? It comes from a heart that adorns itself with a deep trust in God (1 Peter 3:5) and a reverence for the Lord (Proverbs 31:30). It comes from looking to God for sustenance when times and conditions are difficult (Psalm 55:22). It comes from believing God will enable you when your faith is challenged, death is imminent, or relationships are tense (Philippians 4:13). It comes from knowing that God's grace is sufficient for us, whatever life demands of us (2 Corinthians 12:9,10).

Reach for this internal and eternal brand of beauty—the beauty that comes from the Lord—which is available to all women who love God. Reach for it as you study the inspired words of your Bible. Reach for it as you pray. Reach out to the Lord so that the beauty of His strength, faith, courage, and wisdom may fill you.

Listen, O daughter.
Psalm 45:10

There was no Mendelssohn's "Wedding March" as this bride came down the aisle. No video cameras rolled. No photography flashed. But there was the outpouring of "A Song of Love" from the soul of an anonymous observer. In words that move the spirit, this nameless artist extolled both bride and groom. Elegant expressions abounded as the poet declared, "My heart is overflowing with a good theme…my tongue is the pen of a ready writer" (Psalm 45:1).

As women who love God, we especially notice this "ready writer's" words to the princess bride about her expanding life roles. Although we realize now that this psalm was pointing forward to the beauty of our Lord Jesus Christ, we find in it timeless advice for us as wives.

New relationships—To the soon-to-be spouse, the psalmist advises: "Forget your own people…and your father's house" (verse 10). This wisdom echoes the instructions God gave to Adam and Eve, the first couple on earth. In setting forth the basis of marriage, God's Word pronounces, "A man shall leave his father and mother and be joined to his wife" (Genesis 2:24). Leaving and cleaving is the foundational first step for a healthy marriage.

New responsibilities—The joining of a woman to a man for life means a set of new responsibilities. Old loyalties must not compete with the new. From her wedding day forth, this bride (like every other bride through time) would be beside her husband…

- Following him
- Serving with him to better the lives of those around them
- Touching the lives of the next generation with God's truth
- Enjoying her role as wife
- Bringing her husband joy for a lifetime

New recognition—Does this timeless bridal portrait give you a fresh opinion of your own marriage? What riches God has given us in marriage—the privilege of enhancing one another's life, the blessing of family, and the shared joy of furthering the kingdom of God…together!

Sing to God…a defender of widows.
Psalm 68:4,5

Sing praise unto our Lord! All glory to God! Why? Among the many reasons, praise Him because He is "a defender of widows."

Although widowhood is not a subject we enjoy thinking about, the *fact* is that a wife most often outlives her husband. Widows outnumber widowers almost four to one. But the *truth* is that God takes care of His widows. He provides for their needs, He delivers them from danger, and He protects them from injustice.

God's guardianship of widows is one of the many powerful messages in King David's glorious Psalm 68. It is a hymn which points to the absolute victory of Israel's God and His people. David uses six different names for God (Lord, the Lord, God, Almighty God, the Lord God, and God the Lord), and worship and praise cascade out of his heart, mind, and mouth as he celebrates the Almighty King. And for what does David praise God? And for what can you and I praise Him? Psalm 68 tells us:

- *Praise Him for His judgment of the lawless.* Our invisible God is anything but absent! And when He arises, His enemies are judged, convicted, and scattered, but His people are preserved, protected, and delivered!

- *Praise Him for His provision for the helpless.* God cares for those who have lost families, especially the orphans and widows (Exodus 22:22-24; James 1:27). He graciously "sets the solitary in families" (Psalm 68:6). Literally, the Almighty "settles the lonely."

- *Praise Him for His daily benefits.* God, who is constantly at work in our lives, always bearing us up in His all-sufficient care, tirelessly "loading up" or bearing our burdens Himself, ensures our victory day by day.

So in whatever situation you find yourself today, why not sing a song of praise, a song of faith to God? Regardless of your difficulties, trust the Lord because, in due time, He will fulfill all His promises. And in each day's trials, He is an ever-present Helper who blesses and delivers His people. If you are lonely, destitute, bereft, or disadvantaged, take hope in the Lord God, who comforts and cares for widows, prisoners, the fatherless, and all others who are needy in any way. All praise to Him!

> *He grants the barren woman a home,*
> *like a joyful mother of children.*
> PSALM 113:9

*P*raise the LORD!" So begins Psalm 113, one of the festival psalms of Israel. The Hebrew exclamation *Hallelujah* (meaning "Praise ye the Lord!") appears throughout this hymn of praise, calling Israel then—and all who love God now—to praise the Lord!

In this poem of adoration, God is pictured as the God above and as the God below, the God of heaven and the God of earth, the God of the cosmos and the God of hearth and home, the God of the forevermore and the God of the moment. The Lord is truly high above all, yet He touches the humblest life—the poor, the needy, and the barren woman.

Do you have children? If so, don't forget...

- *Their origin*—Children are a heritage from the Lord (Psalm 127:3). Any child we have is a gracious gift from God (Genesis 33:5). Be sure to thank Him daily for each precious blessing!

- *Your attitude*—God prescribes for His mothers and expects them to live out an attitude of joy, and that's certainly the tone of this psalm. Hallelujah! Let your joy flow!

- *God's purpose*—God calls for believing parents to pass on the great truths about Him from generation to generation (Deuteronomy 4:9). In this way, people throughout the ages are blessed.

- *Others' feelings*—When you're with women who have no children, remember to be sensitive and to beseech the Lord on their behalf.

Are you waiting for children? If so...

- *Wait patiently*—This psalm looks back to the song of Hannah (1 Samuel 2, June 11), who waited on the Lord oh so patiently and oh so long!

- *Wait prayerfully*—As Hannah waited patiently, she fasted, prayed for a son, and vowed to give Him into the Lord's service once he was born. Prayer is always appropriate, whatever you're waiting for! And so are songs of joy as you wait in hope on the Lord!

*Your wife shall be like a fruitful vine
in the very heart of your house.*
PSALM 128:3

*W*hat makes a happy home and a home happy? At the heart of any happy, peaceful home is a content wife who is bearing the fruit of love, joy, warmth, and life in rich abundance.

In yet another song from the Bible, this one sung by pilgrims as they climbed the holy hill of Jerusalem to worship, the quiet blessings of an orderly and peaceful home life are lauded. This hymn is launched with the word *blessed*. After all, happy is the home where the wife is like a fruitful vine. And peaceful is the family that flourishes under the care of a wife and mother who, like a fruitful vine, offers shade and shelter in the very heart of her home.

What message does God have in this lovely word picture of fruit and vine, of heart and home, for us women who love Him?

You are the center of your home. In the psalmist's day, an Oriental house was built around an open space laid out with beautiful gardens and planted with various fruits and flowers, vines and trees. Every room looked onto this courtyard and enjoyed its splendor, seclusion, color, and coolness. Married or single, you are the heart of your home, positioned to give gifts of peace and pleasure to your household just as the Oriental courtyards did.

You are the comfort of your home. In the hot and sunny land of the Bible, a vine provided the comfort of pleasant and protective shade. Like those vines, you have the ministry of sheltering and soothing your cherished family.

You are the adornment of your home. The beauty of Palestinian homes was enhanced by the ornamental effects of training vines into designs on a wall or a trellis. They were also used to provide shade in the center courtyard. Here God likens your effect on your family to such vines. As a happy woman who loves God, you bless your loved ones and enhance your home by your gracious and groomed presence.

What a blessing to appreciate God's beautiful imagery in the psalm, to embrace His beautiful plan for your life, and to offer a beautiful song of peace to those who share your home!

That our daughters may be as pillars,
sculptured in palace style.
PSALM 144:12

$\mathcal{W}$ere you inspired yesterday as you considered the structure of an Oriental house and realized that, as a woman of God, you are the center and the heart of your home? Today God offers another admirable portrait of women who love God as the psalmist describes the support posts of a palace. With striking imagery, King David, a master architect (1 Chronicles 28:9-21) suggests that we and our daughters should "be as pillars, sculptured in palace style" (Psalm 144:12). We are to be like the corner columns or pillars of a palace, cut and fit for the structure of a king's palace.

Written long ago, David's image reveals God's ageless desire that the fair daughters of the land be strong and useful, as well as attractive. That message was clear then, and it rings out across the centuries to our hearts today, calling us to God's pattern for beauty and usefulness.

- *A Call to Excellence*—The pillars David described were functional (they supported the building), as well as decorative (in the end, they added to its beauty). They must be superior in strength, as well as pleasing to the eye.

- *A Call to Elegance*—Standing tall and stately, the carved pillars were works of art, adorning their surroundings with statuesque elegance, polished gracefulness, and quiet beauty.

- *A Call to Endurance*—The references to pillars and cornerstones stress the vigor, strength, and dependability of something that needs to last through time. The pillars were intended to support and sustain an edifice.

Stand in awe, dear daughter! Consider the glory and magnificence of God's pillars, of God's women through the ages. Study their "architecture"—their excellence, their elegance, their endurance. Hear and heed the voice of their prompting: "Pursue excellence! Desire elegance! Develop endurance!" Their cry is twofold: First, provide solid support to others. Second, teach and train your daughters (if God has so blessed) in this kind of godly beauty.

The Lord...relieves the...widow.
PSALM 146:9

*T*he Hebrew language defines a widow as "silent one." We immediately sense the pain and sorrow conveyed in those two words. Each of us probably knows a widow, and many of us are widows. But God declares in this magnificent psalm of joyous, triumphant praise that He Himself relieves the dear, desolate widow. Indeed, throughout the Bible, God's personal care for His widows is evident in the law (Deuteronomy 10:18) and in His church (1 Timothy 5:3-16). He takes special care to sustain, protect, defend, and champion this sorority of silent, bereft followers.

Our gracious, compassionate, and powerful God provides happiness for the bereaved, joy for the sorrowful, blessings for the destitute, and delight for those in despair. So take to heart the power and promises of your God from Psalm 146, one of the five "Hallelujah" psalms (146–150) that begin and end with "Hallelujah!" or "Praise the Lord!"

God is...
...the Almighty Creator.
...an Advocate.
...generous and gracious.

God is a God who...
...keeps His promises.
...secures the rights of the needy.
...lifts up the fallen.
...strengthens the fainting.
...tends to the defenseless.

Is your life hard? Do you ever feel like crumbling under its demands, injustices, or trials? Do you wonder how your needs will be met? Then you qualify as one of God's special projects! He delights in caring for the needy and the oppressed. He lends His special help to the weak and afflicted. He sustains and protects those who have no one else.

Still another psalm exclaims, "Happy are the people whose God is the LORD!" (144:15). That's you, dear friend. So why not lift your voice—no matter how weak, tired, sad, or sore-in-heart you are—and join in a hallelujah chorus? Needy ones throughout time have sung to honor our great and gracious God, knowing that His grace will once again prove sufficient for them.

Do not forsake the law of your mother.
PROVERBS 1:8

A woman who loves God undoubtedly has a deep and abiding passion for His Word. And, if she is a mother, her children are to receive the firstfruits of this burning personal passion.

Here in the Book of Proverbs, God calls children to "not forsake the law [or teaching] of your mother," suggesting that we mothers are *on assignment from God to teach His Word to our children*. We can do many things for our children, but teaching God's Word must be our passion. Why? Because God's Word has value for salvation now and for eternity hereafter.

Just how does a mother who loves God, treasures her children, prizes God's Word, and values His wisdom go about teaching truth to her children?

Make some serious decisions—A primary principle of mothering is to give children what they need, not what they want. So every mother who loves God must decide the following: Will I make time in my busy schedule to teach God's Word to my children? Will I strive to speak of the Lord continually? Will I turn off the TV and share with them instead the Bible or a Bible storybook?

Recognize your role as teacher—Ruth Graham, the lovely wife of Billy Graham, said of motherhood, "It's the nicest, most rewarding job in the world, second in importance to none, not even preaching." Then she added, "Maybe it is preaching!" Can you see how your role of mother includes preaching? What are you doing to impart biblical truth to your children at every opportunity?

Consider these mothers of the Bible—Jochebed probably had baby Moses with her for only three brief years, yet she imparted enough truth to Moses in those few years to enable him to lead God's people later in life (Exodus 2). Hannah had her little Samuel for only about the same three years before she left him at the temple, but what she had taught him was enough to make him another powerful guide for God's people (1 Samuel 1–2).

Consider yourself—Are you sowing seeds of God's love and truth in the hearts of your children? It's never too early or even too late to start—and doing something is always better than doing nothing![14]

I was…tender and the only one in the sight of my mother.
PROVERBS 4:3

Ssshhh! Listen and pay close attention! King Solomon, the wisest man ever, is telling us something about how he came to be so wise. Although aware that his wisdom is a gift from the Lord, Solomon also gives credit to his mother. Sharing childhood memories with his own son, Solomon speaks of the love of his mother, Bathsheba (see June 22 and 23), and warmly reminisces, "I was…tender and the only one in the sight of my mother." Put another way, "I was precious and dearly loved by my mother."

Look closely at what is taking place here. The wisdom and knowledge of God is passed from generation to generation to generation, from devoted parents to their children who, in turn, pass it on to theirs. Fierce and faithful mother Edith Schaeffer describes this process well: "A family is a perpetual relay of truth!"[1]

Love makes us mothers the greatest teachers and "relayers" of all because our love helps open the doors to a child's heart, mind, and soul to God's truth. Love paves the way for the wisdom in one heart to be received by another. Love tills the ground of a young spirit and prepares it to receive God's life-giving, life-enhancing, life-preserving wisdom.

As mothers who love our children, we do well to heed these few God-given responsibilities:

- *Stay…faithful as a teacher of truth.* Handing down truth to the next generation is one of God's primary commands to us (see Deuteronomy 6:6,7). As mothers, we are on assignment from God to teach our children His truth and His ways.

- *Pray…passionately.* "Powerful is the heartfelt supplication of a righteous [mother]!" (James 5:16 Weymouth). So pray daily for yourself, that your love of God will grow, and for your offspring, that they will come to love Him deeply, too.

- *Say…regularly and freely.* Speak boldly—and often!—about the Lord. We talk about what is important to us, and when we fail to talk about God, we send a message to our children that He isn't that important.

- *Today…act.* What will you do today to share your love of God with your children?

Rejoice with the wife of your youth.
PROVERBS 5:18

*B*efore he begins, the poet may have wondered how to best communicate his message. He has something on his mind—something God was impressing on him to convey to others. The love between a husband and wife is a vitally important topic, and how can he accurately communicate to his son its significance? Its beauty? Its value?

Finally, he chooses to use imagery that speaks to us even today. Quickly his pen drinks its fill of dark liquid and begins sweeping across the rough parchment with a flurry. *Be generous with the images,* he reminds himself, *so that everyone will see God's stunning picture of marriage!*

"Rejoice with the wife of your youth," Solomon begins. And then, as he strives to communicate that a wife is God's special gift to her husband, the images begin to tumble forth. She is:

- *Like a cistern* built in the center courtyard at home to collect water, an essential for every household (Proverbs 5:15).

- *Like water,* which nourishes life (verse 15).

- *Like running water,* refreshing and cool (verse 15).

- *Like a well,* that taps into fresh underground water sources and sustains life (verse 15).

- *Like a loving deer,* literally "the hind of loves" whose fondness for its young surpasses that of all other creatures (verse 19).

- *Like a graceful doe,* the ultimate image of gracefulness (verse 19).

Dear "loving deer," if you are married, your husband is to rejoice—be glad, be joyful—with you, the wife of his youth! He is to thank God that you bring special delight to his life. He is to live joyfully with you. That's the message of this proverb to him.

God's question to you is, "Are you the kind of wife your husband can rejoice in and rejoice with? The kind of wife who provides joy, pleasure, companionship, and satisfaction?" God's message to you is to love your husband (Titus 2:4). How are you doing? And what can you do today to be a blessing, a fountain of joy, to your precious mate?

Wisdom has built her house.
PROVERBS 9:1

*D*o you ever pray for wisdom, dear lover of the Lord? And have you ever wondered exactly what a woman of wisdom is and does? Well, take heart! God allows you a look into the life and home of a wise woman, and He spells out her greatest achievement in only five words: "Wisdom [personified as a woman] has built her house." As you peek through the window of Proverbs 9:1-6 (be sure you read it!) into the home this woman of wisdom built, notice the kind of place it is. What do you see there? The graciousness of the home is unmistakable.

A place of peace—Instead of arguing, quarreling, fighting, and raised voices, peace is the order of the day. Wisdom's house is a refuge.

A place of quiet—For those arriving after a day of noise, stress, and demand, this home sweet home lacks the blast of TVs and stereos and instead offers the gift of soothing silence. Wisdom's house is a sanctuary.

A place of beauty—Attention has been given to making this home artistically satisfying, to arranging things with love and creativity, to providing a background of beauty for the human relationships developing inside this house.[2] Wisdom's house is a paradise.

A place of order—Every home is an expression of its homemaker and a gift to those who live there. How much more beautiful this gift of "home" is when it is skillfully ordered! Wisdom's house is a haven of rest.

A place of refreshment—Not only are food and drink for physical refreshment prepared and richly arranged on the table, but God's woman of wisdom also provides her family and guests with refreshment for the soul. She offers wisdom—real nourishment, the food that is truly lasting, the words of eternal life. Wisdom's house is a little bit of heaven on earth.

Prayer for your home: May those who enter these doors, dear Lord, find refuge and refreshment for the body, a paradise of beauty and serenity for the spirit, and a sanctuary for the soul.

A gracious woman retains honor.
PROVERBS 11:16

*T*here is no doubt that one quality God desires in His women is graciousness. While men are admired for physical strength, wealth, and achievement, women who love God are admired for the graciousness, charm, and strength of character they possess. So says Proverbs 11:16—"A gracious woman retains honor, but ruthless men retain riches."

With an image that alludes to war, warriors, and the prizes of war taken from the bodies of the dead by the victors, God presents a startling contrast between true feminine grace and brute masculine force. This revealing proverb points to two different ways to the top (graciousness or ruthlessness), two different methods for getting there (character or physical force), and two different prizes (honor or riches). It teaches us that, although a man may be respected for ruthlessness, strength, and fortune, a godly woman is esteemed for the softer but stronger and grander virtues of graciousness, character, and kindness.

Do you, too, desire to wear God's crown of honor, His golden crown of graciousness? Do you yearn for His kind of beauty to characterize your life? Then consider these steps to acquiring God's grace and beauty:

1. *Make graciousness the desire of your heart.* Nothing of value simply happens. Since graciousness is one of God's goals for your life, make it one of your goals to attain—and then retain—honor.

2. *Nurture strength of character.* Put yourself in places (Bible study, prayer time, Scripture study and memorization, worship) where God can transform you. Relying on the Holy Spirit, you'll learn to check your temper, your mouth, your aggression, and your emotions and put your energies into cultivating the spiritual graces of love, joy, peace, patience, kindness, goodness, faithfulness, gentleness, and self-control (Galatians 5:22,23).

3. *Hold a high standard for yourself.* Again, by the power of His Spirit, live according to God's standards. As you do, you'll progress in purity, and your crown of graciousness will shine brighter.

A rich man may lose his wealth at any time, but a gracious woman retains her honor long after her physical beauty fades, long after her bones have mingled with the dust. Godly graciousness carries with it honor *for...and beyond...*a lifetime!

An excellent wife is the crown of her husband.
Proverbs 12:4

Yesterday we admired the crown of graciousness we women who love God so long for. Today we will consider another cherished crown, but this time *we* become the crown worn by another person—and that person is our own husband! As we consider when the words "an excellent wife is the crown of her husband" were written, we discover two meanings for *crown*.

Meaning #1: The marriage ceremony—"Crown" refers to the practice of crowning bridegrooms. When the night for the wedding festivities arrived and it was time for him to go to his bride, the groom dressed up as much like a king as possible, even wearing a gold crown as an emblem of his new position of authority and honor.

Meaning #2: The marriage feast—A crown is a symbol of joy and was worn on all occasions of festivity and gladness, including wedding feasts.

Don't you agree that being a source of honor, joy, and delight to your husband a high calling and privilege? Allow these ten practices to help you, as his crown, shine even brighter:

- *Be a woman who fears the Lord.* The inner person where God's Spirit works is where true godliness and excellence are grown.

- *Be firmly committed to God's standards.* Love the Lord, obey His commands, and follow after Him with all your heart.

- *Be faithful to your marriage vows.* Make the unshakable decision of fidelity to your marriage partner.

- *Be glad when your husband is the center of attention.* Remember, he's the one wearing the crown!

- *Be fiercely loyal to your husband.* Keep any of his shortcomings and failures to yourself.

- *Be a positive emotional influence.* Stand steady and stable at his side.

- *Be a positive physical influence.* Be a master manager of his home.

- *Be a positive financial influence.* Be industrious and frugal.

- *Be a positive influence on the children.* Teach and train them in the way of the Lord. Doing so will bring honor to their father.

- *Be a wife who honors her husband daily as well as for life.*

As such a woman of godliness and excellence, you become your husband's brightest ornament—a glorious crown of excellence!

The wise woman builds her house.
PROVERBS 14:1

*T*here's probably not a Christian woman alive who doesn't want to be—and be known as—a woman of wisdom. That's why this one tiny proverb, tucked into the middle of your Bible, is wisdom for a lifetime, shouting its "Amen!" to Proverbs 9:1—"The wise woman builds her house" (see August 3). "To build" means, literally, to make and to set up a house, but this verse refers not only to the structure and upkeep of the home, but also to the family itself. You see, a home is not only a place; it's also people. In the words of one insightful scholar,

> A house is not always a home and this verse does not speak of house construction, masonry, or carpentry but of home building; the knitting together of family and the day-by-day routine of creating a happy and comfortable place for a family to live.[3]

Who do you think is responsible for the quality of life where you and your family live? God says in Proverbs that it is the woman. Put another way, *you* are the one who sets the atmosphere, creates the refuge, and avoids attitudes and activities that would tear down your precious family members. Making a house a home is a matter of the heart—*your* heart!—and here are a few "how-tos for homebuilding":

✔ *Understand that wisdom builds.* The wise woman—married or single—knows that she is on assignment from God to build her home, and she realizes that building a home is an important lifelong endeavor.

✔ *Decide to begin building.* It's never too late to begin—or begin again—to build your house, to make an oasis of refreshment called "home." And doing so "heartily, as to the Lord" keeps the attitude of your heart right (Colossians 3:23).

✔ *Do one thing each day to build your home.* You don't know where to start? Just do something! Anything! One thing! One thing done each day adds up over a lifetime!

What are you focusing your energy on? Where are you investing your time? Search your heart and your home, and then act on God's wisdom and work on building your home!

The Lord…will establish the boundary of the widow.
Proverbs 15:25

*E*ighty-two times. That's how often God speaks of or on behalf of widows in the Bible. These bereft women who love God and trust in Him are truly some of His precious treasures! Having graduated from dependency on a human being to dependency on God, these women are examples of strong faith in the Lord.

These wonderful women, whom God takes special delight in caring for, find assurance of His care in several places:

—*The law:* "You shall not afflict any widow" (Exodus 22:22). The widow is to be honored and helped.

—*The church:* "Honor…[and] relieve those who are…widows" (1 Timothy 5:3,16). The church is to take on the care of its godly, destitute widows.

—*God Himself:* God is "a defender of widows" (Psalm 68:5) and a heavenly husband (Isaiah 54:5), the One who establishes "the boundary of the widow" (Proverbs 15:25).

Proverbs 15:25 becomes even more meaningful when we remember that it was first spoken when property was defined very simply by landmarks. It was all too easy to move or remove these signposts, thus changing or sometimes even eliminating the widow's property lines. But God Himself promises to protect that which belongs to such a needy and vulnerable woman. Jehovah, the eternal Lord, Yahweh Himself, will personally establish and preserve the widow's property—and woe to anyone who dares to harm His widows!

What does such a promise of God's care mean to women like us? It means that we can:

*Rejoice!…*and smile at the future, enjoying day-to-day life without fear or dread (Proverbs 31:25).

*Rejoice!…*and be confident that nothing can ever separate us from the love of God (Romans 8:35-39).

*Rejoice!…*and know that we walk with the Lord every step of our path—through all the ages and stages, from the beginning, through the middle, and right on to the end when we will dwell in the house of the Lord forever! *Rejoice!*

He who finds a wife finds a good thing.
PROVERBS 18:22

$\mathcal{M}$any a man dreams of finding a good wife to share his life with—a special woman to walk with through the mountains and valleys of his days. In the late nineteenth century, such a man wrote these thoughts:

> Think of an aged pair, who have journeyed together through a long pilgrimage, sharing the joys and the sorrows of their common lot, and, by the sympathy of love, doubling the one and dividing the other—"heirs together of the grace of life"—bound together and mutually endeared by the faith of Christ and the hope of heaven! Their children have risen up, and call them blessed. And at the close of their long day of life, the shadows of the evening are gently lengthened out, and they sleep together in peace! How delightful to think of those who have been one in life, being one in death, and one for ever![4]

The writer is a man who senses the value—and rarity—of a good thing. No price can be put on the blessing of a wife who brings him not only companionship, but also comfort for life. Fortunate is the man who finds in a woman a good thing, literally, "the good graces" of peace, union, and joy.

What would help make you "a good thing" to your own husband? Because godliness is at the core of goodness, the following scriptural qualities are essential and invaluable to a wife who is to be a good thing to her husband:

- *A helper*—God intends for a wife to be her husband's helper (Genesis 2:18).

- *A follower*—A married couple is to travel the journey of life together, with a godly husband leading his family, and his wife graciously following.

- *A worker*—God has much to say about building our home and being a good manager of that home. A good wife gladly gives her best efforts on the home front.

- *A believer*—A believing wife brings to the marriage the favor of the Lord, a fear of the Lord, and a heart knowledge of the Holy One.

It's a good thing, precious sister, to be a good thing!

A prudent wife is from the LORD.
PROVERBS 19:14

Prudent. That word doesn't sound very appealing, does it? Maybe a little old-fashioned, a little stiff? Maybe even a little "prudish"? Today's devotion may help you think more highly of this character trait that God builds into the woman who loves Him. But first some background information....

In its entirety, this verse points out the vast difference between the gifts of men and the gifts of God: "Houses and riches are an inheritance from fathers, but a prudent wife is from the LORD" (Proverbs 19:14). It's true that fathers pass along land, wealth, houses, possessions, and assets to the next generation, often as a form of family blessing. These resources are meant to better the lives of those whom the father leaves behind. These gifts are good and helpful things, but they are limited and temporal.

And how does a prudent wife compare? Oh, she's in a category of her own! You see, such a woman is a blessing direct from the hand of God! Whatever a husband has or does not have in the area of human resources, he is set for life if he has beside him a wife who is prudent.

And just what exactly is a prudent wife, and what exactly does she do that makes her so remarkable?

- Prudence is a virtue that encompasses discipline, reason, and practical management. Therefore a "prudent wife" is a delight to all. In fact, *delight* comes from the same root word as *prudent.*[5]
- She exhibits godly respect toward others.
- She possesses divine wisdom.
- She wisely governs her household…and her life.

Such a wife becomes the joy of her husband. Filled with good sense and godly understanding, she is one of the Lord's greatest gifts to her life partner.

Whether you're married or single, know that prudence is an aspect of godliness and a source of delight to people around you! The fruit of prudence is self-discipline, caution, wisdom, godly respect, and careful reason, and these are displayed in both your conduct and speech. So ask God to help you to…

Stop: Prudence stops and waits.
Look: Prudence takes time to learn.
Listen: Prudence asks before it acts.

...the utterance which his mother taught him.
PROVERBS 31:1

*O*nce upon a time there was a young prince who someday would be king, but he had many lessons to learn before then. So his mother regularly sat down with him beside the hearth in their home and taught him not only how to be a godly king, but also how to find an outstanding wife.

Most scholars agree that Proverbs 31 reflects that wise mother's instruction to her young son. She covers the basics of leadership (verses 1-9) and describes the kind of wife he should seek (verses 10-31). Hers is truly practical instruction.

Are you a mother (or a grandmother)? Then you'll want to show your love for both God and your offspring in the following ways:

Nurture your relationship with your child—A close relationship with your children—a relationship where you are free to talk about anything—serves as a bridge over which you can walk, carrying with you the precious truth of salvation through Jesus Christ.

Open your mouth—Teaching is one aspect of your God-given role as a mother, so speak out! Don't worry about whether your children *want* to hear truth. Ensure that they do! And don't worry about whether they *like* what you share. Be sure you share the gospel of our Lord Jesus. Empowered by the Holy Spirit, God's truth will make its way into the heart and soul of your child, so speak forth that truth!

Share your love for the Lord—You'll want to do more than just teach Bible stories and principles. You'll want to share your own testimony. Kids love to know how God has worked in Mom's life, and they want to know what the Lord means to you. Show them that your relationship with Jesus is personal and vital to your everyday life.

Obey God's law—God's divine law commands mothers to instruct their children: "These words which I command you today...you shall teach them diligently to your children" (Deuteronomy 6:6,7).

Offer practical wisdom—Proverbs 31 offers an index of practical wisdom, rules to live by, and precepts to follow, spoken by a mother who "opens her mouth with wisdom" (verse 26). You'll most certainly want to follow in her footsteps!

...son of my womb...son of my vows...
PROVERBS 31:2

$\mathcal{L}$ ike a tiered fountain, the heart of the Proverbs 31 mother overflows with intense love for her child. Her words seem to spill forth, one upon another, with each phrase repeating something from the prior, yet adding something new. They read literally:

What, son of mine...?

What, son of my womb...?

What, son of my vows...?

This mother who loves God has made a vow and dedicated her boy to God. In prayer, she had asked God for her child and later, in prayer, dedicated him—a child of many prayers, the son of her vows—to her Lord.

We women who love God and our children should also be able to call our sons and daughters "children of many prayers." How?

- *Follow the example of godly and prayerful mothers and grandmothers.* Did you know that, soon after his conversion, Billy Graham's mother set aside a period every day to pray solely for her gifted son and the calling she believed was his? For seven years, she continued those prayers, never missing a day, until Billy was well on his way as a preacher and evangelist. His mother then based her prayers on 2 Timothy 2:15, asking that what he preached would meet with God's approval.[6]

- *Ask God for His vision for your children.* Read about the godly mothers in the Bible and all that their children accomplished for God. Hannah's Samuel ministered to the Lord and led His people. Elizabeth's John the Baptist preached and prepared the way of the Lord Jesus. And dear Mary was blessed among women to teach, train, and love her child, God's Son, our Lord Jesus Christ! What special role does God have for your child? Ask Him to show you.

God is your willing and able partner as you raise your children to know Him and love Him and serve Him. It is His job to work in your children's hearts, but it is your job to pray for them passionately and consistently. So regularly ask God to help your children live for Him. And remember that you'll never know on this side of heaven, precious praying mom, all that your prayers accomplish on behalf of your children!

Who can find a virtuous woman?
Proverbs 31:10 (kjv)

*T*oday we begin looking at God's portrait of a special woman, a treasure whose price is far above rubies and whose image is vividly painted in Proverbs 31:10-31. For 22 verses God presents an overview of godly character for us women to follow through all the ages and stages of our lives. It is literally an alphabet, each verse beginning with one of the 22 letters of the Hebrew alphabet. I invite you to delight yourself in the Lord as you get to know His beautiful woman over the next 22 days.

Are you hesitant? Are you thinking, "I've heard about this outstanding woman all my life! Isn't she the 'ideal woman,' 'the impossible-dream woman'? She always makes me feel inferior, like a first-class failure! *I* could never be like *her!*"

She is indeed a striking figure, but it's not true that you can never be like her. Let the following facts encourage you to follow this God-given and godly role model:

1. Proverbs 31 is taught by a woman. This is a *woman's* estimate of what a woman should be—and can be!

2. The 21 verses of Proverbs 31:11-31 answer the question, "Who can find a virtuous wife?" by defining *virtuous* for us.

3. The wise mother who is teaching her son about women of character is one herself, or she wouldn't be able to describe her as well.

4. Knowing that women of godly character are out there in the world, this mother encourages her son to look for one.

5. And "many daughters have done virtuously" (verse 29, kjv). Count them! *Many!* The Proverbs 31 woman is not a one-of-a-kind fluke!

Oh, God's woman of strength and virtue is indeed a valuable treasure. And, according to God, *you* can become all that she is. How? Follow along for the next few weeks and, as you consider God's ABCs of character, you'll learn how to live out the beauty He describes. Try not to miss a day—or a letter of His alphabet—and you'll discover God's definition of true beauty and learn how to attain it![7]

Who can find a virtuous woman?
For her price is far above rubies.
Proverbs 31:10 (KJV)

*A*ll coins bear images on both sides, and God's use of the word *virtuous* in His rich description of the beautiful Proverbs 31 woman also has a two-sided or double meaning. Both aspects of *virtuous* communicate something of the strength which qualifies her as a precious treasure.

A powerful mind. First, *virtuous* refers to the mind of the Proverbs 31 woman—a mind made strong by her godly mind-set, principles, and attitudes. A quick glance through Proverbs 31:10-31 reveals the opportunities she has to use her sharp mind and how she seizes those opportunities:

- She keeps herself pure (verse 10).
- Her husband trusts her, as do the people around her (verse 11).
- She's a woman of industry (verses 13, 15, 18).
- Ever thrifty, she provides for her loved ones (verse 14).
- She faces life (and death!) with undaunted courage (verse 25).
- Compassion, kindness, and wisdom characterize her life (verses 20, 26).
- Holiness crowns her efforts as she honors the Lord in all she does (verse 30).

These mighty qualities of inner strength—rooted in the virtuous or powerful mind God has blessed her with—enable God's beautiful woman to manage her life, her time, her money, her speech, her home, her relationships, and herself!

A powerful body. Besides referring to her mind, *virtuous* also describes this wonderful woman's ability to put into action all that her powerful mind desires:

- She works willingly with her hands (verse 13).
- She plants a vineyard (verse 16).
- She operates a spindle and distaff (verse 19).
- She works until late at night (verse 15, 18).
- She nurses the needy (verse 20).
- She weaves the family's clothing (verses 21-24).
- Never idle, she watches over and builds her home (verse 27).

These lists may be a lot to take in for one day, but why not—today—ask God to strengthen your mind and your body for this good work? Cultivate the desire to live in God's strength today and everyday for a lifetime. The treasure of virtue lived out in a life that glorifies God is definitely worth your time and prayerful effort!

> *The heart of her husband safely trusts her;*
> *so he will have no lack of gain.*
> Proverbs 31:11

*B*etter than exchanging wedding vows on top of the Rock of Gibraltar (as one well-intentioned couple did) is establishing a marriage on the rock of Jesus Christ and, in His strength, offering your husband the bedrock loyalty of a faithful wife. Truly your partnership would be an unfailing prize!

Character that is trustworthy and reliable is indeed one factor which makes a woman such a prize. But another explanation is veiled in the word *gain* found in Proverbs 31:11. In the day of the Proverbs 31 husband and wife, "gain"—or wealth or war prizes—was obtained in three ways:

By warring and later stripping the valuables off the dead bodies of those who went down to defeat;

By working as an indentured servant, hiring oneself out for long periods of time in faraway places; and

By wrongdoing such as lying, cheating, or stealing.

But a man married to a Proverbs 31 woman knows a different kind of gain. He enjoys the personal contribution that his wife makes to his family's well-being. Verse 11 pictures the wife as a warrior going to battle for her family. Both the Hebrew and Greek languages vividly portray this woman, this unfailing prize, as a mighty warrior who uses her abilities for the benefit of her husband's domain. *She* battles daily on the home front so that *he* doesn't have to engage in war or experience a "lack of gain"![8] Imagine the husband who rests in his wife's character. Not only will she not squander or spend his earnings foolishly, but she herself protects, manages, *and* increases them!

While perhaps the concept of warrior-in-residence is not very appealing, God considers quite beautiful your contribution to the finances of your home, whether you're married or single. You see, God's own beauty—all His virtues, character traits, and holiness—is to be lived out in practical life (day to day), in practical places (at home), and in practical ways (money management). So why not ask God's Spirit to open your eyes to the many opportunities you have right at home to put the godly principles of thrift and wise money management to work—and then go to war!

A Spring of Goodness

AUGUST 15

Proverbs 31

She does him good and not evil
all the days of her life.
PROVERBS 31:12

Can you imagine a dry and dusty land, parched and cracked from a lack of water, relentless sun, and searing heat? Well, that's an apt picture of the land of Israel today as well as when Proverbs 31 was written!

Now imagine the joy, the value, the refreshment, and the life that a year-round spring would introduce into such a bleak existence! That is what a good woman brings into the life of her husband, the atmosphere of her home, and the lives of others. She is a spring of goodness, a welcome relief to those around her who know how hard and demanding life is. The woman who is intent on having her refreshing ministry overflow into the lives of those she loves, does good and not evil all the days of her life!

As women who love God, our calling is to do good and not evil all the days of our lives. We are to follow God's plan and fulfill His pattern for goodness. Aren't you glad that He empowers us when we plan to do the good He calls us to do and then put our plans into action?

Step 1: *Plan to do good*—Proverbs 14:22 says, "Do they not go astray who devise evil? But mercy and truth belong to those who devise good." Sharing his insights into this verse, one preacher pointed to Adolf Hitler, the Nazi leader who masterminded the murder of six million Jews. He noted that Hitler "devised evil," that he planned evil as meticulously as a bride plans her wedding. Just as meticulously we are to "devise good."

Step 2: *Practice your plan*—Don't be content with merely planning to do good. Follow through on your good intentions! Put your plan to work.

What are you planning, dear one? We women who love God are called to do good. So right now whisper a prayer to the God you love and set sail today—and every day—on a course of doing good not only for your husband, but also for others you encounter. God wants His women to be a perpetual spring of goodness!

> *She seeks wool and flax,*
> *and willingly works with her hands.*
> Proverbs 31:13

*D*o you remember the devotional of July 28 and the time we took admiring the pleasant courtyard of an Oriental home? In biblical times, a house was generally built around an open space that was used for a garden. It often included a fountain, which energetically brought happy music of bubbles, gurgles, and splashes to those who lived there.

As a woman with a heart for God, for the people in your life, and for the place you call "home," you bring that same joy to your family when you "willingly" do your work. Thank the Lord for His aid as you serve Him where He has placed you. And thank Him for His grace to live by the following principles for being a fountain of joy at the heart of your home:

- *Pray daily*—Prayer can give you the God-given perspective that lifts your duties in the home from the physical realm and gives them spiritual significance as service to your Lord.

- *Recite Scripture*—Allow God's Word—verses like Colossians 3:23, Philippians 4:13, and Proverbs 14:1, which you have hidden away in your heart—to encourage you as you work.

- *Do your work unto the Lord*—Colossians 3:23 reminds us: "Whatever you do, do it heartily, as to the Lord and not to men." The *What*, the *Who*, and the *Why* of all your work is God Himself!

- *Look for the benefits*—Develop a vision for your work, for the home you are building, and for the ministry of well-being you will offer there.

- *Pause and rest*—There's nothing wrong with a well-earned rest. Pause when you need to and refresh yourself in the Lord (Isaiah 40:31).

- *Value each day*—Your rewards (receiving some "well dones" and enjoying a sense of order in your home and your life) come more frequently when you willingly do your work one task at a time and one day at a time.

What a blessing to know that you can grace your home with the gift of a heart filled with joy! When you choose to work with a willing, happy heart, you become a beautiful source of joy to all, a fountain of God-given joy to those around you!

She is like the merchant ships,
she brings her food from afar.
PROVERBS 31:14

*E*very human being needs food for basic survival, and providing food—not just for survival, but also for enjoyment—is high on the list of services the enterprising woman of Proverbs 31 extends to her loved ones at home. With a real sense of mission, God's beautiful woman sets out, like the majestic, mysterious merchant ships of her day, to bring a high quality of life to those under her roof. Scouring shops that were stocked by ships that regularly sailed the Mediterranean ports, this woman spares no effort to contribute to the well-being and delight of those she cherishes. You can be sure that, when she returned home from her adventures, she carried to her family food, clothing, and all kinds of merchandise from afar!

The picture here, precious sister, is one of a woman who finds genuine satisfaction in providing what's best for her family members and bringing marvelous provision, beauty, and benefits as blessings on their lives. And consider the blessings she herself enjoys in part as a result of her industriousness:

- Health resides under her roof because she sets nutritious foods before her family.

- Savings result as she searches, bargains, and barters to provide the necessary as well as the beautiful for her clan.

- Culture enters her doors with both the goods that come from far-off, exotic places and the tales and information gained when those items were purchased.

- Variety spices up life in her home as foods and furnishings from afar greet and treat those within.

- Quality goods are enjoyed by all because of her keen eye and the uncompromising standards she maintains as she shops.

- Beauty satisfies, invigorates, and ministers to the souls who abide there.

You, too, can provide both the basics and the beauty that will set your household apart from most others. How? Ask God to give you greater resolve and renewed energy so that you can sail off toward the endearing—and enduring—quality of an enterprising spirit. With His love filling your sails, you will find the motivation and desire to give of yourself for the good of others. Set sail—and enjoy the adventure!

> *She also rises while it is yet night,*
> *and provides food for her household,*
> *and a portion for her maidservants.*
> PROVERBS 31:15

For all of us, effective time management is a challenge to one degree or another. In fact, the demand for help—for tips, methods, and solutions—has resulted in entire industries! There are seminars you can attend, time-management systems and notebooks you can buy, magazine articles that herald ultimate keys to success, and books proffered that promise to give busy women like you the help you need to handle the myriad of responsibilities that fall to you.

However, our God who created us, who has defined our role in Scripture, and who knows all about our problems, needs, and challenges, gave us His three pointers—a sure-fire plan for perfect time management—thousands of years ago. You'll find them right here in Proverbs 31 as you watch a busy woman successfully walk through her busy days. Exactly how did she do it?

Step 1: An early start. When a woman gets up a little early each morning, she gets a jump on the day and its list of projects. In the time of the Proverbs 31 woman, one of her first activities was to tend to the home fire in preparation for the day's meals and warmth. The early, quiet part of the day also allowed her the opportunity to tend to her heart fire as this woman who loved God spent time alone with Him.

Step 2: Food for the family. Providing her family's daily bread was another important reason for rising early. Like your family, her family depended on her to prepare the food they needed for another day.

Step 3: A plan for the day. When the Bible says that this woman gave a "portion" to her maidens, it means she gave them their work assignments for the day. She diligently organized herself and her helpers so the housekeeping chores for the day were accomplished.

What a privilege God has given you to set the pattern and tone for your household each new dawn! May He richly bless you as you seek Him early, see to your family's needs, and set in action a plan for the day!

She considers a field and buys it;
from her profits she plants a vineyard.
Proverbs 31:16

God's three steps toward successful home management were such a blessing yesterday! Today, in yet another gem from Proverbs 31, our all-wise and wonderful Lord shows us another helpful trio of pointers for being a Proverbs 31 woman. These steps, however, extend beyond the home front and prompt us to dream beyond the doorposts of home. Proverbs 31:16 is about becoming a visionary and a businesswoman—at the same time! Here's how it happened for the Proverbs 31 woman:

Step 1: Consideration. Hearing that a certain field had come up for sale, this wise woman most likely began to pray to God, ask questions of others, and seek advice from her husband about the possibility of purchasing this field of dreams in order to help her family.

Step 2: Acquisition. Blessed with peace of mind and spirit, practical answers to her questions, and her husband's approval, she took action. This prudent woman purchased her field of dreams with money she had earned and saved through hard work and conscientious thriftiness.

Step 3: Renovation. Next, with her hard-earned, well-managed, faithfully saved money, this capable woman worked to improve her property by planting a vineyard with the best plantings her funds could buy. Nothing but the best for her dear family!

Proverbs 31 calls us not only to labor, but to dream. This noble, accomplished woman dreamed—and then went on to realize her dreams! She dreamed of a better life for her family, of better and more food on their table, of produce she could give and sell to other people, of income she could turn around and use once again to better her family, and of the satisfaction of creatively bringing her dreams to reality. Put differently, she dreamed of blessing others by using the abilities God had blessed her with.

The Proverbs 31 woman certainly calls us to dream. So turn off the TV, the radio, the music, or whatever else keeps you from thinking creatively, from dreaming and wondering and planning. Take time before the Lord to jot down your dream—or ten of them! Then *consider* (ask, seek, and knock), *acquire* (move forward), and *renovate* (improve your acquisition and grow your skills).

> *She girds herself with strength,*
> *and strengthens her arms.*
> Proverbs 31:17

Homemaking. The word stirs a variety of emotions as we think of the people we love who live there and of the effort that goes into making our house a "home sweet home." An eager attitude certainly helps!

The wonderful Proverbs 31 homemaker readied herself—body, soul, spirit, and attitude—to make her house a home. She girded herself with a strong mental attitude and prepared herself for physical work. And we get the impression that she worked eagerly and energetically.

The following ideas can help you develop an eagerness about your work, wherever you are and whomever you serve in the name of the Lord:

1. *Embrace God's will for your life*—The portrait of God's Proverbs 31 woman reflects His will for you.
2. *Stay in God's Word*—There is power in the Word, so make time to read it each day. Listen for what God has just for you.
3. *Develop a vision*—"The big picture" of what you're doing in your home—making it an oasis for your husband, raising your children to love God—fuels your energy for the work you do there.
4. *Tap into the "why"*—Knowing why you do what you do can motivate you to do the task wholeheartedly.
5. *Pray for an eager attitude*—Ask God to change your heart and help you accept with eagerness the tasks He has for you.
6. *Create a schedule*—It helps you not only plan your work, but accomplish it as well!
7. *Develop a routine*—A routine can really help you fly through tasks.
8. *Read books on time management*—Learn efficient ways to do all that you have to do.
9. *Tackle the worst first*—It makes the rest of your day easy.
10. *Play music*—Upbeat music keeps you from sagging.
11. *See how quickly you can work*—Make doing your chores a game. Beat that clock!
12. *Consider the blessings*—Praise God for what your work will mean to you and to those who enter your home.

And please, don't try to apply these 12 suggestions all at once. Pick one, say a prayer, and act on it with eagerness, anticipating what God will show you and how He will use you!

*She perceives that her merchandise is good,
and her lamp does not go out by night.*
Proverbs 31:18

Industrious is a word often used to describe the Proverbs 31 woman, the lady of excellence we've been getting to know. Women always wonder, "How does she do it? What keeps her going? How can she get up early, shop, work, garden, and then sew late into the night?" The answer is her industriousness.

The root of her wonderful and productive busyness is a keen motivation which pushes her along in all her endeavors. She keeps in mind her goal and the reason for doing all that she does. For this dear woman, her consuming love for her family compels her to excel in her efforts for them. Desiring the best for the family she so cherishes, this wonderful woman sets about to provide for them—and to provide with excellence! Her love for her family motivates her to get up early, to shop wisely, to weave clothing and household items for her home, and to purchase and work a field for its sumptuous supply of food and a helpful amount of additional income.

This noble woman's efforts yielded a twofold harvest as she tasted the success of her endeavors. Her family was cared for and her resources grew, pushing her to work just a little longer than normal each day: "Her lamp does not go out by night."

And now for you, precious friend. Do you desire the sweet taste of success? Do you wish you could push yourself a *little* harder, a *little* longer each day? Would you like to accomplish just a *little* more before you turn off the light? Motivation is key, so take time before the Lord to review your motives. Are your efforts fueled by the right motives? Or, put another way, does serving your family come first, before meeting your own needs? Motivated by your love—a love that is fueled by God—you will always try to do your best, and you will find yourself being used by Him to bless your family (and others) in a variety of ways. There's no better taste of success.

"A woman's love is like a light, shining the brightest in the night."[9]

She stretches out her hands to the distaff,
and her hand holds the spindle.
Proverbs 31:19

Jesus teaches that if the tree is good, the fruit will be, too (Matthew 7:15-20). The tree—the heart—of God's beautiful Proverbs 31 woman was good, making all that she did good. And who received the firstfruits of her good heart? Her family! For this woman who loved God, family came first—and no task was too great for her precious ones!

As we saw yesterday, some of all that she did for her household was done at night in the warm glow of a fire and a lamp. Exactly what do you think this beautiful-in-God's-eyes woman did there by her fireside after the sun bowed its brilliant head and God's moon and stars spangled His sky? Today we catch a glimpse of her nighttime efforts.

As evening arrives and her body slows down, this dear woman sits and spins, with distaff and spindle, perfecting her wool and flax for her future weavings. She knows that she must complete the monotonous spinning before she can be more creative and begin her weaving.

Do you have dreams? Are there works of art you would like to create? Skills you desire to gain? Talents you would love to develop? A great, hidden treasure of time is accessible to you at night—a quiet time for growth, a time to perfect skills, learn new arts, read, and study.

How can you begin?

Plan your evenings. Save your daylight hours—your prime energy time—for the work that demands the most from you both physically and mentally. When dusk begins to darken the day and your strength starts to fade, instead of zoning out, kicking back, and plopping down, follow the example of God's beautiful, diligent, and wise Proverbs 31 woman: Simply change activities. During your daylight hours, clean, cook, and cultivate your garden. But after dark pay the bills, fold the clothes, study your cookbooks, and plan your menus. Another proverb tells us, "[She] who has a slack hand [and is negligent] becomes poor, but the hand of the diligent makes rich" (Proverbs 10:4). In other words, the lazy person reaps nothing, but those who are diligent succeed. So plan for diligence, pray for resolve, and proceed! Why not start tonight?

She extends her hand to the poor,
yes, she reaches out her hands to the needy.
PROVERBS 31:20

$\mathcal{K}$eeping watch over the home is one of God's key assignments for women who love Him, and the Proverbs 31 woman definitely models an A+ performance. Her trustworthiness, diligence, industry, thrift, creativity, organization, and micromanagement are quite impressive, aren't they? But aren't you also encouraged to see that mercy is another of her outstanding qualities? In all that she does, she's intent on benefiting others, including people beyond her family. Proverbs 31:20 tells us that "she extends her hand to the poor, yes, [and] reaches out her hands to the needy."

Note carefully several details about this verse: *Her hand* (singular) suggests her generous, giving nature as she lends a helping hand; *her hands* (plural) signifies that these acts of mercy require two hands. Her helping hands clearly reflect her heart—a generous heart of love and compassion, a heart after God.

But how did this gracious woman become a model in giving—and, more importantly, what can you do to grow in this grace?

- *Begin at home*—Each sunrise brings fresh opportunities for you to show mercy to others, especially those within your family.

- *Regularly give to your home church*—Your financial gifts to your local church reach the poor and needy throughout your community, the nation, and even around the world.

- *Err on the side of generosity*—Evangelist Billy Graham smiled proudly as he said this of his wife, Ruth: "She manages the fiscal affairs of the household—with...more generosity than precision!"[10]

It's wonderful to excel in your home, family, and private life, but God highly esteems the great beauty of mercy in your life. Mercy reflects the presence of the Lord in your heart and your life, and it pleases Him to see you extend that presence by what you say and do. Mercy adds the lovely fragrance of the Lord to who you are and to all you do. Don't you sincerely desire to be a generous, helpful, loving, merciful, truly-beautiful-in-the-Lord woman who delights in extending a helping hand to souls in need? Ask God to be with you as you extend mercy and kindness in the name of the Lord and for His sake.

She is not afraid of snow for her household,
for all her household is clothed with scarlet.
PROVERBS 31:21

$\mathcal{L}$ooking to the future and anticipating needs can seem rather unimportant if you're overwhelmed by the demands of the present. But the woman who loves God and her family provides for her family just as the God she loves and serves—and who loves her—provides for her. That's why Proverbs 31:21 sets forth the sparkling virtue of preparation. The foresight of this woman who loves God and her proactive efforts to prepare for the future reveal yet another facet of her great heart of love.

With wisdom and willingness, the Proverbs 31 woman plans ahead and sets all her management skills into motion, providing the blessing of not only food, nursing care, and help, but clothing as well. In winter, her family is handsomely and warmly clothed with scarlet cloaks of wool.

You, too, can begin a chain of blessings for yourself and your family by making preparations for your family's needs, including their clothing.

First, know that the work of preparation is important to God, whose very name is "Jehovah-jireh, God will provide." As God's women, we mirror this aspect of His character when we provide for our loved ones, and our acts of provision happen more easily (if not more bountifully) when we plan and prepare.

Second, when we work to provide clothing and other necessities for our family and when we prepare to meet their future needs, our actions speak forth to them a loud message of love.

Once you have prepared for your family's upcoming needs and placed your trust in our caring, loving, gracious, all-sufficient God, there will be no room in your heart or home for fear. Blessed by your preparations *and* blessed by the promise of God's faithful provision, you and your loved ones will indeed be doubly blessed!

Preparation and provision. Sounds simple, but the blessings are significant to your family and to you.

She makes tapestry for herself;
her clothing is fine linen and purple.
PROVERBS 31:22

*M*oving through Proverbs 31, we've seen that weaving is important in the life of God's beautiful woman and in her Palestinian culture. A creative artist with an end product in mind, this woman spends many late-night hours spinning and weaving her wool and flax into fantastic fabrics with the hands of an artist and then using those textiles to clothe her family—and herself—in the red of royalty, in clothing fit for kings!

Clothing is significant, dear daughter of the King. You see, it's right out there for all to see, and it reflects the heart of the wearer. Hopefully, in your case, your tasteful, modest way of dressing reveals that you, like the Proverbs 31 woman, are a woman who loves God.

The clothing of the Proverbs 31 woman who loved God was a tapestry of beauty. It was *appropriate* to her position as a woman of dignity; it was *appropriate* for her profession as a weaver, making her a walking advertisement for her skill; and it was *appropriate* for her praiseworthy character, robing her in something that spoke of her excellence and her excellent standards.

What are your standards for your attire? As women seeking the kind of beauty that God highly esteems, we want to follow His standards (see 1 Timothy 2:9; Titus 2:5):

- *Modesty*—Observing the conventions of decency

- *Soberness*—Dressing in a proper and sensible manner

- *Moderation*—Wearing neither too much nor too little

- *Discretion*—Showing good judgment and taste

- *Chasteness*—Reflecting a relationship with a holy God

These words may sound old-fashioned, but the choice to dress in a way that reflects these qualities flows out of a heart intent on godliness (1 Timothy 2:9,10). Furthermore, our loving Lord is always more concerned about the clothing of your heart than He is with how you clothe your physical body. As Peter reminds us, "Do not let your adornment be merely outward—arranging the hair, wearing gold, or putting on fine apparel—rather let it be the hidden person of the heart, with the incorruptible beauty of a gentle and quiet spirit, which is very precious in the sight of God" (1 Peter 3:3,4). Amen!

Her husband is known in the gates,
when he sits among the elders of the land.
Proverbs 31:23

Not many people in our culture value God's Word, but His truth teaches us that one of the wife's most important roles is to support her husband (Genesis 2:18). The noble wife of Proverbs 31 certainly knew that, pouring her soul into helping her husband, who became a man of great influence. When he stepped out his front door every morning to serve in the city gates as a counselor and legislator, he was her gift to the fortunate people he served. She, a woman of godly influence in her home, gave to the region a man of godly and moral influence.

So did Susannah Spurgeon, the wife of Charles Spurgeon, famed preacher at London's Metropolitan Tabernacle in the late 1800s. His ministry was thriving, but he became concerned that he might be neglecting his children, so Charles Spurgeon returned home earlier than usual one evening. Opening the door, he was surprised that none of the children were in the hall. Ascending the stairs, he heard his wife's voice and knew that she was praying with the children. One by one she lifted the children before God's throne. When she finished her prayer and her nightly instructions to their little ones, Spurgeon thought, "I can go on with my work. My children are well cared for."[11] Imagine! Because of her faithfulness and diligence at home, Mrs. Spurgeon enabled Charles Haddon Spurgeon, a man of godly influence, to continue to stir and convict hearts even to today. Mrs. Spurgeon also gave the world four sons who became ministers like their father.

What can you do to follow in the footsteps of these two wise women of excellence?

Pray right now and ask God to help you support your husband in ways that will strengthen him and glorify God. Make a Proverbs 31:12 commitment to do your husband good all the days of your life by...

helping him,

praising him,

encouraging him,

nurturing your marriage,

supporting his dreams,

praying for his success that he may be a man of godly influence in his work and his community.

> *She makes linen garments and sells them,*
> *and supplies sashes for the merchants.*
> PROVERBS 31:24

*O*ver the course of time, the contents of a woman's heart and the focus of her life's efforts are sure to be revealed. In the case of God's Proverbs 31 woman, her deep-seated dedication to excellence in all that she did and her personal commitment to creativity hardly stayed hidden.

First, she had apparently made a commitment to excellence. This commitment was born out of her desire to be the woman God wanted her to be, her decision to serve God, and the very grace of God. This noble woman loved God, desired what He wanted for her and from her, decided to expend her energies to strive for God's goals, and was richly blessed by Him.

Next, she had made a commitment to creativity, to actively and consciously cultivate her God-given abilities and talents. Fueled by her love for God and for her family, our woman of excellence sought ways to creatively express herself in the commonplace tasks of daily life. Clothes woven for her family became works of art. Food prepared in the kitchen became exceptional delights to sight and taste. Items made or purchased for the house turned it into a study in beauty.

Oh, happy the home where one of God's creative servants resides! And happy the woman who takes advantage of every task to grow in her creativity and skills. What this woman faithfully did for her family with her own signature flair, soon became a sideline profession. In other words, *something personal* (doing all things excellently for her precious family and treasured home) became *something professional* (selling her excellent goods to others). How can you, too, dear woman created in the image of our creative God, soar to creative excellence?

- *Be alert*—Notice how others express themselves and learn from them.
- *Plan*—Plan your projects and plan to further develop your skills.
- *Take initiative*—Act on your desires for a more creative life-style.
- *Work hard*—Work eagerly and diligently to achieve all that your heart desires and all that God desires from you.

Strength and honor are her clothing;
she shall rejoice in time to come.
PROVERBS 31:25

*P*ut on godliness, the Bible tells us (Ephesians 4:22-32; Colossians 3:8-17). In the same way that we put clothes on, God calls us to wear the garment of godly character worn by God's Proverbs 31 woman. What exactly has she put on?

Strength—The Proverbs 31 woman has faithfully built up economic strength and made diligent preparations for temporal changes even as she trusts deeply in the Lord, drawing His strength for any sorrow or care. This woman is also strong in wisdom and in her knowledge of God. She possesses a measure of physical strength and enjoys the social strength that results from a life of virtue. Adding to her wardrobe of virtues, her powerful mind gives her inward vigor and resolution. Strength received from the Lord is also among the clothing of grace she wears.

Dignity—The literal Hebrew translation is "splendor." Apparently the noble spirit of the Proverbs 31 woman gives her an aura of majesty. We who know her through words alone marvel at her virtuous character, her godly behavior, and her regal bearing. There is nothing common, low, or little in her wardrobe of character. Her greatness of soul—coupled with her gracious conduct—spells goodness to all who are blessed to know her. All that she is, is touched with the beauty of dignity.

Hope—Robed in such virtuous splendor, this dear woman rejoices—or, literally, laughs—at the future, and you can, too! Being able to rejoice in the future requires clothing yourself today with the garment of strength, the ornament of dignity, and the robe of faith. Your faith in an ever-faithful God will certainly fuel in you hope for the future.

So, starting today, give your life afresh to God and proceed full faith ahead into your beautiful day. Also, today make the commitment to wake up every day of your life and put on the virtues of strength, dignity, and hope, all of which are rooted in your knowledge of your heavenly Father. Then you, too, can stand comfortably clothed in your God-given virtues, look down the corridor of time toward your unknown future, and rejoice!

She opens her mouth with wisdom,
and on her tongue is the law of kindness.
PROVERBS 31:26

Quenching thirst was a serious and everyday challenge for the Proverbs 31 woman and others in her day who lived in the deadly dry land of Israel. The basic struggle to survive was—and remains—the rule of the day there. Brutal heat and life-threatening thirst are two facts of daily life.

Against this harsh background, Proverbs 10:11 says, "The mouth of the righteous is a fountain of life" (NASB). Godly speech is likened to water, which is essential for sustaining life. And godly speech can meet our emotional needs just as water meets our physical needs. Being in the presence of a woman who speaks words of wisdom and kindness is like finding a fountain in the desert—both give life!

Now God uses very few words to describe the Proverbs 31 woman and her words, which are also very few. Two basic comments seem to nicely describe her speech:

Wise in Speech—"She opens her mouth with wisdom" and

Kind in Heart—"On her tongue is the law of kindness."

When this godly woman does speak, she is wise and kind, and her wisdom and kindness are apparent not only in *what* she says but also in *how* she says it.

Think again about that fountain of life in the desert. Then think of the hurting, stressed, struggling people who fill your daily world. While they may wear brave smiles, other proverbs suggest the truth behind every smile: "The heart know[s] its own bitterness....Even in laughter the heart is sorrowful; and the end of that mirth is heaviness" (Proverbs 14:10,13 KJV).

Won't you ask God to use you to refresh and encourage everyone you encounter with life-giving words, with words that are wise and kind? With God's blessing, with His love in your heart, and with a careful choice of wise and kind words, you can help heal the downhearted. You, too, can be a fountain of life.

She watches over the ways of her household,
and does not eat the bread of idleness.
PROVERBS 31:27

*R*unning a household is a responsibility God gives to all His women, married or single, and Proverbs 31:27 describes that task with the image of a watchman (or a watchwoman!). The woman who loves God and accepts His call will literally "watch over" her family and the household affairs.

The image of the watch-keeper suggests that God's woman stands guard, keeping her eyes moving back and forth to see who is coming and who is going, in order to fulfill her divine assignment as overseer of her precious family and property. Alert and energetic, the Proverbs 31 woman has her finger on the pulse of her household. Her job assignment from God is to maintain a watchful eye, to know what's going on under her roof, and to care for the people as well as the place. Nothing escapes her oversight and care. Indeed, she seems to have eyes in the back of her head!

How does she manage this huge assignment? The proverb explains, "She...does not eat the bread of idleness" (31:27). This woman who loves her God and her family watches over herself, too. She has no place for idleness in her schedule. How could she afford to be idle? How could she even find the time? Busy managing her house and watching over her flock, she has no time to partake of ("eat of") laziness and idleness. The reverse is equally true: Because she is not idly wasting away the hours, she has the time she needs to keep a watchful eye on her home and be sure that it's well-managed.

Working (and watching!) at home may not sound very inviting or very exciting, but your home is definitely a place most worthy of your diligent watching! In fact, dear homemaker, your home is the most important place in the world for you to be spending your time and investing your energy. Why? Because the work you do in your home is important work, significant work, eternal work. The work you do in your home is your supreme service to God. Enjoy the beauty of serving there because...there's no place like home!

> *Her children rise up and call her blessed;*
> *her husband also, and he praises her.*
> Proverbs 31:28

Says Edith Schaeffer, a woman—and mother—who loves God, "Being a mother is worth fighting for, worth calling a career, worth the dignity of hard work."[12] At this point of getting to know God's Proverbs 31 woman, a model for us to emulate, God allows us to meet this wonderful lady's wonderful children.

And these children are celebrating—celebrating their mother! They rise up and bless her; they praise her with their words and their lives. This dear woman receives her highest accolades not from the community or the townspeople or the folks at church, at work, or in the neighborhood. That blessing of appreciation comes from those who matter most, those who know her best, and those who have received a lifetime of the firstfruits of her day-in, day-out love: her family!

How did this praise come to be? Consider these essentials in the heart of a mother:

- *Essential #1: A mother cares*...and shows her care in daily life and practical ways. She gives gifts of the basics (food, clothing, shelter, and rest), the gift of time, and the gift of love, and she gives all of these for the short term and the long term.

- *Essential #2: A mother focuses*...all her mothering energies and efforts on one goal: to raise each child to love and serve the Lord.

- *Essential #3: A mother plans*...the daily operations of the home and trusts God with final outcomes.

- *Essential #4: A mother works*...expending herself in the work of love, willingly putting her love into action.

When it comes to mothering, there is no place for neutrality, coasting, aloofness, or a hands-thrown-up-in-the-air, I-give-up attitude. The kind of mothering God calls us to requires constant attention, ongoing efforts, a never-give-up attitude, and the commitment to give 100 percent-plus! Being God's kind of mother touches generations of children with His love. Won't you commit yourself and your children to the Lord right now? Then do the work of mothering heartily as a service to Him, and trust the God you love as you raise your children for His kingdom and His glory.

> *"Many daughters have done well,*
> *but you excel them all."*
> PROVERBS 31:29

The grand finale of praise for God's Proverbs 31 woman continues! Yesterday wasn't it delightful to hear this noble woman's cherished children pay her tribute? Today is even more heartwarming as her dear husband joins in their song of praise, adding his voice in recognition and appreciation of all she does for him. The recitation of her numerous selfless works rises to a crowning chorus: "You excel them all! You are the best of all!"

What has she done to earn this tribute? A quick review of Proverbs 31 reveals this woman's many shining virtues and provides us with a checklist for evaluating our own character and life. Whether you are young or old, single or married (to a husband who may or may not praise you), God wants your character to reflect His presence in your life. So whisper a prayer and ask God to use the following questions to prompt good works in your life:

- *As a woman*—Do you put the power of your mind and your body to work on behalf of your husband, your family, and your home? At the same time, is it your deepest desire to not only *do* worthily, but to *be* a worthy woman, exemplary in character in every situation?

- *As a homemaker*—Do you provide for the needs at home? Do you carefully and attentively look over the ways of your household?

- *As a mother*—Are you, in obedience to God and for His glory, raising your children to love and serve the Lord, thereby giving your husband peace of mind and strengthening his reputation in the community?

- *As a wife*—Does your behavior bring honor to your husband's name and reputation? Do you contribute positively to his financial well-being through careful management of the household funds? Does your husband trust you and your faithfulness? Do your words encourage and build him up for the demands of life? In your honest opinion, has your husband found a virtuous woman in you, a woman who loves God? Pray that he has—and keep pursuing the heights of excellence!

Charm is deceitful and beauty is passing,
but a woman who fears the LORD, she shall be praised.
PROVERBS 31:30

*U*nderneath all that we admire in the Proverbs 31 woman—and any other woman who loves God—is her deep reverence for the Lord. Although our world values charm and beauty, God is concerned with something else: a heart that fears the Lord. As you grow in your own love for the Lord, why not follow these time-honored practices?

Commit yourself to Christ—In our New Testament day and age, a woman who loves God is a woman who enjoys a personal relationship with God through His Son, Jesus Christ. When Jesus Christ rules your heart and life, all that you do is an act of worship done *as to the Lord* and not to men (Colossians 3:23).

Schedule time with the Lord—As one who names Jesus as Lord, you are privileged to behold the beauty of the Lord and worship Him in the beauty of His holiness (Psalm 29:2). So figure out a way to balance the demands of your daily life with a regular, daily time of being in God's presence and nurturing there an inner beauty that pleases Him—and then do your best to maintain that balance!

Embrace God's plan—Proverbs 31 lays out God's plan for your life. A woman who loves God finds herself able to embrace it, glory in it, delight in its every aspect, excel in it, and experience it more fully day by day as she walks with her Lord.

Be sure—If you're not sure about how to begin a relationship with Jesus Christ, you can do so now. By earnestly praying the following words, you will set foot on the path of growing in godly beauty:

> *Jesus, I know I am a sinner, but I want to turn away from my sins and follow You. I believe that You died for my sins and rose again victorious over the power of sin and death, and I want to accept You as my personal Savior. Come into my life, Lord Jesus, and help me obey You from this day forward. Amen!*

Give her of the fruit of her hands,
and let her own works praise her in the gates.
PROVERBS 31:31

Voices—indeed, many voices!—are heard as we gaze in wonder and awe at God's finished portrait of all He finds worthy in His women. As Proverbs 31 comes to a close (and with it the Book of Proverbs itself, God's book of wisdom), we see the fruit that is born over a lifetime of loving and serving others out of a heart that loves and follows after God.

O what joy! What glory! What a wonderful harvest of praise! Every voice possible is praising this woman who is so very beautiful in God's eyes! In these words of Proverbs 31, preserved through the centuries, we hear:

- The voice of her children sound out her praise.
- The voice of her husband issue forth praise in the gates.
- The voice of God praise her.
- Even the voice of her works praise her.

But there is one voice yet to be heard—and that is yours. The rich beauty of the Proverbs 31 woman is not appreciated by our culture. Our enemy Satan, as well as the fallen world in which we live, labels her beauty undesirable. Oh, how very wrong they are! Dear follower of God, this Proverbs 31 woman is true beauty personified. She lives out all that is beautiful in God's eyes.

Your praise will indicate that you recognize the splendor of all that is beautiful in God's eyes. And the richest kind of praise you can offer is to follow in her footsteps.

Won't you bow your head now and offer your voice in praise to God for His beautiful woman? She is indeed one of His precious gifts to you. She is here in Proverbs 31 to inspire, instruct, and encourage you when you find your vision dimming, when you sense your priorities shifting, when you fail to be the woman of God you want to be. A fresh visit with the woman who is beautiful in God's eyes, this woman who loves God, will renew your vision, restore your strength, and rekindle both your love for God and your commitment to His plan for making you and your life beautiful in His eyes!

Live joyfully with the wife whom you love
all the days...which He has given you under the sun.
ECCLESIASTES 9:9

*I*t's been said before in God's Word (and in this book!) that married life is meant to be a blessing. A home inhabited by a happily married husband and wife is indeed one of life's graces. Now, here among the wisdom literature of the Bible, King Solomon shares some God-given insights on making the most of daily life, including married life.

Although "all is vanity" is a theme throughout the Book of Ecclesiastes (1:1), Solomon cautions us to live life to the best advantage. Aware of the uncertainty of life's journey and the inevitable reality of death, the Preacher (as Solomon is called throughout Ecclesiastes) bids us to make the most of each and every day—and especially each and every day with our mate! Why? Because a happy marriage is one of the few pleasures in an otherwise difficult life.

Are you married? Thank God now for His high calling in marriage and let these words about marriage written by Martin Luther, the father of the Reformation, help you make each day a blessing for your dear husband:

> The greatest blessing is to have a wife to whom you may entrust
>   your affairs.
> Marriage is no joke; it must be worked on, and prayed over.
> Love begins when we wish to serve others.
> Nothing is more sweet than harmony in marriage, and nothing
>   more distressing than dissension.
> Let the wife make her husband glad to come home.[1]

A high calling indeed for those women of God who are married! Rely on the Lord to help you fulfill that calling!

Are you single? Then yours is truly a high calling to love and serve God with all your heart, soul, mind, and strength. Paul, another wise and inspired writer of Scripture, has this word for you: While "she who is married cares about the things of the world—how she may please her husband...the unmarried woman cares about the things of the Lord" (1 Corinthians 7:34). There is no happier life than a life of heartfelt service to the God you love. Thank Him now for His holy calling of singleness.

The song of songs, which is Solomon's.
SONG OF SOLOMON 1:1

Song of Solomon," "Song of Songs," "Poem of Love," "Canticles"—these titles have been given to a tiny book tucked in the middle of your Bible. And these titles tell us that the Song of Solomon is a song of pure love penned by King Solomon as he reflected upon his wife, an unnamed maiden from Shunem. Note the stages of Solomon's growing and deepening relationship with his bride:

Knowing—"Getting to know you" is the all-important first step in any relationship. An individual's values, character, and personality are revealed over time. Time spent together also gives one person the opportunity to observe another's love for and commitment to God (Song 1:1–3:5).

Marrying—A wedding marks the beginning of two lives becoming one and the blessing of sex and greater intimacy between partners (Song 3:6–5:1).

Cleaving—Count on it: Every marriage will be tested! As challenges and afflictions come, both partners must follow through on their commitment to the Lord and to the commitment of marriage. Properly handled with God's wisdom and grace, problems will press a couple more closely to one another and to their heavenly Father (5:2–8:4).

Journeying—Hand in hand, a husband and wife who love and honor both God and one another can face the trials and tribulations of life (Song 8:5-14).

Even today, some 3000 years after it was written, Jews around the world read this exquisite song each year at their Passover celebration. Why not pause right now, set aside the demands and hassles of your daily life for about five minutes, curl up with your Bible, and enjoy God's choicest love song? Consider the courtship, marriage, and maturing grace of a couple who loved God. Join them for a moment on their journey through life. And listen for the spiritual music this song provides for a lifetime of marital harmony. It is given to us by God to reveal His intention for romance and loveliness in marriage, the most precious of human relations and "the grace of life" (1 Peter 3:7).[2]

The book of the genealogy of Jesus Christ.
MATTHEW 1:1

*H*ave you ever experienced the pleasure of ambling along a seashore and gathering an assortment of rocks and shells to carry home? If so, you probably never bothered to pick up and save any dull, dirty, ragged, unremarkable rocks. If you think about it, you've always chosen the smooth, polished, shiny stones.

But have you ever thought about *how* these stones came to be so polished and refined? Their attractive smoothness was a direct result of the storms that tossed and buffeted them, eventually eliminating rough edges and tarnished spots so that the surface glistened.

Today, dear one, God allows us to gather and take home to our heart the lives of four women who forever stand as trophies of God's great grace, four women who were honored to be part of the lineage of our holy Lord and Savior, Jesus Christ.

- *Tamar* leads off this small group of privileged women. Her blemished past includes deception and fornication (Genesis 38).

- *Rahab* follows—a wanton heathen known in the Bible as "Rahab, the harlot" (Joshua 2).

- *Ruth* is next, another pagan, hailing from a degenerate, idol-worshiping tribe in Moab (Ruth 1).

- *Bathsheba*, the woman who committed adultery with Israel's King David, rounds out this quartet of sinners (2 Samuel 11).

What an unlikely group to be among the holy Savior's ancestors! But God's Word clearly teaches that "there is none righteous, no, not one" and that "all have sinned and fall short of the glory of God" (Romans 3:10, 23). And that "all," dear believer, includes every one of us who loves God!

Aren't you grateful for God's grace, for His undeserved favor which He pours on those of us who love Him and follow Him? Each of us has a past that's blemished by sin, yet God has provided for the forgiveness of our sins and the redemption of our lives through the death of Jesus, His perfect, sinless Son. Through the suffering of God's only Son, we are cleansed, polished, and perfected, made ready to be displayed as further trophies of God's grace, and fit only through Jesus to be called joint heirs with Christ (Romans 8:17). Oh, do thank Him now!

The book of the genealogy of Jesus Christ...
Mary, of whom was born Jesus who is called Christ.
MATTHEW 1:1,16

*I*n a few days we'll be delving into the Book of Luke and examining the details of Mary's life more carefully, but first we'll consider a few facts about this woman who loved God that we find only in the Book of Matthew. We are initially introduced to Mary when her name appears here in Jesus' genealogy where she is referred to as wife to her husband, Joseph. She is soon to become known as the mother of our Lord and Savior.

Have you ever wondered what kind of woman God chose to be "blessed...among women" (Luke 1:28), to carry within her womb God-become-man, to love and cherish Him as her firstborn son, to raise Him in the knowledge of the Lord God, to be the mother of His precious and only Son?

- *A chaste virgin*—The prophet Isaiah stated that God's Son would be born of a virgin (Isaiah 7:14). Young Mary was unmarried, a pure and godly woman.

- *A humble maiden*—Hailing from the village of Nazareth, Mary was a small-town girl, not a princess from a powerful nation or a sophisticated city girl from the best of society.

- *A devoted follower*—God always looks at the heart, not the outward appearance (1 Samuel 16:7). When He looked at dear Mary, He found in her a woman after His own heart, a woman who would live according to His will (Acts 13:22).

- *A faithful Jew*—Of the tribe of Judah and the line of David, Mary worshiped the one true God and apparently did so in spirit and truth (John 4:24). Only such a woman would qualify for God's important assignment.

What four phrases would you use to describe yourself? As you think about that, let yourself enjoy the relief that comes with knowing that, no matter how humble, how simple, how poor, how ordinary, how intelligent, or how successful we are, God looks on our heart just as He did Mary's. And like her, you can be blessed among women and used by God to do great things for Him. How? Simply love Him...love Him humbly, devotedly, faithfully...love Him with all your heart, soul, strength, and mind!

They saw the young Child with Mary His mother,
and fell down and worshiped Him.
Matthew 2:11

*T*oday, as we glimpse once again into Matthew's life of Mary, at details not recorded in the other Gospels, we realize immediately that ours is a glorious glimpse!

The humble Mary has given birth to Jesus and is now welcoming "wise men from the East" into her home. Perhaps there was some confusion as these exotic foreigners tried to explain their presence. These Magi had seen "His star" in the East and had come to worship Him. First they had gone to King Herod, who was quite disturbed that someone other than himself was deemed worthy of worship and the title of *king*. Not even Herod's priests and scribes knew who this royal person might be!

But the Magi would soon find out. At last, the star which had directed these sincere seekers on a journey of hundreds of miles, led them to Mary's doorstep in Bethlehem. They had come to worship her child, her little boy Jesus, as King of the Jews!

Mary, a woman who pondered things in her heart, surely felt her heart encouraged by these mysterious travelers:

Vision—These men had come to Bethlehem to worship the Christ Child, the King of the Jews. The fact that they had traveled several months from a faraway place may have given Mary an even greater vision and clearer understanding of the future and the kingdom God had for her child.

Provision—These wise men from the East paid homage to Mary's infant not only with their worship but also with costly gifts. These gifts may have financed Joseph and Mary's flight-for-life to Egypt—a hasty journey made in order to protect their precious baby from the slaughter of all baby boys in and around Bethlehem initiated by a jealous King Herod.

Dear one, God knows His people's needs—including *your* needs—and He acts to provide what they need *and* what you need. Whether you need the encouragement of greater vision or provision, your God has promised to "supply all your need according to His riches in glory by Christ Jesus" (Philippians 4:19). Look to Him now. Lift up your needs to Him. Remind yourself anew that, "The Lord is my shepherd; I shall not want" (Psalm 23:1)!

> *[And Joseph]…took the young Child and His mother*
> *by night and departed for Egypt.*
> Matthew 2:14

*G*od not only granted Mary's family vision and provision (as we saw yesterday), but He also gave them guidance.

King Herod was angry, *exceedingly* angry, so angry when he learned of a child being called "King of the Jews" that he ordered the murder of every male child under the age of two in and around the city of Bethlehem. Surely the threat of another king would be eliminated by such a command!

But in a dream, God instructed Joseph—the sacred infant's earthly guardian—to take his family and flee immediately to Egypt. There they would escape Herod's deadly plan.

We never know what marriage, motherhood, or even a given day will bring, do we? Mary—a woman who loved God, who was "highly favored" and "blessed…among women," who had found "honor with God" (Luke 1:28,30)—nevertheless had lessons to learn about faith in God and following Him.

First, following. Can you imagine being awakened in the middle of a dark night by your husband's declaration that you were leaving, moving—right now? "But where are we going, Honey?"

"To Egypt. It's *only* a 10- to 15-day journey."

"But why, Honey?"

"Because, you see, I had this dream and God told me to go."

Imagine what would happen under most roofs after that kind of announcement and explanation! (What would you have done in those circumstances?) Mary, however, followed God's plan for her as a wife and followed her husband…an act which saved their young son's life.

Next, faith. Do you realize that faith in God is what enables us women who love God to follow our husband? Just like the holy women of old—women like Mary—who loved God and trusted in Him, we are to adorn ourselves with God's beautiful, submissive spirit and follow our husbands (1 Peter 3:5,6). Faith in God enables us to do so.

> Father, grant that I may be a woman with faith in You that is strong enough to enable me to follow others as they lead me into Your good and acceptable and perfect will. Thank You for working in my life through the leadership of others. Amen.

> *Then [Joseph]…took the young Child and His mother,*
> *and came into the land of Israel.*
> MATTHEW 2:21

Since the Gospel writer Matthew is the only one to record Mary, Joseph, and Jesus' flight *to* Egypt, he is understandably the only one who reports their return *from* Egypt to set up their home in Nazareth. Both journeys were prompted in the same divine way. Once again an angel of the Lord visited Joseph in a dream, this time announcing Herod's death and instructing Joseph to take his little family back to the land of Israel.

So back to the Holy Land they went and settled down in Nazareth, the hometown of both Mary and Joseph. They were home! Looking back over the past few years, they could thank God for how He had guided them and protected them. But what about the future? Mary indeed would face many of life's joys…and sorrows. It has been well stated, "Motherhood is a painful privilege."[3] Mary would taste:

The Joys of…	The Sorrows of…
Loving a child	Watching that child die
Raising a child	Not understanding Him
Knowing God through Jesus	Witnessing His death for her sins

Oh, there were other joys for Mary: the happy sounds of a brood of children; joyous pilgrimages together to worship the true God; family meals and cozy times gathered around a warm fire; hearing her son—the Son of God—preach, observing His miracles, and later witnessing His resurrection from the dead. But there were other sorrows as well: the death of her husband, Joseph; her fellow townspeople's rejection of her son; and letting go of her son to go about His heavenly Father's business.

And through it all, the lows and the highs, the pains and the pleasures, the sorrows and the joys, Mary loved God and looked to Him for His strength which is always made perfect in weakness (2 Corinthians 12:9). Truly, Mary shows us how to trust the Lord as we, too, walk the unpredictable road of life—a road of joys and sorrows that God uses to conform us into the lovely image of His Son.

Then the mother of Zebedee's sons came to Him...
kneeling down and asking something from Him.
MATTHEW 20:20

*T*oday we meet a mother who, like many other mothers, loves God and desires that her children serve the Lord. This mother happened to be the mother of James and John, the sons of Zebedee, who had left their father's boat and business to answer Jesus' call to "follow Me" (Matthew 4:19) and become His disciples. In this brief scene, covered in only four verses, we see a caring mother bring the desires of her heart before her Savior.

Person—There is no doubt that the mother of Zebedee's sons sensed Jesus' authority.

Posture—As this devoted worshiper approached her sovereign Lord, the only fitting posture was one of humility, so this mother of two knelt before her Lord.

Petition—A faithful follower (see Matthew 27:56), the mother of James and John asked something of the only One who could grant it. She dared to ask, "Grant that these two sons of mine may sit, one on Your right hand and the other on the left, in Your kingdom." In other words, "Let them rule together with You in special positions of greatness."

This faithful mom, who wanted her sons to love and serve Jesus forever, may have misunderstood Jesus' teachings on service, rewards, and His kingdom, but she does show us a pattern for true spiritual concern in the heart of a mother.

Person—Is Jesus Christ your personal Lord and Savior? Do you let Him reign as Lord over every aspect of your life?

Posture—Do you nurture a posture of humility that honors Jesus as Lord over every aspect of your life? Does God have in you a reverent and true worshiper, a woman of prayer and contrite in heart?

Petition—Do you bring your every concern for your children to your heavenly Father? Do you "ask...seek...and knock" on behalf of your sons and daughters (Matthew 7:7-9)? O lift up your soul unto the Lord on their behalf *now!*

While he was sitting on the judgment seat,
his wife sent to him…
Matthew 27:19

*A*t the darkest time in the history of the world, the woman currently before us experienced a brief flicker of the light of understanding about who Jesus was. Our Lord had already prayed in the Garden of Gethsemane, preparing Himself for betrayal, arrest, trial, torture, and death. There He stood—a lamb led to the slaughter (Isaiah 53:7)—before Pontius Pilate, the Roman governor of Judea. As Jesus awaited the death sentence which Pilate alone could authorize, a messenger suddenly appeared with a note. It was a warning from Pilate's wife: "Have nothing to do with that just Man, for I have suffered many things today in a dream because of Him." Everything leading up to her message was brief, just a flicker:

- *A brief dream*—We don't know the content of Pilate's wife's dream, but clearly it was troubling enough to prompt her to warn her powerful husband before he acted.

- *A brief insight*—This woman's dream either revealed to her or helped her conclude that Jesus was a "just Man."

- *A brief note*—Acting quickly, Pilate's wife dashed off a succinct message to him.

A series of brief flickers of light had led up to her brief Gospel appearance of only 38 words. Was this woman's faith real? Did the flicker of the light of her understanding, her moment of insight, last? Oh, don't you hope and pray so? We can't know about her, but we can know about *ourselves*, precious one! We know, for instance, that:

- A lifetime commitment to *living for God*, renewed day by day, fans the flame of faith.

- A lifetime of *studying the Bible* fuels an accurate understanding of God's living and powerful Word.

- A lifetime of *obeying in faithfulness* causes our light to shine brightly among people.

- A lifetime of *praying with passion* allows us to see into the blaze of God's glory!

Are you fanning the flame of your faith? Are you fueling the light of your knowledge of Christ? And are you letting the light of Christ within you shine outwardly in the world?

> *Behold, Jesus met them...[and] they came*
> *and held Him by the feet and worshiped Him.*
> Matthew 28:9,10

The Good News of Jesus Christ is rooted in the fact that He rose from the dead. Our Savior was crucified for our sins, died, and was buried—but then He rose from the grave (1 Corinthians 15:3,4). No other religious leader in history can make that claim. Only Jesus Christ, the one true God, has proven victorious over sin and death!

Today we meet a small group of faithful women who celebrated that victory firsthand. Though they had witnessed the worst moment in history—Jesus' gruesome death—three long days later they received the greatest blessing of all: They saw and spoke with the resurrected, glorified, transformed Jesus! Their story appears in each of the four Gospels, but only Matthew lets us hear what the risen Jesus said to these loyal ladies—words of reassurance ("Do not be afraid"), of instruction ("Go and tell My brethren"), and promise ("There they will see Me"). Note now the path these women walked that led right to the feet of the resurrected Christ—and beyond!

- *The Path of Faithfulness*—Jesus' disciples deserted Him, but these women lingered at the cross to the very end, then followed at a distance to see where He was buried, and later returned to the tomb to tend to His body.

- *The Path of Learning*—At the tomb on Sunday morning, an angel instructed this little band of women to tell the disciples that Jesus was alive.

- *The Path of Obedience*—Matthew tells us they departed *quickly* to carry out the angel's instructions. As they went in obedience to that divine order, Jesus met and spoke with them.

Think about how you might have responded to the Savior's words. Probably in the same reverential, awestruck way these women did—probably with breathless worship!

After all, dear lover of the Lord, it is on our close walk with Jesus—a walk marked by faithfulness, learning, and obedience; by service, worship, and a faith that overcomes doubt—that the many and various blessings reserved for those who love most, trust most, obey most, and believe most are revealed!

"And are not His sisters here with us?"
MARK 6:3

*M*ary was indeed "blessed...among women" to be Jesus' mother (Luke 1:28). But at least two other women were also blessed. These unnamed women were Jesus' sisters, women who spent their lives near to the incarnate God. We don't usually think much about Jesus' sisters, but today we want to do just that. Imagine all that they must have experienced as they daily beheld Jesus, God in the flesh and Savior of the world! They could...

- *Hear Him teach*...His wonderful words of truth and life.
- *Seek His counsel*...and go and sin no more.
- *Bask in His love*...and learn how to love others.
- *Enjoy His healing touch*...and be restored and refreshed.
- *Listen to His prayers*...as He spoke to His holy Father.
- *Marvel at His faith*...that could move mountains.
- *Observe His miracles*...as He exercised authority over evil.
- *Learn from His sinless behavior*...and follow in His steps.
- *Witness His concern for others*...as He reached out in compassion.
- *Follow Him*...to the end of the age and on to heaven.

Obviously, you are a woman who loves God or you wouldn't be reading a book entitled *Women Who Loved God*. And you probably spend time with Jesus when you read God's Word. In the Scriptures you, too, hear Jesus teach, seek His counsel, bask in His love, enjoy His healing touch, listen to His prayers, marvel at His faith, observe His miracles, learn from His sinless behavior, and witness His concern for others.

But these nine activities become significant and truly life-changing *only* when you have personally decided to follow Jesus. You must desire not only to live your life "near to the heart of God," but also to be in Christ Jesus the Lord (2 Corinthians 5:17). Can you sing, say, and pray today, "I have decided to follow Jesus...no turning back, no turning back"?[4] If so, the first nine activities listed will bring you near to the heart of God, and you'll know rich blessings and deep joy.

*She kept asking Him to
cast the demon out of her daughter.*
Mark 7:26

*A*rtists never depict Christ with His back turned," reports scholar Dr. Herbert Lockyer.[5] Yet today we meet an anguished mother to whom Jesus turned His back.

The Syro-Phoenician woman knew constant anguish as she helplessly watched her daughter suffer from a demon. It's quite likely that this Canaanite woman was wondering what to do, where to go, and how to find help when Jesus arrived in her heathen, Baal-worshiping region. She had heard of Jesus, His kindness, and His powerful miracles. Perhaps her heart leaped as she thought, "I know! Jesus can help!"

Humbling herself before the Mighty God, this dear woman fell at Jesus' feet and asked Him politely and respectfully to cast the demon out of her young daughter.

Jesus' response? NO!

This mother kept asking, begging again and again.

Jesus' response? NO! "It is not good to take the children [of Israel]'s bread and throw it to the little dogs [the Gentiles]."

She tried again: "Yes, Lord, yet even the little dogs under the table eat from the children's crumbs."

Jesus' response? YES! "For this saying go your way; the demon has gone out of your daughter." And when she arrived home, the demon had indeed left her daughter—just as Jesus had said. There was no physical touch. No laying on of hands. No spittle mixed with dirt. No drama. No calling down of fire. No casting out of any demon. No face-to-face showdown. Only a few words spoken from a distance, but they were spoken by the very breath of God. At the same time that Jesus' words offered peace, comfort, and assurance to the mother, they wrenched the young girl free from the vile demon's control.

Note three lessons for us here as we seek to love God even more: *First,* we must have enough faith in God to boldly ask—and ask again…and again…and again—for what we need. *Second,* we must believe that Jesus can help us. *Third,* we must have enough faith to boldly trust in the power and efficiency of the Word of God—even before we see its results. We need to be like this dear Syro-Phoenician woman and place in God our bold and trusting faith.

A woman came having an alabaster flask of very costly oil…
[and] she broke the flask and poured it on His head.
MARK 14:3

*E*very woman who loves God desires the ornament that is precious in His sight: a gentle and quiet spirit (1 Peter 3:4). Such a spirit has been aptly described as "the silent preaching of a lovely life."[6] Let's see how this ornament glittered in the life of Mary of Bethany.

Her emotion—In this scene, the heart of Mary, a sister of Lazarus, is overflowing with joy and love for the Savior who had raised her brother from the dead. Imagine! Her beloved Lazarus, who was dead, was alive again! Mary must somehow demonstrate her gratitude to Jesus for this miracle. But how?

Her devotion—The greater the gift received, the greater the challenge of sufficiently expressing thanks. Mary chose the most costly gift she could give: the contents of an alabaster flask. This graceful, long-necked bottle made of precious marble contained fragrant oil worth a year's wages. In her devotion, though, Mary thought nothing of breaking the bottle's neck and pouring the ointment on her Master's head.

A commotion—Mary probably never dreamed that her expression of thanksgiving and worship would be criticized, yet censure came. But as she silently poured out both her devotion and her ointment, she heard the voice of God Himself rebuke her accusers: "Let her alone….She has done a good work for Me."

Pouring out the ointment of her worship revealed in Mary the ornament of a gentle and quiet spirit as she said nothing and did nothing in her defense. Hers was not an argumentative, combative, or defensive spirit. Instead we see only the beauty of her gentle and quiet spirit—the silent preaching of her lovely life of devotion to her Lord.

Dear sister, there is no place for defensiveness in a woman who loves God. After all, God Himself has promised to "tread down our enemies" (Psalm 60:12)! Should you ever be criticized for your acts of devotion, follow Mary's example. Let the ornament of a gentle and quiet spirit speak volumes.

His wife was of the daughters of Aaron,
and her name was Elizabeth.
LUKE 1:5

*T*oday we meet Elizabeth, a woman blessed by God with a heritage of kinsmen who loved God. Not only was Elizabeth from the priestly line of Aaron (Exodus 6:23), but she was married to Zacharias, himself a priest. Don't you thank the Lord that the ancestors of both members of this dear couple were faithful to train them in godliness? Training one's children to love and serve the Lord is a parent's primary responsibility.

No wonder, then, that some time ago an unnamed saint wrote "Ten Reasons for a Family Altar,"[7] a phrase referring to family devotional time. For the next several days, we'll look at the life of Elizabeth and see how her family heritage and the truths about God that were passed on to her around "the family altar" prepared and equipped her to walk bravely through a difficult and pain-filled life.

> *Reason #1 for a Devotional Time*—"It will send you forth to your daily task with cheerful heart, stronger for the work and truer to duty, and determined in whatever is done therein to glorify God."

Jumping ahead in Elizabeth's life story, we see that she passed the age of childbearing...and never had a child. That statement points to decades of marriage under the dark cloud of barrenness in a culture that considered childlessness both a calamity and God's judgment for sin.

How did Elizabeth keep going? Perhaps her faithfulness to a devotional time with her God exposed her to empowering truths about Him—truths which fortified her for the day-in, day-out reality of her childless life. Only regular time with the Lord could have given her a cheerful heart, strength for her work, and the determination to glorify God in all she did.

Do you have a daily devotional time? If not, begin today! See that you spend time each day being quiet before the Lord, studying His Word, and praying. Worship Him. Look to Him for strength for the day. And if you have children, gather them daily to pray and hear God's sacred Word. This daily practice will help your children stand strong in the Lord and His truth, seeking to glorify God in all they do.

*And they were both righteous before God, walking
in all the commandments and ordinances of the Lord blameless.*
LUKE 1:6

$\mathcal{C}$onsider God's portrait of Elizabeth and Zacharias. These dear people of God were blessed recipients of a godly, priestly heritage, but they were nevertheless ordained to walk down a difficult road. You see, they had no children—no little ones to love, no grandchildren to cherish, no one with whom to share their heritage of faith, no offspring to carry forth the family name.

Despite this painful fact in a time when childlessness was considered a sign of God's judgment for sin, Luke tells us in no uncertain terms that Elizabeth and Zacharias "were both righteous before God, walking in all the commandments and ordinances of the Lord blameless."

- *Righteous*—Elizabeth and her husband followed God's law in the most technical sense of strict legal observance.

- *Obedient*—Elizabeth walked alongside her husband in all the Lord's commandments (moral obedience) and ordinances (ceremonial obedience).

- *Blameless*—Elizabeth and Zacharias lived lives that were pleasing to God. Outwardly obedient to the Law of Moses, they were also inwardly obedient to the Lord.

But still they suffered—and aren't you glad God tells us about that suffering? Elizabeth shows us the way to love God and follow hard after Him even when life is hard! What contributed to her faith and faithfulness? Perhaps—and probably—a daily devotional time.

Reason #2 for a Devotional Time—"It will make you conscious throughout the day of the attending presence of the unseen Divine One, who will bring you through more than [a] conqueror."

Throughout the day, moment-by-moment awareness of God's unfailing presence with you will enable you to bear every cross and face every crucible as far more than a conqueror!

Dear one, there is no other way to endure difficult times *and* remain righteous, obedient, and blameless but to visit with the Lord and look to the Divine One...daily, diligently, and devoutly. Seek Him now! Experience what it is to be, in Christ, more than a conqueror as you face life's challenges and hardships.

They had no child, because Elizabeth was barren,
and they were both well advanced in years.
LUKE 1:7

$\mathscr{T}$he childlessness that Elizabeth and her husband knew may not sound too troublesome to us in a time when many couples choose not to have children. But in Elizabeth's day, the Jewish rabbis believed that seven kinds of people were to be excommunicated from God. Their list began with these searing words: "A Jew who has no wife, or a Jew who has a wife and who has no child." Besides being a great stigma in the Jewish culture, having no children was even valid grounds for divorce.

While a husband could divorce a barren wife, there was a weight much heavier than the fear of divorce in the heart of a woman who had no children. You see, every Hebrew woman hoped to bear the long-awaited Messiah. As a faithful, righteous, and obedient Jew, surely Elizabeth had also dreamed of being so privileged. Sadly, however, the flame on Elizabeth's candle of hope died as her childbearing years flickered out.

How does one cope with discouragement, disappointment, adversity, and blighted hopes, dear pilgrim? By spending time with God. *Elizabeth* means "God is my oath" or "a worshiper of God." Don't you think she looked to Him for strength for each day? And so must you!

> *Reason #3 for a Devotional Time*—"It will bring you strength to meet the discouragements, the disappointments, the unexpected adversities, and sometimes the blighted hopes that may fall to your lot."

A woman who loves God looks not to the day's problems, but to the power of her God to assist her with those problems! Only a quiet visit with God gives you strength for today, strength to face the discouragements, the disappointments, the unexpected adversities, and the blighted hopes that may sometimes fall to your lot. The light received from the Lord each new day fuels our love relationship with Him, keeps the flame of our hope burning, and kindles strength for one more day, whatever it may hold.

So, like Elizabeth, cling to God, whatever your circumstances. And cling to His promise: "Be strong and of good courage; do not be afraid, nor be dismayed, for the LORD your God is with you wherever [and through whatever!] you go" (Joshua 1:9).

Now after those days his wife Elizabeth conceived;
and she hid herself five months....
LUKE 1:24

*I*t was a miracle! No, it was many miracles!

First Miracle—As Elizabeth's husband, Zacharias, performed his priestly duty at the temple, a glorious messenger of the Lord suddenly appeared to him. "Your prayer is heard," he announced, "and your wife Elizabeth will bear you a son." The good news continued: "And you will have joy and gladness, and many will rejoice at his birth. For he will be great in the sight of the Lord, and...will also go before Him in the spirit and power of Elijah."

Second Miracle—Unfortunately, Zacharias questioned the angel's glad tidings and was struck dumb for his unbelief.

Third Miracle—Just as the angelic visitor had predicted, Elizabeth did conceive despite her old age! What bright hope for tomorrow!

How did Elizabeth respond to the miracle of pregnancy? Did she boast? Did she parade around town, spreading the news? Did she raise her hand and "share" at the local prayer-'n'-share group? No. Elizabeth chose to stay out of sight, nestled quietly near the Lord she loved, for a full five months. Why?

- *She was joyful!*—A baby was on the way! And this baby would be the forerunner of the Messiah, who was also on the way!

- *She was grateful!*—She may have spent a good deal of those many months at home bowed in thanksgiving before the Lord.

- *She was realistic!*—The expected child was to play a mighty part in the history of God's people, and the responsibility of training him in godliness demanded serious and prayerful preparation on her part.

Do you go to the Lord with not only your sorrows, but also with your joys, your gratitude, your responsibilities, and your bright hopes for your tomorrows?

Reason #4 for a Devotional Life—"It will sweeten home life and enrich home relationships as nothing else can do."

God will fill you anew with His love and hope, peace and strength, the fruit of His Spirit, when you spend time with Him—and your home life and family relationships will be sweetly blessed.

The virgin's name was Mary.
LUKE 1:27

*Y*esterday we celebrated with Zacharias and Elizabeth that the Messiah, the Savior of the world, was on His way! At long last, 400 years after the last prophecy concerning His arrival, the blessed event was about to happen!

But exactly *how* would He arrive? The answer, in a word, is *Mary*. Little is known about this woman so richly blessed by God to bring His Son into the world. The Bible reports that she was a virgin from the city of Nazareth, of the tribe of Judah, of the royal line of David, and that she was engaged to Joseph. Let's allow the culture of Mary's day to fill in some of the details of her life.

Parents—Although Mary's parents are never mentioned, we can believe, based on Mary's character and knowledge of God's Word, that she came from a godly home of devout Jews.

Training—As they grew up, girls were trained not only in household tasks, but also in the things of the Lord. It is evident in the richness of her praise-filled "Magnificat" (verses 47-55) that Mary knew the Scriptures well and had hidden portions of God's Word in her young heart.

Engagement—Mary was engaged to Joseph in an era when betrothal was binding. The engagement, made official by a signed, written document of marriage, came at least one year before the wedding.

Age—Most Israelite boys married by their late teens, but women wed even earlier. The rabbis, however, had set the minimum age for marriage at 12 for girls.[8] Mary was most likely a young adolescent.

Although she was probably young and, from all appearances, poor, Mary had something priceless on the inside: She was a woman who loved God deeply, obediently, supremely, and passionately. Is it any wonder, then, that God chose this woman to bring His Son into the world?

With God, it's always what's inside that counts! When He shines His holy light into the corners of your heart, what does He discover there? Make it your heart's primary desire to nurture a deep, obedient, supreme, passionate love for God! Such love is a priceless and eternal treasure.

*"Do not be afraid, Mary,
for you have found favor with God."*
LUKE 1:30

*W*hat kind of woman did God choose to be the mother of His only Son, the mother of our Lord Jesus? The Bible tells us that Mary was...

- *Young*—She was unseasoned, inexperienced, unaccomplished, and unmarried. She had never been a mother.
- *Poor*—She possessed no fortune, no wealth, and no family inheritance.
- *Unknown*—She boasted no fame or social status; she was unknown. No one had ever heard of her father or mother—or her. Nothing is said about her physical appearance or beauty.

No one would choose Mary to be the mother of God's Son—except God! Despite what she lacked in the world's eyes, God sent His angel Gabriel to this poor, humble teenage girl.

Can you imagine the scene? Mary herself could hardly believe her eyes! Imagine what this angelic messenger from God looked like! But more startling was the announcement Mary heard. She could hardly believe her ears either as this magnificent creature uttered, "Rejoice, highly favored one, the Lord is with you; blessed are you among women!...You have found favor with God."

When the Lord went looking for a woman to bless as mother to His Son, He searched for a woman who loved God. From the world's perspective, Mary seemed completely *un*fit, *un*usable for any task, and you may often feel that way. You may feel that you are no one special, that you are deficient in areas that the world deems essential, that you need more education, better clothes, a better resumé, a better pedigree—the list goes on. But if you love God—if you seek after Him in your heart—you'll find favor with Him and He will use you.

Do you want to do extraordinary things for God? Then start by simply loving and obeying Him. Her love for God qualified Mary to be used by God. She was poor, young, and unknown, but she possessed a faith which was pleasing in God's sight, so she found favor with Him. Beloved, when you love God enough to pay the high price of obedience, then you, too, will be highly favored by Him. Just imagine—and pray about—how He might use you!

Then Mary said to the angel, "How can this be?"
Luke 1:34

The sun rose that morning just as it had risen every day of her life. As she considered her list of chores, she found no hint that on this day her life would be transformed and transported from the mundane to the realm of the mysterious. But something happened that day which changed everything—forever.

Seconds after it happened, gone were any hopes of a quiet life. Gone were the comfort and safety that come with a predictable routine. Gone was the peaceful existence she had known—the existence which had led her to expect a simple and unremarkable future in Nazareth.

When the angel Gabriel appeared before young Mary, the words he spoke to her completely changed her life. Nothing would ever be the same for Mary, for God had chosen her to be the mother of His Son. She would bring into the world its Savior, Lord, and King. Nothing could ever be the same for Mary....

All women who love God can learn much from Mary about how to handle the turning points of life. We see in the Gospel of Luke that, at this major turning point in her life, Mary humbly accepted the news from Gabriel that she would bear God's Son. Notice her initial response—"How can this be, since I am a virgin?" (NASB). This perfectly natural question received an answer that pointed to the supernatural: "The Holy Spirit will come upon you, and the power of the Highest will overshadow you; therefore, also, that Holy One who is to be born will be called the Son of God." The birth would be a miracle, and that was all the explanation Mary got.

Perhaps you, too, dear lover of the Lord, can point to a day in your life that changed everything for you—a day after which nothing was ever the same, perhaps a day when dark clouds hid the sun. Such turning points in life can shake us to the core. Such turning points can also send us to God, His Word, and His promises...and to the acceptance of the fact that full understanding of the "how" and any "whys" lies in the realm of God.[9]

"Behold the maidservant of the Lord!"
LUKE 1:38

*H*asn't it been inspiring these past few days to be armchair observers of a young maiden's encounter with Gabriel, the mighty messenger of God? First we noted what kind of woman Mary was: a woman of character and a virgin. Then we considered the challenge she faced: being the mother of Jesus, God's own Son. Finally we listened to her careful and reverent question, spoken in a whisper: "How can this be?"

Two clues found in the Scriptures (one today and another tomorrow) help us understand how Mary was able to put her faith in her God at this life-changing moment.

> *Clue #1: The Heart of a Handmaiden*—After God's messenger told Mary her part in God's glorious plan, her first words were "Behold the maidservant of the Lord!"

In the Bible, *maidservant* or *handmaid* refers to a female slave whose will was not her own. Instead, she was obligated to perform her master's will without question or delay. A handmaiden would sit silently, watching for hand signals from her mistress (Psalm 123:2), which she would obey without question or hesitation.

Clearly, Mary had cultivated the heart of a handmaiden and a devoted attentiveness to her Lord. No longer regarding her will as her own and instead considering herself as having no personal rights, she was wholly committed to her God. Her one purpose in life was to obey her Master's will.

So that day in Nazareth when God moved His hand and signaled His will, His devoted young handmaiden noticed and responded. A model for every woman who loves God, Mary accepted God's will for her life. Whatever God wanted, this humble handmaiden was willing to do, even though obedience meant that everything in her life changed—forever.

Spend some time in prayer. Ask God to help you let go of those circumstances of your life that you don't understand…and to embrace His good, acceptable, and perfect will for you (Romans 12:2). Thank Him for what He is teaching you through the life of Mary. Ask Him to continue to teach you to love—and trust—Him even more and to grow in you the heart of a handmaiden.

> *"Let it be to me according to your word."*
> Luke 1:38

Yesterday we marveled at the remarkable heart of servanthood which Mary exhibited as God revealed His extraordinary plan to her. Today we note another amazing characteristic of the young Mary who loved our God so very much:

> *Clue #2: An Attitude of Acceptance*—Having acknowledged herself as "the maidservant of the Lord," Mary then said to God's representative, "Let it be to me according to your word."

When God spoke through Gabriel and told Mary that she had been chosen to be the mother of Jesus, she willingly accepted God's plan for her, and her life changed completely. God's choice meant that Mary would be pregnant before she was married and therefore branded a fornicator (John 8:41). God's choice meant trouble with her husband-to-be, trouble at home, trouble in Nazareth, and trouble among the children she would one day have. His choice meant a life of tension as she and her baby were hunted down, as she fled from country to country, and as her firstborn Son caused violent reactions in the hearts of the people He met. And God's choice meant that Mary's soul would be pierced with great sorrow (Luke 2:35) as she followed her son on His path of pain to the foot of the cross (John 19:25). Yet when the angel appeared with his news, Mary's attitude of acceptance was clear: "Let it be to me according to your word."

Do you wonder why Mary was able to accept God's radical plan for her life? Mary's own words answer that question. She saw herself as God's handmaiden and, as such, accepted His will for her life. Furthermore, Mary knew her heavenly Father well enough to trust Him, to rest in His love for her, and to accept what He ordained for her life.

And you, dear friend? Is yours an attitude of acceptance? Prayerfully consider this checklist:

✓ How do you generally handle shocking news or unfair circumstances?

✓ What keeps you from replying to the events of life with "let it be to me according to your word"?

✓ What could you do to learn more about the character of our trustworthy God?

✓ What step toward that goal will you take today?

And [Mary] entered the house
of Zacharias and greeted Elizabeth.
LUKE 1:40

*T*oday we see God weaving together the lives of two women who loved Him: Mary so young and Elizabeth so old. Both women were miraculously pregnant—Elizabeth with the one who would announce the coming of Jesus, and Mary with the Lord Himself. Truly, the women's friendship illustrates God's design that His older women encourage younger ones in just such a May-December relationship (Titus 2:3-5).

Two women who loved God. Two pregnancies. Two miracles! And oh, what sweet fellowship these two lovers of the Lord enjoyed in Elizabeth's home, showing us yet another blessing enjoyed in the household that regularly spends time with the Lord [begun September 17]:

> *Reason #5 for a Devotional Time*—"It will exert a helpful, hallowed influence over those who may at any time be guests within your home."

Certainly such "a helpful, hallowed influence" greeted young Mary as she crossed the threshold into Elizabeth's warm and welcoming home. And as she entered, the give-and-take of blessing and encouragement, of assurance and edification, of praying and sharing, of *koinonia* and godly fellowship, began. Blessed, indeed, was the hallowed influence of Elizabeth's home on her young guest!

And you, precious sister to this twosome? Do you realize that the moments you spend bent over God's Word and kneeling in devoted prayer are a holy time of preparation not only for yourself, but for ministry to others, for ministry within your home? As Ray and Anne Ortlund have rightly observed, "The greater the proportion of your day—of your life— spent hidden in quiet, in reflection, in prayer, [in study,] in scheduling, in preparation, the greater will be the effectiveness, the impact, the power, of the part of your life that shows."[10] The effectiveness of your ministry to people will be in direct proportion to the time you spend away from people and with God in a quiet time of preparation.

Are you a May—a young woman whose love for God is growing? Ask God to lead you to someone older who can fan the flame of your growing love. Or are you a December—a woman who has loving guidance to offer? Seek out those who need your godly influence in their lives.

And it happened, when Elizabeth heard the greeting of Mary...
Elizabeth was filled with the Holy Spirit.
LUKE 1:41

*W*hat a joyous scene of exultant worship is painted here in the opening chapter of Luke! Elizabeth, a woman well past the age of child-bearing, is expecting a baby. But rather than shouting her good news from her rooftop, Elizabeth chose instead to hide herself for five months to wonder over this wonder.

What do you, dear reader, think Elizabeth did there, huddled alone at home? Don't you suspect that she lingered in worship before God, joyfully exalting Him who is the Giver of all good gifts and the Source of every blessing? In such secluded moments of adoration, Elizabeth, a woman who loved God, exemplified yet another reason for solitary spiritual preparation at home with the Lord:

> *Reason #6 for a Devotional Time*—"We honor Him who is the giver of all good and the source of all blessings."

The lovely Elizabeth sought the Lord in the seclusion of her home, pri-vately praising Him that the Messiah was on the way and thanking Him for her baby who was destined to prepare God's people for the Christ's coming.

It was into such a godly environment that Elizabeth's cousin, the also-expectant Mary, arrived, possibly wondering if the events of the past few days of her young life were real. As Mary entered, Elizabeth revealed an extraordi-nary understanding of the situation. She greeted Mary with utmost joy and not a hint of skepticism about the working of the Lord. As the babe in her womb leaped for joy in response to the Holy One in Mary's, Elizabeth under-stood the response of her unborn child and acknowledged the great impor-tance of the Christ Child whom Mary carried. The illuminating work of God's Spirit in Elizabeth's carefully prepared heart led to discernment, insight, and understanding about God's will. Her quiet time alone with her God enabled her to believe in His amazing plan...and to rejoice!

Surely you, too, desire to love God more deeply. Then seek the sanctity of solitude and allow God to open your eyes that you may behold won-drous things from His law (Psalm 119:18) and His working in your life. Such time alone with your heavenly Father does indeed honor Him, the Source of all the blessings you know.

Then she spoke out…and said,
"Blessed are you among women,
and blessed is the fruit of your womb!"
LUKE 1:42

*T*oday we'll consider more details of the Spirit-empowered encounter of Mary and Elizabeth, the electric scene we first looked at yesterday. When these two women who loved God came together, they offered from their hearts "blessing and glory and wisdom, thanksgiving and honor and power and might…to our God forever and ever" (Revelation 7:12)! Consider the scene….

Both Mary and Elizabeth are filled with the Spirit of God, and each is expecting a baby whose role is central to God's eternal plan for His people. So it's no surprise that, at this moment, the souls of both are drawn upward in worship of the Almighty. In the shelter of Elizabeth's home, these two cousins in the flesh and sisters in the Lord commune with their God, drawing much-needed strength for today and bright hope for tomorrow from Him as well as from one another. Imagine the joy as they share in their adoration of the omnipotent God. Consider the rich sisterhood in the Lord they share and how that is enhanced by God's visible work in their lives. Note, too, the sweet ministry they offer to one another in the quiet retreat of Elizabeth's home.

Sounds like a lovely moment, a sweet relationship, a tender time, doesn't it? But remember what awaited each of these lovely women who loved the God who led them. Church history suggests that Elizabeth would soon see the death of her husband, and she would soon follow him, enjoying only a brief taste of motherhood. And we know that Mary's soul would be pierced through with sorrow as her precious Jesus walked the path to Calvary's rugged cross.

Do you have such a Mary or Elizabeth who is a friend in Christ? More importantly, *are you* such a friend to others? The Christian art of encouragement is both a command to be obeyed and a gift God graciously gives to His people. As we who are God's pilgrims walk through treacherous valleys and clouded byways, we are to strengthen and be strengthened by one another in the Lord.

And Mary said: "My soul magnifies the Lord."
Luke 1:46

*J*esus Himself once said, "A good man out of the good treasure of his heart brings forth good...for out of the abundance of the heart his mouth speaks" (Luke 6:45). The surest test of a heart is indeed the caliber of its speech—the quality of the words which issue forth from it.

Today God allows us to see through her words the condition of Mary's heart. As she arrived at Elizabeth's residence, this young woman—who ponders things in her heart and, in biblical accounts, rarely speaks (Luke 2:19)—opened her mouth and spoke from the abundance of her heart.

And what issued forth were the rich words of praise in Luke 1:45-55, a song known as the "Magnificat." "My soul magnifies the Lord," Mary begins, and the inspired words which follow contain 15 quotations from the Old Testament. As one author has observed, the number of Scriptures quoted in the "Magnificat" shows that "Mary knew God, through the books of Moses, the Psalms and the writings of the prophets. She had a deep reverence for the Lord God in her heart because she knew what He had done in the history of her people."[11]

Clearly, Mary had tuned her heartstrings to the heart and the Word of God! Indeed, her heart was saturated with the Word of God. Knowing God and knowing about His mercy, His provision, and His faithfulness to her ancestors, Mary sang. What was the content of her heart song? It was...

- *A song of joy* characterized by gladness and celebration.

- *A song of substance* drawn from the Scriptures.

- *A song from the past* reflecting Hannah's song (1 Samuel 2).

- *A song for today* since God is the same yesterday and today.

- *A song for eternity* because God's Word—where the song is recorded—will stand forever!

Knowing God and recognizing His infinite power enables you to join with Mary in her chorus of praise. Why not make Mary's solo a duet? Spend a golden minute now reading her beautiful and joyful words. Then add your voice to her sweet melody and echo her praise: "My soul magnifies the Lord!"

"My spirit has rejoiced in God my Savior."
LUKE 1:47

A testimony is an outpouring of gratitude to God for all that He has done. As we begin today to plumb the depths of Mary's testimony and savor the richness of her lovely "Magnificat," we can't help but notice that the mother of our Savior begins where every testimony begins: in praise to God for salvation. You see, Mary's little baby Jesus was the long-awaited Savior. He would take away the sins of the world—including the sins of Mary, His mother! Therefore, this cascading song of her heart begins, "My spirit has rejoiced in God my Savior."

Mary needed a Savior, and she freely acknowledged that fact. She recognized that her only hope for salvation was the divine grace of God revealed in His Son, her Messiah.

Perhaps you are wondering, "Why do I need a Savior?" Consider all that Jesus the Christ, the Savior God sent, offers you and me. He:

> **S** ubstitutes His sinless life for our sinful one (2 Corinthians 5:21);
>
> **A** ssures us of eternal life (John 10:28, 29);
>
> **V** anquishes Satan's hold on our life (2 Timothy 2:26);
>
> **I** nitiates us into the family of God (Galatians 4:4-6);
>
> **O** verthrows the power of sin (Romans 6:1-10); and
>
> **R** econciles us to a holy God (2 Corinthians 5:19).

Are you saved? Do you enjoy in Jesus Christ all that the word *Savior* represents: the forgiveness of sin, the assurance of heaven, freedom from Satan's power, fellowship with the saints, and a relationship with God through His Son? If not, name Jesus your Savior right now! Pray, "Forgive my sins! Come into my heart, Lord Jesus!" You can begin your walk with the Savior today.

Then, whether you have belonged to the Savior for a minute or a lifetime, pause right now. Pray and thank God for the truths touched upon in the above acrostic. Sing and shout, "Hallelujah, what a Savior!"

> *"For He who is mighty*
> *has done great things for me."*
> Luke 1:49

Worship, or the act of paying divine honors to a deity, "is as old as humanity. It [is]…a necessity of the human soul as native to it as the consciousness of God itself, which impels it to testify by word and act its love and gratitude to the Author of life and the Giver of all good."[1]

And worshiping was exactly what Mary, the mother of our Savior, was doing 20 centuries ago when she spoke her famous "Magnificat." Her full heart offered words of love and gratitude to the Author of life and Giver of all good things for the great works He had done and now was doing for His people and for her.

Do you ever wonder how to express your appreciation to your Savior? He has done so much for us, His beloved children. We were lost, and He found us. We were spiritually blind, but now we see. We were dead in our trespasses and sins, and He has made us alive (Ephesians 2:1). He has called us out of darkness into His marvelous light (1 Peter 2:9). And He has given us sufficiency in all things (2 Corinthians 9:8), blessed us with all spiritual blessings (Ephesians 1:3), and opened the door to abundant life in Him (John 10:10).

So why not do as Mary did and fall before Him now in praise and worship? Remember and name specifically the many awesome things God has done for you, dear woman who loves Him and is loved by Him.

Also think about what acts of worship you can offer Him today and every day—acts that befit such a mighty, protecting, saving, and loving Lord. Consider these possible gifts of worship:

Time—in His Word, in service, in prayer.

Money—given not for a tax deduction or a cause, but given solely out of love for God.

Faith—for the future, to offer a sacrifice, or to give extravagantly.

Witnessing—to those who know Him not.

Praise—to Him for all to hear, praise for what He has done for you.

Oh, worship now! Extravagantly! Loudly! Sincerely! For He who is mighty has done great things for *you!*

"Holy is His name."
LUKE 1:49

*D*o you long to be a woman of great faith? Then plan to spend your life filling your heart and mind with the Word of God, for its truth is the sure foundation for a faith that pleases God. That Mary, Jesus' mother, had such a heart is obvious in her hymn of faith. Her words reveal a heart filled to overflowing with the Old Testament law, the psalms, the prophets, and the prayers of other believers. When this young woman spoke of God, she spoke of His nature, His character, and His attributes, often using the words of those who had gone before her:

- *God's holiness*—"Holy is His name!" (verse 49)—God is wholly pure and totally "other," set apart from sinful, self-centered human beings. In Jesus, God revealed His holiness.

- *God's mercy*—"His mercy is on those who fear Him from generation to generation" (verse 50)—Behold the patience and the mercy of the Lord! In Jesus, God extended His mercy to us in the act of salvation, His Son's death on the cross for our sin.

- *God's power*—"He has shown strength with His arm; He has scattered the proud in the imagination of their hearts. He has put down the mighty from their thrones, and exalted the lowly" (verses 51, 52)—Stand in awe of God's power! In Jesus, the proud and mighty are put down, while those who in the world's eyes are of low degree, the poor and the humble, are exalted.

- *God's goodness*—"He has filled the hungry with good things, and the rich He has sent away empty" (verse 53)—God is good, and Jesus' life and teachings reflect that goodness. He taught that God is kind even to the unthankful and evil (Luke 6:35).

- *God's faithfulness*—"He has helped His servant Israel, in remembrance of His mercy, as He spoke to our fathers, to Abraham and to his seed forever" (verses 54,55)—God is eternally faithful to His Word and to His chosen people. In Jesus, God sent the Redeemer He had promised to Abraham and to us, Abraham's seed.

Dear sister, get to know these things about God—and more!—by personally studying His Word, the foundation for faith.

Now Elizabeth's full time came...
and she brought forth a son.
LUKE 1:57

We saw two days ago that He who is mighty performs great things for those who love Him, for Mary and for you. That same mighty God accomplished great things for Elizabeth, too. Leading off her "great things" list was a miraculous pregnancy in her old age and the delivery of her son, John the Baptist. "When her neighbors and relatives heard how the Lord had shown great mercy to her, they rejoiced with her."

It's hard for us to imagine Elizabeth's complete and utter joy at God's goodness to her. She had been so long without a child, and yet—miracle of miracles—God chose her to bear John, the forerunner of the Lord! Her little baby would grow up to be great in the sight of the Lord, to be filled with the Holy Spirit, to turn the hearts of many in Israel to the Lord, and to make ready a people prepared to receive the Messiah. The blazing light of God's goodness made many decades of darkness fade into a distant memory.

- Do you think about the great things God has done for you? Verse 24 tells us that Elizabeth hid herself for five months to contemplate God's goodness in her life.

- If you are a mother, do you consider that role to be one of life's greatest blessings? And do your children bring you great joy? When John was born, his mother's heart was filled with overflowing joy. Elizabeth relished the thought of—at long last—being a mother!

- Do you rejoice with others over the great things God does in their lives? Elizabeth's neighbors gathered to rejoice with her over her newborn. The Bible teaches that "love does not envy" (1 Corinthians 13:4) and calls us to "rejoice with those who rejoice" (Romans 12:15).

- Do you remain faithful to God and choose to trust in His goodness even in the darkness when you see no sign of His love? In times like that we women who love God are to "walk by faith, not by sight" (2 Corinthians 5:7), choosing to trust in God's redemptive goodness and unfailing love as we wait once again to experience it.

And she brought forth her firstborn Son, and wrapped Him
in swaddling cloths, and laid Him in a manger.
LUKE 2:7

These much-loved words, breathed by God, speak of an event that changed the course of history, the fate of man, and the path of our lives. Yet the path Mary walked to the manger was not an easy one.

Oh, the most wonderful thing that could happen to a young woman happened to Mary. She was chosen by God to bring Jesus, His only Son and His best gift to mankind, into the world. But consider what Mary encountered on that road to the stable:

- Her husband-to-be wanted to quietly divorce her.
- The timing of the Roman tax caused Mary to make a treacherous trip in her final weeks of pregnancy.
- Mary was away from her home—and her family and friends—when it was time to deliver her first child.
- And because there was no room in the town's inn, the bed for Mary's little baby was an animal stall, a manger!

These are hardly the ideal circumstances for childbirth! But Mary's God transformed each one of these potential stumbling blocks into stepping-stones for her:

- Obeying God, Joseph did not divorce Mary, but stayed by her side.
- The timing of the tax meant that Mary was in exactly the right place. The prophecy that Immanuel would be born in Bethlehem was fulfilled (Micah 5:2).
- Mary's family and friends were far away, but her God (and yours) is all-sufficient in all things. He always provides all that we need. He more than adequately stands in as Head of the family of God and is a Friend who sticks closer than any brother or sister, parent or friend.
- When the world closes its doors to us, God is our refuge (Psalm 46:1), and He provides us with His power whenever we are weak or in need (2 Corinthians 12:9,10).

What difficulties, what potential stumbling blocks, line the path of your life? Turn to God and lean on Him. Just as He took care of Mary, your faithful, loving, caring heavenly Father will take care of you as you walk your path of faith!

But Mary kept all these things and pondered them in her heart.
Luke 2:19

*G*ood news! Christ the Savior is born! God wanted this message spread, and He chose a divine means to proclaim the news and an unlikely group to receive it and share it.

On the night of Jesus' birth, God's angels appeared to a group of lowly shepherds. These radiant messengers lighted up the sky with their presence and praise as they heralded the birth of Christ the Lord. Then, wasting no time, the shepherds went to Bethlehem to verify the angels' message. Once they had done so, they broadcast the glad tidings for all to hear. Some who heard the Word of God from the shepherds merely wondered about it, but Mary, Jesus' mother, quietly treasured it in her heart and pondered upon it.

Do you know what it means to *treasure* something in your heart? It means to guard that thing so surely and faithfully that, as a result, you will keep it safely and securely. Mary guarded the treasure of God's truth so closely and faithfully that it became hers, kept within herself, safe within her heart.

And as she treasured the truth, she *pondered* it. Again and again Mary thought through the words and events together, considering how they fit together, comparing them to prophecy, weighing them against what she knew of her God, carrying their message in her heart.

We noted earlier that Mary may have been a woman of few words. Here we see her as a woman who kept the many wonders she saw and heard within her heart, treasuring them because they came from God. As you read about the birth of Jesus in Luke 2, an account probably told to the Gospel writer by Mary herself, aren't you glad that she treasured and pondered the events surrounding the birth of her son, your Savior? That act of treasuring gave us details about our Savior that now we, too, can treasure.

Prayer: O Lord! May Mary's valuable habit of treasuring and pondering Your truth become mine! May I be a woman who loves You *and* loves Your Word. May I use the mind You've given me to think on what is true, to hide that truth in my heart, and to seek to better understand it.

*They brought Him to Jerusalem to present Him to the Lord...
and to offer a sacrifice according to...the law.*
LUKE 2:22,24

God never makes a mistake, and He certainly didn't make one when He chose Mary to be the mother of His Son!

The responsibility of raising Jesus, the Righteous Branch of David, called for righteous parents who followed God's law. As some verses in Luke 2 show, Mary and Joseph clearly met that criterion. Four verses address the temple rituals surrounding Jesus' birth, and in those verses the law of the Lord—and its fulfillment—is mentioned three times:

- Jesus was circumcised exactly eight days after His birth, just as God's law required.

- Mary's purification after childbirth took place exactly 40 days after the birth of her male child, and the prescribed sacrificial offering (a pair of turtledoves) was made, just as God's law required.

- Mary presented Jesus, her firstborn son, to the Lord exactly according to the requirements of God's law.

In Mary we see the kind of woman God delights in—a woman after His own heart, a woman willing to do all His will. While it's true that, because of Jesus Christ's perfect fulfillment of God's law, we live in the age of God's marvelous grace, our obedience and wholehearted commitment to walking in the ways of the Lord are still essential. Are you one who loves God by walking in His ways?

- Do you love others? All of God's law is fulfilled in one word: *love* (Galatians 5:14)!

- Do you confess sin instantly, consistently, and sincerely? Fellowship with God is all the sweeter when we confess our sin immediately and then turn completely away from it (1 John 1:9).

- Are you faithfully training your children in the nurture and admonition of the Lord? God's primary command to parents is to teach and train our children in His truth and His ways (Ephesians 6:4).

Spend time with the Lord now and affirm your desire to be, like Mary, a woman after God's own heart.

*"Yes, a sword will pierce
through your own soul also."*
LUKE 2:35

*N*one of us knows exactly what the future holds, but God allowed Mary a hint about what awaited her: A sword would pierce her soul. True, Mary was highly favored by God and greatly blessed to be the mother of His Son, but this privilege also meant real agony. Her joy would be mingled with sorrow....

It was a day of great bliss when Mary and Joseph took their infant son to the temple to dedicate Him to God. Surely their hopes and dreams soared as they considered His bright future! As if to affirm their thoughts, an old man named Simeon—a devout man of God who worshiped regularly in the temple, waiting expectantly to see the coming of the Lord—took Jesus in his arms and prophesied concerning Jesus' ministry to the world.

But as Simeon finished his blessing, he turned to Mary and said, "A sword will pierce through your own soul." Mary, a woman after God's own heart, would find her heart pierced to its core by what would happen to her son.

We will never fully know the depth or degree of Mary's anguish, but Simeon's choice of words paints a gruesome picture. The word he used for *sword* was the same word found in the Old Testament to describe the giant Goliath's large, broad sword (1 Samuel 17:51). The pain Mary would know when her son was nailed to the cross would be like the pain inflicted by a huge and cruel weapon.

Dear one, God's blessings on another woman are never cause for jealousy or envy. A woman who is blessed by God, who shines for Him and radiates His favor, may tempt us in our sinfulness to respond with scorn, disdain, or pettiness. But be assured that God's great blessing tends to come with a great price. Perhaps that is why the Bible encourages us to highly regard those we may be tempted to envy and to instead...

- Rejoice with those who rejoice (Romans 12:15).
- Esteem highly those who are over you in the Lord (1 Thessalonians 5:12,13).
- Remember to pray for and be sure to obey those who rule over you (Hebrews 13:7,17).

We don't always know the price of God's favor.

> *Now there was one, Anna, a prophetess....*
> LUKE 2:36

So far on our journey through God's sacred Word—a journey of meeting and learning from women who loved God—we've encountered a handful of prophetesses. These women (listed here) were empowered to speak God's Word, bringing light into darkness:

> *Miriam* led the Israelite women in praise when God defeated Pharaoh and his army (Exodus 15:20).
>
> *Deborah* served as a judge in Israel and gave Barak instructions from God that led to victory against Sisera (Judges 4:4-7).
>
> *Huldah* counseled King Josiah regarding the book of the law (2 Kings 22:14).

Today, even as our minds may still be reeling from the prophet Simeon's words to Mary, God once again sends light into darkness—to Mary and to us—through the words of the prophetess Anna. At the very moment Simeon made his somber pronouncement, Anna "gave thanks to the Lord, and spoke of Him to all those who looked for redemption in Jerusalem." Perhaps her words momentarily lifted the dark cloud that had crossed Mary's happy heart with Simeon's warning of the sorrow that lay ahead. Perhaps Anna's words brightened her *own* overcast heart!

Anna's life was touched by darkness. Her own dear husband had died after only seven years of marriage. For the intervening years, 84-year-old Anna had daily lifted up her eyes to the hills and looked for help and redemption from the Lord. On this particular day, the Light of the world entered the temple of the Lord. Mary arrived, carrying the long-awaited Christ Child in her arms—the One who would dispel the world's darkness. No wonder Anna praised and thanked God!

And how gracious of God to use Anna to remind Mary that her own dear son—her Savior, her Lord, and her Master—would bring the brilliance of His light to her needy heart as well. Everyone needs light—the light of God's Word, the light of His promises, and the light of your joyful trust in Him. Won't you share that light with someone today—with someone who walks in darkness?

[She] did not depart from the temple,
but served God with fastings and prayers night and day.
LUKE 2:37

*I*n just a few verses, God gives us all we know about Anna, a godly woman who loved God in her sunset years. We learn that...

> *Anna was a widow.* Having lost her husband after only seven years of marriage, this woman knew sorrow. But she had apparently allowed her suffering to soften her fiber and strengthen her faith. Anna spent the rest of her long life in faithful service to the Lord both night and day.

> *Anna was a senior citizen.* At age 84, Anna still looked for "the deliverance of Jerusalem," for the Messiah, for the Savior, for Jesus! How truly blessed she was when God rewarded her many years of faith by allowing her to see—in the flesh—the Hope of Israel!

How did this joyful event come about? When Mary took young Jesus to the temple according to the requirements of the law, God prompted Simeon to proclaim Jesus' role in history and to prophesy regarding His ministry and Mary's sorrow. On the heels of Simeon's prediction of pain, God prompted Anna to focus once again on the fact that Jesus would fulfill the prophecies and bring redemption to the world.

The life of Anna offers us two important lessons. First, we see the fruit of long-term faith, and faith "is the substance of things hoped for" (Hebrews 11:1). Is your faith ever-burning—never dimming, never cooling, never faltering—as you look to God for the hope of Jesus' Second Coming?

Second, we learn a lesson about encouraging one another. How Anna's joyous outpouring of faith must have sunk deep into Mary's pierced soul! As she held her precious infant and pondered Simeon's warning, Anna's words of encouragement must have been a wave of refreshment, soothing her bruised spirit. Do you seek to lift up, encourage, and restore those who are cast down? To speak a timely word of ever-burning faith in God to those who are weary is indeed a divine art!

[She] did not depart from the temple,
but served God with fastings and prayers night and day.
LUKE 2:37

The apostle Paul spoke for all of us when he so rightly declared that "our outward man is perishing" (2 Corinthians 4:16). We all feel it, sense it, and know it. The body gives way day by day. But in his next breath, Paul offers the secret of enduring such decline: "Yet the inward man is renewed day by day." Hear the eloquent William Barclay on this secret of endurance:

> All through life it must happen that a man's bodily strength fades away, but all through life it ought to happen that a man's soul keeps growing. The sufferings which leave a man with a weakened body may be the very things which strengthen the sinews of his soul. It was the prayer of the poet, "Let me grow lovely growing old." From the physical point of view life may be a slow but inevitable slipping down the slope that leads to death. But from the spiritual point of view life is a climbing up the hill that leads to the presence of God. No man need fear the years, for they bring him nearer, not to death, but to God.[2]

Certainly the prophetess Anna must have been one who grew lovely growing old. At 84 years old and undoubtedly enduring the ailments which age delivers to us all, this dear saint knew how to draw nearer to God: She fasted and prayed continuously.

Anna never ceased to pray. When life looked hopeless (no husband, no children, no apparent means of support), Anna prayed. Day by day, she renewed her mind and her inner person through prayer—prayer regularly accompanied and enhanced by fasting. This daily, continual, faithful contact with God, the Source of all strength, enabled Anna to climb up the hill that leads to His very presence. Indeed, Anna's day-by-day faithfulness was rewarded as she saw God-in-flesh, as she beheld—and held—the baby Jesus, the Lord and Savior come at last!

May you follow in Anna's footsteps and look to the Lord for His renewing strength and grace...day by day.

His parents went to Jerusalem every year
at the Feast of the Passover.
LUKE 2:41

*H*asn't it been inspiring to see how faithfully Mary and Joseph followed God's law? We can learn much from their lives—lessons we can apply in our own hearts and homes! Today, for instance, we fast-forward 12 years and find further evidence of Mary and Joseph's obedience to the law of the Lord.

A Jewish boy became a man at age 12, and God required every adult male to attend the annual Passover celebration. So when He was 12, Jesus joined His parents in worshiping the Lord at Passover. Many wonderful things happened there on the Temple Mount (we'll enjoy those tomorrow), but right now let's consider ways we can ensure that ours—like Mary's—is a family that worships together.

Worship—God calls believers to come together on the first day of the week for worship, and He tells us to be careful not to forsake such assembling together (Acts 20:7; Hebrews 10:25). So a wise and godly woman and mother will do whatever must be done to ensure that she and her family worship together on Sundays. She does exactly what Mary did: She takes her young ones to church!

Observe—God has given the church the foundational rites of baptism and communion (Matthew 28:19; 1 Corinthians 11:23-25). Just as Jesus' parents made sure He observed the Jewish rites and feasts according to God's instructions, we must—for ourselves and for our children—follow the Lord's instructions to us for worship, baptism, and communion.

Celebrate—Does your church mark special seasons of worship like Advent and Lent? Does it celebrate the church anniversary and ministry dedications; revival meetings, and praise and prayer meetings; baby dedications or baptisms; worship services on Thanksgiving Eve, Christmas Eve, Good Friday, and Easter morning? Whatever your church chooses to celebrate, be there! These special times of worship will further your family's dedication to God and His church (and your dedication to your local church) as they sow seeds in the soil of sacred memories!

Every godly mother you meet will tell you that she wishes she had done more during her children's formative years to impress upon their moldable hearts the importance and joy of family life in the church! Begin today... and persevere!

So when they saw Him, they were amazed.
LUKE 2:48

ine verses describe Jesus' journey to Jerusalem and the time He spent there celebrating Passover. Those verses hardly begin to describe all the emotion and insight which resulted from that trip. So much happened!

First, imagine the worship. We can be sure it was glorious and meaningful, especially since it was the first time Jesus could participate!

Then, Jesus was missing from the great company of people traveling home to Nazareth together. Only late in the evening of their first day's journey did Mary and Joseph realize that Jesus was not with either parent or with any family member or friend. We shudder to imagine the fear and even terror Mary must have felt in her heart! Her young son was alone in that crowded, bustling city!

Next, Mary and Joseph hurried back to Jerusalem, looking for Jesus all along the way. Once in the city, Mary and Joseph spent three frantic days searching for their son.

At last, they found Jesus in the temple, sitting among the teachers there and calmly interacting with them.

Then, as any other mother would have, Mary exclaimed, "Son, why have You done this to us? Look, Your father and I have sought You anxiously."

Finally, giving Mary a few more thoughts to ponder in her heart, Jesus spoke the first of His words that are preserved for us: "Why did you seek Me? Did you not know that I must be about My Father's business?"

The result? Mary was amazed—literally "driven out of her senses"—and did not understand.

"Mary, Did You Know?" the title of a contemporary Christian song, echoes Jesus' words to His mother.[3] Didn't she remember what the angel Gabriel had said about Him? Didn't she remember what Elizabeth had said about her unborn child? Didn't she remember what the shepherds had told her, what Simeon had prophesied, what Anna had announced? Didn't she *yet* know?

Do you know Jesus as not merely a baby in a manger, a wise teacher, or a good man, but as God in flesh, the Savior of the world? O, believe it now!

> *Then He went down with them...*
> *and was subject to them.*
> LUKE 2:51

*E*ven though the young Jesus obviously felt "at home" in His Father's house, and even though He was gaining a more complete understanding of His calling and purpose as the Son of God, the Holy Child still needed a mother and a home. As someone has marveled, "Not even to the angels fell such an honor as to the parents of Jesus!"[4] Instead, the high calling of mothering the Master fell to sweet Mary.

So after leaving the religious teachers there in the temple area, Jesus returned to Nazareth with Mary and Joseph. The Scriptures say He "was subject to them": He was obedient while He lived under their authority. So Mary continued raising Jesus, the Son of God. What exactly did Mary give to Messiah?

1. *Mary gave Jesus life,* humanly speaking. Hers was the body that brought God's precious Son into this world.

2. *Mary gave Jesus a home.* The Man of Sorrows—who all too soon would have no place to lay His head, who would make the Mount of Olives his "home away from heaven," and who would spend time at Mary and Martha's house—received from the heart and hands of dear Mary the gift of a home.

3. *Mary gave Jesus training in godliness.* God had carefully selected Mary for the special job of mothering the Master. Surely she who found such favor with the Almighty would model godly virtues in her home and guide those in her care toward a life devoted to Him.

Like Mary, we who have children can give them these same three gifts of life, a home, and training in godliness. Blessed are the offspring raised in such a heaven on earth! Even those of us who have no children can both model godly character and, as the sisters Mary and Martha did for our Lord, give the gift of home to all who enter our doors. Like Mary the mother of Jesus, we have the high calling to give life, a home, and training in godliness as we serve God and His people.

But Simon's wife's mother was sick with a high fever.
LUKE 4:38

- The penalty for bigamy is two mothers-in-law.
- The wife isn't always boss in the American home. Sometimes it's her mother.
- To the average husband, the "blessed event" is when his mother-in-law goes home.
- "Double trouble" is a mother-in-law with a twin sister.

These one-liners make gentle fun of mothers-in-law, but they don't reflect everyone's experience. Consider, for instance, the apostle Peter. He opened his home to his mother-in-law and let the Master know her needs.

One Sabbath, the apostle approached Jesus with the news that his wife's mother was extremely ill with a high fever. Peter asked Jesus to help her. Soon, standing by her bed, Jesus "rebuked the fever, and it left her. And immediately she arose and served them."

This scene, painted for us in only two verses, invites us to consider at least three situations:

1. *Do you have a mother-in-law?* If so, examine your heart. Look for evidence of the kind of generous and gracious spirit Peter showed toward his wife's mother. Ask God to give you a sincere concern for your mother-in-law's well-being. You may even want to go back and review the beautiful relationship Ruth and Naomi enjoyed (see May 19-31). A woman who loves God also loves her mother-in-law!

2. *Are you a mother-in-law?* Peter's mother-in-law was obviously accustomed to loving those in her son-in-law's home by serving them. Are you a generous and gracious giver, seeking to make life a little easier for your family? Ask God to reveal greater ways for you to express your love for your family and your gratitude for the blessing that they are to you.

3. *Do you—or do those you know and love—have any needs?* If so, go to Jesus. God's Son, your Savior, is the Helper. Our compassionate Lord is "touched with the feeling of our infirmities" (Hebrews 4:15,16 KJV) and powerful enough to do something about our weakness and pain.

Your family matters matter to Jesus. So invite Him not only to meet your needs, but also to enable you to love one another with His love.

> *A dead man was being carried out,*
> *the only son of his mother; and she was a widow.*
> LUKE 7:12

*T*oday we meet yet another in the ranks of the sorrowing. She is referred to simply as "the widow of Nain."

This dear woman had already lost her husband, and today we read that she lost her son—her *only* son—as well. Jesus noticed this weeping woman as she followed her son's coffin along its funeral procession. What can a woman who has no husband or son do? How would she survive in this world? To what source of income and means of protection could she look? What could she do in such an apparently hopeless situation?

Jesus—whose own mother was probably a widow by this time—was deeply moved by this widow's painful predicament. So He reached out and touched the coffin of her dear son...and literally gave him back to his mother! We can only imagine the joy both mother and son experienced as God graciously gave each of them new life! Jesus overcame the power of death and revealed His awesome power.

We, too, can know the awesome power of God in our life. Consider, for example, this single truth and promise: "The Lord is my shepherd; I shall not want" (Psalm 23:1). Did you know that the English words "I shall not want" are the translation of the great name of God *Jehovah-Jireh*? Consider its wondrous meaning:

- God is able to foresee the needs of His children.

- God is able to meet the needs of His children.

- God's faithful and loving character demands that He provide for the needs of His children.

- God not only knows and sees what we need, but He provides for these needs as well. The one is connected to the other: God cannot know of a need and not provide. For God, to know *is* to provide!

If you, beloved sister, feel that you, like the humble widow of Nain, lack in any area of life, take heart! God knows your plight, whatever it is. And God acts on your behalf to meet all your true and real needs. O glorify Him now, as those did who witnessed His miraculous provision for the widow of Nain!

*And behold, a woman…who was a sinner…began to wash His
feet with her tears…and anointed them with the fragrant oil.*
LUKE 7:37,38

*D*o you know this simple acrostic that guides the prayer life of many
Christians?

> **A**—Adoration of God
> **C**—Confession of sin
> **T**—Thanksgiving for blessings
> **S**—Supplication for concerns

As we'll see today, it's also an acrostic for a godly life.

In Luke 7 we meet a woman who poured out her devotion to Jesus in a
multitude of ways. She is not identified by name, but God made sure her
love for the Lord is recorded forever in His Word. At a dinner given for
Jesus, this woman was scorned by the host for her many sins. Yet this
"woman…who was a sinner" washed Jesus' feet with her tears, wiped them
with her hair, kissed His feet, and anointed them with fragrant oil. Her
actions follow the pattern of the acrostic:

A—She adored Jesus.

C—A sinner, probably a prostitute, she knew her sins were many,
and she acknowledged and confessed them with true penitence,
heartfelt grief, and genuine remorse.

T—She poured out her thanks to the only One who could—and
did—forgive, cleanse, and change her, the only One who
could—and did—make her whole.

S—Perhaps she put words to her supplication for forgiveness, a gift
she clearly received. Jesus said to her, "Your sins are forgiven."

How can you follow this acrostic for prayer and worship in your own
life? Take time right now to follow this woman's example:

A—Adore the One who opens the life gates to heaven.

C—Confess any sin that would block the kind of relationship with
God you so desire.

T—Thank Jesus for His blood which makes the vilest clean and
washes us whiter than snow.

S—Go before God in humble supplication. What situation in your
life is impossible without God? For what do you need His guidance, His help, His power? Ask Him boldly!

*Certain women…provided for Him
from their substance.*
Luke 8:2,3

When our Lord Jesus walked this earth, these "certain women" who loved Him enjoyed a very special role that is "absolutely unique in the gospels," explains theologian Charles Caldwell Ryrie.[5] They were allowed to minister to the Lord—a role that His male followers and disciples did not have. We more fully appreciate the uniqueness of this role when we realize that the Greek word used here meaning "to serve" appears in the four Gospels only when the ministry being spoken of is ministry being rendered directly to Jesus—and in those cases it is the ministry of either angels or women! What a wondrous honor to serve the Savior!

Exactly who comprised this honored band of faithful feminine followers? The roll call here in the Gospel of Luke includes Mary Magdalene, Joanna, Susanna, and "many others." As Jesus traveled about, He extended divine healing and deliverance to people. These women whom Jesus had healed and delivered then chose to follow Him and support His ministry, giving of their substance and their service.

> *Substance*—By funding Jesus' ministry and supporting Him and His disciples as they preached, these noble women met a very practical need.

> *Service*—Graciously and unobtrusively, these dear women who loved Jesus also saw to His personal comfort and well-being.

Today we serve the Lord by serving His people. As one godly person has noted regarding our service to those who labor for the Lord, "It is not always the person in the foreground who is doing the greatest work. Many a man who occupies a public position could not sustain it for one week without the help of [others]. There is no gift that cannot be used in the service of Christ. Many of His greatest servants are in the background, unseen but essential to His cause."[6]

What can you do to follow the example of these women who loved Jesus, to advance Christ's cause by offering your substance and service? Remember that Jesus said, "Inasmuch as you did it to one of the least of these My brethren, you did it to Me" (Matthew 25:40)!

*Certain women who had been healed
of evil spirits and infirmities—Mary called Magdalene,
out of whom had come seven demons…*
<small>Luke 8:2</small>

*H*ave you heard the saying "the worst first"? Well, dear follower of the Lord, on Luke's roster of those women whom Jesus had healed and delivered, "the worst" is "the first" to be named. We can only imagine the destruction, the pain, the torment, the suffering that seven—*seven!*—demons caused in the tortured life of Mary Magdalene.

But Jesus—God Incarnate, the God not only of compassion but also of power—delivered this desperate, seemingly incurable woman from bondage. The detail "out of whom had come seven demons" and the fact that she was from the town Magdala on the coast of the Sea of Galilee are all we know about her. But we see that, from the moment of her release, she seems to have spent her life following Jesus. Wherever He was, Mary Magdalene could be found in His shadow. She who was delivered from much loved much!

How blessed is our assurance, beloved of the Lord, that the past has no hold on our present or our future! Consider these truths from God's truth—truths which teach us that He replaces a crippling past with a gloriously transformed present and future:

- "Therefore, if anyone is in Christ, he is a new creation; old things have passed away; behold, all things have become new" (2 Corinthians 5:17).

- "It is no longer I who live, but Christ lives in me" (Galatians 2:20).

- "I press on…forgetting those things which are behind and reaching forward to those things which are ahead" (Philippians 3:12,13).

- "Seek those things which are above….Set your mind on things above, not on things on the earth. For you died, and your life is hidden with Christ in God" (Colossians 3:1-3).

Choose one of these passages and hide its freeing truth in your heart and mind. Like Mary Magdalene, you can—in God's power—rise up from your past and press on. You can be like the sheep that follows closest to the Shepherd—in His shadow, enjoying the most intimate fellowship with Him, and partaking of His choicest provision.

> *Certain women who had been healed*
> *of evil spirits and infirmities...*
> *Joanna...and Susanna...*
> LUKE 8:2,3

*H*ow refreshing to marvel over the goodness of the Lord who freed Mary Magdalene from the dark power of seven demons! And now we are privileged to meet two other women whom Jesus touched with His healing hand. They are:

Joanna	*Susanna*
Her name means *Jehovah has shown favor.*	Her name means *a white lily.*
She was the wife of Chuza, the house steward of Herod the Tetrarch.	No husband's name is given.

Both of these women had tasted and seen that the Lord is good (Psalm 34:8). Both had tasted much, both were loved much, and both loved the Lord much!

But how does someone thank God for the miracle of healing? These two women gave their money to Jesus. Evidently they had funds at their disposal which they delighted in giving to Him in support of the ministry by which they had been so blessed. Ponder these principles for giving:

- *Freely*—"Freely you have received, freely give" (Matthew 10:8).

- *Bountifully*—"He who sows bountifully will also reap bountifully" (2 Corinthians 9:6).

- *Cheerfully*—"Let each one give as he purposes in his heart, not grudgingly or of necessity; for God loves a cheerful giver" (2 Corinthians 9:7).

What a good time to consider your personal practice of giving to the Lord's work and to pray about what He would have you do for His kingdom! Ask yourself, "Am I giving freely...bountifully...and cheerfully?...Should I be giving more?...Does my giving reflect my belief that it is impossible to outgive God?"

One final challenge comes our way from the heart of a saint of old who wrote, "I would not like to meet God with a large bank account. That would be a terrible calamity. He expects me to invest it somehow before I die, for Him."[7] Ask God to reveal His greater purposes for your finances, as well as specific ways you can be more generous.

*He had an only daughter about twelve years
of age, and she was dying.*
LUKE 8:42

*A*s we've seen, many women—the widow of Nain, Peter's mother-in-law, Mary Magdalene, Joanna, Susanna, and "many others"—were blessed by many gracious miracles Jesus worked on their behalf. Today we meet a young girl—her parents' only child, not identified by name—who desperately needed the touch of God. But the scene of the miracle involves many people:

- *The young girl's father, Jairus*—A VIP who served as the "president" of the synagogue, Jairus was nevertheless powerless over his daughter's illness and death.

- *Jairus's daughter*—The young girl stood at death's door. Would the crowd that surrounded Jesus and the needs of another keep Him from arriving in time to save her life?

- *People*—As Jairus led the Healer to his house where his precious daughter lay, a crowd of people pressed in and slowed their progress. Then, as Jesus stopped to heal a woman in the crowd, a messenger rushed up to announce that the girl had died. When Jesus finally arrived at Jairus's house, the wailing women had already been hired (as was the custom) and were mourning the girl's death.

We can only imagine the desperate father's various emotions—the fear, the impatience, the fading hope—as he watched the Master's progress be slowed by both the crowd and the needs of another suffering person.

While the assault of the crowd and the need of the hemorrhaging woman caused Jairus and his family twice the pain and twice the tragedy as his daughter's sickness became death, these circumstances afforded our Lord the glorious opportunity to do twice the miracle!

Dear woman of faith, Jesus' miraculous raising of Jairus's daughter from death is about faith—faith when time seems to be running out, faith when circumstances seem to turn against you, faith when Jesus seems slow to respond. Jesus' miraculous raising of Jairus's daughter from death is about faith in the darkness. When every trace of light is extinguished—as it may have seemed to Jairus—do you still believe in the power of God? As Jesus told Jairus, "Only believe."

> *Now a woman…came from behind and*
> *touched the border of His garment.*
> LUKE 8:43,44

*"W*hy not?" she may have thought, spotting Jesus in the throng of people. "But Jairus seems distraught and in a hurry, so I'd better not interrupt. But a simple touch of the Miracle Worker's robe wouldn't slow them down."

So as Jesus passed by on the way to the home of Jairus, the ruler of the synagogue, this diseased but full-of-hope-in-Jesus woman summoned all her courage and faith and put forth her trembling fingers until she felt the garment of God flutter through them.

Instantly two things happened. First, this dear woman noticed that she was healed. After suffering a dozen years from incurable hemorrhaging and after spending all she had on doctors who were unable to help, the flow of blood simply stopped!

And at the same second, Jesus turned and asked, "Who touched Me?"

"How could He have possibly noticed?" she wondered.

The disciples wondered the same thing: "Master, the multitudes crowd around You, yet You say, '*Who touched Me?*'"

But Almighty God had perceived His healing power going out from Him, and He wanted to know who had, in faith, been made well.

Perhaps our sister-in-suffering thought she could quietly return home healed. How much more comfortable if touching the garment of God didn't turn into a big deal! But she knew she couldn't let Jesus' question go unanswered. Shaking, she stepped forth, fell before His feet, and shared her secret for all to hear, telling why she had touched the Master's robe and noting that she had been healed immediately.

What a model for us! Blessed by Jesus' miraculous touch, this dear woman spoke her testimony before many witnesses. She gave God the glory He so richly deserves and received Jesus' benediction—"Daughter, be of good cheer; your faith has made you well. Go in peace."

What wondrous thing has God done for you? Have you publicly given Him the glory? Have you told others of His goodness to you and His power in your life? O shout of His excellencies from the housetop!

He permitted no one to go in except...
the father and mother of the girl.
LUKE 8:51

*T*he multitude of people surrounding Jesus had a multitude of needs. Among them, Jairus, the ruler of the synagogue, needed his 12-year-old daughter healed, and the woman with the issue of blood needed it to stop. Only God Himself could meet such needs, so Jesus, God-in-flesh, did exactly that. He healed the dear woman who now worshiped at His feet. Her 12-year hemorrhage ended. Then He assured Jairus that his daughter who had just died would be restored—if he would "only believe."

That brings us to another dear woman who needed the Lord, and she is the unnamed mother of Jairus's daughter, whose precious child lay at home...dead.

The little girl was so ill that her father had gone to Jesus to beg Him to come to his house and heal his daughter. Left behind, the anxious mother tended to their dying daughter, doing all she could—hoping...praying... waiting....

The minutes of the nursing and waiting continued. Where *was* Jesus? This mother's hope turned to hopelessness as she witnessed her beloved daughter's final breath.

Perhaps this devastated mother sent the messenger to her husband to let him know it was too late, that their only child was gone. Perhaps she also called in the mourners to begin their vigil of sorrow.

Despite the message He had received, in strode the Master, filled with all strength and power and honor and glory and majesty. Jesus dismissed everyone but the girl's parents and His three closest disciples, took the dead child's hand, and spoke three words: "Little girl, arise." In response to the Word of God, her spirit returned and she arose immediately.

Have you known the power of the Word of God in your life, dear one? Have you clung to it as you've hoped and prayed and waited? We are called to believe God's Word regardless of life's events, regardless of seemingly hopeless circumstances, regardless of what appears to be, regardless of timing and events that seem to be all wrong. We are to "look [not] at the things which are seen, but at the things which are not seen....For we walk by faith, not by sight" (2 Corinthians 4:18; 5:7).

A certain woman named Martha welcomed Him into her house.
And she had a sister called Mary.
LUKE 10:38,39

*O*ur world today offers women—even women who love God—pressure from many sources. We never seem to have enough time—pressure! We want to do well as a wife and a parent—pressure! We are called to be good stewards of finances and effective managers of a home—pressure! How do you handle the pressures of life—with peace or panic?

In sisters Mary and Martha, God presents us women with a classic study in opposites when it comes to managing the demands of life. When Jesus went to their home, Martha welcomed Him in for dinner, but she became distracted by all her preparations. Busy in the kitchen, lots of details on her mind, and anxious that everything go well, Martha was a whirlwind of activity.

How did her lack of peace show itself? First of all, Martha was stirring the pot not only in the kitchen, but also in the family room! There she stood, accusing Christ ("Don't you care?") and accusing Mary ("She's left me to serve alone"), complaining about the burden she had assumed. She's bossy, blaming, distracted from what mattered most. And she's yarping—which, you'll notice, is "praying" spelled backwards!

In contrast to this hurricane of female hyperactivity, we find the lovely Mary...

—resting at the Lord's feet while Martha is restless...

—worshiping while Martha worries...

—at peace while Martha's panic level rises...

—sitting while Martha is stewing...

—listening while Martha is lashing out...and

—commended by Jesus while Martha is confronted by Him.

Would an outside observer see Martha or Mary in you as you cope with life's schedules, commitments, and pressure? Are you in turmoil—or are you trusting and at peace? Are you prone to running around in circles—or do you rest in the Lord? Is your relationship with Jesus your first priority—or are you too busy to sit at His feet and enjoy His presence? The woman whose heart and soul are at rest is the woman who knows one theological truth: *Our times are in God's hands.* And this truth makes all the difference when it comes to peace or panic![8]

*And behold, there was a woman who had a spirit of
infirmity eighteen years, and was bent over
and could in no way raise herself up.*
LUKE 13:11

*W*hat a scene—and caught in the middle of it all was a solitary woman. The scene began with Jesus teaching in a synagogue on the Sabbath, and, as He spoke, He spotted her.

- *Malady*—Imagine 18 years of being prisoner to a deforming condition that bowed this woman's back so completely that she could not stand up straight!

- *Mercy*—Our great and compassionate Savior could not let such a tragedy go unaddressed. After first announcing that she was released from her infirmity, Jesus reached forth His healing hands, laid them tenderly—and powerfully—on her back, and made her whole again.

- *Murmuring*—Can you believe that the ruler of the synagogue was indignant? He thought the miracle ought not to have been performed on the Sabbath day!

- *Masterful defense*—Beware the wrath of the Lord! "Hypocrite!" He exclaimed. "Does not each one of you on the Sabbath loose his ox or his donkey from the stall, and lead it away to water it? So ought not this woman, being a daughter of Abraham, whom Satan has bound—think of it—for eighteen years, be loosed from this bond on the Sabbath?" Who could stand against the Lord's reasoning, logic, and gracious interpretation of God's law?

- *Merriment*—Jesus' adversaries hung their heads low after He spoke, but the crowd of people who witnessed this scene rejoiced for the glorious things He was doing among them!

Jesus teaches us many lessons, doesn't He? Here He shows us the wisdom of searching for the spirit of God's love behind the letter of His law. Surely a human being is more important than an animal! Surely a handicapped woman deserved to be released from her physical bondage no matter what day of the week it was! Dear sister, ask God to grace you with a portion of Jesus' divine wisdom, His discernment, and above all, His great heart of mercy. Indeed, every person in need is an opportunity for us to show Jesus' kind of love.

He saw also a certain poor widow putting in two mites.
Luke 21:2

O how we love to sing,

> I surrender all…
> All to Thee I freely give…
> I surrender all![9]

These simple words touch a chord deep within the heart of every woman who loves God and wants to relinquish her all to Him, to fully accept His perfect will, and to live what is called by some "the surrendered life." Today we come face to face with just such a woman—a woman who truly surrendered her all.

As Jesus sat in the temple area, He watched many people deposit their money into the collection boxes. These gifts were for the day-in, day-out operation and upkeep of God's temple. Oh, the rich were there, "casting" in their gifts. But what caught Christ's eye was a certain poor widow quietly putting in two small coins. Omniscience knew how many, and Omniscience knew how much: Her gift was two *lepta*, two of the smallest coins in existence, two of "the thin ones."

But Omniscience knew something else as well. Perhaps clearing His throat before He spoke, He stated to those around Him, "Truly I say to you that this poor widow has put in more than all; for all these out of their abundance have put in offerings for God, but she out of her poverty has put in all the livelihood that she had."

Omniscience has praised this dear widow's sacrificial giving and preserved the account of her gift in His Word. While others gave out of their abundance, this woman of poverty—this woman with few resources for making money but who loved God—gave all that she had!

What might be written about your giving pattern and purposes? Do you give regularly, give freely, and give sacrificially? How much we give of what we have and how we give that gift—these are true measures of our love for God. As Jesus Himself said, "Where your treasure is, there your heart will be also" (Matthew 6:21). Where is your heart?

All His acquaintances, and the women who followed
Him from Galilee, stood at a distance, watching these things.
Luke 23:49

*W*hat was the worst day of your life, dear reader? Perhaps your personal experience with dark and difficult times will help you to relate to the faithful group of women who followed Jesus. And because they followed Him to the end, they were eyewitnesses of the worst day the world has ever known.

The Bible says that the loyal group of ladies who followed Jesus "stood at a distance, watching these things." What exactly were those "things"? What did those who were true friends to Jesus—those who stuck closer than a brother and loved at all times (Proverbs 18:24; 17:17)—witness? Hear the Bible's account of the vile events:

- Jesus was arrested as He prayed in the garden.
- Jesus' closest friends, His disciples, fled, leaving Him to fend for Himself and to die alone.
- Jesus was tried unjustly, sentenced to death, whipped, beaten, spit upon, and scoffed at.
- Jesus was marched through the crowded streets of Jerusalem to the site of His crucifixion.
- Jesus was nailed to a cross alongside two criminals.
- As Jesus hung dying, soldiers gambled for His cloak, mocked Him, sneered at Him, ridiculed Him, and gave Him only vinegar to drink.
- The noonday sky became as dark as night for three hours. The ground shook, rocks split, and the graves of the dead were opened (Matthew 27:52,53).
- After Jesus died, His body was run through with a sword.
- Jesus' body was laid in a stone sepulcher, unprepared for burial.

It's one thing to follow Jesus and be near Him, to quietly sit and listen to His wonderful words of life, to give of your goods to sustain His ministry, to benefit from His miracles, to fix Him a meal and enjoy the pleasure of His company. But it's quite another thing to love God and follow Him faithfully when times are hard. Pray that God will give you the faithfulness that these women who loved God had: a to-the-end faithfulness to your Friend and Savior, a faithfulness to Jesus through good times *and* bad!

And the women who had come with Him
from Galilee followed after, and they observed the tomb
and how His body was laid.
LUKE 23:55

*H*ow is true love measured? In the case of the faithful women who loved and followed Jesus, their great devotion was evident in little things. This band of believing women was limited in what they could do for the Lord of the universe, but on history's darkest day their devotion nevertheless shone brilliantly through their little acts of love.

Love stayed. Although Jesus' disciples fled in fright, these dear women who loved God stayed with His Son through His crucifixion, never wavering, ever watching, modeling a to-the-end devotion. Perfect love cast out all fear (1 John 4:18).

Love followed. We don't know how many people followed the crucified Jesus to His tomb (were there church officials, government representatives, the merely curious, or professional mourners?), but we do know that this loyal company of ladies walked behind those who carried His body. And they went for one reason: to learn the way to Jesus' tomb.

Love cared. These gallant, caring women realized that no one had properly prepared Jesus' body for burial. Their hearts were moved with compassion, and they decided to meet their Master's final earthly need. It was a little thing, perhaps in their minds even an after-the-fact matter, yet they decided that they must see to the proper care of their dead Friend's body.

Love worked. And so these dear women returned home after a long, tiring, gruesome, agonizing day at the base of Golgotha and prepared spices and ointments for the proper embalming of Jesus' body.

Little things. Simple acts. Yet each one revealed a heart that loves God! And what joy to know that little is often much when our giving is the natural outgrowth of our devotion to Jesus.

Can you think of some little thing you can do today for your Friend and Savior? Can you stay a little longer in prayer, follow a little closer in obedience, care a little more for His people, work a little harder for His kingdom? Ask for His guidance and His grace now.

> *Very early in the morning, they, and certain*
> *other women with them, came to the tomb.*
> Luke 24:1

Sunrise sent forth its signal. The Sabbath was over. And so was the most dreadful day in the history of the world: the day Jesus died. Now it was time for the faithful women of the cross—those who had stayed through the crucifixion, witnessed every vile abuse, and followed Jesus' body to the tomb—to carry out the last offices of love and embalm His body. It was early—*very early*, the Bible tells us—when this little fellowship of faithful followers went to the tomb.

But why didn't others go along? What might have been some of their reasons—or excuses?

> **Excuse #1:** *Someone else will do it.* "I'm sure *someone else* noticed that Jesus' body wasn't properly prepared for burial. Surely *someone else* will do it! Why duplicate what *someone else* will surely do?"

> **Excuse #2:** *We're tired.* "Oh, wasn't it awful? That horrible sight of Jesus hanging on the cross! I thought the day would never end—and my feet are still killing me!"

> **Excuse #3:** *Jesus' disciples should do it.* "Can you believe it! His 12 followers leaving Him to die alone! They ought to at least show up today and take care of things!"

> **Excuse #4:** *It can't be done!* "Didn't you see that giant stone they rolled across the opening of Jesus' tomb? There's no way we could push that massive thing aside!"

Such "reasons" may have seemed legitimate enough to some, yet acting out of respect for their Sovereign, affection for their Friend, and a faithfulness born of love, these exemplary women allowed nothing to keep them from doing what they wanted to do for the One they had followed to the end. They loved Jesus, and this love precluded all excuses and persisted against overwhelming obstacles, despite personal discomfort and inconvenience.

How do you serve the Savior? With diligence? With faithfulness? With follow-through? Without excuses? And how do you serve your family? Your Christian brothers and sisters? Your friends, neighbors, and coworkers? Hopefully, you serve with the fervency of a love that surrenders to no excuses!

*Then they returned from the tomb and
told all these things to the eleven and to all the rest.*
LUKE 24:9

*W*hat does it mean to truly follow Jesus? We talk about, we desire, and we pray for a life spent faithfully walking with Jesus. Today, as we say farewell to a circle of women who loved Jesus and faithfully followed Him to the end, we see in them more of what it means to truly follow God. Note how they model for us an unwavering devotion to their Lord:

- *They followed Him in life.* As Jesus walked, talked, and ministered throughout Jerusalem, Judea, and Samaria, these women were there, ministering to Him physically and financially (Luke 8:2,3).

- *They followed Him in death.* Never wavering, these faithful followers of Jesus waited at the foot of the cross, watched as His body was removed, and walked behind those who took Him to the burial tomb.

- *They followed through in duty.* Walking toward the tomb, these dear women realized that Jesus' body had not been properly prepared for burial. The next morning, as they followed through on this final duty to their departed Friend, they were blessed to be the first to witness His resurrection from the dead and to talk with the risen Lord (John 20:11-18)!

- *They followed His instructions.* When they spoke with Jesus, He gave them an assignment: Go, to My brethren and tell them all these things (John 20:17). Of course, these women who loved God rushed to do just that!

Dear one, surely you desire to truly follow Jesus. And exactly what does such discipleship require of you? That you follow Him in life, in death, in duty, and in obedience. Make the words of this old familiar hymn the prayer of your heart, and ask God to help you follow His lead in every aspect of your life:

> He leadeth me, He leadeth me,
> By His own hand He leadeth me;
> His faithful foll'wer I would be,
> For by His hand He leadeth me.[10]

*When they ran out of wine, the mother of Jesus
said to Him, "They have no wine."*
JOHN 2:3

*T*he mother of Jesus." The phrase sounds glorious, doesn't it? But as we might imagine, being the mother of Jesus was not without its challenges. Consider today's passage.

Mary, Jesus' mother, may have been a woman who spoke very little, a woman more thoughtful than conversant. But when the wine ran out at this wedding in Cana, Mary may have wondered, "What can I do to help? I know! I'll tell Jesus!" We don't know exactly what she hoped for or expected. But we do know that Jesus' response to her words reminded her that He was more—much more!—than her firstborn son. He reminded her of His position and duties as Deity.

Jesus' response to His mother can instruct us in the ways of the Lord:

God's purposes—God does not exist to serve man; man exists to serve God. Although Jesus did provide some wine, He performed this miracle in order to serve His own divine purposes, not merely grant His mother's veiled request. In the case of this water turned to wine, God's purpose was far greater than merely supplying drink for wedding festivities. As the Bible reports, Jesus' purpose in the miracle was to manifest His glory and deity so that others might believe. Mary was concerned with the temporal, while Jesus was primarily concerned about the eternal.

Where do your interests lie? Do you worry about unimportant details, about trivialities? Are you overly concerned with the minutiae of daily life, with secondary things? Receive with grace Jesus' rebuke of Mary's earthly preoccupation and set your affection on things above—on the eternal and, therefore, more significant issues of life.

God's timing—God's timing is governed by His great wisdom and knowledge. Mary may have feared that no one had noticed the lack of drink and felt the need to point it out to Jesus. But Omniscience, who knows all things, knew and—in *His* time, on *His* divine schedule—acted miraculously as only Omnipotence can.

Are there things you "need"? Are there matters you fear have gone unnoticed? Then wait on the Lord, on the wisdom of His timing, on the ways of Deity.

A woman of Samaria came to draw water.
JOHN 4:7

*O*ne of the blessings of coming alongside the women of the Bible who loved God is learning the lessons which each of their lives offers us. Consider today another woman from the past—a woman who came to love God and walk with Jesus. She is known simply as "a woman of Samaria." As Jesus traveled through her region, He stopped to rest by a well where she came to draw water. Exactly what message does her story have for us?

Message to the Samaritan Woman	*Message to Us*
She had sinned. She had had five husbands, and now the man she lived with was not her husband.	*We have sinned.* That's the clear message of Romans 3:23—"For all have sinned."
She was saved. After talking with Jesus, the woman drank of the water Jesus offered her: living water springing up into everlasting life.	*We can be saved.* Jesus extends the same living water to us. He promises, "I give them eternal life, and they shall never perish" (John 10:28).
She shared the good news. Rushing into the city, this woman spread the news of Jesus' presence and testified of His message.	*We must share the good news.* The Bible asks us who know the Lord, "How shall they believe in Him of whom they have not heard?" (Romans 10:14).

When the Savior stopped and visited with one sinful woman, she was saved—and others were saved as well ("Many of the Samaritans of that city believed in Him because of the word of the woman who testified...."). Won't you, too, talk first with the Savior? Speak with God about everlasting life, about yourself, about the sin that mars your life, about your loved ones who still do not know Him. Drink deeply from the refreshing resource of His Word. Then tell others the good news of Jesus Christ. Open up the living waters of everlasting life to friends and enemies alike. Make sure that you do your part to spread the truth of the gospel to the ends of the earth (Romans 10:18)!

> *Then the scribes and Pharisees brought to Him*
> *a woman caught in adultery.*
> John 8:3

*A*ccusations flew! The scribes and Pharisees were doing the flinging, and their words were a trap. Hoping to catch Jesus making a judgment that ran counter to their understanding of the law, these self-righteous leaders went to Him, dragging with them a poor woman they knew had sinned. "Teacher, this woman was caught in adultery, in the very act. Now Moses, in the law, commanded us that such should be stoned. But what do you say?"

Jesus' response was twofold. He wisely advised, "He who is without sin among you, let him throw a stone at her first." Then, after the accusers had departed (without throwing a single stone!), Jesus graciously forgave the woman.

Let's consider now some components of true forgiveness—forgiveness we receive from God, as well as the grace of forgiveness we extend to others. As you read through the items on this list, ask God to engrave them on your heart:

> **F** orget the offense. It's commonly stated that we are to forgive *and* forget. Perhaps this noble thought has its roots in Jeremiah 31:34—"I will forgive their iniquity, and their sin I will remember no more."

> **O** ur forgiveness is in Christ. In Him "we have redemption through His blood, the forgiveness of sins" (Colossians 1:14).

> **R** epentance refuses to sin again. The forgiven sinner repents of his sin and, like the adulterous woman was instructed, goes his way and does not sin again.

> **G** o on. All have sinned (Romans 3:23), and those who are forgiven must go forward, leaving behind their sinful ways and pressing on in God's purposes (Philippians 3:13,14).

> **I** nfinite forgiveness. Forgiveness covers offenses again and again. When Peter asked, "Lord, how often shall my brother sin against me, and I forgive him? Up to seven times?" Jesus answered, "Up to seventy times seven" (Matthew 18:21, 22).

> **V** alue the sinner just as God does. Here is our model: "While we were still sinners, Christ died for us" (Romans 5:8), offering us the forgiveness of sin.

> **E** mulate God. We are to forgive one another just as God in Christ also forgave us (Ephesians 4:32). Such is the grace of forgiveness!

Now a certain man was sick, Lazarus of Bethany,
the town of Mary and her sister Martha.
JOHN 11:1

What do you do when trouble comes your way? How do you handle the problems that touch your life? Do you tend to...

Tell a friend?	Take a pill?
Call a counselor?	Hide in a novel?
Join a group?	Watch a movie?
Go shopping?	Fall apart?
Get a new hairstyle?	Eat something?

Today we visit two sisters who faced real life-and-death trouble. We've seen Mary and Martha before as they welcomed Jesus and His disciples into their home for a meal (see October 23), but today we see them face a crisis in their family. Their beloved brother, Lazarus, was sick. Besides being dear to them, he was probably their sole means of support. (The Bible never mentions that Mary or Martha has a husband or children.) Their brother's serious illness meant not only great sadness, but an unknown, insecure future as well. These two women who loved God knew they must tell Jesus. They knew of His deep love for their brother, and they knew of His powerful miracles. So they sent for the Teacher.

O that we would follow in this wise pair's footsteps! Why should we turn solely to a friend, a counselor, or a support group when we have Jesus, the Friend who sticks closer than a brother? Why should we women who profess to love God dabble in the world's quick fixes and appealing escapes (pleasure, entertainment, vanity) when we face serious trouble? And why should we give in to the flesh when we have the ultimate Resource in God? As a simple message from an eloquent psalm reminds us:

> I will lift up my eyes to the hills—
> From whence comes my help?
> My help comes from the LORD,
> Who made heaven and earth (Psalm 121:1).

May the psalmist's pattern be ours as we follow the example of Mary and Martha and call on Jesus, the ultimate Resource and Friend, when problems arise and crises come.

> *Then Martha, as soon as she heard that Jesus*
> *was coming, went and met Him.*
> John 11:20

$\mathcal{W}$hat do you think of when you hear the phrase "the odd couple"? This phrase has come to describe two people who handle life in contrasting ways, and sisters Mary and Martha certainly qualify as an "odd couple." As we saw when Jesus and His disciples visited their home for dinner, Martha bustled with unbridled energy while Mary worshiped at the feet of the Master.

Today we see this "odd couple" in another life situation. Their brother, Lazarus, was seriously ill. Mary and Martha had sent for Jesus, but He did not come, so their beloved brother died. At that point the sisters heard that Jesus was approaching their village. Let's look today at Martha's response and consider Mary's tomorrow.

How did Martha respond—or, perhaps in her case, how did she *react*—when she learned that the Savior was approaching? True to form, Martha leaped up, rushed out the door, and ran down the road to meet the Master.

Martha's statement of faith—Martha may have been abrupt and hurried, but her heart was right. She believed in Jesus and trusted in His power to heal. "Lord," she ventured, "if You had been here, my brother would not have died."

Martha's lesson in faith—Martha was right to go to Jesus, but she had missed a central truth about Jesus. When she volunteered, "I know that whatever You ask of God, God will give You," Jesus corrected her by stating, "I am the resurrection and the life. He who believes in Me, though he may die, he shall live." He was saying, "Martha, I don't have to ask of God. *I am* God, and life is in *Me!* He who believes in *Me* shall live!"

Precious one, who do you believe Jesus is? Martha recognized His power, but her understanding of His deity was incomplete until He corrected her. Do you believe that Jesus is God—God-in-flesh—and that belief in Him, though you die, gives you eternal life? That is the message dear Martha heard from the lips of the incarnate God Himself, and it is His message to us, too. As Jesus asked Martha, "Do you believe this?"

But Mary was sitting in the house.
JOHN 11:20

*Y*esterday we saw how Martha, one member of the "odd couple" of sisters, responded to Jesus after her brother's death. Almost on cue, the energetic, do-it-yourself Martha leaped up and bolted out of the house to meet Jesus before He reached their doorway.

But the ever-pensive Mary stayed in the house, waiting for the Savior. Soon word arrived: "The Teacher has come and is calling for you."

Joining Jesus outside the town, dear Mary could only fall at His holy feet and declare her faith: "Lord, if You had been here, my brother would not have died."

These sisters show us two ways of managing life, and each way has its benefits. Martha definitely gets things done and makes things happen, but don't miss the importance of spending time in "the Mary mode," of spending time waiting on the Lord. When we choose to spend time out of sight and close to Jesus, important things can happen:

- We read and study God's Word.
- We linger in sweet prayer.
- We commit to memory favorite Scriptures.
- We meditate on things of the Lord.

In our busy world, we may be tempted to think that time alone with God, time spent waiting on the Lord, doesn't accomplish much. We may think it's unimportant. After all, no one sees it, and there is no glory, no splash, no notice, nothing to measure or count. Yet time regularly spent with God bears fruit that can grow only in the shade of His presence. Consider these thought-provoking words of nineteenth-century Scottish lecturer Henry Drummond: "Talent develops itself in solitude; the talent of prayer, of faith, of meditation, of seeing the unseen."[1]

Do you desire to bear this kind of heavenly fruit that grows only in the shade of God's presence? Then, today and everyday, seek the solitude such divine fruit requires.

> *There they made Him a supper; and Martha served*
> *[and] Mary…anointed the feet of Jesus,*
> *and wiped His feet with her hair.*
> John 12:2,3

efore we bid Mary and Martha Godspeed, let's peek through the window into their home. The whole family is there: Mary, Martha, and their brother, Lazarus, whom Jesus raised from the dead. We see a truly joyous celebration as these grateful folks prepare another meal for their beloved Jesus. The scene is both priceless and instructive.

Both Martha and Mary loved God, but Martha showed her love for Him in practical matters and Mary in the pious. Please take these two images of two aspects of love along with you today…and every day…as you express to God your love for Him.

Service—As usual, Martha served. Are we surprised? Service is Martha's way of expressing love. She was a practical woman, and hers was a practical love. She delighted in meeting the needs of the One she loved so dearly.

And you? Are you faithful to serve wherever God has placed you, remembering that whatever you do, you are to do heartily, "as to the Lord and not to man" (Colossians 3:23)? Do you regard the practical tasks at home—meals to prepare, floors to sweep, and clothes to wash—as ways of expressing your love for God? While these daily duties may seem insignificant, God knows the sacrifice involved and is pleased when we serve as unto Him!

Worship—As usual, Mary worshiped. Are we surprised? Mary was ever desirous of worshiping the Lord. This evening she poured her expensive oil over Jesus' feet in an act of extravagant love and then wiped His feet with her hair.

Are you, fellow lover of the Lord, an uninhibited worshiper of God? Do you seek new ways to show your love for Him? Oh, your acts of adoration may be scoffed at, as were Mary's. People may consider your sacrifices of worship unwise, wasteful, even foolish. But once again, God welcomes the gifts of worship you bring to pour out at His feet. So make them lavish— and make them every day!

Now there stood by the cross of Jesus His mother....
John 19:25

*Y*es, a sword will pierce through your own soul also." My, how these words must have suddenly rung loudly in Mary's ears! Thirty-three years earlier when Mary took the newborn Jesus to the temple in Jerusalem, the elderly Simeon had solemnly pronounced these prophetic words (Luke 2:35).

What a wonderful day that had been! Mary and Joseph were so pleased with their tiny baby, so humbled that God had chosen them to care for His Son, and so excited to present Jesus to God. Simeon himself was ecstatic in the blessing of being able to see the long-awaited Messiah. Yet there had been that word, spoken directly to Mary, about a piercing sword.

Yes, Mary's path as the mother of Jesus had many precious moments, but that path had its pain, too, as she witnessed people's violent reactions to Jesus and His message. And now Mary stood at the foot of Jesus' cross, watching her firstborn Son die a criminal's torturous death. A sword was indeed piercing her soul!

Then, in the horrible quiet, Mary heard the clear voice of Jesus speaking to His disciple John. And He was speaking about *her:* "Behold your mother!" No, she (by now a widow) wasn't being forgotten or overlooked! God was taking care of her! Having loved His own, Jesus loved them to the end (John 13:1), and "His own" included His mother, Mary!

Consider two lessons from Mary's difficult life that we can take with us along life's often painful path:

> *Lesson #1: Life's pain should never allow us to neglect caring for our loved ones.* Jesus shows us that. Despite the agonizing pain He felt as He hung dying on the cross, He was thinking of Mary, and He called John to provide for her.

> *Lesson #2: Life's pain should never cause us to doubt God's care for us.* The Almighty is with us always, even to the end of the age (Matthew 28:20), and He will not fail to provide for us (Psalm 23:1) or to love us to the end.

Thank God for His unfailing love and care for you...and then follow His example by caring for your loved ones, even in the midst of your own personal pain.

*These all continued...in prayer
and supplication, with the women and Mary
the mother of Jesus, and with His brothers.*
ACTS 1:14

*P*artings are indeed such sweet sorrow, aren't they? Today we say farewell to Mary, the mother of Jesus. She isn't mentioned again in the Bible after today's Scripture passage, so let's examine carefully the details of her final appearance:

Fact #1: Mary is in the upper room. Perhaps the very spot where Jesus shared His last meal with His disciples, this room became the meeting place for His followers after His glorious resurrection.

Fact #2: Mary is among Jesus' faithful followers. No single believer in Christ is ever more important than another. Here we see Mary and others who followed Jesus standing on equal ground.

Fact #3: Mary is praying. Kneeling shoulder to shoulder with the other saints, Mary joins with the group, persisting in prayer for much-needed strength and the grace to carry on without Jesus.

Fact #4: Mary is with other women. Jesus' followers included a small band of women who supported His ministry, as well as the wives of some of the disciples.

Fact #5: Mary's other sons are present. We can imagine Mary's joy! Her sons had never believed in Jesus before His death (John 7:5), but they were brought to faith by His death and resurrection. Finally, all her sons were united in faith!

What a beautiful portrait of godly devotion we find in the life of Jesus' beloved mother! Mary worshiped and fellowshipped with other believers, persisted in prayer, spent time with sisters in the faith, and valued her family's faith. Do these phrases describe your life, too? If not, which areas do you need to develop so that your life reflects your devotion to God just as precious Mary's did?

P.S. Aren't you glad that we never have to truly say good-bye to the women in the Bible who loved God? They are preserved forever in God's Word, and you can renew your acquaintance with them anytime by simply opening up your Bible. Why not make it your practice to take time each day to drop in on one of these women who loved God?

> *At Joppa there was a certain disciple named...Dorcas.*
> *This woman was full of good works and*
> *charitable deeds which she did.*
> ACTS 9:36

*C*ome along, dear and faithful traveler through the Bible, to Joppa, a city on the seacoast of the Mediterranean. Let's look in on a situation in the local church there.

The People. Serving in the congregation at Joppa was a lovely saint named Dorcas. Her name—meaning "gazelle"—suggested her loveliness and beauty. In what ways did this dear woman minister to those in her church? She spent her hours and energy making coats and garments for the widows who were among the most needy persons in her day and culture. Dorcas didn't merely dream, make grand plans, or passionately desire to better the lives of her suffering sisters—she acted! And she was adored by the Christians in Joppa for her good works and acts of charity.

The Problem. When Dorcas died, the church mourned and grieved. Such a gracious, giving saint had been taken from them!

Tomorrow we'll consider the resolution of this problem, but today let's pause and ponder Dorcas's ministry. Note that we don't see her teaching, evangelizing, or counseling. Instead, we see her working quietly, doing some hands-on labor of love, putting forth practical efforts for the good of other people. Hers was not a "sowing" ministry, but a "sewing" ministry!

Do you want your life to count? Do you yearn for your life to matter for the kingdom? Do you long to influence others for the Lord and touch them with His love? Then, as the Bible says, put on a heart of compassion and kindness (Colossians 3:12). Learn to look at people and situations through Jesus' eyes of love and consider the afflictions and hardships you see. Then ask God, "What would ease the lives of the unfortunate? What would better their condition? What can I do—big or small—to help?" When you, like Dorcas, work to meet the needs of others, your life will count for Christ.

> Thought: She who does good for good's sake (and God's sake!), seeking neither praise nor reward, is sure of both in the end!

Then [Peter]...presented her alive.
ACTS 9:41

*W*asn't it challenging yesterday to meet Dorcas, a woman who loved God; who loved His people with deeds, not mere words; and who was in turn loved by them? To realize that she loved people through the very practical acts of sewing coats and garments was a second challenge! In light of Dorcas's love gifts of clothes for the widows in the church, we can easily understand why her death caused the people such sadness and prompted their heartfelt petition to God.

The Petition. As the church contemplated the loss of their much-loved Dorcas, two of Christ's disciples from her hometown went to the apostle Peter. Hadn't Peter just healed a paralyzed man in Lydda? Perhaps Peter could use this divine power on behalf of Dorcas, too!

The Presentation. Peter followed these men back to the crowded house of dear Dorcas. The widows had assembled to show him the many clothes this thoughtful woman had made for them. Emptying the death chamber, Peter knelt, prayed, and commanded the corpse, "Arise." As the dead Dorcas began to stir, Peter helped her up and then presented her to the saints and widows—alive!

Our glimpse into this gathering of believers is a glimpse into goodness. We know Dorcas possessed a good and godly heart. But consider other elements of good—those good things that happened as a result of the Lord's goodness in miraculously resurrecting Dorcas:

1. *God was glorified.* No person but God has the power to raise someone from the dead. Oh, how He must have been praised!

2. *Faith was generated.* We are told that many believed as a result of Peter's miracle. May God be praised for that, too!

3. *The people were gladdened.* Joy rippled through the church at Joppa: Dorcas was back! This loving, caring, generous woman who loved them—and God—was alive!

Check your own heart, dear one. Filled with God's love and goodness, does your heart prompt you to do good works for Him and His people? Do your lips overflow with praise for God's goodness? As the psalmist says, "Oh, that men would give thanks to the LORD for His goodness, and for His wonderful works to the children of men!" (Psalm 107:8). Do so now!

So…[Peter] came to the house of Mary…
where many were gathered together praying.
Acts 12:12

Webster's defines *generosity* as "liberality in spirit or act," and today we meet another generous woman who loved God and His people. Her name is Mary.

- *This Mary was the sister of Barnabas.* This wonderful man of God, described as "a good man, full of the Holy Spirit and of faith" (Acts 11:24), gladly sold the property he owned and gave the funds to benefit the body of Christ (Acts 4:36,37). Barnabas was generous in both spirit and deed.

- *This Mary was the devoted mother of John Mark.* This wonderful son was an evangelist who accompanied the apostle Paul on his travels and later wrote the Gospel of Mark. He lived his entire life not to get, but instead to give all that he was and all that he had for the cause of Christ.

Now we witness the generous spirit and brave actions of his mother, Mary. At a time when Christians were being relentlessly persecuted, Mary opened her home so that the saints would have a place to worship. In fact, as we meet her, the believers have gathered at her house to pray for Peter, who was in prison awaiting execution by King Herod. James was already dead by Herod's hand, and Peter was next.

What would you have done? Would you have followed in Mary's noble footsteps and willingly risked your life and generously sacrificed your time, effort, and money to serve the Lord? It takes *time* to serve God—to say no to lesser things, to make time for His worthy purposes, to prepare for ministry, to be with God's people. And it takes *effort* to serve others—to clean your house, to put fresh sheets on the bed, to prepare meals for guests. And it takes *money* to love with deeds, not just words—to purchase groceries, to provide a shelter for those in need, to build a house for a family that is without a home, to give to the church, to support pastors and missionaries as they serve God.

Why not ask God what you can do today—and every day—to nurture a generous spirit? Seek to live life with open hands.

And as Peter knocked at the door of the gate,
a girl named Rhoda came to answer.
ACTS 12:13

*D*o you remember yesterday's visit to the home of Mary, the mother of Mark? This brave woman was hosting a late-night prayer meeting at her house. As the believers asked God to deliver Peter from imprisonment and certain execution, there was a knock at the door of the gate.

Mary's maid Rhoda now enters the story. While the others prayed, she went to the door to see who was at the gate. (Note that she was also on duty late at night as others—and maybe she herself—prayed!) When she recognized Peter at the gate, the flesh-and-blood answer to the group's fervent prayers, she was so excited that, instead of opening the door, she ran back inside to share the good news with the others. Imagine her shrieks of joy as she burst into the room filled with pious pray-ers: "It's Peter! It's Peter! Peter's standing at the gate! Hallelujah! Our prayers have been answered! He's here!"

And yet, faithful in her duties and effervescent in her excitement, this dear girl (whose name means "rose") was called *Manias* by the others: "Maniac! Mad woman! You are beside yourself!" As the story ends, we—and those who scorned her—see that Rhoda was right. Peter was indeed out of prison and knocking on their door....

Do you wonder how Rhoda handled the name-calling, the put-downs, and the unjust criticism she received? We're not told the details, but we do know what God calls women who love Him to do in such circumstances. Consider the Bible's words of instruction:

> Put on a gentle and quiet spirit, which is very precious in the sight of God (1 Peter 3:4).

> A servant of the Lord must not quarrel, but be gentle to all and patient (2 Timothy 2:24).

> Love suffers long, is kind, does not behave rudely, and is not provoked (1 Corinthians 13:4,5).

> The fruit of the Spirit is love, joy, peace, longsuffering, kindness, goodness, faithfulness, gentleness, and self-control (Galatians 5:22-23).

The next time you are misunderstood or unjustly criticized as Rhoda was, look to the Lord's good Word for His guidance and to His Spirit for the ability to exhibit a gracious spirit.

> *And behold, a certain disciple was there, named Timothy,*
> *the son of a certain Jewish woman who believed,*
> *but his father was Greek.*
> Acts 16:1

*A*re you familiar with the name *Nike?* Yes, it's a familiar brand of athletic wear, but do you know its origin? *Nike* is the Greek goddess of victory, and the name means "conquering well." Today we meet Eunice, and her very name comes from *Nike*. What victory do we see in her life?

We know that she was the mother of Timothy, the man who became the apostle Paul's most trusted companion and disciple. We'll look at Eunice as mother next month (see December 13), but today let's focus on her marriage to a Greek man, a Gentile and therefore an unbeliever. What instruction does the Bible give to those of us who are also married to an unbeliever?

- *Display*—Be sure you demonstrate your affection and respect for your beloved unbeliever (Ephesians 5:33).

- *Pray*—Prayer certainly helps any situation, and marriage to an unbelieving husband will benefit as well (James 5:16)—so pray!

- *Say*—Never fail to praise, encourage, build up, and communicate your love to your man (Colossians 4:6).

- *Array*—Each and every day be sure to put on a gentle and quiet spirit (1 Peter 3:4). Such a spirit is priceless to the Lord and helpful in any marriage.

- *Delay*—Make delay your first tactic when trouble arises. Hold your tongue, breathe a quick prayer, and find in the Lord the wisdom and grace you need to give a soft and appropriate answer (Proverbs 15:1, 28).

- *Pay*—Pay attention to the women in the Bible who loved God and were married to men who were not believers. Esther (the Book of Esther) and Abigail (1 Samuel 25) stand out as victors in this special role.

- *Stay*—The Bible encourages a wife not to depart from her husband (1 Corinthians 7:10). Talk to your pastor about your situation.

- *Repay*—Be sure to repay evil with good (Romans 12:21). It's hard to do, but doing so gives you the *Nike*—the victory!

Allow sweet Eunice to encourage you, and remember that your faith in Jesus can and will sustain you in your marriage—and may even be used by Him to soften the heart of your beloved unbeliever!

Now a certain woman named Lydia heard us....
The Lord opened her heart to heed the things spoken by Paul.
ACTS 16:14

*N*ever underestimate the power of a woman," the old cliché warns. And today we'll certainly see the power of a woman named Lydia when God was at work through her. Into her tender heart were sown the seeds from which the church at Philippi grew. Consider some of the threads that make up the tapestry of Lydia's life:

- *She was a woman.* This obvious fact is important to the story. You see, ten men were required to organize a synagogue, and apparently this quorum was missing in Philippi. Not having a synagogue in which to gather, the women met outside of town to pray.

- *She was a worshiper.* Lydia believed in the God of Israel, but she had not yet become a follower of Jesus Christ.

- *She was attentive.* One day, down by the riverside, the apostle Paul showed up at the women's prayer meeting, sat down, and began talking about Jesus—and Lydia listened.

- *She was baptized.* As the truth about Jesus Christ penetrated Lydia's open heart, God graciously and sovereignly enabled her to receive the truth of salvation. The first thing Lydia did as a Christian, her first act of obedience and faithfulness to her Lord, was to be baptized.

- *She was influential.* And Lydia wasn't baptized alone. Evidently she was instrumental in her entire household—relatives and servants alike—becoming believers.

- *She was hospitable.* Not only did she open her heart, but she also opened her home. Paul's message had helped her, and now she wanted to help him and his friends by providing a home-away-from-home for them.

Dear woman who loves God, in what ways is your life similar to Lydia's? Are you worshiping regularly with other believers? Are you attentive to the teaching of God's Word? Have you been baptized according to the Lord's command to New Testament believers? Are you sharing with other people, especially with those closest to you, the truth about salvation in Christ which you possess? And are you, like Lydia, opening your home to the Lord's workers and His people?

"Never underestimate the power of a woman"—and that includes you—especially when she's serving the Lord!

*So they went out of the prison
and entered the house of Lydia.*
ACTS 16:40

*E*veryone enjoys the intricacies of an attractive tapestry, and yesterday we began noticing the various strands in the life-weaving of Lydia. Today we want to consider two other threads in the lovely tapestry of her life.

- *She was a businesswoman.* Lydia had lived in Thyatira, a city famous for its expensive purple dye. Now living in Philippi, Lydia sold clothes made from her deep-dyed purple fabrics. Because of the great cost of these goods, only the rich and the royal could afford them. And, as a dealer of these highly prized and costly garments, Lydia prospered.

- *She was generous.* How did Lydia use her wealth? She cared for her relatives and household servants, but she also opened her home for the cause of Christ. Immediately after her conversion and baptism, she compelled Paul and his traveling companions to stay with her. Evidently her house was spacious because the budding church in Philippi met in Lydia's home.

There is nothing wrong or sinful with being successful in what you do. God blessed Lydia with ability, creativity, and a strong work ethic, just as He has other women who love Him. He undoubtedly expects us to live out our priorities (Titus 2:3-5), to work willingly with our hands (Proverbs 31:13), and to do whatever we do heartily as unto Him (Colossians 3:23). But with the blessings of ability and prosperity comes responsibility. To whom much is given, much is also required (Luke 12:48). So we who love Him must always remember...

The source of wealth: We are not to think, "My power and the might of my hand have gained me this wealth." We are to "remember the LORD your God, for it is He who gives you power to get wealth" (Deuteronomy 8:17,18).

The purpose of wealth: We are "not to be haughty, nor to trust in uncertain riches but in the living God, who gives us richly all things to enjoy...[and to] do good, that [we may] be rich in good works, ready to give, willing to share" (1 Timothy 6:17,18).

And [Paul] found a certain Jew named Aquila...
with his wife Priscilla…and he came to them.
ACTS 18:2

ℬookends. That image may come to mind as we look at both another woman who loves God and her husband. This woman and her husband are a magnificent team. Like a pair of bookends, they each hold up their end as they serve God's kingdom. Her name is Priscilla, and her mate-for-life was Aquila. Take a look at their twin traits:

- *Servants*—Always mentioned together, Priscilla and Aquila stand as a team in both marriage and ministry.

- *Itinerants*—Each time this dear couple is named, they're in a different location. They trekked from Rome to Corinth to Ephesus and back again to Rome, and each city was a key site for ministry.

- *Industrious*—Both husband and wife shared in their joint occupation of tentmaking and leatherworks.

- *Hospitable*—This twosome opened up not only their hearts but also their tent flaps and took the homeless apostle Paul into their quarters. In fact, the church in Ephesus met in their home (1 Corinthians 16:19).

- *Perseverant*—Expelled from Rome, this pair knew a life of relentless persecution, yet they remained faithful to their Lord.

- *Knowledgeable*—With heartstrings tuned to God, Priscilla and Aquila listened attentively to Paul as he taught Jews and Greeks alike, gaining the knowledge they needed to serve Him in other places and other ways.

- *Willing*—This husband-wife duo was willing to do anything and go anywhere, at any time and at any cost, for the cause of Christ. At one point, they even left Corinth with Paul to help him build up the body of Christ.

If you are married, do you complement your husband's efforts? That's our calling (Ephesians 5:22), whether or not our husband is a Christian (1 Peter 3:1). As godly wives, we are to support our husband's dreams, hold up our end of the responsibility for family and home, and shoulder our part of the load of life. It takes both our husband and us—and the Lord's blessing!—to build a marriage and a family that glorify Him. One more word: If you are single, remember that the pursuit of the godly qualities outlined above is important for you, too!

Now this man had four virgin daughters who prophesied.
ACTS 21:9

*I*f you are single…" Today, as we meet four single women who loved God, we see in their lives another way to complete this sentence which closed yesterday's devotional reading. Although only one verse in the Holy Scriptures speaks about these women, it reveals that they were devoted to God. We don't know their names, but we do know that they served God in a unique way. What made their service so unique?

Their father—The first men selected to serve in the church after Jesus ascended into heaven were described as "men of good reputation, full of the Holy Spirit and wisdom" and "full of faith" (Acts 6:3,5). Philip, the evangelist, was among the seven men who met these standards, and he was the father of these four single women. What a blessing to have such a godly heritage in their family and spiritual model right in their own home!

Their ministry—As we've seen throughout this devotional book, only a handful of women were empowered by God to prophesy to His people, and these four beloved sisters are among that number. Along with Miriam, Deborah, Huldah, and Anna, these four women served God by speaking forth His Word to His people.

Their singleness—The sacred Scriptures set forth singleness as a truly sacred calling: "There is a difference between a wife and a virgin. The unmarried woman cares about the things of the Lord, that she may be holy both in body and in spirit. But she who is married cares about the things of the world—how she may please her husband" (1 Corinthians 7:34). In other words, a single woman is free from the earthly concerns of serving a husband to consecrate herself completely to the Lord's work, to be wholly His.

"If you are single…" Dear one, if you are single, please don't succumb to any pressure you may feel to get married. After all, it is the Lord who completes each woman's life, whether she is married or single. Furthermore, as a single saint, you are better able to devote yourself wholly and solely to God and His work. So, as a single, embrace your special opportunity—a high calling and high privilege—to serve Christ wholeheartedly!

I commend to you Phoebe our sister,
who is a servant of the church in Cenchrea.
ROMANS 16:1

*E*veryone needs help! If you're not sure of this truth, simply consider the challenges, stresses, and pressures of every day. Daily life brings with it much to do and many responsibilities to juggle, not to mention sorrows of heart to bear and physical ailments to cope with. Yes, everyone needs help!

And the apostle Paul, God's choice servant, was no different. Second Corinthians 11 lists the many trials he faced, and in the face of those trials God gave Paul, His faithful servant, a servant to help him. Her name was Phoebe, meaning "bright and radiant," and Phoebe definitely stands as a bright and radiant example of the faithful servanthood God desires in each of His children—including us! Three special titles describe her shining faithfulness:

1. *A sister*—Paul calls Phoebe "our sister." A devoted and committed member of the family of God, Phoebe was a Christian sister not only to Paul, but also to each and every saint in their fellowship.

2. *A servant*—The apostle next commends Phoebe as "a servant of the church in Cenchrea." The honored title *servant,* from which our English words for *deacon* and *deaconess* come, denotes one who serves any and all in the church.

3. *A succorer*—Paul further praises Phoebe: "She has been a helper of many and of myself also." In classical Greek, *helper* refers to a trainer in the Olympic games who stood by the athletes to see that they were properly trained and rightly girded for competition. *Helper* literally means "one who stands by in case of need."

God's message to us is clear. As sisters who love God and whom He calls to love His people, we are to be in faithful attendance, to stand by in case of need, and then to willingly meet that need. Such dedicated, selfless service shines oh so brilliantly in our dark world!

P.S. Like Paul, you, too, can thank God for such a servant as Phoebe, for she most likely delivered the priceless Book of Romans to Rome for Paul. As one scholar has so aptly written, "Phoebe carried under the folds of her robe the whole future of Christian theology."[2]

> *I commend to you Phoebe our sister,*
> *who…has been a helper of many and of myself also.*
> ROMANS 16:1,2

*A*s someone has quipped, "Some folks are poor spellers. They think *service* is spelled *serve us!*"[3] But that's not the Bible's picture! God's Word, for instance, shows us Phoebe, described by the apostle Paul as a sister, servant, and succorer (see yesterday's devotion). Before we leave Phoebe's bright and shining life of ministry, take to heart these thoughts about helping others.

Serve all—Phoebe not only served the famous and well-known apostle Paul, but she also humbly served those in her small-town home church at Cenchrea. *Check:* Do you offer the same kind of heartfelt service to anyone and everyone, regardless of their stature, or do you pick and choose whom you will serve?

Serve humbly—In the early church a servant and a helper was one who cared for the sick and the poor, ministered to martyrs and prisoners, and quietly assisted the people and ministry of the church whenever help was needed. *Check:* Are you happy to serve in the shadows when—and so that—others shine, satisfied that the work of Christ is furthered, glad to be assisting those efforts and meeting the needs of others? Do you serve faithfully, quietly, and selflessly, seeking nothing for yourself, desiring no recognition, glory, or notice?

Serve always—Dear Phoebe's service seems constant. Probably a widow, she "has been a helper," so she continues to do in the present what she had done in the past. Hers was a long-distance track record of faithfulness. Having served faithfully in the past, she was still serving as she carried Paul's precious parchment letter from Corinth to Rome. She was faithful yesterday…today…and undoubtedly would be tomorrow. *Check:* Are you a servant not only in days gone by, but also in the present, and brimming with plans for serving in the future?

Dear fellow servant, our Jesus—the Son of Man who did not come to be served, but to serve, and to give His life a ransom for many (Matthew 20:28)—is the ultimate model for selfless service for those who love Him. Look to His example and to Phoebe, and follow in their faithful footsteps of selfless service.

Greet Priscilla and Aquila...
who risked their own necks for my life.
ROMANS 16:3,4

*T*hroughout his ministry, Louis B. Talbot, the founder of Talbot Theological Seminary, kept a copy of *Foxe's Book of Martyrs* on his bedstand and each night, before turning out his light, read about the persecution and suffering of one of God's saints.

Today, dear pilgrim, we visit again with Priscilla, a sister and saint who probably came close to death as a martyr. She and her husband, Aquila, somehow, at some time, intervened to save the apostle Paul's life. We have no details other than Paul's acknowledgment that they laid down their lives on his account. Literally, they had "placed their necks under the ax" for him.

While we may shudder to think of such a situation, the Bible is not shy about addressing the subject of persecution and suffering. Consider these two teachings:

Expect suffering. To live a godly life is to be a clear witness for the light of God's truth and love. Therefore, faithful believers must expect persecution and suffering in this dark and fallen world. In fact, Scripture promises it: "All who desire to live godly in Christ Jesus will suffer persecution" (2 Timothy 3:12). Another passage clearly states, "For to you it has been granted on behalf of Christ, not only to believe in Him, but also to suffer for His sake" (Philippians 1:29).

Rejoice in suffering. Overflowing joy in Christ—joy in the future as well as in the present, whatever the current circumstances—is the reward of those who suffer for righteousness in this life. "Beloved, do not think it strange concerning the fiery trial which is to try you, as though some strange thing happened to you; but rejoice to the extent that you partake of Christ's sufferings, that when His glory is revealed, you may also be glad with exceeding joy" (1 Peter 4:12,13).

What awaits those of us who might meet a martyr's death like Priscilla faced? As Dr. Talbot loved to say, "It would be wonderful for a martyr to die with tears in his eyes, only to open his eyes and find the hand of the Lord Jesus wiping those tears away."[4] This joy and glory is the very *worst* that awaits God's faithful martyrs!

Greet Mary…Junia…Tryphena and Tryphosa…Persis…
Rufus['s mother]…Julia…Nereus['s sister]….
ROMANS 16:6-15

esser lights" is a descriptive term coined by writer and preacher Chuck Swindoll to identify those saints in Scripture who, although in God's economy are no less important than others, are lesser known to us because so very little is written about them. Today's roll call of "lesser lights" includes eight women whom Paul personally greeted in his letter to the Christians in Rome. What do we learn about each?

- *Mary*—Paul declares that this particular Mary worked hard for the Roman church, literally toiling to the point of weariness and exhaustion.

- *Junia*—Paul greeted her as a kinsman.

- *Tryphena and Tryphosa*—These two sisters in Christ may have been twin sisters by blood. Although their names mean *delicate* and *dainty*, they labored strenuously for the Lord.

- *Persis*—Beloved by all who knew her, this woman also worked hard for the cause of Christ.

- *Rufus's mother*—Somehow and in some way this dear woman had cared for Paul as if he were her own son.

- *Julia and Nereus's sister*—These two women were also outstanding members of and leaders in the local church at Rome.[5]

What does it take to stand tall among Paul's friends and colaborers listed here? The bottom-line quality seems to be hard work for God's kingdom. These women labored to the point of weariness and fatigue. They tirelessly served the Lord and His people.

Dear worker in the Lord, this faithful corps of women who loved God seem to offer two words for our hearts. *First,* we must prayerfully consider the intensity of our own labor for Christ's church and for His sheep. Does our intensity need to be turned up a notch or two?

Second, if you ever feel like a "lesser light," remember that no matter who does or does not know about your efforts for the Lord, He does! Your name is known in heaven. Indeed, it is written in the Lamb's Book of Life (Revelation 21:27)! You, beloved child of the King and perhaps a "lesser light," are never unnoticed by the God you serve!

> *Now to the married I command...*
> *a wife is not to depart from her husband.*
> 1 CORINTHIANS 7:10

$\mathcal{U}$nequally yoked" is a term often used to describe a Christian who is married to an unbelieving spouse. Because so many women who love God find themselves in this situation, the devotions for today and tomorrow share some of the guidelines the Bible gives us for marriage that apply to dear women who are unequally yoked. First, carefully read through 1 Corinthians 7:10-16 and then take to heart these fine words of advice from the book *Women Helping Women:*[6]

Remain in your marriage—God's first word to a woman unequally yoked in marriage is to remain, if at all possible, in that relationship. Why? "For the unbelieving husband is sanctified by the wife" (1 Corinthians 7:14). In other words, he is set apart for God's blessing because of his wife. The presence of a believing wife in the home exposes the members of her household to God and sets them apart for God's grace.

Trust in the Lord—God has promised us His presence and His help when we face trials, and that promise extends to our marriage, even a difficult one. Our gracious God has also assured us of a way of escape through any difficulty that might tempt us to give in to sin (1 Corinthians 10:13). God will enable us to stand strong in the face of any trial—including those that come in our marriage.

Plan your tactics—Wisdom involves having a plan, and the wise woman plans how to better live in her situation. Her plan should involve living according to God's Word, living without bitterness or anger, and having others prayerfully hold her accountable for godly attitudes.

If your dear husband is not a Christian, you undoubtedly have many unique opportunities to grow in grace. Remaining in your marriage, trusting in the Lord, and planning to live in a more Christlike way can only produce much fruit in your life. So look to the Lord now. Choose to walk with Him through every day, o'er all the way. Cling to His hand as you walk with Him. Claim His every promise. And rejoice that the power of Christ rests on you (2 Corinthians 12:9)!

*For how do you know, O wife,
whether you will save your husband?*
1 Corinthians 7:16

*A*re you married to a beloved unbeliever? Then prayerfully read
1 Corinthians 7:10-16 and consider these biblical strategies for living with
an unsaved husband—strategies which are good for any and every wife![7]

1. *Build your relationship with God.* A wife's union with Christ is an even higher union than the marriage bond.

2. *Don't return evil for evil or provoke your husband to evil.* Sometimes you may be hard to live with, too!

3. *Think biblically about the demands your husband makes.* Looking to the Lord will help you discern if his requests are reasonable.

4. *Develop a forgiving, forbearing spirit.* Christian wives must forgive husbands (unbelieving and otherwise) and refuse to hold a grudge.

5. *Do good.* Put yourself to work doing good for your husband. Be creative, study your man, and find ways to help him.

6. *Respect your husband.* Respect the position of authority God gives your husband as head of the household.

7. *Act wisely and decisively.* You may be called to act boldly according to the Lord's leading as Abigail did for the good of your husband (see June 17).

8. *Persevere and endure.* God is interested in changing you right *in* your circumstances.

9. *Challenge tyranny appropriately.* Love your husband, but graciously resist any harsh misuse of his authority.

10. *Know the limits of your responsibility.* Consider any criticism from your husband, obey God's Word, and leave the rest to God.

11. *Build rest and recreation into your schedule.* Living with a loved one who disregards the Lord can be very tiring.

12. *Meet regularly with a mature Christian woman.* Have others hold you accountable to being a faithful Christian wife.

13. *Actively use your spiritual gifts to serve the Lord.* Find a way to serve God's people from your home.

Paul asks, "How do you know, O wife, whether you will save your husband?" Only God can "save" anyone, but He does use the faithful witness of a Christian wife to teach an unbelieving husband about His light, His truth, Himself. Evangelism begins at home, and your beloved unbeliever just might be won by your conduct (1 Peter 3:1). Oh, pray so now!

There is a difference between a wife and a virgin.
The unmarried woman cares about the things of the Lord....
1 CORINTHIANS 7:34

We've seen it before on our journey through the Bible, and it has come up again. That "it" is singleness. Today we pause once again to behold the beautiful holiness God has in mind for His single women.

In today's passage, the Bible states, "There is a difference between a wife and a virgin." The married woman's interests are divided between the earthly and the heavenly. She is called to love God, but also to love, serve, and please her husband. But the unmarried woman is called to wholly love, serve, and please the Lord.

If you are single, have you set yourself apart *from* the things of this life and *for* the Lord's work? Fewer family demands and obligations enable you to be more devoted to God. And these fewer hindrances can mean more opportunities and greater freedom to live out an undistracted devotion to God. Consider these possibilities:

Missions work—Whether in full-time or short-term missions work, you can use your freedom to serve Christ around the world.

Full-time work in a Christian organization—Churches, Christian schools, colleges, seminaries, and ministry organizations can definitely benefit from your God-given talents and skills on a full-time basis.

Giving of money—If you have a well-paying career, be a generous giver to your church's ministry.

Witnessing for Christ on your job—Of course, your very presence as God's light in the world serves as a refreshing witness for Jesus and helps draw others to Him.

Dear single friend, the opportunity to be fully devoted to God, to serve Him with a wholehearted, no-holds-barred devotion is yours. And remember that a longing for marriage (or anything else!) should never be allowed to rob you of the complete joy and fulfillment God means for you to know each day. Our eyes should be forever focused on what has graciously come from the hand of God, not on what seems to be withheld. Make it your practice to choose every day to live that day fully and gloriously unto the Lord. Ask God for His help in focusing fully on the opportunities that are yours today as a single woman who loves God.

> *There is a difference between a wife and a virgin....*
> *She who is married cares about the things of the world—*
> *how she may please her husband.*
> 1 CORINTHIANS 7:34

*Y*esterday we considered the freedom to wholeheartedly devote herself to God which a single woman enjoys. Today's Scripture passage, however, offers instruction for a married woman.

While marriage does not prevent great devotion to the Lord, nurturing a marriage relationship does require time, effort, and emotion that might otherwise be devoted to our heavenly Father. Married women cannot avoid being concerned about the earthly needs of their spouse, about "the things of the world." Since caring for our husband is part of our calling from the Lord, how can we do a better job at it?

- *Pray for him daily*—Focusing on your husband in prayer will help you focus on him in your heart.

- *Plan for him daily*—Nothing just happens—including a great marriage! Planning helps you focus your thoughts on your man.

- *Prepare for him daily*—Preparing (the house, the meals, your words) for your husband helps you focus on him with your actions.

- *Please him*—Pay attention to your husband's wants, likes, and dislikes, and then make the effort to please him.

- *Protect your time with him*—If your husband is at home, try to be there, too.

- *Physically love him*—Take a minute to read 1 Corinthians 7:3-5. A little affection goes a long way in caring for your man!

- *Positively respond to him*—Answering his words and responding to his actions immediately and graciously will help create a non-threatening atmosphere for communication.

- *Praise him*—Blessing your husband in public as well as in private is one way to sow in your heart seeds of love for him.

- *Pray always*—A woman who loves God (and her husband!) is a woman who prays. Ask God throughout the day to enable you to be the kind of loving and supportive wife He wants you to be.[8]

> *But I want you to know that the head of every man is Christ,*
> *the head of woman is man, and the head of Christ is God.*
> 1 C<small>ORINTHIANS</small> 11:3

*H*ow can a marriage run smoothly? How can a husband and wife, who are equals in God's eyes, work together to achieve all that He wants them to accomplish for His purposes and His glory?

Today we see God's plan for order and harmony in marriage expressed in the callings to *headship* and *submission*. Look at the three examples of gracious submission God gives us in this one sacred verse:

Christ was subject to God. Headship and therefore submission exist in the Godhead. Jesus Christ, equal in every way with God the Father, nevertheless willingly submitted to the Father and carried out His plan of salvation for mankind.

Man is subject to Christ. The Bible clearly declares Jesus Christ's headship: God "put all things [and all people] under [Christ's] feet, and gave Him to be head over all things to the church" (Ephesians 1:22).

Woman is subject to man. Here we see the need for headship in a marriage. Although equal to man under God (Galatians 3:28), the wife is called upon by God to willingly submit to her husband for the sake of their marriage and family.

All Christians are called to a life of submission, a life of graciously yielding to others for the good of all. In fact, the Christian life *is* a life of submission! Every single one of us who names Jesus as Lord is called to be subject to other people. We are to submit to the government and to our employers (1 Peter 2:13-25), we are to submit to one another (Ephesians 5:21), and of course we are to submit to God (1 Peter 5:6).

Sometimes following our husband comes easily, but no one will dispute the fact that sometimes it's difficult. But when you submit to God and to His guidelines for headship and submission, you'll be on the path to greater godliness in your marriage and home. This godly submission will also make you more like Jesus and work for the good of all.

Woman is the glory of man.
1 Corinthians 11:7

There is never a reason for you to feel in any way inferior to your husband. No matter what others may say, what the world may say, what feminist leaders may say, God says you are the "glory" of your husband. And, oh, what a *glorious* word God chose when He said that! Hide these precious Scriptures in your heart and allow them to guide your thinking:

- "Woman is the glory of man" (1 Corinthians 11:7). As man reflects the glory of God, so a woman reflects the glory of man. Together a husband and wife reflect the glory of God and show Christ to the world.

- "An excellent wife is the crown of her husband" (Proverbs 12:4). We can especially rejoice when our husband is noticed and praised if we have contributed to his success.

- "He who finds a wife finds a good thing" (Proverbs 18:22). One of the greatest blessings God gives a man is a good wife—one who will work with him to live out God's purposes for him.

- "A prudent wife is from the Lord" (Proverbs 19:14). It is the prudent wife who will strengthen her husband's reputation.

It is our privilege as wives to bring goodness to our husband and glory to his name. As the Bible says of our great model, the Proverbs 31 woman, "Her husband is known in the gates" (Proverbs 31:23). With the Lord's help, we too will live in a way that brings honor to our husband and helps his reputation.

Being a wife who brings glory and honor to her husband is a challenge. So take a moment now to pray and ask God to help you support your husband in ways that will strengthen him and glorify God. Make a Proverbs 31:12 commitment to do your husband good all the days of your life by praising and encouraging him, nurturing your marriage, serving your family, tending to your home, watching over the finances, supporting his dreams, and praying for his success—all this so that he may be a man of godly influence in his home, his church, his work, and his community. It's a blessing to have your husband known as having a worthy wife![9]

*For man is not from woman,
but woman from man.*
1 CORINTHIANS 11:8

efore reading the next few days of devotions, look again at the first two chapters of Genesis and the wondrous details of God's glorious creation of both the world and mankind. Marvel anew at the order of God's design, His purposes, and the dignity He assigns human beings!

One fact from the Bible's account of Creation continues to impact our lives as women who love God, and that is the fact that we women have our origin in the man. God first formed Adam out of the dust of the ground. Then later, while Adam slept, God removed one of his ribs, closed up the flesh, and made Adam's rib into a woman. God made woman *from* the man.

Today's Scripture verse echoes this Creation truth that woman is from man. In fact, *woman* means "man-ess" in the Hebrew language. As some unknown saint of old has commented, "Woman was taken not from man's head to rule over him, nor from his feet to be trampled upon, but from his side, under his arm, to be protected, and closest to his heart, to be loved, to be near his heart, to be dear to him."

These thoughts should stir our hearts to act in the following ways toward our husband:

- *Cherish him.* He who is called to nourish his marriage and cherish his wife (Ephesians 5:28-33) deserves to be cherished by his cherished mate.

- *Love him.* He who is called to love his wife as Christ loved the church and gave Himself for it (Ephesians 5:25) deserves the devoted and self-sacrificing love of a grateful wife.

- *Serve him.* He who is called to protect and provide for his wife and family (1 Corinthians 11:3) deserves to be cared for by that wife.

Ask God today, dear wife, for a greater understanding and appreciation of the tremendous charge God has given your husband, the one nearest and dearest to you. Then fall on your knees and...

- *Pray for him.* He who is called to bear the God-given responsibility outlined above deserves (and needs!) the ongoing prayers and heartfelt supplications of a faithful wife and partner!

Nor was man created for the woman, but woman for the man.
1 CORINTHIANS 11:9

$\mathcal{A}$ll was finished. Creation was complete. Yet sad words described the condition of Adam, the first man: "For Adam there was not found a helper comparable to him" (Genesis 2:20). Every beast of the field, every bird of the air, and every fish in the sea had a mate, a counterpart, but Adam had none. No sooner did God assess the situation ("It is not good that man should be alone...") than He offered a solution ("I will make him a helper comparable to him" [verse 18]).

Have you ever wondered what your purpose is as a wife? In His creation of Eve we have God's answer: God created her, the first woman, *for* the man, to be man's helper. Therefore, any woman who loves God and who is married is *on assignment from God to help her husband!*

So what can a wife do so that God can grow in her a heart committed to helping her husband and fulfilling her God-given assignment? Consider these suggestions:

- *Make a commitment to help your husband*—The decision to serve is yours, beloved. No one can decide for you, and no one can force you to decide. *You* must make the decision to help your husband. And as a woman who loves God, you'll undoubtedly want to follow through on His assignment for you to be a helper to your man.

- *Focus on your husband*—God wants us wives to focus our energy and efforts on our husbands—on *his* tasks, *his* goals, *his* responsibilities. But beware! Our sin nature cries out all too freely, "Me first!" But God wants us to say to our husband, "You first!"

- *Ask of your actions, "Will this help or hinder my husband?"*—By asking this simple question of ourselves before we act, we have a better chance of choosing conduct that will help our husband.

Helping. It's a simple yet noble assignment—and one that reaps rich rewards. Not only does our husband benefit, but we benefit as well as we learn to serve as Christ Himself did![10]

*Wives, submit to your own husbands,
as to the Lord.*
EPHESIANS 5:22

People love the Old Testament books of the Bible with their exciting stories about the heroes of the faith. We easily relate to the challenges faced by those saints who loved God, to their struggles to trust the Almighty and to live out their faith in obedience to Him and with confidence in Him.

Then the psalms bring to the surface feelings of joy and hopelessness, of praise and isolation, of assurance and questioning—feelings which offer us an exquisite nearness to God that few other parts of the Bible excite.

And who doesn't benefit from the proverbs, those pithy sayings of pure wisdom that make us think and, when we learn from them, make our lives better?

And, ah, the Gospels! How we adore our Jesus and how we love to read the pages that illuminate His life for us! Truly, through these four eyewitness accounts, we can almost see the unseen Savior!

The epistles come next, and they are different from what has come before. An epistle is a letter written, in this case, by one of God's servants to believers. Epistles address and correct specific problems in the Christian life and the Christian church. Some of the issues addressed in these ancient letters hit close to home. Certain issues which were problems then are problems now.

Why all this background in today's devotion? Two reasons:

First, because the rest of this book's devotions are based on passages from the epistles. Please be encouraged to continue reading, learning, growing, and grappling as we press on toward the end. Don't quit, don't tire, and don't give up! In these little letters God gives us sound advice and answers our questions about how to live for Him today.

Second, because submission to husbands has come up again—and it will come up again...and again...and again! The reason for this recurrent theme is that submission was a challenge when the epistles were written, it is a challenge for us today, and it will be a challenge tomorrow! Today God says once again, "Wives, submit to your own husbands, as to the Lord." Submission, just like helping (see yesterday's devotion), is a noble calling from God to all women who love Him. So press on!

"Honor your father and mother,"
which is the first commandment with promise.
EPHESIANS 6:2

$\mathcal{M}$uch is written about living life in such a way that, at the end, you have no regrets. The best way to have no regrets when it comes to your relationship with your parents is to follow God's commandment: "Honor your father and mother." God calls us—no matter what our age—to love and respect our parents. As one expositor of the Bible explains, "To honor a parent means to evaluate that person accurately and honestly, and treat him with the deference, respect, reverence, kindness, courtesy, and obedience which his station in life or his character demands."[11]

How can we as women who love God, better honor our dear parents? Consider these suggestions drawn from the above comment:

- *Evaluate.* Your parents may not be all you desire them to be, but God highly esteems their position of authority and commands that they be honored because of that position. As women who love God, we must make sure our evaluation of father and mother matches up with God's!

- *Defer.* While the opposite may be seen under some roofs and in some clans, God did not intend family gatherings to become an arena for feuding. How can we work to ensure a more civil and peaceful family climate? By deferring to our parents. Every situation improves when we willingly yield to our parents because of the honored position God has granted them.

- *Respect.* Lived out in thought, word, and deed, respect brings about the kinds of relationships God wants in His families. Besides, an attitude of respect can give birth to active admiration.

- *Revere.* We who love God revere Him, and God wants us to revere our father and mother as well. Reverence is respect mingled with love and awe. An attitude of reverence toward our parents moves us to treat them with kindness, courtesy, and obedience.

In short, a woman who loves God will love her mother and father! What can you do today both to nurture and to express your love for your parents?

Euodia and…Syntyche…
these women who labored with me in the gospel…
PHILIPPIANS 4:2,3

$\mathcal{T}$hey were heroes (or should we say heroines?) in the church. Euodia and Syntyche were prominent members of the church in Philippi. As workers for Christ in their local church, they apparently accomplished many great deeds for God and played a leading role in the early days at the church in Philippi. What exactly do we know about this dynamic duo?

- They were probably among the women who met to pray with Lydia by the river outside of Philippi when the apostle Paul arrived there and preached the gospel (Acts 16:13, see November 13). Quite possibly that was the day of their salvation.

- They were probably deaconesses in the church that was founded in Philippi. In that position, they would have been involved in serving the body and teaching other women.

- They toiled side by side with Paul in the work of the ministry. Using the language of the arena, Paul reports that Euodia and Syntyche labored and strove as fellow athletes in the arena with him.

We, too, can make a meaningful contribution to the Lord's causes. As women who love God, we are gifted by Him to profit other believers (1 Corinthians 12:7). While our work will not be alongside an apostle like Paul, we are assured that our efforts are important and count greatly in the kingdom (1 Corinthians 15:58). When we do our part, when we labor selflessly for God's kingdom, the gospel is shared, other people are introduced to Jesus, members of the body of Christ are edified, and the world sees the reality of Jesus Christ.

Warning! Just one more word about this ministry team: Their efforts for Christ were tarnished by their problems with one another, with their inability "to agree with each other." After all they did for the cause of Christ and for Paul himself and after all the energy they valiantly expended in the arena for Christ, the final word on these women points to their contention and their disruption of the Lord's work. As you serve, pray that this kind of closing statement will never be made about your ministry! May your labor for the Lord never be tarnished by sin.

*Wives, submit to your own husbands,
as is fitting in the Lord.*
COLOSSIANS 3:18

*D*o you want to be in harmony with God's will? Do you desire to be a woman after God's own heart? Is the aim of your life to bring glory to God in all that you do? Do you long to live for God and do things His way?

Well, today's passage from God's Holy Word again gives us wives one way to walk according to His plan for women who love God. For the eighth time in the Bible[1] we are exhorted to not only love and help our husband, but also to follow his leadership. In a passage that clearly lays out God's guidelines for husbands, children, fathers, and servants, Paul also addresses wives: "Wives, submit to your own husbands, as is fitting in the Lord." Note that this kind of submission to our husband's leadership is described as "fitting in the Lord." Adapting ourselves to our husband's direction is appropriate to us as women who belong to God.

As you live out this command with action befitting a believer, embrace these befitting attitudes:

- *A willingness to honor God's Word*—A woman who loves God heeds God's Word simply because it *is* God's Word! As another Scripture tells us, we are to be "obedient to [our] own husbands, that the word of God may not be blasphemed" (Titus 2:5).

- *A willingness to pray for your husband*—Prayer for another changes both the pray-er and the one prayed for. As you pray for your precious spouse, watch for wonderful things to happen to both of you—individually and together!

- *A willingness to look to the Lord in your actions*—If things get tough in your new effort to follow your husband, look to the Lord. *He*, the God of the Universe—not he, the man who is your husband—is the reason you are doing what you need to do.

- *A willingness to grow in God's grace*—As you venture forward and make the hard decisions and tough choices required to obey the Lord and submit to your husband, you will experience the marvelous, all-sufficient grace of our great God! Hallelujah!

> *I desire...that the women adorn themselves*
> *in modest apparel, with propriety and moderation...*
> *which is proper for women professing*
> *godliness, with good works.*
> 1 Timothy 2:8-10

*T*he everyday issue of what to wear has always raised questions for women, especially for women who love God. We face that question each new morning when we approach our closet. But what does *God* say about what we should wear? What guidelines does His Word offer us? Today's reading definitely helps us understand more of the mind of the Lord on this day-in, day-out challenge. Here we find the following criteria for the beauty of our dress:

Adorn yourself with modesty—God's Word counsels us women who desire to be beautiful in God's eyes to wear what is appropriate, proper, and suitable for the day's activities. Modesty also calls for clothing that is becoming, seemly, and orderly—for apparel that is decent and in order, that fits the order of the day.

Adorn yourself with propriety—Our dress should reflect our deep reverence for the God we love. He is holy, and our clothing should send forth a message about that holiness, indicating a woman who is concerned with inner purity, a woman who is set apart in heart to the Lord. Our God is worthy of respect, so shouldn't our clothing invite the respect of others, rather than their stares, shock, or scorn?

Adorn yourself with moderation—Our calling as a daughter of the King is a serious one, so our attire should indicate the seriousness with which we regard our privileged position in Christ. Our dress is to reveal a refined moderation to signal that we are women of self-restraint and discretion.

Adorn yourself with good works—God wants people to notice our good deeds: our godly actions and the gracious ornament of our good works, not our clothing!

One final word, dear beautiful sister. When God tells us to *adorn* ourselves, He means to *arrange* ourselves in an appropriate and graceful order.[2] So make sure that what you are wearing today...and every day... reflects the beauty and order of the Lord and your love for Him. Your goal each new day is to put on apparel that is fitting for a child of God and displays your devotion to Him.

Let a woman learn in silence....
1 TIMOTHY 2:11

*W*hen Jesus walked this earth, women had long been suppressed by both society and religion. Our Lord, however, established a new social and religious order based on the once unheard-of principle that "there is neither Jew nor Greek, there is neither slave nor free, there is neither male nor female; for you are all one in Christ Jesus" (Galatians 3:28).

But as we approach 1 Timothy 2 and today's issue of silence in the church, it appears that some women in the early church took their newfound freedom a little too far and were disrupting public worship with their outspokenness and verbal outbursts. So Paul writes a corrective word to help restore godly order and beauty to the worship services. In short, he asks that the women listen in silence and learn.

Even though these words were written to address a specific problem in a specific church at a specific time, we women today who love God would also do well to "listen and learn." These two wonderful principles not only speak to us about our personal conduct in our own church assembly, but they also offer wise advice for our daily life in general.

The principle of listening—The wisdom literature of the Bible tells us that "he who restrains his lips is wise." Why? Because "in the multitude of words sin is not lacking" (Proverbs 10:19). Less is best when it comes to speech! And we all know it's hard to talk and listen at the same time!

The principle of learning—The Bible tells us that learning is a decision. Therefore a woman who loves God chooses...

- *To seek knowledge*—"The heart of him who has understanding seeks knowledge" and "wise people store up knowledge" (Proverbs 15:14; 10:14).

- *To grow in knowledge*—The wisdom of the Proverbs says to "incline your ear and hear the words of the wise, and apply your heart to my knowledge" and teaches that "a wise man is strong, yes, a man of knowledge increases strength" (Proverbs 22:17; 24:5). The woman who listens and learns can experience the reality of brains over brawn!

How are you doing, dear sister, in the vital areas of listening and learning, of seeking and growing in godly wisdom and knowledge?

She will be saved in childbearing....
1 TIMOTHY 2:15

$\mathcal{O}$nce again some historical information will help us appreciate today's passage and the insight it offers into God's will for His women.

In an effort to redirect women's hearts and focus their energies on their most meaningful role in His kingdom, God reminds us of the beauty and significance of motherhood with the statement, "She will be saved in child-bearing." Evidently, some of the women in the early church who aspired to congregational leadership were usurping the roles laid out by the Lord for the male members of the assembly. In that context, a reminder of the dignity and distinction of nurturing their children seemed to be in order.

Paul's words are a sweet reminder for us today, too. As the voices of our culture call us away from the home front, it's easy for us to think that being a mother is not important. We all know those days when it seems we do nothing significant, nothing meaningful, nothing to make a mark upon our world. But nothing could be less true! No one can raise up your children for God and for society as you can. No one can love your little ones as genuinely and fervently as you do. And no one can give mankind the gift of a godly man or woman for the next generation like you—with God's help!—can.

How can we be sure we are investing our efforts and energies in what is most meaningful? How can we make a significant contribution to Christ's church and the world?

Embrace your calling as a mother—God established mothering as a high and vitally important calling, and His Word invites us to wholeheartedly embrace the privilege of parenting. As we raise our children, we can know genuine joy and fulfillment. When they leave the nest to go forth and serve the Lord and nurture yet another generation in the things of the Lord, we can know that our life has counted...greatly!

Excel in your efforts as a mother—The Proverbs 31 woman truly excelled in her role as mother. She became "the best of the best" and challenges us to do the same. Don't just *be* a mother. With the Lord's help and in His power, be the *best* mother you can be! Indeed, excel in your calling!

Likewise, their wives must be reverent....
1 TIMOTHY 3:11

*T*oday we meet a special group of women who have come to be known as *deaconesses*. As the early church grew, new needs arose. Who, for instance, would teach the new female believers? Who would counsel them regarding their marriage and family problems? Who would tend to them in childbirth, illness, destitution, and death? Who would visit them in their homes? Who would guide them through the baptism ceremony? It seemed appropriate that a woman should help another woman in such works of charity. Thus the wives of the male leaders naturally came to fill this much-needed ministry.

Because of the importance of these personal ministries, God set forth some high standards for those women who would care for the needs of other women in the church. Today we look at the first of the four criteria God established for women in leadership. Exactly what kind of woman does the Lord use?

1. *The woman God uses is dignified*—Since God is first and foremost in the heart of a woman who loves Him, hers is a life of worship. This woman lives in the presence of the God she loves, and that position gives her actions dignity and decorum. As a daughter of the King, she unconsciously acts with a certain nobility and regality. Her devotion to God is evident in all that she says and does, and there is seriousness and purpose to her life which cannot be missed. Even in her slightest acts—like entering a room, speaking to another, sitting in a meeting—people will notice something regal, something grand, something magnificent and noble. Why? Because of the God who lives within her and because of her continuous worship of the God she loves.

Dear sister, does your behavior reflect a certain godly dignity that invites the respect of other people? Does your conduct reflect something of the majesty of the Lord? When others have contact with you, do they sense that you are a dignitary for Deity? These questions give us much to think about and pray about...and perhaps alter!

Likewise, their wives must be...not slanderers....
1 TIMOTHY 3:11

$\mathcal{A}$s you may remember from yesterday's reading, leaders in the early church realized that women needed special assistance that would best come from other women. The female members of the church needed, for instance, to be visited, cared for in their homes, and nursed in their difficulties. They also needed encouragement, counsel, and instruction as they were preparing for baptism and attempting to live a godly life. So in His infinite wisdom, God set forth His standard of woman-to-woman ministry in areas of life where women should supply the hands-on help other women needed.

But what kind of woman qualified for such intimate ministry? As we've seen, first *the woman God uses is dignified.* Her behavior reflects a certain dignity that invites the respect of others, and her conduct reflects something of the majesty of the Lord.

> 2. *The woman God uses is not a gossip*—Just as a young doctor pledges in the Hippocratic oath never to repeat anything that he has heard from or about a patient, so the woman God uses is not to repeat anything she sees or hears about the women God calls her to help.

A person who does talk maliciously about others is called a gossip—a word used in the Bible of the devil himself. His very name is *diabolos*, "slanderer." In fact, "slanderer" is used 34 times in Scripture as a title for Satan and once to refer to Judas, the one who betrayed our Jesus (John 6:70). This is frightening company, and no woman who loves God and whom He calls to serve His women in the church should be a gossip and a slanderer! The two extremes—helping women by our works and hurting women by our words—just do not go together!

What can you do today, fellow lover of the Lord, to eliminate gossip from your life? Do you need to ask the Lord to help you resist that temptation? Do you simply need to speak less? Do you need to ask God to give you a greater love for His women? To echo Paul, "Let no corrupt word proceed out of your mouth" (Ephesians 4:29). Oh, please, choose to help and not hurt one another!

Likewise, their wives must be...temperate....
1 TIMOTHY 3:11

*M*any Christians who visit the Holy Land also journey north into Lebanon to see the well-preserved ruins of Baalbek. There the remains of the temple of Bacchus overlook flourishing vineyards. It was certainly a pretty site for a building, but what went on inside that ancient structure was *not* pretty! This temple was devoted to the worship of Dionysus, whose domain was "the liquid fire in the grape." As worshipers, both male and female, drank freely of the potent, abundant wine of the fields, their worship turned into "dancing madness" and "orgies."[3]

Because many of the women in the early church came from such a vile background where drunkenness and excess were a way of life and a way of worship, God called the women who ministered in the church to the discipline of temperance. We've already learned that the woman God uses must be dignified and must not be a gossip. Today God adds to His list of qualifications for a woman in ministry this third guideline:

3. *The woman God uses is temperate*—The call to temperance is more than a call to abstain from alcoholic excess. God's women are to be calm, dispassionate, grave, and sober. Their lives are to be characterized by moderation and restraint in all things. Although 1 Timothy 3:11 specifically addresses drunkenness, it also calls women to self-control in all areas of life. One translation says, "Women are to be serious in behavior, saying no evil of others, *controlling themselves*" (emphasis added).[4] In what areas of your life is God calling you to temperance?

Food	Possessions	Caffeine	Sleep
Alcohol	Talents	Tobacco	Sports
Clothes	Money	Drugs	Career

The woman God uses in ministry is free from excesses in and addiction to *anything!*

If any areas in your life call for a dose of self-restraint, follow in the steps of Daniel. He purposed in his heart that he would not defile himself with the king's rich foods and wine (Daniel 1:8). God will give you the same strength He gave Daniel. In fact, He promises both to never let you be tempted beyond what you can bear and to provide you a way out when temptation does arise (1 Corinthians 10:13). What a glorious and hope-filled promise!

Likewise, their wives must be…
faithful in all things….
1 TIMOTHY 3:11

$\mathcal{T}$he final criterion that will be used by God to judge us is not success but faithfulness."[5] These thought-provoking words in 1 Timothy remind us how vitally important it is that God's faithfulness is part of our character. Indeed, God calls us Christian women who love Him to be "faithful in all things."

As we've noted these past few days, the early church was growing as people embraced Jesus Christ as their Savior. These increased numbers meant new ministry challenges, especially among the women. For instance, what kind of woman should be appointed to minister to the female members of the church? Who could walk among her sisters in need, meet their needs, and keep to herself what she heard and witnessed? The early church leaders decided that such responsibilities should fall upon those women who were dignified, not gossips, and temperate in all aspects of their lives. And they singled out one more crucial characteristic as necessary:

4. *The woman God uses is faithful in all things*—She must be absolutely reliable and completely trustworthy as she carried out the business of the church. These ministering saints would live out the love of Christ as they performed their God-given duties according to the instructions they received. Truly, a faithful-in-all-things woman would be a blessing to the church body she served!

Exactly what does a woman who is faithful in all things do—and how can we women who love God develop this priceless quality? Begin by being faithful in these day-in, day-out practices:

• *Faithfulness follows through* on whatever must be done, no matter what the task.

• *Faithfulness delivers the goods,* whether a message or a meal.

• *Faithfulness keeps her word*: Her yes means yes and her no means no (James 5:12).

• *Faithfulness keeps her commitments and appointment*s. You won't find her canceling plans!

God rewards not our success, but the faithfulness with which we do His will. He is far more concerned about us being faithful women after His own heart than He is about any success we achieve in the world's eyes—and we should be, too!

Now she who is really a widow, and left alone,
trusts in God and continues in
supplication and prayers night and day.
1 TIMOTHY 5:5

To the Greek poet Euripides, the most haunting sin ever was failure in one's duty to a parent, and God's judgment is no less scathing. We've already noted several times His Old and New Testament commandment to "honor your father and your mother" (see April 11 and November 30). In fact, honoring and caring for our parents is an essential part of our duty as Christians. May we never forget God's instruction to us "to repay" our parents and grandparents (verse 4)!

But what about those dear widows who have no children to, in response to this command, care for them? God places the responsibility for these widows fully on the church—as long as these widows first meet certain criteria, two of which we'll look at now. Take these character issues to heart, because they paint a picture of godly senior sainthood:

> *A woman of faith*—What does a woman who loves God do when she finds herself desolate and utterly alone? She trusts in Him. Literally, she fixes her hope in the direction of God. She has her hope set unshakably on Him, and because she has so consistently set her hope on the Lord, that hope has become a permanent attitude and mindset. Hers is a settled and immovable trust in her Almighty God and heavenly Father. Is this widow alone? Never! She has the Lord!

> *A woman of prayer*—What does a woman who loves God do when she has no one to help provide for her daily needs? She looks to the Lord and faithfully lifts her needs before Him, the One who has promised she shall never want (Psalm 23:1). She addresses to God her supplications and prayers for her personal needs. Like the senior saint Anna (see October 10), she is a woman of faithful prayer, continuing in an attitude of prayer both night and day.

Oh, the manifold blessings of a life of faith! Taste them now! May it be said of you in years to come, "She is a woman of faith who truly loves God and trusts in Him completely!"

Honor widows who are...well reported for good works:
if she has brought up children...lodged strangers...
washed the saints' feet...relieved the afflicted...
[and] diligently followed every good work.
1 TIMOTHY 5:3,10

*H*ow can a woman know, beyond a shadow of a doubt, that her life has counted? Women who love God and long to do His will look to His Word for answers to this important question.

In today's passage, God gives us a checklist for godly character and a life of good works. Although these criteria were originally used to determine which Christian widows in the early church qualified for financial care, they present the Lord's standards for those who yearn to lead a lovely and useful life. Take a moment to compare your life to God's standards.

✓ *Overall conduct:* Good words are spoken of women who love God. Nothing ill is said or heard of her conduct in the home or anywhere else. She has earned the reputation of doing good deeds of all kinds, including the following.

✓ *Nurtured children:* The order in which this godly woman's good works are listed is significant. Caring for children ranks first. If you ever wonder how important caring for your children is in God's eyes, consider this verse!

✓ *Hospitality to strangers:* Next on the list comes using home and hearth to welcome traveling Christians and to entertain fellow believers.

✓ *Help for those in trouble:* The woman who loves God uses her strength to assist those who suffer. Her humble service means hands-on ministry that gives glory to God.

✓ *Washing the feet of the saints:* Love for God is reflected in a general manner of compassion and benevolence and perhaps, more specifically, visits to the needy, the ill, the shut-in and even—literally, as well as metaphorically—tending to the menial service of foot-washing.

✓ *Devotion to every good work:* The woman who loves God diligently pursues a life of good works.

Now ask the Lord for His great grace in emulating this grand group of women who loved Him and desired to serve Him and His people!

> *...the genuine faith that is in you,*
> *which dwelt first in your grandmother Lois*
> *and your mother Eunice...*
> 2 Timothy 1:5

*Y*ou've probably seen the kind of picture frame that displays two photographs instead of only one. Similarly, today's Scripture passage pairs the portraits of two women who loved God: the mother/daughter team of Lois and Eunice. Both mother and daughter are heralded as outstanding mothers. Let's get to know Lois today and then meet her daughter tomorrow.

What do we learn here about Lois?

- *Her name*—First of all, Lois's name most likely means "agreeable"—and we know the apostle Paul found that to be true about her! These 2 Timothy words of praise flow from his pen.

- *Her background*—A devout Jewess, Lois apparently instructed her daughter, Eunice, and her grandson, Timothy, in the Old Testament Scriptures, thus preparing their hearts to hear the words about eternal life through Jesus Christ, which Paul preached when he passed through their hometown of Lystra (Acts 16:1).

- *Her faith*—Commendations by others always tell us much about the one complimented. Here Paul lauds Lois's faith as genuine and sincere.

- *Her legacy*—Have you heard of Timothy? He's the young Christian who accompanied Paul, God's mighty messenger, as he preached the gospel of Jesus Christ and helped establish churches throughout the Mediterranean world. This young man became Paul's true son in the faith (verse 2) and the one person Paul could point to as "like-minded" with himself (Philippians 2:20).

- *Her title*—Many grandmothers are mentioned in the Bible, but Lois is the only one referred to by the honored and revered label *grandmother*.

The Bible speaks of "the law" or teaching of the mother (Proverbs 1:8; 6:20), indicating that those of us who are mothers—and, like Lois, grandmothers—are on assignment from God to teach His Word to our children and to our children's children. We are to pass on the spiritual truths which will ensure a godly heritage for generations to come. Teaching God's Word *must* be our passion, just as it was for Lois!

...the genuine faith that is in you,
which dwelt first in your grandmother Lois
and your mother Eunice...
2 TIMOTHY 1:5

Yesterday we met Lois, the godly grandmother whose precious portrait God has preserved for us in His Word, and today we can look at the accompanying picture of Eunice, Lois's daughter. As we consider her portrait, we are surprised by one of the brush strokes that make up the details of Eunice's daily life: *Eunice had an unbelieving husband.* Eunice was a believing Jewess who had passed her faith along to her son Timothy without the help of a believing mate (Acts 16:1).

Are you married to a man who is not a Christian? Or do you know women who love God who are in this position? Be encouraged! If you've ever wondered whether your children will be able to discern the truth when two belief systems and two set of values are lived out in front of them daily, be assured that truth always shines brighter! Also remember that your children are "holy," that is, set apart unto the Lord by the godly presence of one believing parent, by the presence of Christ in you (1 Corinthians 7:14). And because Christ lives in you, Christ lives in your home! That means that your children are exposed to a godly witness, whether or not they want it and whether or not they are even aware of it. They will also know divine blessing and protection because of their believing mother.[6]

So take heart! Be faithful to sow the seeds not only of love, but also of divine truth. Be diligent to share the Scriptures with your little ones. Take every opportunity to pray with them and for them. Share with them the wonderful stories about Jesus and the specifics about how He can become their Savior. Be steadfast in your faith...and in your faith for your children's spiritual development. Above all, live out God's love in your own life. And when you are discouraged or when it appears that your godly efforts for your children are failing, press on, remembering that "He who is in you is greater than he who is in the world" (1 John 4:4)!

The older women [are to]...
admonish the young women...
TITUS 2:3,4

*D*o you feel sad when you think of growing older? Do you wonder what you will do in your sunset years?

Although modern society may not respect its elders, today's passage of Scripture clearly shows the church honoring its older women and giving them an important responsibility. Indeed, senior saints play a vital part in the church when they respond to God's call to teach and admonish, to train and encourage, the younger women in the body of Christ. Truly, older women in whom the years have nurtured serenity, compassion, patience, practical understanding, and godly knowledge have a crucial role to play in the life of the church and in their community.

For the next few weeks, we will look at Titus 2:3-5 and marvel at the beauty and dignity God bestows upon us women. We will see what His Holy Word teaches about our sacred roles and, ideally, we will see more clearly all God has in mind for our lives.

But for now, take time out and enjoy a few minutes in prayer. Set aside your to-do list for a while, curl up with your Bible, and look once again at God's words of wisdom to us in Titus 2:3-5. As you do, remember that "to everything there is a season, a time for every purpose under heaven" (Ecclesiastes 3:1) and consider these two "seasons" in your life as a woman who loves God:

Are you a younger woman? Your assignment from God is to devote yourself to loving your husband and children. If you have no husband and children, God nevertheless wants you to dedicate yourself to growing as a home manager and to pursuing the godly qualities of discretion, purity, kindness, and a servant's heart.

Are you an older woman? Your assignment from God is to share what you know with younger women who love God. Through the years, you have gained some precious knowledge—pearls, if you will!—that you can pass on to those who are learning. As you exhibit a reverent spirit, guard your speech, walk with careful discipline, and pass on what you know, you give a priceless gift—indeed, your priceless pearls of beauty and dignity—to God, to His church, and to His women!

The older women likewise...[are to] be
reverent in behavior.
TITUS 2:3

𝒯he Bible often speaks of godly character qualities as gems and jewels, so let's think of the godly traits described in Titus 2:3-5 as a breathtakingly beautiful string of cultured pearls. Who doesn't admire a lovely strand of pearls? Their soft luster adds a touch of grace and beauty to any woman's appearance. So each day, as we grow in our understanding of God's kind of beauty, may we slip another pearl onto the exquisite strand of virtues which give glory to Him!

Now it shouldn't surprise us that God begins this gracious strand of character traits with the pearl of piety: "The older women likewise...[are to] be reverent in behavior." What a dazzling pearl this one is! Consider these two aspects of reverent behavior:

> *Sacred*—*Sacred* is used to describe services, items, and temples set apart for religious use. As women of God, we, too, are sacred. We are a band of people living in the presence of the Most Sacred Person, going about the sacred duties His Holy Word calls us to. We are indeed "a royal priesthood," called to lives of holiness (1 Peter 2:9). Indeed, our every word and our every action should speak of our sacred service to God Most High!

> *Sanctified*—*Sanctified* also refers to being set apart and dedicated to some person, place, or purpose. We who belong to the Lord are consecrated unto Him for His pleasure and His purposes (Ephesians 1:9,11). God calls us to a life-style that reflects His values and His priorities. And because He is "holy, holy, holy" (Isaiah 6:3), we who belong to Him should behave in a way that honors and glorifies Him. Such behavior will reveal the beauty of Jesus in us and even inspire other people to a similar life of joyful piety and worship.

Dear one, look into the mirror of God's Word. Does your life reflect a worshipful heart and a soul in tune with the Lord? Is the priceless pearl of joyous piety the first thing others notice about you? Is all that you do done with the presence of the Lord in mind and done as unto Him? May the pearl of piety grace all you say and do!

The older women likewise...
[are not to] be...slanderers.
TITUS 2:3

*N*o pearl shows off its deep luster more than the pearl of silence does. Now that doesn't mean that we can't speak up or share words of encouragement and edification. But the virtue of silence does mean that *what* we share should in fact be encouraging and edifying!

As Paul instructs young pastor Timothy about ministering in the church, Paul wisely delegates the teaching and training of the congregation's young women to its godly older women. But Paul cautions that these older women are not to be slanderers. Although old age may too often bring out intolerance, criticism, and bitterness in people, Christ's aged saints are to use their voice for better things than these![7]

Hear what Dr. Gene Getz, author of *The Measure of a Woman*, says about our speech: "How we use our tongues serves as a precise measurement of our Christian maturity...[and] reflects on every thing we do and affects every thing we do, and every person we come in contact with."[8] So as guidelines for our speech, Dr. Getz suggests that we ask these questions before sharing any information about another person:

- Is this information pure?
- Will it contribute to the building up of this person (or persons)?
- Will it create harmony and peace in the body of Christ?
- Is it the most merciful thing to do?
- Will it produce good fruit?
- Does it reflect a submissive attitude on my part?
- Am I truly sincere and unselfish in wanting to share this information?
- Am I being impartial and objective?
- Do I really have the facts?
- Am I truly being considerate of this person in sharing this information?

When it comes to the words we speak, less is best: "In the multitude of words sin is not lacking, but he who restrains his lips is wise" (Proverbs 10:19). So pray before you say!

> *The older women likewise...*
> *[are not to] be...given to much wine.*
> TITUS 2:2

*N*o race is won without focusing one's full attention on the finish line, and the Christian life is a race—indeed, a *lifelong* race! Scripture calls us to run the race and tells us *how* to run it well: "Let us lay aside every weight, and the sin which so easily ensnares us, and let us run with endurance the race that is set before us" (Hebrews 12:1).

As we consider the Titus 2 qualifications for those women worthy to teach and guide the congregation's younger women, God points today to *temperance*, that is, to a life of moderation and discipline. Instead of being given to excesses and addictions of any kind, godly women are to maintain a strict control over their desires and habits. No excesses, no "weights," and no encumbrances are to mar their reputation or impair their service to the Lord. These women desire to "lay aside every weight, and the sin which so easily ensnares." Totally devoted to God, they constantly look to Jesus with every step they take as they run the race of life.

Let the following biblical and practical set of guidelines for freedom from excess help you slip the invaluable pearl of discipline onto your growing strand of godly traits:

- *Excess*—Will this practice slow me down? (Hebrews 12:1)

- *Expediency*—Is it useful, profitable, and beneficial? (1 Corinthians 6:12)

- *Emulation*—Is it what Jesus would do in the same situation? (1 John 2:6)

- *Evangelism*—Will it spread the gospel to unbelievers, enhance my testimony, or serve as a strong basis for personal evangelism? (Colossians 4:5)

- *Edification*—Will it build me up in Christ? (1 Corinthians 10:23)

- *Exaltation*—Will God be glorified? (1 Corinthians 10:31)

- *Example*—Will this action offer my Christian sisters the proper kind of example—a righteous path—to follow? Will it harm my weaker sister in Christ or strengthen her? (1 Corinthians 8:13)[9]

Clearly the pearl of discipline is a precious one indeed! Focus on it, desire it, grasp it, display it, and point others to it. Oh, how this pearl beautifies every woman who loves God!

> *The older women...[are to] be...*
> *teachers of good things.*
> Titus 2:3

*T*oday we read more about that faithful group of "older" women who are to be about the business of teaching their younger sisters how to follow God. Known for their devotion to the Lord instead of gossip and indulgences, these women were to assist the women in the church who were younger in age and newer in the faith.

Whether or not we qualify as an "older" woman in terms of our age, we can be sure that teaching "good things"—sharing pearls of wisdom—is a godly goal which we reach in two ways:

First, we teach by what we do. By living out your priorities and exhibiting godly behavior, you teach and disciple others without saying a word. Truly, the best way to teach God's standards is to model them moment by moment in your everyday life. We all need role models for a life of faith, and we all know that a single picture is worth a thousand words. So by God's grace and in His power, you can teach others "good things" by what you do.

Second, we teach by what we say. Formal instruction has long been the companion teaching tool to a sincere example, and God has given you a long list of topics to talk about. For starters, here are three:

- *Do you know Jesus?* Just as all roads lead to Rome, all your teaching should lead to Christ! Share with other people how to become a Christian, how to enjoy the assurance of salvation and the security of their position in Christ, and how to grow in Christlikeness.

- *Have you been married or had children?* Oh, how your younger sisters need to hear what you have learned! Consider all you've learned along the way as a wife and mother and then pass those pearls of wisdom on to others.

- *Have you learned how to manage your home?* Once again, bless those who are still struggling in this area with all that you have learned. Encourage them! Give them a vision for their homes! Instruct them in the basics!

Give of yourself, precious sister! Share your experiences, your knowledge, and your God-given wisdom. Offer who you are and what you know in service of the Lord and of those women who love Him!

*Admonish the young women to
love their husbands.*
Titus 2:4

*W*omen who love God know what His Word says about the priority position a husband is to hold in the heart and soul of a married woman. In fact, the very first thing that godly older women are to teach and encourage younger ones to do is "to love their husbands." And this verse is a call to friendship love. The word used here is *phileo*, meaning "friendship love," a love that cherishes, enjoys, and *likes* our husband! God calls us to value our dear husband and to build a friendship with him. In fact, he is to be our best friend.

But how can we women who love God (and our husbands!) make this kind of love a reality in our life? What we can do to slip this pearl of devotion onto our strand of lovely graces? Follow these ABCs:

*A*sk yourself, *"Am I spoiling my husband rotten?"* Loving your husband is all about spoiling him rotten! Lavishing love on him! Showing him that he truly is the number one person in your life. Are you doing that in your day-in, day-out routine?

*B*egin to choose your husband over all other human relationships. And "all other" includes your children! Two family counselors have observed, "The point at which many marriages jump the track is in OVERinvesting in children and UNDERinvesting in the marriage."[10]

*C*ommit to making your husband your number-one human relationship. Our relationship with our husband is to be more important than all the other relationships we enjoy—and that "all others" includes our parents, friends, and neighbors; a brother, sister, best friend, and even our children. Your husband has to be number one—and he has to know it. (And "all others" need to know it, too!)

Our calling, dear wife, is to love our husband. So do all you can to communicate your love to your precious husband. Be creative and have fun. Invest your energy and your time. And remember that a heart that loves is a heart that plans. So spend time in prayer, put on your thinking cap, and get to work showing your husband the love that is in your heart![11]

Admonish the young women to…
love their children.
TITUS 2:4

*B*ehold the luster of this next priceless pearl! Behold the beauty of motherhood! If you have been graced and honored to wear this title, then you'll be most interested in the fact that, after our husband, our children are to take precedence over all other people in our life and in our schedule. That's clearly the teaching here in Titus 2.

In the lesson plans He gives older women to teach younger women, God calls us to first love our husbands and, second, to love our children. We can best respond to this divine call when we have a heart of passion:

- *A passion for teaching God's Word*—Our precious children—not the children at church; not the women at church; not friends, neighbors, or anyone else—are to receive the firstfruits of our burning passion for God's holy truth. The Bible is clear: We mothers are *on assignment from God to teach His Word to our children* (Proverbs 1:8; 6:20). We can do many things for our children, but teaching God's Word to our sons and daughters must be our passion.

- *A passion for teaching God's wisdom*—Closely related to our call to teach God's Word to our children is our call to instruct them in His wisdom. We are to pass on to our sons and daughters the principles and counsel, the models of praise and guidelines for decision-making, and the godly practices and spiritual instruction found in the Bible. We must have a passion for teaching our children practical and scriptural wisdom for their daily lives.

- *A passion for prayer*—What a blessing is the mother who thinks, loves, acts, speaks, and *prays* with passion! You are to focus your most energetic and fervent prayers on your child (James 5:16). We mothers who love God—and our sons and daughters—will never know on this side of heaven all that our prayers accomplish on behalf of our children, but we are to faithfully and passionately pray for them. No one else is in a better position to do so!

Dear mother (and grandmother!), know that God is our willing and able Partner as we raise our children to know Him and love Him and serve Him—as we do so with passion!

Admonish the young women to…be discreet.
Titus 2:4,5

Prudence is a wonderful old word that, like *discreet*, means "to use good judgment" [see August 9]. Again, we see that prudence or discretion has to do with self-control in all aspects of daily life. As one teacher states, "No quality of life stands out more boldly in Scripture as a mark of Christian maturity than being 'self-controlled'…being 'sensible,' 'sober,' and of a 'sound mind.' "[12] But just how does this quality of prudent self-control come about in our lives? And what does it look like in a woman who loves God?

- *Prudence is reflected in balance.* The woman who wears the pearl of prudence is admired for the gracious beauty and order in her life. Habitually self-controlled, she is able to avoid wild emotional and behavioral extremes, teeter-totter patterns, and radical highs and lows. Because caution and good judgment guide her decisions, she knows an evenness and stability in life. She experiences fewer failures, crises, "eeks!" and "oh no's!"

- *Prudence is reflected in sensibility.* The woman of discretion weighs all her options before making decisions and commitments. She asks, "Where will this decision lead? What might be the far-reaching results of this choice? Will this option benefit my precious family, and will it be good for me?" With an eye to the future and her heart filled with concern for God's honor and her family's good, this wise woman looks to the Lord, weighs all her options, and then exercises good judgment as she makes sensible decisions.

- *Prudence is reflected in neutrality.* Finally, a woman of wisdom and discretion is a woman whose heart is quiet in its passions. Because her soul looks to the Lord and trusts in Him, she can live with or without the things of this world. Matters of position, possession, and passion fail to unnerve or control God's woman of wisdom. She finds all she truly needs in the Lord and rests in Him. As the Proverbs teach us, "A sound [or tranquil] heart is life to the body" (Proverbs 14:30).

We cultivate the fine pearl of prudence when we stop, wait, pray, weigh our choices, search the Scriptures, and seek wise counsel…*before* we make our decisions!

Admonish the young women to...be...chaste.
TITUS 2:4,5

*W*hen you think of pearls, don't you almost automatically think of purity? Our heavenly Father wants the lives of the women who love Him to radiate the chastity or purity that comes with being His in heart, soul, mind, and body.

As women who are saved by a holy God, we, too, precious sister, are to be holy, to be sacred vessels unto the Lord. Our passage today bids us to be modest and pure, set apart for the Lord, and free from defilement and over-concern for the things of this world. God calls us to scrupulously and actively avoid impurity and immorality in thought, word, and deed.

Why would God include *purity* in His call to us? As Dr. Gene Getz explains, "The subjects emphasized by biblical writers reflect the major problems in New Testament churches, and no problem is dealt with more consistently than immorality. Hardly a letter was penned that did not treat this subject specifically, graphically, and with candor."[13] So we read much of God's concern for the purity of His women and of His church.

The best way to keep our lives pure is to fill our minds with God's Word. As the psalmist declares,

> The law of the LORD is perfect...
> The testimony of the LORD is sure...
> The statutes of the LORD are right...
> The commandment of the LORD is pure...
> The fear of the LORD is clean...
> The judgments of the LORD are true
>   and righteous altogether (Psalm 19:7-9).

As we seek those things above, as we refuse to become too attached to what is merely temporary; as we set our minds and affections on things above, not on things of the earth (Colossians 3:1, 2); as we turn our eyes upon Jesus, the pure Word of God, the Holy Person of God, and the spotless Son, then the things of this world will indeed grow strangely dim and unappealing.

So think on whatever things are true, noble, just, pure, lovely, of good report, virtuous, and praiseworthy (Philippians 4:8). Since thoughts precede actions, let this be the first step you take toward adding the pearl of purity to your strand of godly virtues.

*Admonish the young women
to…be…homemakers.*
TITUS 2:4,5

*A*s you may know, pearls come in a surprising variety of colors. And today we will look at a new and perhaps surprising shade of pearl in this strand of godly virtues we've been examining.

We've been noting the qualities God wants to characterize the lives of the women who love Him. We've seen the importance He places on our roles as wives, mothers, and servants in the church. And today we behold the lovely luster God has in mind for our homemaking! Too many women don't see the value of caring for their home. They are instead tempted to view home management as a tedious burden to bear.

But God knows your talents—indeed, He's created them in you!—and has designed the perfect place for many of those talents to blossom, and that place is your home. As we "build our home" God's way (Proverbs 14:1), He blesses us in these ways:

- *Order becomes the order of the day*—Paying a little attention each day to the place you call home can bring order from chaos, grow your talent for management, and make your home a peaceful oasis in a loud and busy world.

- *Family members and guests are blessed*—How fortunate is the loved one who enters the refuge of *home* after a hard day at work or school!

- *Relationships under your roof are improved*—Home is where family members form relationships. When the pearls of beauty, peace, order, joy, and love shine there, people can know a sense of safety and genuine well-being. When home is a place of calmness and love, family relationships can blossom.

- *You become the resident artist as your talent grows*—Consider yourself on assignment from God to bring beauty into your home. And, precious homemaker, as you work to fulfill that assignment, you'll be pleasantly surprised to discover that the pearl of your homemaking talents adds a rich, lustrous quality to your life.

Ask God now to renew your energy and spark your creativity so that you can use—and enjoy using—the talents He has given you to enhance your home life, better care for your family, and glorify Him in your role as homemaker.

Admonish the young women to...be...good.
Titus 2:4,5

God's calling to the women who love Him to cultivate such character qualities as discipline and dignity, piety and wisdom, also includes a softer pearl of grace, the pearl of goodness. And how lovely this gem is! For starters, goodness is the kindheartedness we extend to others while we work hard disciplining ourselves! As someone has said, "Deal ruthlessly with yourself, compassionately with others." That's goodness.

Consider other beautiful aspects of this precious pearl:

Goodness is active—Goodness is more than a topic for meditation and prayer. Goodness is something we do. In fact, the word itself (*agathos* in the Greek) means "doing good."

> Who needs your goodness today? Think of your husband and children, parents and in-laws, coworkers and neighbors. Are there widows, the elderly, or ill folks who need your touch of compassion?

Goodness is a heart condition—A kind heart—a heart that cares about other people, that yearns to improve their lives, that notices their needs and thinks about their well-being—precedes active goodness.

> Would those who know you best consider you to be kind? Are you one who regularly asks, "What can I do for you today?" Does your heart look out through eyes of love and see people as Jesus does?

Goodness is a choice—As women who love God, every day we are to "put on" a heart of kindness, compassion, and goodness, just as we put on our clothes (Ephesians 4:32; Colossians 3:12). Make sure you choose to wear this soft garment of grace and goodness!

> Look to the Lord in prayer, beloved. Speak to Him about goodness: His goodness, your goodness (or your lack!), and the goodness that you so want to shine forth from you, His child. Ask for His filling, His help, His grace as you choose to walk in His light wearing the pearl of goodness.

Admonish the young women to...
be...obedient to their own husbands,
that the word of God may not be blasphemed.
Titus 2:4,5

*I*t's Christmas Day! As we celebrate the birth of our Savior, let us consider an important way we can bring honor and glory to God and to His Son.

In Titus 2, we've been looking at God's roles and standards for women who love Him. Today the passage ends with the clarion call to honor Him by obeying His commands, which Jesus summarized by saying to love God with all we are and to love our neighbors (Mark 12:30,31). When we live according to these two basic laws, the Word of God is not blasphemed, not discredited, by our words or our actions.

After all, *how* we live out our daily life as women who love God sends a message to the watching world. When we walk according to God's standards, He is glorified and the message of salvation is clearly proclaimed. Conversely, when we are lacking in such vital areas as love, self-control, purity, love of home, kindness, and humility, God and His ways are dishonored and people readily "blaspheme" and slander Him and His truth.

What a gift of glory—what a radiant pearl—we give to the Lord when we honor Him by walking in His ways! As we leave this precious section of Scripture, may we measure our life against it, allow it to give us fresh insights, and invite God to be at work transforming us and conforming us to His holy standards.

- Does my behavior reflect a heart that worships God and loves Him above all else?

- Do I love God by obeying His commands?

- Am I loving other people by being careful with my speech, in control of my passions, and generous with God-given wisdom?

- Do I love other people by praying passionately for them and freely sharing my God-given talents with them?

- Am I willingly serving my husband and children with a selfless, sacrificial love?

- Am I cautious, chaste, and compassionate?

On this Christmas Day when we remember how much God has given us in His Son—His unspeakably wonderful Gift!—let us offer to Him the gift of obedience, that precious and lustrous pearl which gives Him both great joy and great glory!

> *By faith Sarah herself also received strength*
> *to conceive seed, and she bore a child*
> *when she was past the age, because she*
> *judged Him faithful who had promised.*
> HEBREWS 11:11

Shhh! Today we tiptoe into the hallowed halls of Hebrews 11, God's portrait gallery of great men and women who have loved Him through the ages. We can't help but notice the larger-than-life pictures of Noah, Abraham, Isaac, Jacob, Joseph, Moses, and Joshua. But just as grand is the portrait of the gentle and quiet-spirited Sarah who possessed a strong-as-steel faith (see 1 Peter 3:1-6). Her faith shines as brightly as that of the other people listed on this holy roster!

What merited dear Sarah's inclusion in faith's Hall of Fame?

Motherhood—This blessing came late to the long-barren Sarah, who, at age 90, finally bore Isaac! And once the blessing was bestowed, Sarah was a fierce, loyal mother to her precious son (see Genesis 21)!

Mother of a nation—Sarah has been esteemed throughout time as a kind of mother figure to God's chosen nation of Israel. From Sarah and her husband, Abraham, and through their son, Isaac, come—through faith—all true believers, God's chosen people through time (Romans 4:16).

Mother of faith—Hebrew 11 points to the acts of faith of those who preceded us in time, and Sarah is the first woman named. And what was her outstanding act of faith? Sarah considered God faithful and able to follow through on His promise of a son in her old age.

We're nearing the end of our year-long journey through the Bible. Along the way we've met women just like us who have walked with God by faith. And we need to remember, as many of them did, that "with God nothing will be impossible" (Luke 1:37).

What trials and temptations do you currently face? Does some difficulty or affliction affect your every moment? Do you live alone? Are your days or your health waning? Are you stretched to the limit by the demands of each day? Identify your greatest challenge, and then look to the Lord with the greatest of faith. As Hebrews 11:1 tells us, "Faith is the substance of things hoped for, the evidence of things not seen."

Then ask yourself what the angel of the Lord asked Sarah: "Is anything too hard for the LORD?" (Genesis 18:14). What is your answer, dear one?

By faith Moses, when he was born,
was hidden three months by his parents,
because…they were not afraid of the king's command.
HEBREWS 11:23

*A*s we continue walking through God's gallery of faith's heroes, noting the women honored there, we next pause before His glowing portrait of Jochebed. As we look at her picture, we behold a quiet strength in her—the strength that comes with faith in our unchanging God:

- *Faith of her fathers*—Consider the roots of this woman's grand faith. Both her father, Levi, and her brother Kohath were priests—a fact that suggests much about Jochebed's heritage and upbringing. Hers was a family set apart to serve the Lord!

- *Faith as a wife*—When Jochebed became the wife of Amram, himself a priest as well, her faith joined with his, and another family of faith was born.

- *Faith as a mother*—Jochebed passed her godly heritage on to her three children: Aaron, Moses, and Miriam. Aaron and Moses were priests, and Miriam served alongside them (Micah 6:4). But long before the three of them began serving the Lord, we see their mother's greatest act of faith. Defying Pharaoh's command that every son born to the Hebrew people be killed (Exodus 1:22), Jochebed hid baby Moses. *She* was not afraid of the king's command! As the Bible declares, "Perfect love casts out fear" (1 John 4:18). Jochebed loved God *and* Moses, and that love dispelled all fear and enabled her to act in faith and, therefore, with courage!

We've grown much this year, but what can we do next year to further grow in our love for God and our faith in Him? *First,* we can spend more time in His Word. Empowered by His Holy Spirit, the truth of Scripture at work in your heart will help you to be strong and stand fast in the faith (1 Corinthians 16:13). *Second,* we can look for ways to live out our faith. Even seemingly small choices can require a measure of faith and courage, and those situations can help perfect our faith. As we focus on God's all-sufficient power and grace, problems dim and obstacles diminish as He demonstrates His faithfulness and our faith in Him grows.

> *By faith the harlot Rahab did not perish*
> *with those who did not believe,*
> *when she had received the spies with peace.*
> Hebrews 11:31

*I*t's been a long-time practice of artists to paint over their less impressive works. Sometimes when they do so, they end up creating a grand masterpiece on a canvas that once held a less-than-remarkable picture. Today, dear woman of faith, we come across just such a canvas in God's Hebrews 11 portrait gallery. It's His picture of Rahab. As we look intently at Rahab's portrait, we see that hers is a picture on a picture, a "before-and-after" composition:

- *A harlot*—Our now-shining Rahab is a woman with a past that isn't pretty! Making her living and providing for her family in the worst of ways, Rahab is referred to as "Rahab the harlot."

- *A heroine*—Rahab hid Joshua's spies from her king, saved their lives by sending them out of town a secret way, declared her faith in their God, marked out her home with a scarlet cord, and, trusting Joshua's word, waited for his army to return and counted on his mercy toward her. These many acts of faith made Rahab a heroine to the people of Israel.

- *A hallowed vessel*—Believing in the holy and mighty God of Israel transformed Rahab into a hallowed and holy vessel fit for God's use, giving her a heart of faith and compelling her to act in faith. What the prophet promised became true of Rahab: "Though your sins are like scarlet, they shall be as white as snow; though they are red like crimson, they shall be as wool" (Isaiah 1:18).

Do you consider your life to be permanently tainted by past failures, poor decisions, and sickening sin? If so, enjoy the cleansing that is yours through faith in the only One who can wash away your sins. Declare along with Rahab that "the Lord...God, He is God in heaven above and on earth beneath" (Joshua 2:11) and allow Him to wash your crimson sins as white as snow. Let the Lord transform your life, your "before" picture, into something lovely and hallowed, something worthy to hang in the halls of heaven!

> *Let it be the hidden person of the heart,*
> *with the incorruptible beauty of a gentle and quiet spirit,*
> *which is very precious in the sight of God.*
> 1 PETER 3:4

*D*id you read carefully the sacred words of Scripture written above? For centuries, these lovely words have moved women who love God to clothe their hidden person of the heart with the garment of God's gentle and quiet spirit. Gentleness and quietness—these twin traits are so very precious in the sight of the God we so love!

But many women (perhaps you, too, dear one?) have sighed and wondered, "Exactly what does a gentle and quiet spirit look like? And how do I go about putting on the two beautiful jewels of this gracious ornament?"

A simple but wonderful definition serves us well on our quest for this gentle and quiet bearing: *Gentle* (or meek) means "not creating disturbances," and *quiet* means "bearing with tranquillity the disturbances caused by others."[14] Today let's look at *gentleness*, and we'll consider *quietness* tomorrow.

Gentle means not creating disturbances. Think of this definition in light of Jesus' life and model. When describing Himself, Jesus said, "I am *gentle* and lowly in heart" (Matthew 11:29, emphasis added). Furthermore, He who is the King of the universe came to us not as a mighty, conquering warrior leading an army, but as a lowly and *gentle* man sitting on a donkey (Matthew 21:5), refusing to strive, quarrel, or even bruise a single reed (Matthew 12:19, 20).

Are you getting the idea? Do you sense the gentle beauty God has in mind for you as one of His chosen women? We are called not to aggression, combativeness, and contention, but to gentleness, mildness, forbearance, and patience. Instead of being harsh, violent, or forceful, provoking other people and causing disturbances, we are to exhibit all that is winsome, pleasant, and agreeable. A high calling, indeed!

Do you want to wear the precious jewel of gentleness? Then first put on the Lord Jesus Christ (Romans 13:14). With Jesus as your chief and basic adornment, His gentleness will be evident as you walk through life…gently and *not* creating disturbances!

The incorruptible beauty of a gentle and quiet spirit...
is very precious in the sight of God.
1 PETER 3:4

Yesterday we considered the beauty of a gentle spirit which does not cause disturbances. Now, dear gentlewoman, we behold its twin grace of *quietness*. Both qualities are "very precious in the sight of God," and both add a loveliness to our life and to the lives of those around us. As we've seen, a gentle spirit does not create disturbances. Now we'll see that *a quiet spirit does not respond to the disturbances caused by other people.* Instead it tranquilly, quietly bears with any distress brought about by people's words and deeds.

What would such a quiet spirit mean in your life, and how would it show forth its sparkle? It would mean...

- *A refusal to be bothered by things within or without*—Resting in Christ, we allow our faith and confidence in Him to quiet our heart regarding matters outside our control.

- *A desire for a life of peace and order*—A woman with a quiet heart enjoys a quiet life (1 Timothy 2:2), and she does what she can to make such peace and order happen (Proverbs 31:27).

- *A quietness in word*—The definition of a "quiet spirit" leaves room for quietness in word as well as in manner and actions. Absent from the behavior of a quiet-spirited woman are the outbursts, tongue-lashings, and exclamations that betray a heart that is not at rest in the Lord.

The secret to obtaining this rare jewel, the secret behind a quiet heart, is *trust in God.* Having urged us to adorn ourselves with a gentle and quiet spirit, Peter explains, "For in this manner, in former times, the holy women who *trusted in God* also adorned themselves" (verse 5, emphasis added). And this entire book has been about those precious, holy women of the Bible who loved God and trusted in Him. That trust is what causes these two jewels to glisten!

Do you, dear one, want to possess the jewels of quietness and gentleness? Then trust in the Lord. Look to Him when disturbances arise. Call upon Him in times of trouble. Draw near to Him in faith. And walk with Him each step of the way.

> *And the Spirit and the bride say, "Come!"*
> Revelation 22:17

*C*ongratulations, dear friend! You've finished your journey through the Bible—a trip which has given you the opportunity to meet some very special women who loved God. And how fitting it is to end our spiritual pilgrimage in the final book of the Bible, in the final chapter of the Bible, on the final page of the Bible where we come face-to-face with "the bride of Christ." In the Scriptures, the church is called "the bride, the Lamb's wife" (Revelation 21:9). The picture suggested by that phrase is truly beautiful: Just as a bridegroom rejoices over his bride, so the Lord, the church's Bridegroom, shall forever rejoice in His people—and His people will rejoice in Him!

Jesus has promised to come again, and we need to consider the significance of His promise.

First, if you have not yet named Jesus as your Savior and Lord, let the cry of both the Spirit and the bride of Christ be your cry! Welcome the Bridegroom into your heart. Don't let another year—or day or minute!—go by without taking this all-important step. Begin the fresh new year as a child of God!

Second, if you love God and follow Jesus Christ, resolve to spend each new day keeping yourself spotless and without wrinkle, holy and without blemish, so that you may present yourself to your holy Bridegroom like a bride adorned for her husband in the clean, white linen of righteousness (Ephesians 5:27; Revelation 19:8; 21:2).

Third, as you stand on the threshold of a new year, consider the prayer of young Joan of Arc. When, at age 19, this courageous French woman learned that she was sentenced to die at the stake, she offered this prayer to the God she loved: "I shall only last a year; use me as You can."

Use me as You can. These words come from a heart wholly set apart for God. Beloved pilgrim, as you look to your bright new year, make this prayer your own each and every day! Setting your heart wholly apart for your heavenly Father and asking Him to use you as He can will mark you as a woman who truly loves God.

Notes

JANUARY

1. John Milton, *Eve.*
2. Herbert Lockyer, *All the Promises of the Bible,* p. 10.
3. J. B. Phillips.
4. "Safely Through the Night," Leech/Fred Brock Music ASCAP. Paul Sandberg.
5. Donald Grey Barnhouse, *Let Me Illustrate* (Grand Rapids, MI: Fleming H. Revell, 1967), pp. 253-54.

FEBRUARY

1. Herbert Lockyer, *The Women of the Bible* (Grand Rapids, MI: Zondervan Publishing House, 1975), p. 111.
2. Elisabeth Elliot, *Let Me Be a Woman* (Wheaton, IL: Tyndale House Publishers, Inc., 1977), p. 42.
3. Lockyer, *Women of the Bible,* p. 137.
4. Drawn from *The Handbook of Bible Application*, Neil S. Wilson, ed. (Wheaton, IL: Tyndale House Publishers, Inc., 1992), p. 485.

MARCH

1. Philip Melancthon.
2. Elizabeth George, *A Woman After God's Own Heart* (Eugene, OR: Harvest House Publishers, 1997), p. 29.
3. Mrs. Charles E. Cowman, *Streams in the Desert—Volume 1* (Grand Rapids, MI: Zondervan Publishing House, 1965), p. 331.
4. Ben Patterson, *Waiting* (Downers Grove, IL: InterVarsity Press, 1989), p. i.
5. Anne Ortlund, *Building a Great Marriage* (Old Tappan, NJ: Fleming H. Revell Company, 1984), p. 146.
6. V. Raymond Edman.
7. Merrill F. Unger, *Unger's Bible Dictionary* (Chicago: Moody Press, 1972), p. 348.
8. Lord Dewar.
9. Horace Bushnell.
10. Phil Whisenhunt.
11. Stephen G. Green.
12. Ruth Vaughn.

APRIL

1. Merrill C. Tenney, ed., *The Zondervan Pictorial Encyclopedia of the Bible, Vol. 4* (Grand Rapids, MI: Zondervan Publishing House, 1975), p. 875.
2. Drawn from principles found in *Spiritual Leadership,* by J. Oswald Sanders (Chicago: Moody Press, 1967).
3. Charles W. Landon.

4. *Worldwide Challenge,* "Elisabeth Elliot Leitch: Held by God's Sovereignty," January 1978, pp. 39-40.
5. M. R. DeHaan and Henry G. Bosch, *Bread for Each Day* (Grand Rapids, MI: Zondervan Publishing House, 1962), June 23.
6. *Akron Baptist Journal.*
7. Matthew Henry.
8. *The Zondervan Pictorial Encyclopedia of the Bible, Vol. 5,* p. 575.
9. Drawn from Herbert Lockyer, *The Women of the Bible* (Grand Rapids, MI: Zondervan Publishing House, 1975), p. 180.
10. Drawn from *The Zondervan Pictorial Encyclopedia, Vol. 5,* pp. 890-91.
11. John Oxenham.
12. Samuel Johnson.

MAY

1. Elizabeth George, *Beautiful in God's Eyes* (Eugene, OR: Harvest House Publishers, 1998), pp. 13-16.
2. Julie Nixon Eisenhower, *Special People* (New York: Ballantine Books, 1977), pp. 3-37.
3. Stanley High, *Billy Graham* (New York: McGraw Hill, 1956), p. 71.
4. J. H. Morrison.
5. Charles Dickens, *A Tale of Two Cities.*
6. Matthew Henry, *Matthew Henry Commentary,* vol. 2, pp. 204-05.
7. Information from Kenneth W. Osbeck, *Amazing Grace* (Grand Rapids, MI: Kregel Publications, 1990), p. 216.
8. John MacArthur, *The MacArthur Study Bible* (Nashville: Word Publishing, 1997), p. 373.
9. Herbert Lockyer, *The Women of the Bible* (Grand Rapids, MI: Zondervan Publishing House, 1975), pp. 144-49.

JUNE

1. Herbert Lockyer, *Dark Threads the Weaver Needs* (Old Tappan, NJ: Fleming H. Revell Company, 1979).
2. William Temple, Archbishop of Canterbury.
3. James Strong, *Strong's Exhaustive Concordance of the Bible* (Nashville: Abingdon Press, 1973), p. 95.
4. Curtis Vaughan, gen. ed., *The Old Testament Books of Poetry from 26-Translations* (Grand Rapids, MI: Zondervan Bible Publishers, 1973), p. 578.
5. Henri Frederic Amiel.
6. John Mason.
7. Elisabeth Elliot, *The Shaping of a Christian Family* (Nashville: Thomas Nelson Publishers, 1992), p. 201.
8. John MacArthur, *The MacArthur Study Bible* (Nashville: Word Publishing, 1997), p. 407.

9. Herbert Lockyer, *The Women of the Bible* (Grand Rapids, MI: Zondervan Publishing House, 1975), p. 36.
10. Drawn from Herbert Lockyer, *All the Kings and Queens of the Bible* (Grand Rapids, MI: Zondervan Publishing House, 1971), p. 212.
11. J. D. Douglas.

JULY

1. Madeline Bridges.
2. R. K. Harrison, *The Psalms for Today: A New Translation from the Hebrew into Current English* (Grand Rapids, MI: Zondervan Publishing House, 1961).
3. Peter Scholtes.
4. Merrill F. Unger, *Unger's Bible Dictionary* (Chicago: Moody Press, 1972), p. 420.
5. Bill Gothard Ministries.
6. Drawn from Russell Kelso Carter's 1849–1928 hymn, "Standing on the Promises."
7. Unger, *Unger's Bible Dictionary*, p. 498.
8. Lewis Barrett Lehrman, *Being an Artist* (Cincinnati, OH: North Light Books, 1992), p. 5.
9. Suggested reading: *Amazing Grace, 101 Hymn Stories* and *101 More Hymn Stories*, by Kenneth W. Osbeck (Grand Rapids, MI: Kregel Publications).
10. Two quotes on this page, author unknown, quoted from *Amazing Grace* by Kenneth W. Osbeck, p. 8.
11. Mrs. Howard Taylor, *John and Betty Stam, A Story of Triumph* (Chicago: Moody Press, revised edition, 1982), p. 130.
12. Reverend E. H. Hamilton, China Inland Mission missionary.
13. Richard C. Halverson, "Perspective" newsletter, Oct. 26, 1977. (Gender changed.)
14. Drawn from *A Woman After God's Own Heart*, by Elizabeth George (Eugene, OR: Harvest House Publishers, 1997), pp. 97-106.

AUGUST

1. Edith Schaeffer, *What Is a Family?* (Old Tappan, NJ: Fleming H. Revell Company, 1975), p. 119.
2. Edith Schaeffer, *Hidden Art* (Wheaton, IL: Tyndale House Publishers, 1971).
3. Robert Alden, *Proverbs* (Grand Rapids, MI: Baker Book House, 1983), p. 110.
4. Ralph Wardlaw, *Lectures on the Book of Proverbs, Vol. II* (Minneapolis: Klock & Klock Christian Publishers, Inc., 1981 reprint of 1861 edition), p. 209.
5. Charles F. Pfeiffer and Everett Y. Harrison, eds., *Wycliffe Bible Commentary* (Chicago: Moody Press, 1973), p. 572.
6. Stanley High, *Billy Graham* (New York: McGraw Hill, 1956), p. 71.
7. The contents regarding the Proverbs 31 woman are drawn from *Beautiful in God's Eyes: The Treasures of the Proverbs 31 Woman* by Elizabeth George (Eugene, OR: Harvest House Publishers, 1998). For further insights into the

Proverbs 31 woman, read this practical and inspirational verse-by-verse summary.

8. Cheryl Julia Dunn, *A Study of Proverbs,* master thesis (Biola University, 1993), p. 25.
9. "A Woman's Love" by Douglas Malloch.
10. High, *Billy Graham,* p. 127.
11. John MacArthur, "God's High Calling for Women," Part 4 (Panorama City, CA: Word of Grace, #GC-54-17, 1986).
12. Schaeffer, *What Is a Family?* p. 121.

SEPTEMBER

1. William J. Petersen, *Martin Luther Had a Wife* (Wheaton, IL: Tyndale House Publishers, Inc., 1983), pp. 13-37.
2. John MacArthur, *The MacArthur Study Bible* (Nashville: Word Publishing, 1997), p. 941.
3. *Life Application Bible* (Wheaton, IL: Tyndale House Publishers, Inc. and Youth for Christ, 1988), p. 1471.
4. "I Have Decided to Follow Jesus," Indian melody arranged by Norman Johnson.
5. Herbert Lockyer, *The Women of the Bible* (Grand Rapids, MI: Zondervan Publishing House, 1975), p. 225.
6. William Barclay, *The Letters of James and Peter,* revised edition (Philadelphia: The Westminster Press, 1976), p. 217.
7. Walter B. Knight, *Knight's Master Book of New Illustrations* (Grand Rapids, MI: Wm. B. Eerdmans Publishing Company, 1979), pp. 204-05. This is the source for the "Reasons for Devotional Time" found in the next several pages.
8. J. A. Thompson, *Handbook of Life in Bible Times* (Downers Grove, IL: Inter-Varsity Press, 1986), pp. 83-85.
9. The contents of this devotion are drawn from *Loving God with All Your Mind* by Elizabeth George (Eugene, OR: Harvest House Publishers, 1994), p. 183.
10. Ray and Anne Ortlund, *The Best Half of Life* (Glendale, CA: Regal Books, 1976), p. 79.
11. Gien Karssen, *Her Name Is Woman* (Colorado Springs: NavPress, 1975), p. 131.

OCTOBER

1. Merrill F. Unger, *Unger's Bible Dictionary,* quoting Keil (Chicago: Moody Press, 1972), p. 1172.
2. William Barclay, *The Letters to the Corinthians,* rev. ed. (Philadelphia: The Westminster Press, 1975), p. 201.
3. Song title by Mark Lowry and Buddy Greene.
4. German scholar Johann Albrecht Bengel.
5. Charles Caldwell Ryrie, *The Role of Women in the Church,* quoted material by Walter F. Adeney (Chicago: Moody Press, 1970), p. 34.

6. William Barclay, *The Gospel of Luke,* rev. ed. (Philadelphia: The Westminister Press, 1975), p. 97.

7. Oswald J. Smith, *The Man God Uses* (London: Marshall, Morgan, and Scott, 1932), pp. 52-57.

8. Drawn from *God's Garden of Grace: Growing in the Fruit of the Spirit* by Elizabeth George (Eugene OR: Harvest House Publishers, 1996), pp. 66-69.

9. Hymn by Judson W. VandeVenter and Winfield S. Weeden.

10. Hymn by Joseph H Gilmore, 1834–1918.

NOVEMBER

1. From *The Greatest Thing in the World.*

2. Marvin R. Vincent, *World Studies in the New Testament—Vol. III, The Epistles of Paul,* quoting Renan (Grand Rapids, MI: Wm. B. Eerdmans Publishing Co., 1973), p. 177.

3. Robert C. Cunningham.

4. Carol Talbot, *For This I Was Born* (Chicago: Moody Press, 1977), p. 208.

5. All information drawn from John MacArthur, Jr., *The MacArthur New Testament Commentary—Romans 9–16* (Chicago: Moody Press, 1994), pp. 364-69.

6. Elyse Fitzpatrick and Carol Cornish, *Women Helping Women* (Eugene, OR: Harvest House Publishers, 1997), pp. 207-19.

7. Ibid., thirteen strategies abbreviated from those offered by Carol Cornish, *Women Helping Women,* pp. 219-30.

8. Drawn from Elizabeth George, *A Woman After God's Own Heart* (Eugene, OR: Harvest House Publishers, 1997), pp. 77-95.

9. Drawn from Elizabeth George, *Beautiful in God's Eyes* (Eugene, OR: Harvest House Publishers, 1998), pp. 161-70.

10. Drawn from Elizabeth George, *A Woman After God's Own Heart,* pp. 60-63.

11. Kenneth S. Wuest, *Wuest's Word Studies*—vol. 1, Galatians and Ephesians (Grand Rapids, MI: Wm. B. Eerdmans Publishing Company, 1973), p. 136.

DECEMBER

1. William Hendriksen, *New Testament Commentary—Exposition of Colossians and Philemon* (Grand Rapids, MI: Baker Book House, 1975), p. 168.

2. Kenneth S. Wuest, *Wuest's Word Studies*—vol. 2 (Grand Rapids, MI: Wm. B. Eerdmans Publishing Company, 1974), p. 46.

3. Drawn from *The Zondervan Pictorial Encyclopedia of the Bible—Volumes One and Two,* Merrill C. Tenney, gen. ed. (Grand Rapids, MI: Zondervan Publishing House, 1975).

4. Curtis Vaughan, gen. ed., *The New Testament from 26 Translations*—The New Testament in Basic English (Grand Rapids, MI: Zondervan Publishing House, 1967), pp. 970-71.

5. Albert M. Wells, Jr., ed., *Inspiring Quotations Contemporary & Classical* (Nashville: Thomas Nelson Publishers, 1988), p. 69.

6. John MacArthur, *The MacArthur Study Bible* (Nashville: Word Publishing, 1997), p. 1738.
7. D. Edmond Hiebert, *Everyman's Bible Commentary—Titus and Philemon* (Chicago: Moody Press, 1957), p. 39 (quoting Spence).
8. Gene A. Getz, *The Measure of a Woman* (Ventura, CA: Regal Books, 1977), pp. 28-29.
9. John F. MacArthur, audiotapes #1833 and #1834 entitled "The Limits of Our Liberty, Part 1 and 2" [1 Corinthians 8:1-13] (Grace to You, P.O. Box 4000, Panorama City, CA 91412). © 1975 by John MacArthur.
10. Howard and Charlotte Clinebell.
11. Drawn from Elizabeth George, *A Woman After God's Own Heart* (Eugene, OR: Harvest House Publishers, 1997), pp. 77-95.
12. Getz, *The Measure of a Woman,* pp. 93-94.
13. Ibid., pp. 103-05.
14. Robert Jamieson, A. R. Fausset, and David Brown, *Commentary on the Whole Bible* (Grand Rapids, MI: Zondervan Publishing House, 1973), p. 1475 (quoting Bengel).

Bibliography

Blaiklock, E. M. and H. H. Rowdon. *Bible Characters and Doctrines*. Grand Rapids, MI: William B. Eerdmans Publishing Company, 1973.

Hendricks, Jeanne. *A Woman for All Seasons*. Nashville: Thomas Nelson Inc., 1977.

Henry, Matthew. *Matthew Henry's Commentary on the Whole Bible*. Peabody, MA: Hendrickson Publishers, Inc., 1996.

Jamieson, Robert, A. R. Fausset, and David Brown. *Commentary on the Whole Bible*. Grand Rapids, MI: Zondervan Publishing House, 1973.

Karssen, Gien. *Her Name Is Woman*. Colorado Springs: NavPress, 1975 and 1977.

Kidner, Derek. *Genesis*. Downers Grove, IL: InterVarsity Press, 1973.

Life Application Bible. Wheaton, IL: Tyndale House Publishers, Inc., 1988.

Lockyer, Herbert. *The Women of the Bible*. Grand Rapids, MI: Zondervan Publishing House, 1975.

MacArthur, John. *The MacArthur Study Bible*. Nashville: Word Publishing, 1997.

Matthews, Victor H. *Manners and Customs in the Bible* (rev. ed.). Peabody, MA: Hendrickson Publishers, Inc., 1996.

Pfeiffer, Charles F. and Everett F. Harrison. *The Wycliffe Bible Commentary*. Chicago: Moody Press, 1973.

Phillips, John. *Exploring Genesis*. Neptune, NJ: Loizeaux Brothers, 1980.

Ryrie, Charles Caldwell. *The Ryrie Study Bible*. Chicago: Moody Press, 1978.

Spence, H. D. M., and Joseph S. Exell. *The Pulpit Commentary*. Grand Rapids, MI: William B. Eerdmans Publishing Company, 1978.

Spurgeon, Charles Haddon. *Spurgeon's Sermons on Old and New Testament Women*. Grand Rapids, MI: Kregel Publications, 1995.

Unger, Merrill. *Unger's Bible Dictionary*. Chicago: Moody Press, 1972.

Index of Women

Index of Scriptures